The Mammoth Book of

DIRTY, SICK,
X-RATED &
POLITICALLY INCORRECT
JOKES

D1147587

Rob

Also available

The Mammoth Book of 20th Century Science Fiction
The Mammoth Book of Awesome Comic Fantasy
The Mammoth Book of Best New Erotica 3
The Mammoth Book of Best New Horror 14
The Mammoth Book of Best New Science Fiction 16
The Mammoth Book of British Kings & Queens
The Mammoth Book of Celtic Myths and Legends
The Mammoth Book of Fighter Pilots
The Mammoth Book of Future Cops
The Mammoth Book of Great Detective Stories
The Mammoth Book of Great Inventions
The Mammoth Book of Hearts of Oak
The Mammoth Book of Heroes
The Mammoth Book of Historical Whodunnits
The Mammoth Book of How It Happened
The Mammoth Book of How It Happened: America
The Mammoth Book of How It Happened: Ancient Egypt
The Mammoth Book of How It Happened: Ancient Rome
The Mammoth Book of How It Happened: Battles
The Mammoth Book of How It Happened In Britain
The Mammoth Book of How It Happened: Everest
The Mammoth Book of How It Happened Naval Battles
The Mammoth Book of How It Happened WWI
The Mammoth Book of How It Happened World War II
The Mammoth Book of International Erotica
The Mammoth Book of Jack the Ripper
The Mammoth Book of Maneaters
The Mammoth Book of Mountain Disasters
The Mammoth Book of Native Americans
The Mammoth Book of New Terror
The Mammoth Book of Private Eye Stories
The Mammoth Book of Prophecies
The Mammoth Book of Pulp Action
The Mammoth Book of Roaring Twenties Whodunnits
The Mammoth Book of Roman Whodunnits
The Mammoth Book of Roaring Twenties Whodunnits
The Mammoth Book of SAS & Elite Forces
The Mammoth Book of Science Fiction Century Volume 1
The Mammoth Book of Seriously Comic Fantasy
The Mammoth Book of Sex, Drugs & Rock 'n' Roll
The Mammoth Book of Sorcerer's Tales
The Mammoth Book of Space Exploration and Disasters
The Mammoth Book of Special Forces
The Mammoth Book of Storms & Sea Disasters
The Mammoth Book of Short Erotic Novels
The Mammoth Book of Sword and Honour
The Mammoth Book of The Edge
The Mammoth Book of Travel in Dangerous Places
The Mammoth Book of True War Stories
The Mammoth Book of UFOs
The Mammoth Book of Vampires
The Mammoth Book of War Correspondents
The Mammoth Book of Women Who Kill
The Mammoth Encyclopedia of Extraterrestrial Encounters
The Mammoth Encyclopedia of Modern Crime Fiction
The Mammoth Encyclopedia of Unsolved Mysteries

The Mammoth Book of

DIRTY, SICK,
X-RATED &
POLITICALLY INCORRECT
JOKES

Edited by

GEOFF TIBBALLS

ROBINSON
London

Constable & Robinson Ltd
3 The Lanchesters
162 Fulham Palace Road
London W6 9ER
www.constablerobinson.com

First published in the UK by Robinson,
an imprint of Constable & Robinson Ltd, 2005

Copyright © Geoff Tibballs, 2005

All rights reserved. This book is sold subject to the condition that
it shall not, by way of trade or otherwise, be lent, re-sold, hired out
or otherwise circulated in any form of binding or cover other than that in
which it is published and without a similar condition including this
condition being imposed on the subsequent purchaser.

A copy of the British Library Cataloguing in
Publication Data is available from the British Library.

ISBN 1–84119–967–2

Printed and bound in the EU

3 5 7 9 10 8 6 4

CONTENTS

INTRODUCTION

If you're looking for a nice joke book to give your old grandma a chuckle at Christmas, put this book down immediately! Unless, that is, your grandma happens to be a cross-dressing, hard-drinking, sex-crazed, dwarf Mexican nun with a penchant for bikers and donkeys. For be warned, the contents of this bumper collection of brand spanking new, dirty, X-rated, and decidedly politically incorrect jokes is not for the faint-hearted. Even a blonde would blush . . . if she got any of them.

All of the usual suspects are here — jokes about sex, religion, health, old age, politics, different nationalities, men and women bashing, plus a selection of particularly filthy limericks. My only concession to political correctness is that I have tried to be scrupulously fair in ensuring that men receive just as much stick as women and that the English are ridiculed to the same extent as other nations, not least because I firmly believe that the ability to laugh at yourself is one of the keys to a reasonably contented life. Besides, it's always good to get the jibe in first. Equally we all need somebody else to laugh at, as long it is not vindictive. After all, the Americans laugh at the Canadians, the Canadians make fun of the Newfies, and they in turn probably mock mercilessly the inhabitants of a tiny island somewhere off the coast of Newfoundland. It's what makes the world of mirth go round. But if you are offended by any of the jokes in this book, then I guess I've succeeded in my task.

At Constable & Robinson thanks are due to Nick Robinson and Pete Duncan, and also to Eryl Humphrey Jones for some excellent jokes.

Geoff Tibballs
January 2005

ACCIDENTS

1 Five people – four guys and a young woman – were on a plane when it suddenly plunged into the sea. Miraculously all five survived the crash but found themselves stranded on a desert island. Since the guys needed to satisfy their natural urges, with the woman's agreement they drew up a rota whereby each would take it in turns to screw her as much as possible for a week at a time. The arrangement worked really well for the next six years, satisfying both the guys and the nymphomaniac woman until she died unexpectedly. The first month went by and it was awful for the guys; the second month was really bad; the third month was almost unbearable; by the fourth month they couldn't take it any more, so they buried her.

2 A police officer arrived at the scene of a horrific road accident with several fatalities. Body parts were strewn everywhere. He was making notes of where everything was when he suddenly came across a decapitated human head. He wrote in his notebook 'Head on bullevard' but couldn't spell it. He tried 'bouelevard' and 'boolevard', but still couldn't get it right. So when no one was looking, he kicked the head and wrote 'Head on kerb'.

3 A guy working at a lumberyard accidentally sheared off all ten of his fingers. At the hospital, the surgeon said: 'Give me the fingers and I'll see what I can do.'
   'I haven't got them,' said the man.
   'Why not?' asked the surgeon. 'This is 2005, we've got microsurgery and all kinds of amazing techniques. I could have put them back on and made you like new. So why didn't you bring the fingers?'
   The man said: 'I couldn't pick them up.'

4 Driving his date down a country lane one night, a guy pretended to run out of gas in the hope of being able to have sex with her in the back seat. But she wasn't falling for such an old trick, and said that she had a $100 bill in her purse.
   'If you walk into town,' she said, 'you can use the money to buy gas.'
   He said he had to pee first. But while he was peeing, she decided to light a match near the gas tank to see if there was any gas in it. There was a big explosion, scattering things far and wide.
   As the bang subsided, she called out: 'Help me find my purse. It's got $100 in it!'

He yelled back: 'Never mind about that! Help me find my right hand. It's got my dick in it!'

5   What's the difference between a guy falling from the first floor and one falling from the sixteenth floor? – The guy falling from the first floor goes 'Splat, aaaargh!' and the one falling from the sixteenth floor goes 'Aaaargh, splat!'

6   One evening a man was at home watching TV and eating peanuts, tossing them in the air and catching them in his mouth. While he was in the middle of catching one, his wife asked him a question and as he turned to answer, the peanut landed in his ear. The wife tried to remove the peanut but only succeeded in pushing it deeper into his ear. With all subsequent attempts to remove the peanut failing miserably, the pair began to panic and decided to go to the hospital but, just as they were about to leave, their daughter came home with her date. Hearing of the problem, the young man told the father to sit down, then proceeded to shove two fingers up the father's nose and told him to blow hard. Sure enough, when the father blew, the peanut flew out of his ear.

Everyone congratulated the young man, and the daughter took him into the kitchen to get him something to eat as a reward. The relieved wife turned to her husband and said: 'Isn't he smart? What do you think he's going to be when he grows older?'

The father replied: 'From the smell of his fingers, our son-in-law!'

7   A small plane crashed in the middle of the desert. The pilot and co-pilot wandered around for days in search of food, but could find nothing. Finally the co-pilot announced: 'I'm so hungry, I'm going to chop off my dick and eat it.'

'Before you do,' said the pilot. 'Think of your girlfriend.'

'What's the point? At this rate I will never see her again anyway.'

'I know, but if you think of her first, hopefully there will be enough for both of us.'

8   A farmer was so concerned about drivers speeding down the country lane where he lived and endangering his sheep that he asked the police to put up a sign. So they put up a 'Slow' sign, but it had no effect. Then they erected a 'Hazard Ahead' sign, but that had no effect either. Finally they tried a 'Children Crossing' sign, but still the motorists failed to reduce their speed.

As a last resort, the farmer asked the police if he could put up his own sign. The police agreed, and when an officer called on the farmer a week later to see whether there had been any improvement, he was amazed to see the traffic crawling slowly along the lane. Then he noticed the farmer's handmade sign by the roadside. It read: 'Nudist Colony.'

9 One day two brothers, Jack and Jim, decided to go out diving for seafood. After filling the first sack, Jack took it back to shore to grab a replacement, but while Jim was left alone out at sea, he suddenly spotted a shark swimming towards him.

Jim frantically called out to his brother: 'Jack, help me! There's a shark heading straight for me!'

Jack called back: 'OK, I'm coming, bro.'

Jim was freaking out as the shark swam right up to him and bit off his left leg. Again he called out to Jack, who was still at the shoreline: 'Jack, come and help me, the shark's bitten off one of my legs!'

Jack yelled back: 'Hold on, bro, I'm coming.'

Jim tried to stay calm and wait for his brother but then the shark bit off his left arm. He shouted to Jack: 'Hurry up! Come and help me! The shark has bitten off my arm and my leg!'

Jack called back: 'Hold on, I'm coming.'

Then the shark bit off Jim's right leg. Jim screamed: 'Jack, you have to come and save me! The shark has bitten off both my legs and an arm!'

Jack called back: 'Just wait, I'm coming.'

The shark then bit off Jim's other arm. Now Jim had no arms or legs.

Jack finally arrived to save him. 'Come on, bro,' said Jack, 'get on my back and I'll swim you back to shore.'

When they finally made it back to the shore, Jack said with an exhausted sigh: 'I feel fucked.'

Jim replied: 'Well, I had to hold on somehow!'

10 A cop arrived at the scene of a car smash. He rushed over and asked the driver: 'Are you seriously hurt?'

'I don't know,' said the driver. 'I haven't spoken to my lawyer yet.'

11 Two guys were sitting in a bar. One said: 'Did you hear the news — Mike is dead?'

'How?' gasped the other. 'What happened to him?'

'Well, he was on his way over to my house the other day and when he pulled up outside, he didn't brake properly and — bang — he hit the pavement, the car flipped over and he went crashing through the sunroof. He went flying through the air and smashed through my upstairs bedroom window.'

'Wow! What a horrible way to die!'

'No, no, he survived that. That didn't kill him. So, after landing in my upstairs bedroom, he was lying on the floor covered in broken glass. Then he spotted the big antique wardrobe we have in the room and reached for the handle to try and pull himself up. He was just dragging himself up when – bang – this massive wardrobe came crashing down on top of him, crushing him and breaking most of his bones.'

'What a way to go! That's terrible!'

'No, no, that didn't kill him: he survived that. He managed to get the wardrobe off him and crawled out onto the landing. There, he tried to pull himself up on the banister, but under his weight the banister broke and he fell down to the first floor. In mid-air, all the broken banister poles spun and fell on him, pinning him to the floor, sticking right through him.'

'Gee! That is an awful way to go!'

'No, no, that didn't kill him, he even survived that. So he was on the downstairs landing, just beside the kitchen. He crawled in to the kitchen, tried to pull himself up by the cooker, but accidentally reached for a big pot of boiling water. Whoosh! The whole thing came down on him and burned off most of his skin.'

'Man! What a way to go!'

'No, no, he survived that. He was lying on the ground, covered in boiling water, and he spotted the phone. He thought he'd reach for the phone to call for help but instead he grabbed the light switch and pulled the whole thing off the wall. Well, water and electricity don't mix, so he got electrocuted – boom – 10,000 volts shot through him.'

'Now that is one horrible way to go!'

'No, no, that didn't kill him. He survived that, he . . .'

'Hold on now, just how the hell did Mike die?'

'I shot him!'

'You shot him? What the hell did you shoot him for?'

'He was wrecking my house!'

12 A man fell out of an eleventh-storey window. He was lying on the ground with a crowd gathered around him when a cop walked over and said: 'What happened?'

The guy said: 'I don't know. I just got here.'

13 On vacation, a little boy asked his mother: 'Can I go swimming in the sea?'

'No, darling, you can't,' she replied. 'The sea's way too rough, there's a dangerous offshore current, and this stretch of coastline is supposed to be plagued with jellyfish and sharks.'

'But Daddy's gone swimming in the sea,' protested the boy.

'I know,' said the mother. 'But Daddy has excellent life insurance.'

14 A woman was drying herself after taking a shower when she slipped and landed on the floor with her legs spread wide apart. Worse still, her pussy created a vacuum so that she was unable to move. She called her husband to help but, hard though he tried, he couldn't prise her pussy away from the floor tiles. In desperation, he then summoned a neighbour, who also tried unsuccessfully to shift her. Finally the neighbour suggested: 'Why don't we get a hammer and break the tiles around her legs and lift her that way?'

'Great idea,' said the husband, 'but let me just rub her tits a little so I can push her over to the kitchen. The tiles are cheaper in there.'

15 Two bums were sitting talking. The first started bragging: 'Today was the best day ever! I found a brand new pack of smokes just sitting on the ground. So you know what I did? I sat and smoked every last one of them – had the best day ever!'

The second bum just laughed. 'That's nothing. Today I was walking along the railroad tracks when I found this girl lying on the tracks. You know what I did? I shagged her all day long. It was my best day ever!'

The first bum sneered: 'No way did you do it all day long!'

'OK,' conceded the second bum, 'but it was for a good few hours – best day of my life!'

'So,' persisted the first bum, 'did she give you a blow job?'

'No.'

'Huh! How could you possibly be screwing this girl for hours, and she didn't even give you a blow job?'

'How could she?' protested the second bum. 'She didn't have a head!'

ADULTERY

16 Arriving home from a shopping trip, a wife was horrified to find her husband in bed with a pretty girl. Just as the wife was about to storm out of the house, her husband called out: 'Before you go, I want you to hear how all this came about. Driving home, I saw this young girl, looking poor and tired. I offered her a ride. She was hungry, so I brought her home and fed her some of the roast you had forgotten about in the refrigerator. Her shoes were worn out, so I gave her a pair of your shoes that you don't wear because they are out of fashion. She was cold, so I gave her the new birthday sweater you never wear because the colour doesn't suit you. Her trousers had holes in them, so I gave her a pair of yours that don't fit you any more. Then, as this poor girl was about to leave the house, she paused and asked, "Is there anything else that your wife doesn't use any more?" . . . So here we are!'

17 A doctor was having an affair with his nurse and soon she told him she was pregnant. Not wanting his wife to know, he gave the nurse a sum of money and told her to go to Italy and have the baby there.

'But how will I let you know the baby is born?' asked the nurse.

'Just send me a postcard and write "spaghetti" on the back.'

Six months later the doctor's wife called him at the office and said that he had received a strange postcard from Europe. When the doctor arrived home that evening, he read the card and immediately collapsed to the floor with a heart attack. While the paramedics were preparing to rush him to hospital, one asked the wife what had precipitated the cardiac arrest. Still mystified, she picked up the card and read: 'Spaghetti, Spaghetti, Spaghetti, Spaghetti – two with sausage and meatballs, two without.'

18 A guy arrived home from work to find a stranger screwing his wife.

'What the hell are you two doing?' demanded the husband.

His wife turned to the stranger and said: 'See, I told you he was stupid.'

19 After telling his wife he was working late at the office, a man took his secretary to a hotel and had wild sex with her. But on his way home, he noticed a huge love bite on his neck and began to panic. What would he tell his wife?

Walking in the door, he was greeted by his excited dog. In a moment of inspiration, he dropped to the floor and pretended to fight off the affectionate dog. Holding his neck with one hand, he went into the living room and exclaimed: 'Honey, look what the dog did to my neck!'

His wife jumped up, ripped open her blouse and said: 'That's nothing. Look what he did to my tits!'

20 A married couple invited a male friend over to their house for the evening, but when a sudden blizzard blew up, the friend was prevented from travelling home. Since the couple didn't have a guest room, he said he would book into a nearby hotel, but the wife wouldn't hear of it.

'Nonsense,' she insisted. 'Our bed is plenty big enough for all three of us, and we're all friends here.'

The husband agreed, so they settled down in bed together: the husband was in the middle, the wife on his left, and the friend on his right. Soon the husband began snoring loudly, and the wife sneaked over to the friend's side of the bed and invited him to have sex with her.

'Look, I'd really like to,' said the friend. 'You know I've always fancied you. But it wouldn't be right, not in the same bed as your husband. Anyway, he'll wake up, and then he'll kill me!'

'Don't worry about him,' said the wife. 'He's such a heavy sleeper, he'll never notice. If you don't believe me, just yank a hair out of his ass. He won't even wake up.'

So the friend pulled a hair from the husband's ass, and sure enough he didn't even flinch. Reassured, he proceeded to have sex with the wife who then returned to her side of the bed.

But she was restless, and thirty minutes later she was back on the friend's side of the bed, pleading for more sex. The friend was sure the husband would wake up this time, but once more the wife persuaded him to yank a hair from the husband's ass. And when the husband failed to stir, they had sex again. They carried on like this for the next four hours, always first making sure that it was safe by yanking a hair from the husband's ass. Finally after about the seventh bout of sex, the wife returned to her side of the bed.

The husband then rolled over and whispered to his friend: 'Listen, I don't care if you screw my wife, but could you please stop using my ass for a scoreboard?'

21 A few guys always used to meet up on Fridays after work for a drink. One Friday, Pete showed up late, sat down forlornly at the bar and knocked back his first beer in one gulp.

'You OK?' asked Bill, another of the gang.

'Not really,' sighed Pete. 'This morning my wife told me that she's rationing our sex life – she's cutting me back to just once a week. I can't believe it.'

Bill put a consoling arm around Pete's shoulder. 'You think you've got it bad – she's cut some guys out altogether!'

22 When her husband had to cancel his vacation to the Caribbean because of business commitments, a wife decided to go alone. Making the most of her freedom, she allowed herself to be seduced by a black man. After a passionate night of sex, she asked him his name.

'I'm not going to tell you,' he said, 'because you'll laugh.'

'No, I won't,' she said.

'You will.'

'I won't – I promise.'

'OK, my first name is Snow.'

The woman immediately started laughing.

'I knew you'd make fun of it!' he said.

'No, it's just that my husband won't believe me when I tell him that I had ten inches of Snow every day in the Caribbean!'

23 A husband staggered home at two o'clock in the morning. He opened the bedroom door to find another man in bed with his wife. The wife pushed the man off her and demanded to know why her husband was so late home.

The husband yelled: 'Who the hell is this guy, and what's he doing in bed with you?'

The wife shouted back: 'Don't go changing the subject! Where the hell have you been till this time of night?'

24 A guy walked into a bar, ordered a double scotch and moaned to the bartender: 'An irate husband has written to me, threatening to have me killed unless I stop screwing his wife.'

'So why don't you just stop?' said the bartender.

'It's not as easy as that,' replied the guy. 'He didn't sign his name.'

25 An old priest was getting fed up with the number of people in his parish who were confessing to adultery. One Sunday in the pulpit, he announced: 'If I hear one more person confess to adultery, I'm quitting!'

Since he was so popular, the parishioners came up with a code word to avoid incurring his wrath: anyone who had committed adultery would say they had 'fallen'.

The arrangement appeared to satisfy the old priest right up until his death. His young replacement soon settled into parish life and visited the mayor to express his concern about safety in the town: 'You have to do something about the sidewalks,' the new priest told the mayor. 'When people come into the confessional, they keep talking about having fallen.'

The mayor began to laugh, realizing that nobody had told the new priest about the code word.

Before the mayor could explain, the priest shook an accusing finger at him and said: 'I don't know what you're laughing about. Your wife has fallen three times already this week!'

26 A guy came home late and very drunk. His wife was waiting for him.

'You've been kissing someone, haven't you?' she barked.

'No.'

'Then explain the lipstick on your shirt.'

'That's easy,' he said. 'I used my shirt to wipe my dick.'

27 A missionary was sent to live with a primitive native tribe that lived in the depths of the jungle. He spent several years with the people, during which time he taught them English, and how to read and write. He also taught them the Christian ways of the white man, and one thing that he stressed in particular was the evil of sexual sin, namely no adultery and no fornication.

One day, the wife of one of the tribe's noblemen gave birth to a child. But to everyone's horror, the child was white. Not surprisingly, this caused a veritable stir in the village. The chief sent for the missionary and said: 'You have taught us the evils of sexual sin, but here is a black woman who gives birth to a white child. You are the only white man who has been in the village for many years. What is the explanation?'

The missionary said: 'No, my good man, you are mistaken. This is a natural occurrence, what we English call an albino. Nature does this on some occasions. For example, look at that flock of sheep. They are all white except among them, look, there is one black sheep.'

The chief thought it over for a moment, called the missionary forward, and whispered in his ear: 'OK. Tell you what. You don't say anything about the black sheep, and I won't say anything about the white child.'

28 A woman was having an affair with an inspector from a pest-control company. One afternoon they were having sex when her husband arrived home unexpectedly.

'Quick,' she said to her lover. 'Into the closet!'

When the husband reached the bedroom, he spotted two drinking glasses on the table and immediately became suspicious. He started searching the room and eventually discovered the man in the closet.

'Who are you?' asked the husband.

'I'm an inspector from Bugzap.'

'What are you doing in there?'

'I'm investigating a complaint regarding an infestation of moths.'

'And where are your clothes?'

The lover looked down at his naked body and said: 'Those little bastards!'

29 A wife arrived home flashing a new diamond ring. 'Where did you get that?' asked her husband suspiciously.

She said: 'My boss and I played the lotto and we won, so I bought the ring with my share of the winnings.'

A week later, she arrived home wearing a new Italian leather coat. 'Where did you get that?' asked her husband.

'My boss and I played the lotto, and guess what, we won again. So I bought the coat with my share of the winnings.'

Three weeks later, she arrived home driving a new Ferrari. 'Where did you get that?' asked the husband.

'My boss and I played the lotto, and you'll never believe it, but we won again. So I bought the car with my share of the winnings.'

That night she asked her husband to run her a nice warm bath, but when she went into the bathroom she found that the bath water was only a couple of inches deep.

'Why did you only run a little amount of water?' she asked.

'Well,' he mumbled sourly, 'we don't want you to get your lotto ticket wet, do we?'

30 Exhausted from a long day at work, a business executive arrived home to find his wife in bed with a neighbour.

'That's it!' stormed the husband. 'If you're in bed screwing *my* wife, I'm going next door to sleep with yours!'

'Go ahead,' replied the neighbour. 'The rest will do you good.'

31 A couple had been married for over forty years, but with the husband in serious financial trouble, he told his wife that he was thinking of committing suicide.

'Don't worry, honey,' she said reassuringly. 'We're not as hard up as you think because right from the start of our marriage I've been putting aside two dollars every time we had sex. Our savings have now grown to over $100,000!'

'Oh, that's wonderful!' he exclaimed. 'What an amazing woman you are! What an ingenious idea! I'm only sorry now that I didn't give you all my business!'

32 Although scheduled for all-night duty at the station, a police officer was allowed to go home early. Creeping into the house at two o'clock in the morning, he took great pains not to wake his wife. He undressed in the dark, crept into the bedroom and began climbing gingerly into bed. But just as he pulled back the sheet, his wife sat up sleepily and said: 'Darling, would you go down to the all-night drug store on the next block and get some aspirin? I've got a splitting headache.'

'Sure, honey,' he said and, feeling his way across the room, he got dressed again in the dark and walked to the drug store.

As he entered, the pharmacist looked up in surprise and asked: 'Aren't you Officer Maloney of the 10th District?'

'Yes, that's right,' said the officer.

'Then why on earth are you wearing the Fire Chief's uniform?'

33 In bed with her lover, a woman heard her husband turn the key in the front door. Since there was no time for the lover to escape, the wife covered him in talcum powder and made him stand in the corner. 'Just stay still and pretend you're a statue,' she ordered.

When the husband entered the bedroom, the wife asked innocently: 'What do you think of our new statue? Remember the Carters bought one for their bedroom? So I've bought one for ours.'

'Very nice, honey,' said the husband disinterestedly before going downstairs for dinner.

An hour and a half later, he returned alone to the bedroom carrying a beer and a sandwich. He put them on the dressing table and said: 'These are for you. When I was playing statues at the Carters', I stood there for three days without so much as a drink of water.'

34 An English Lord of the Manor returned home early from his grouse shoot to find his wife having sex in bed with his best friend, the local MP.

'How could you, Miranda?' he cried. 'After everything I've done for you. I've given you this beautiful house, I've always provided you with the most expensive clothes and jewels, I bought you a Ferrari for your birthday, I've tried to be a kind husband, and this is how you repay me!'

Hearing this, the wife burst into tears.

The Lord then turned to the MP: 'And as for you, Reggie, you might at least have the decency to stop while I'm talking!'

35 A woman was having an affair while her husband was out at work. One day she was in bed with her boyfriend when she heard her husband's car pull into the driveway.

'Quick!' she shouted to her boyfriend. 'Grab your clothes and jump out the window. My husband is home early!'

The boyfriend looked out the window and said: 'I can't jump! It's raining like crazy out there and I'm naked!'

'I don't care,' she insisted. 'If my husband catches us, he'll kill the pair of us.'

So the boyfriend grabbed his clothes and jumped from the bedroom window. When he landed, he found himself in the middle of a group of marathon runners. Hoping to blend in even though he was naked, he started running alongside them, carrying his clothes over his arm.

One of the runners asked: 'Do you always run in the nude?'

Thinking on his feet, the boyfriend replied breathlessly: 'Yes, always. It feels so free having the air blow over my skin while I'm running.'

'Do you always run carrying your clothes on your arm?' queried the athlete.

'Oh, yes,' panted the boyfriend. 'That way I can get dressed at the end of the run, get in my car and just go straight home without a shower.'

'And,' persisted the athlete, 'do you always wear a condom when you run?'

'Only if it's raining.'

AIRPLANES

36 A famous French wartime pilot named Pierre was having dinner with a brunette, and when they finished they headed to a hotel where he called room service and asked for a bottle of red wine. When it arrived, he put some red wine on the woman's lips and began kissing her passionately.

'What is the red wine for?' she panted.

The pilot replied suavely: 'For when Pierre the famous fighter pilot has red meat, he has red wine.'

'Ooooh!' she sighed, and they carried on.

A few minutes of heavy kissing later, he reached for the phone and ordered a bottle of white wine. When it arrived, he splashed it on her chest and began kissing her breasts.

'What is the white wine for?' she gasped.

The pilot replied suavely: 'For when Pierre the famous fighter pilot has white meat, he has white wine.'

'Ooooh!' she groaned.

Soon he worked his way down to her pussy, pulled out a can of lighter fluid and a match, sprinkled it on her muff and set fire to it.

'Aaagh! Why the fuck did you do that?' she screamed.

The pilot replied proudly: 'For when Pierre the famous fighter pilot goes down, he goes down in flames!'

37 'Flight 1234,' advised the control tower, 'turn right 45 degrees for noise abatement.'

'Roger,' the pilot responded, 'but we're at 35,000 feet. How much noise can we make up here?'

'Sir,' replied the radar man, 'have you ever heard the noise a 727 makes when it hits a 747?'

38 What did the kamikaze pilot instructor say to his students? – Watch closely. I'm only going to do this once.

39 A passenger was sitting on an airplane, sweating profusely and chewing his nails. The flight attendant said: 'Sir, can I get you something from the bar to calm you down?'

She got him a whiskey, and he knocked it back, but twenty minutes later she noticed that he was shaking like a leaf.

'Would another drink help?' she asked sympathetically.

He nodded feverishly. So she fetched him another whiskey, and he gulped it down.

But a quarter of an hour later, there was no improvement. In fact, he was worse than ever, and was sobbing audibly.

The flight attendant remarked: 'I've never seen anyone so afraid of flying.'

'I'm not afraid of flying,' said the man. 'I'm trying to give up drinking!'

40 As an airplane prepared for takeoff, the flight attendant concluded her announcement by saying: 'And on behalf of your captain, Jill Duncan, we wish you all a pleasant journey.'

A male passenger in row B was appalled to hear that the plane had a woman pilot. When the attendant came around to make the last-minute checks, he said: 'Is that right? This plane is being flown by a woman?'

'Yes,' replied the attendant politely. 'In fact the entire crew is female.'

'In that case,' he grumbled, 'I'll need a stiff drink once we get under way. I don't know what to think of all those women up there in the cockpit.'

'That's another thing,' said the attendant. 'We no longer call it the cockpit. Now it's the box office.'

Signs That You've Chosen a 'No Frills' Airline:

41 • Tickets are sold through lottery terminals.

42 • At the airport all the insurance machines are sold out.

43 • Before the flight, the passengers get together and elect a pilot.

44 • You can't board the plane unless you have the exact change.

45 • Before you take off, the flight attendant tells you to fasten your Velcro.

46 • The captain asks all the passengers to chip in a little for gas.

47 • When they pull the steps away, the plane starts rocking.

48 • The captain yells at the ground crew to get the cows off the runway.

49 • All planes have both a toilet and a chapel.

50 • No movie. You don't need one. Your life keeps flashing before your eyes.

51 • You see a man with a gun, but he's demanding to be let off the plane.

52 With a plane about to crash, the captain asked the passengers: 'Does anyone on board believe in the power of prayer?'

A preacher immediately put his hand up.

'Good,' said the captain. 'We're one parachute short.'

53 The airplane was just taking off when the pilot, making a routine announcement, suddenly screamed: 'Oh, my God!'

A few minutes later, he came back on the intercom and apologized if he had scared any of the passengers. He explained: 'While I was talking, the flight attendant brought me a cup of coffee and spilled hot coffee in my lap. You should see the front of my trousers!'

One of the passengers said: 'That's nothing. He should see the back of mine!'

54 Three women were on a flight when the captain suddenly announced: 'Please prepare for a crash landing!'

The first woman immediately began putting on all her jewellery.

'Why are you doing that?' asked the other two.

'Well, when they come to rescue us they will see that I am rich and will rescue me first.'

The second woman, not wishing to be outdone, then began removing her top and bra.

'Why are you doing that?' asked her two friends.

'Well, when they come to rescue us they will see what great tits I have and will pick me up first.'

Not wishing to be outdone, the third woman, who was West Indian, started taking off her skirt and panties.

'Why are you doing that?' asked the other two.

'Well, they always search for the black box first!'

ALASKA

55 It was forty below zero one winter's night in Alaska. In the town saloon, the bartender told Ed: 'You owe me quite a bit on your tab.'

'Sorry,' said Ed, 'I'm flat broke this week.'

'OK,' said the bartender, 'I'll just write your name and the amount you owe me right here on the wall.'

Ed looked concerned. 'I don't want any of my friends to see that.'

'They won't,' said the bartender. 'I'll just hang your parka over it until it's paid . . .'

ALCOHOL

56 A guy went to a doctor and said: 'I'm having problems with sex. I think my privates are too small.'

The doctor asked him what he drinks when he goes to the pub.

'Er, lager,' he replied, bemused.

'Ha, that's your problem,' said the doctor. 'Lager shrinks things. You should try drinking Guinness instead — that makes things grow.'

Two months later, the man returned to the doctor's with a big smile on his face. He shook the doctor warmly by the hand and thanked him.

'I take it you now drink Guinness?' said the doctor.

'No,' replied the man, 'but I've got the wife on lager.'

57 When are beer and your mother-in-law at their best? — When they're cold, opened up, and on the table.

58 A man walked into a bar and ordered a scotch. 'And,' he added ominously, 'I want a ten-year-old scotch. And don't try to fob me off with something younger because I can tell the difference.'

The bartender thought the customer was all talk and decided to trick him by giving him a five-year-old scotch. But the man took one sip, grimaced, and snapped: 'Bartender, this is five-year-old scotch. I told you I wanted ten-year-old scotch.'

The bartender was still not convinced and tried to fool the customer with a seven-year-old scotch, but once again the man said: 'I told you I wanted ten-year-old scotch. This is only seven years old.'

Admitting defeat, the bartender served him the ten-year-old scotch, and the customer purred. 'Perfect. At last, the real thing.'

Observing all this was a drunk, who then staggered over, slammed a glass down in front of the whiskey connoisseur, and said: 'Here, try this one.'

The man took a sip and immediately spat it out. 'Ugh! It tastes like piss!'

'Yeah,' said the drunk. 'Now tell me how old I am.'

59 A suave playboy picked up an elegant young lady in a bar and took her back to his apartment. Eager to impress her, he showed her his collected works of art and some rare first editions. He then offered her a drink, asking her whether she would prefer a glass of sherry or port.

'Oh, definitely sherry,' she said. 'Sherry is like the nectar of the gods. Just looking at it in this crystal decanter fills me with anticipation. When the stopper is removed and the beautiful liquid is poured into the glass and I inhale the delicious tangy aroma, I am lifted on the wings of ecstasy. As I taste the magical potion, my whole being glows, it seems like a thousand violins are playing in my ears, and I'm transported into another world. Port, on the other hand, makes me fart.'

60 Why did God invent alcohol? – So that fat women can get laid too.

61 A blonde walked into a bar and ordered a triple Jack Daniels . . . followed by another . . . and another . . . and another . . . and another. She ended up spreadeagled on the floor, and all the guys in the bar took advantage of her.

It was the same story for the next two nights: she downed a succession of Jack Daniels, collapsed on the floor, and all the guys in the bar had sex with her.

On the fourth night, she asked the bartender for a martini.

'I thought you drank Jack Daniels?' he said.

'Not any more,' she replied. 'It makes my pussy sore.'

62 An ex-US Marine Virginian hillbilly came to town carrying a jug of moonshine in one hand and a shotgun in the other. He stopped a man on the street and said: 'Here, friend, take a drink outta my jug.'

The guy protested, saying he never drank, but the hillbilly levelled the shotgun at him and commanded: 'Drink!'

The stranger drank, shuddered, shook, shivered, and coughed. 'My God!' he said. 'That's awful stuff you've got there!'

'Ain't it, though!' replied the hillbilly. 'Now, you hold the gun on me while I take a swig.'

63 Fred started chatting up a good-looking girl in a bar. Seeing that she didn't back off, he asked her name.

'Carmen,' she replied.

'That's a nice name,' he said, warming up the conversation. 'Who named you, your mother?'

'No, as a matter of fact, I named myself.'

'That's interesting. Why Carmen?'

'Because I like cars, and I like men.' Looking directly into his eyes, she asked: 'What's your name?'

He said: 'Beerfuck.'

ALZHEIMER'S

64 After playing bridge together for many years, two old ladies had got to know each other pretty well. Then one day, during a game of cards, one lady suddenly looked up at the other and said: 'I realize we've known each other for many years but, for the life of me, I just can't bring it to mind. Would you please tell me your name again, dear?'

There was silence for a couple of minutes, and then the other lady answered: 'How soon do you need to know?'

65 What's the best thing about Alzheimer's? – You never have to watch reruns on TV.

66 What's the best thing about having kids with Alzheimer's? – You can give them the same presents year after year.

67 Did you hear about the Easter egg hunt for Alzheimer's patients? – They hid their own eggs!

68 What was the name of Ronald Reagan's last movie? – *Partial Recall.*

69 An old guy walked up to an old woman at a dance and said: 'So, tell me, do I come here often?'

70 Three friends with Alzheimer's were chatting together at a train station. They were so engrossed in their conversation that they didn't hear the guard blow his whistle to signal the train's departure. Just as the train began to pull away, two of the men managed to scramble aboard, but the third didn't make it.

The guard came over to console him: 'Never mind,' said the guard. 'Two of you made it, and there's another train in an hour.'

'No, you don't understand,' said the man. 'They came to see *me* off.'

AMERICANS

71 A New England cabbie picked up a woman passenger late at night. She was very drunk and flopped in the front seat next to him, hitching up her short skirt to give him a good view of her pussy.

'Where to, lady?' he asked, trying to avert his gaze.

Wrapping an arm around his neck and opening her legs even wider, she whispered: 'I want you to go where it smells.'

He said: 'Lady, there's no way I'm taking you to Pittsburgh at this time of night!'

72 A group of American tourists were visiting Windsor Castle, which is situated directly in the flight path of Heathrow Airport. While they were admiring the castle walls, a plane flew overhead at a relatively low altitude, making a tremendous amount of noise. One of the American tourists complained: 'Why the heck did they build the castle so close to the airport?'

73 Why do American eighteen-year-olds take sex education courses? – So they can learn what they've been doing wrong for the past five years.

74 What do Americans call a TV set that goes five years without need of repair? – An import.

75 A city slicker pulled into a one-street town in the middle of Wyoming. The place seemed deserted apart from an old timer sitting in a rocking chair at the front of the general store.
   'What do you folks do around here?' asked the city slicker.
   The old timer replied slowly: 'We don't do nothin' but hunt 'n' fuck.'
   'What do you hunt?'
   'Something to fuck.'

Signs That You Might Be Trailer Trash:

76 • Your wife's hairdo was once ruined by a ceiling fan.
77 • You've been married three times and still have the same in-laws.
78 • You can't get married to your sweetheart because there's a law against it.
79 • You think loading a dishwasher means getting your wife drunk.
80 • Your toilet paper has numbers on it.
81 • A tornado hits your home and causes $10,000 of improvement.
82 • You think Dom Perignon is a Mafia boss.
83 • You think a woman who is 'out of your league' bowls on a different night.

84 A Canadian man was having coffee and croissants with butter and jam in a Toronto diner when an American guy, chewing gum, sat down next to him. The Canadian ignored the American, who nevertheless started up a conversation.
   The American snapped his gum and said: 'You Canadian folk eat the whole bread?'

Annoyed at having his leisurely breakfast interrupted, the Canadian frowned and replied: 'Of course.'

The American blew a huge bubble and grinned. 'We don't. In the States, we only eat what's inside. We collect the crusts in a container, recycle them, transform them into croissants and sell them to Canada.'

The Canadian listened in silence, but the American persisted. 'D'ya eat jelly with the bread?'

The Canadian sighed. 'Of course.'

Cracking his gum between his teeth, the American said: 'We don't. In the States, we eat fresh fruit for breakfast, then we put all the peels, seeds and leftovers in containers, recycle them, transform them into jam and sell it to Canada.'

The Canadian then asked: 'Do you have sex in the States?'

The American smiled and said: 'Of course we do.'

The Canadian leaned closer and asked: 'And what do you do with the condoms once you've used them?'

'We throw them away, of course.'

Now it was the Canadian's turn to smile. 'We don't. In Canada, we put them in a container, recycle them, melt them down into chewing gum and sell them to the United States.'

85 What's the difference between a Northern fairytale and a Southern fairytale? – A Northern fairytale starts, 'Once upon a time . . .' A Southern fairytale starts, 'Y'all ain't gonna believe this shit . . .'

86 An aborigine was fishing in Queensland, Australia, when a crocodile suddenly leaped from the water and grabbed him by the legs. The crocodile was halfway through devouring the man when a boatload of American tourists passed by. One woman said: 'I thought aborigines were meant to be poor. Well, there's one over there with a Lacoste sleeping bag.'

87 An American inventor went to the US Patents Office to register a new folding bottle.

'What's it called?' asked the clerk.

'A fottle,' replied the inventor. 'It's short for "folding bottle".'

'That's a silly name,' said the clerk.

'And I've also invented a folding carton called a farton.'

'I'm sorry, there's no way we can allow that. It's too rude.'

'Oh, dear,' said the inventor. 'Then you're gonna hate the name of my folding bucket!'

88 A Swiss man, looking for directions, pulled up at a bus stop where two Americans were waiting.

'Entschuldigung, koennen Sie Deutsch sprechen?' he asked. The two Americans just stared at him.

He tried again. 'Excusez-moi, parlez-vous Français?' The two Americans continued to stare.

'Parlare Italiano?' asked the Swiss. No response.

'Hablan ustedes Español?' he ventured. Still nothing.

The Swiss man then drove off, disgusted.

The first American turned to the other and said: 'Y' know, maybe we should learn a foreign language.'

'Why?' said the other. 'That guy knew four languages, and it didn't do him any good.'

Some Rejected State Slogans:

89 • Alabama: Literassy Ain't Everything. Ya Want Fries With That?

90 • Alaska: 11,623 Eskimos Can't Be Wrong.

91 • California: As Seen On TV.

92 • Colorado: If You Don't Ski, Don't Bother.

93 • Florida: Ask Us About Our Grandchildren.

94 • Georgia: We Put The 'Fun' In Fundamentalist Extremism.

95 • Hawaii: Haka Tiki Mou Sha'ami Leeki Toru (Death To Mainland Scum, But Leave Your Money)

96 • Iowa: We Do Amazing Things With Corn.

97 • Kentucky: Tobacco Is a Vegetable.

98 • Michigan: First Line Of Defense From The Canadians.

99 • Minnesota: 10,000 Lakes And 10,000,000 Mosquitoes.

100 • Mississippi: Come And Feel Better About Your Own State.

101 • New Jersey: You Have The Right To Remain Silent, You Have The Right To An Attorney.

102 • North Carolina: Five Million People; Fifteen Last Names.

103 • Utah: Our Jesus Is Better Than Your Jesus.

104 • Wyoming: Miles And Miles Of Nothing Since 1890.

AMISH

105 A young Amish girl was going out on her first date. As it was a bitterly cold night, she put on some gloves, only to be chastised by her mother who thought gloves were unbecoming of a lady.

The girl protested. 'What am I supposed to do with my hands if they get cold from riding in the buggy?'

The mother advised: 'Just stick your hands between your legs and they will get warm.'

The girl obeyed her mother's wishes and went off on her date. On their way home, her hands got cold, so she placed them between her legs. Her young escort looked across and asked: 'Why on earth have you got your hands between your legs?'

She replied: 'My mother told me that if my hands got cold, I should stick them between my legs to get them warm.'

Her date said: 'Well, my dick is frozen solid. So would you mind if I stick it between your legs to get it warm?'

The girl could see no harm in the idea and allowed him to stick his dick between her legs.

When she arrived home, she asked her mother: 'What do you know about dicks?'

Her mother was startled. 'Why, what do you know about dicks?'

The girl said: 'All I know is that when they thaw out they make an awful mess!'

106 Two Amish women were picking potatoes one day. Holding two potatoes in her hand, the first Amish woman turned to the other and said: 'These potatoes remind me of my husband's testicles.'

The second woman said: 'Are his testicles that big?'

'No, they're that dirty.'

107 What goes clippity-clop, clippity-clop, clippity-clop, bang, bang, bang? – An Amish drive-by shooting.

108 An Amish boy and his father made their first visit to a big city shopping mall. They were amazed by everything they saw, especially the two shiny silver walls that could move apart and then slide back together again.

'What is it?' asked the boy.

The father, never having seen an elevator before, said: 'I don't know.'

They watched intently as an old lady went over to the moving walls and pressed a button. They saw the walls open and the old lady went into a small room. Then the walls closed, and the boy and his father were transfixed as the small numbers above the walls lit up in sequence. The pair continued to gaze in awe until the light reached the last number, and then the numbers began to light in reverse order. Finally the walls opened again and out stepped a beautiful young woman.

The father turned to the boy and said: 'Go get your mother.'

Signs That Your Amish Teen Is In Trouble:

109 • He sometimes stays in bed until after 6 a.m.

110 • Under his bed, you find pictures of women without bonnets.

111 • He defiantly says, 'If I had a radio, I'd listen to rap.'

112 • When you criticize him, he yells, 'Thou suck!'

113 • His name is Jebediah but he prefers to be known as 'Jeb Daddy'.

114 • You discover his secret stash of colourful socks.

115 • He uses the slang expression: 'Talk to the hand 'cos the beard ain't listening.'

116 • He was recently pulled over for driving under the influence of cottage cheese.

117 • He has taken to wearing his big black hat backwards.

ANIMALS

118 Three bulls heard that the farmer was introducing a new bull. The three were reluctant to give up any of their cows to the newcomer.

The first bull said proudly: 'I've been here five years, I've got a hundred cows, and I'm keeping them.'

The second bull announced: 'I've been here five years, I've got fifty cows, and I intend keeping them.'

The third bull, the youngest of the three, warned: 'I've been here a year and although I only have ten cows, I'm gonna keep them.'

A few minutes after their shows of bravado, a lorry pulled up to the farm and out stepped the biggest bull they had ever seen — a truly awesome creature. The first two bulls immediately backed down and said the newcomer could have as many of their cows as he wanted. Meanwhile the third bull began pawing the dirt, shaking his horns and snorting.

The first bull went over to him and said: 'Son, let me give you some advice real quick. Let him have some of your cows and live to tell the tale.'

The third bull said: 'Hey, as far as I'm concerned he can have *all* my cows. I'm just making sure he knows I'm a bull!'

119 A female elephant was walking through the jungle one day when she got a thorn in her foot. The further she walked, the more it hurt until eventually she began to limp. After a while, an ant came over to her and asked: 'What's the matter?'

The elephant replied: 'I've got this thorn in my foot, and I would do anything to get it out.'

The ant said: 'Anything?' Would you let me butt-fuck you?'

The elephant thought about it for a minute and decided what the hell. How bad could an ant be? So she agreed. The ant started pulling on the thorn and soon got it out. True to her word, the elephant lay down on her side and moved her tail out of the way. The ant crawled up on her and started getting to work.

This unlikely scene was watched from the top of a tree by a monkey who laughed so much that he accidentally knocked a coconut out of the tree. The coconut crashed down on the elephant's head, right between her ears.

'Aaaaargh!' moaned the elephant in pain.

The ant yelled: 'Take it all bitch, take it all!'

120 What's the difference between a dog and a fox? – About eight beers.

121 What's the difference between a hamster and a cow? – Cows survive the branding.

122 A man went to the doctor and said: 'I've got a huge hole in my ass.'

The doctor said: 'Drop your pants, bend over and I'll take a look.'

The man did as requested, and the doctor examined him. 'My God!' exclaimed the doctor. 'What on earth could have made a hole as big as that?'

The patient replied: 'I've been fucked by an elephant!'

The doctor said: 'But an elephant's penis is long and thin, this hole is enormous.'

'Yes,' said the patient, 'but he fingered me first.'

123 What do you get when you cross an alligator and a railroad track? – Three pieces of alligator.

124 A little girl walked into a pet shop and asked in the sweetest little lisp: 'Excuthe me, mithter, do you keep widdle wabbits?'

As the shopkeeper's heart melted, he got down on his knees to her level and asked: 'Do you want a widdle white wabbit or a thoft and fuwwy bwack wabbit or maybe one like this cute widdle bwown wabbit over there?'

The little girl leaned forward and said in a quiet voice: 'I don't fink my pet python weally gives a thit.'

125 Why do mice have such tiny balls? – Because so few of them can dance.

126 Some of the animals went to see God in order to complain about their lot in life.

The elephant moaned: 'I really hate this long trunk – it's always getting in the way. It makes me so clumsy, and if I'm not careful I trip over it.'

'Maybe,' said God, 'but your trunk makes you useful to humans. It allows you to lift huge weights that they cannot manage. Without it, you would serve no purpose.'

While the elephant thought about what God had said, the giraffe butted in. 'I hate my long neck,' said the giraffe. 'It's such a nuisance in high winds. Why can't I have something more normal?'

God replied: 'But your long neck enables you to reach succulent leaves at the very tops of trees – places where no other animal can get to. It gives you a tremendous advantage. Without your long neck, you would always have to battle with shorter creatures for food.'

While the giraffe digested God's words, the hen interrupted: 'Either let me have a bigger arse or smaller eggs . . .'

127 Two cows were chatting in a field. The first said: 'I was artificaly inseminated this morning.'

'I don't believe you.'

'It's true, no bull!'

128 A gorilla and a rhino were best friends until one day, as the rhino bent over to drink from a watering hole, the gorilla took advantage of the situation and buggered him. The rhino reacted angrily and chased the gorilla all over the game reserve. Half an hour later and still hotly pursued by the charging rhino, the gorilla spotted an explorer sitting in a chair, reading a newspaper. Creeping up behind the explorer, the gorilla killed him, grabbed his clothes and paper, threw the body behind a bush, and sat down in the chair to read.

Moments later, the rhino came charging onto the scene. 'Excuse me,' he said. 'Have you seen a gorilla around here?'

Holding up the newspaper to hide his face, the gorilla replied: 'What, the one that buggered a rhino by the watering hole?'

'Oh, God!' said the rhino. 'Don't tell me it's in the papers already!'

129 A mouse was drinking heavily in a bar, and the more he drank, the hornier he became. Having recently split up from his girlfriend, he was desperate for sex, but the only female in the bar was a giraffe. Still, she was a nice-looking giraffe and, after buying her a couple of drinks, the mouse left with her.

An hour later, the mouse staggered back into the bar alone, looking thoroughly exhausted.

'Why are you so tired?' asked the bartender.

The mouse explained: 'Between the "Kiss me, Fuck me, Kiss me, Fuck me", I must have run twenty miles!'

130 Did you hear about the bisexual donkey? – It had a hee in the morning and a haw at night.

131 Hearing howls from his basement one night, a man went downstairs to see a female cat being raped by a mouse. The man was intrigued by the sight and, after gaining the mouse's trust with a few pieces of cheese, he persuaded the rodent to repeat the act on next door's German Shepherd dog.

Excited by this bizarre discovery, the man was desperate to show off the mouse to his wife. 'Look what I've brought to show you,' he called, entering the bedroom. But before he could explain, the wife took one look at the mouse, screamed, and hid under the bedclothes.

'It's only a mouse, honey,' he said.

'Get out! Get out!' she yelled. 'And take that sex maniac with you!'

132 It's spring, and a bear cub emerges from a cave. His knees were wobbling, his paws were weak, and he had big circles under his eyes.

His mother looked at the state of him and said: 'Junior, did you hibernate all winter like you were supposed to?'

'Hibernate?' said the bear cub. 'Damn. I thought you said masturbate!'

133 What's the only animal with an asshole in the middle of its back? – A police horse.

134 It was that time of the year when the bulls were called upon to service the local cows. Entrusted with the task were a young bull by the name of Henry and an older one called Sam. As the senior partner, Sam felt obliged to take charge of the organization. A stickler for neatness, he suggested that they wait until the cows were lined up at the feeding trough and then work their way along the line from either end. 'You start at one end,' he told Henry, 'I'll start at the other, and we'll meet in the middle. It will all be conducted in a nice orderly fashion. And remember, you have to treat the cows with respect and courtesy. Always be polite after inseminating them.'

Henry promised to treat the cows gently but when he saw them lined up at the trough, youthful exuberance took over and he raced along the line at breakneck speed. 'Thank you ma'am, thank you ma'am, thank you ma'am, thank you ma'am, sorry Sam, thank you ma'am . . .'

135 What has four legs and flies? – A dead horse.

136 When the Ark's door was closed, Noah called a meeting with all the animals. 'Listen up,' he said. 'There will be no sex on this trip. All of you males take off your penis and hand it to my sons. I will sit at that table over there and write you a receipt. After we see land, you can get your penis back.'

A week into the journey, Mr Rabbit hopped excitedly into his wife's cage and said: 'Quick! Get on my shoulders and look out the window to see if you can see land.'

She got onto his shoulders but said: 'Sorry, no sign of land yet.'

'Damn!' he said.

This went on every day for the next week. Each day Mr Rabbit would rush in excitedly and ask Mrs Rabbit if she could see land yet. Each time the answer was the same. Eventually she got fed up with him. 'What's wrong with you?' she asked. 'You know it will rain for forty days and forty nights. Only after the water has drained will we be able to see land. Why are you acting so excited?'

'Look,' said Mr Rabbit slyly, producing a slip of paper from his pocket. 'I've got the horse's receipt!'

137 What did the slug say to the snail? – '*Big Issue*, mate?'

138   A woman living near Nairobi was eating breakfast on her patio when she noticed a huge gorilla climbing her palm tree. Scared, she ran into her house and phoned the local gorilla handler. He told her not to worry, and said that he would be right over. When he arrived, he explained that it was a fairly common problem and should only take a few minutes. He then went to his truck and fetched a stepladder, a shotgun, an 8ft pole, a pair of handcuffs, and a vicious pit bull terrier.

'What is all that stuff for?' asked the woman.

He said: 'First, I climb up on the stepladder and ram the pole up the gorilla's ass. This will cause the gorilla to fall from the tree, at which point the mean pit bull will bite the gorilla in the balls. This temporarily paralyses the gorilla, and at that point I handcuff the gorilla and take him away.'

The woman looked puzzled. 'So, what's the shotgun for?'

'In case I fall off the ladder, you shoot the pit bull!'

139   Two small boys – Timmy and Michael – were playing with their pet tortoises in the garden. Timmy boasted that his tortoise was the faster, so they agreed to have a race to the garden wall. Michael's tortoise lumbered away, but Timmy's just sat there in its shell.

'You're gonna lose! You're gonna lose!' laughed Michael as his pet headed off up the garden.

'No, I'm not!' yelled Timmy. And with that he picked up his tortoise and hurled it at the wall.

140   What does a bull do to stay warm on a cold day? – It goes into a barn and slips into a nice warm Jersey.

141   Two naturalists were observing wildlife in the forests of Canada.

One said: 'Did you see that bear over there?'

'No,' replied the second. 'I didn't.'

A few minutes later the first naturalist said: 'Did you just see that eagle flying overheard?'

'No, I missed that,' said the second, dejected.

Five minutes later, the first naturalist said: 'Did you see that moose go behind those trees?'

'Damn!' said the second. 'I missed that, too!'

'You really ought to keep your eyes open,' said the first. 'That way you won't keep missing things.'

A few minutes later, the first naturalist said: 'Hey, did you see that?'

'As a matter of fact I did,' snapped the second man, determined not to be ridiculed further. 'Indeed, I probably spotted it before you!'

'Oh, yes?' said the first naturalist. 'So why did you step in it?'

142 How many animals can you get into a pair of tights? – Ten little piggies, two calves, one beaver, one ass, one pussy, thousands of hares, and a dead fish no one can ever find.

ART

143 At an art exhibition, two women were staring at a painting entitled *Home for Lunch*. The painting was of three very naked and very black men, sitting on a park bench. What was unusual was that the man on either end of the bench had black penises, but the man in the middle had a pink penis. The two women were standing there, staring at the picture, scratching their heads and trying to figure this out.

Then the artist walked by and, noticing the women's confusion, asked: 'Can I help you at all?'

'Well, yes,' said one of the women. 'We were curious about the picture of the black men on the bench. Why does the man in the middle have a pink penis?'

'Oh,' said the artist. 'I'm afraid you've misunderstood the painting. The three men are not African-Americans, they're coal miners, and the fellow in the middle went "Home for Lunch".'

ATHEISTS

144 An atheist was walking through a Canadian forest when a huge grizzly bear began chasing him. Cornered in a cave, the terrified atheist sank to his knees, shouting: 'Lord, save me!'

God called down: 'You hypocrite! All these years you've denied my very existence, and now you want my help!'

'I know, I know,' pleaded the atheist. 'I have no right to ask for your help, but could you at least meet me halfway on this and make the bear a Christian? Please, God, I'm begging you.'

'Very well,' sighed God, and he made the bear a Christian.

The atheist breathed a huge sigh of relief and boldly approached the bear. But as he tried to pass, the bear bared his teeth and gored the atheist to death. Standing over the corpse, the bear then put his paws together and said: 'Lord, for this sumptuous meal I thank you . . .'

AUSTRALIANS

145 Bruce was driving over Sydney Harbour Bridge when he spotted his girlfriend Sheila about to throw herself off. Bruce slammed on the brakes and yelled: 'Sheila, what the hell d'ya think you're doing?'

Sheila turned around with a tear in her eye and said: 'G'day Bruce. Ya got me pregnant and so now I'm gonna kill myself.'

Bruce got a lump in his throat when he heard this. 'Struth, Sheila,' he said, 'not only are you a great shag, but you're a real sport too.'

Then he drove off.

146 What's the definition of Australian aristocracy? – A man who can trace his lineage back to his father.

147 On a visit to London, an Australian applied for a job as a royal footman. Armed with his references from his previous job, he went along to the interview, where he was asked to drop his trousers.

Seeing the Australian's puzzled expression, the interviewer explained: 'Don't worry, it's merely a formality. You see, footmen are often required to wear kilts when accompanying the Queen to Balmoral, so we like to examine the knees of applicants to check for any unsightly scars.'

The Aussie duly dropped his trousers to allow his knees to be inspected.

'Excellent,' said the interviewer. 'Now could you show me your testimonials?'

Thirty seconds later, the Aussie found himself lying in the corridor, nursing a black eye. 'Struth,' he said, picking himself up and dusting himself down. 'I reckon I'd have got that job if I'd known the lingo a little better.'

148 How do you know when an Australian woman is having her period? – She's only wearing one sock.

149 An Australian had been wandering through the outback for months when he came to an isolated farm with a pretty girl standing at the gate.

'D'ya shag?' he asked.

'No, but you've talked me into it, you silver-tongued bastard!'

150 An Englishman wanted to become an Irishman, so he visited a doctor to find out how to go about it. The doctor said: 'This is a very delicate and dangerous operation. You see, in order to make you Irish, I'll have to remove half your brain. Are you happy with that?'

'Yes, that's OK,' said the Englishman. 'I've always wanted to be Irish, and I'm prepared to take the risk.'

The operation went ahead, but the Englishman woke to find a look of horror on the doctor's face. 'I'm so terribly sorry,' said the doctor. 'Instead of removing half the brain, I've taken the whole brain out.'

The patient replied: 'No worries, mate.'

AUTOMOBILES

How To Identify Where a Driver Is From:

151 • One hand on wheel, one hand on horn – Chicago

152 • One hand on wheel, one finger out window – New York City

153 • One hand on wheel, one hand on newspaper, foot solidly on accelerator – Boston

154 • One hand on wheel, cradling mobile phone, brick on accelerator, with gun in lap – Los Angeles

155 • Both hands on wheel, eyes shut, both feet on brake, quivering in terror – Ohio, but driving in California

156 • Both hands in air, gesturing, both feet on accelerator, head turned to talk to someone in back seat – Italy

157 • One hand on latte, one knee on wheel, cradling cell phone, foot on brake, mind on game – Seattle

158 • One hand on wheel, one hand on hunting rifle, throwing McDonald's bag out of window – Texas male

159 • One hand constantly refocusing rearview mirror to show different angles of big hair, poodle steering car, chrome .38 revolver with mother of pearl inlaid handle in glove compartment – Texas female

160 • Four-wheel drive pickup truck, shotgun mounted in rear window, beer cans on floor, squirrel tails attached to antenna — Arkansas

161 • Two hands gripping wheel, blue hair barely visible above window level, driving 35 mph on the interstate in the left lane with the blinker on — Florida

162 A wealthy lady was being driven by her chauffeur when their car got a flat tyre. The chauffeur got out and began trying to remove the hubcap. After watching him struggle for five minutes, she leaned out of the window and asked: 'Would you like a screwdriver?'

'We might as well,' he said. 'I can't get this bloody wheel off!'

163 How can you tell when an auto mechanic just had sex? — One of his fingers is clean.

164 A hitch-hiker was standing by the roadside, making vulgar gestures at passing cars.

Another hiker came over to him and said: 'You'll never get a lift like that.'

'I don't care,' said the first. 'It's my lunch break.'

165 Having just bought a small sports car, a young guy was keen to show it off to his girlfriend. So they went for a drive in the country where she began to feel decidedly amorous. As he stopped the car in a quiet lane, she said: 'There's no room in here; let's go and screw behind that grassy bank. Hurry up and get out of the car before I get out of the mood!'

The guy struggled for a minute, then said dejectedly: 'Until I get out of the mood, I can't get out of the car!'

166 A speeding car smashed through a guardrail, rolled down a cliff, bounced off a tree, and landed upside down, wheels spinning frantically.

As the driver climbed slowly back up to the road, a passing motorist said: 'Are you drunk?'

'Of course,' he said. 'What do you think I am, a stunt driver?'

167 Out on a date, a young couple went for a drive in the countryside. Starting to feel randy, they looked for a quiet lane and tried to have sex in the back seat. However the car was too small and instead they decided to carry on underneath the vehicle where there was more legroom.

A few minutes later, a police officer happened to be passing. He immediately announced that he was arresting the couple for indecent exposure.

'But I'm not doing anything illegal,' protested the man. 'I'm just fixing my car.'

'You're having sex,' replied the officer coldly. 'And I know that to be a fact for three reasons. Firstly, you have no tools out. Secondly, I can see a second pair of legs in addition to yours. And thirdly, your car's been stolen.'

168 How can an American be certain that the car he's just bought is actually new? – When it's recalled by the factory.

169 John was driving around town in a Rolls-Royce when he saw his friend Alec waving to him.

'Hey, where did you get the car?' asked Alec.

'Well,' explained John, 'I was walking down the road to the general store when a beautiful blonde pulled up in this car and offered me a ride. I got in, but instead of going into town, she drove up to the lane by the lake and removed all of her clothes except her black lacy knickers. She then lay back in the seat, spread her legs and said: "Take anything you want from me." Well, I could see her underwear would never fit me, so I took the car . . .'

170 What's the difference between a Jehovah's Witness and a Skoda? – You can shut the door on a Jehovah's Witness.

171 What's the difference between a Skoda and a tampon? – The tampon comes with its own tow rope.

172 What's the difference between being caught inside Kylie Minogue's bra and being caught inside a Skoda? – You feel a bigger tit in a Skoda!

173 A lady went to a car dealership to buy a Skoda, only to be told that, due to new EC regulations, she had to provide an account of her medical history before she could purchase the car. Mildly irritated, she complied, and returned the following day with the required information.

The salesman read through her documents but said: 'Sorry, madam, you can't buy a Skoda.'

'Why on earth not?' she asked.

'Because,' said the salesman, 'it says here that you've had a hysterectomy, and you have to be a complete cunt to buy a Skoda!'

174 Why do men pay more than women for car insurance? – Because women don't get blow jobs while they're driving.

175 Did you hear about the new device that makes your car run ninety-five per cent quieter? – It fits right over her mouth.

176 It was a perfect summer's day, and a guy was driving along the highway to a scenic lake where he intended spending the afternoon fishing. About an hour from his destination, he spotted a man dressed from head to toe in red standing by the side of the highway and gesturing him to stop. The fisherman pulled over, wound down his window and asked: 'How can I help you?'

'I am the red asshole of the asphalt,' replied the man in red. 'You got anything to eat?'

Blessed with a generous spirit on such a beautiful day, the fisherman handed the man one of his sandwiches before resuming his journey.

A few miles down the road, he noticed a man dressed all in yellow standing by the side of the road and beckoning him to stop. Mildly irritated by a second interruption to his progress, the fisherman called out: 'What do you want?'

'I am the yellow asshole of the asphalt,' replied the man in yellow. 'Got anything to drink?'

The fisherman handed him a can of Coke and quickly drove off. Not wanting to lose any more time, he put his foot down in an attempt to reach the lake by lunchtime, but a few miles further down the road he saw a guy dressed all in blue standing by the side of the road gesturing him to stop. Frustrated at yet another delay, the fisherman pulled over, wound down the window and yelled: 'Let me guess, you're the blue asshole of the asphalt. What the hell do you want?'

The man in blue replied: 'Driver's licence and registration, please.'

BABIES

177 A woman went to her doctor and said. 'Doctor, I can't sleep at night. When I'm in the next room, I have this terrible fear that I won't hear the baby if he falls out of the crib at night. What should I do?'

'Easy,' said the doctor. 'Just take the carpet off the floor.'

178 While waiting for a train, a man was holding two babies, one in each arm.

A woman came up to him and said: 'Aren't they cute? What are their names?'

'I don't know,' said the guy, irritated.

'Are they boys or girls?', continued the woman.

'I don't know,' snapped the guy.

'What kind of a father are you?' she said.

He answered: 'I'm not their father, I'm a condom salesman. And these are the two complaints I'm taking back to my company!'

179 What's the difference between a seagull and a baby? – A seagull flits along the shore.

180 Two storks – father stork and baby stork – were sitting on the nest. Baby stork was crying incessantly, and father stork was trying to calm him down. 'Don't worry, your mother will come back. She's only bringing people babies and making them happy.'

The following night it was the father's turn to do the rounds. So as mother and baby stork sat on the nest, she told him: 'Don't worry, your father will be back as soon as possible. But for now he's bringing joy to new mommies and daddies.'

A few days later, mother and father stork were sick with worry: baby stork had been gone from the nest all night. When he finally returned the next morning, they said: 'Where on earth have you been?'

'Aw,' he said, 'just scaring the shit out of college kids!'

181 What's the bad news about being a test tube baby? – You know for sure that your dad is a wanker.

182 Two young guys, Rick and Jamie, were sleeping with the same girl, so when she fell pregnant there was no way of knowing which was the father. Not wishing to be burdened with responsibility, they paid for her to have the baby out of town, but then months went by without any news. Eventually Rick phoned the girl. The following day he phoned Jamie.

'There's good and bad news,' said Rick. 'The good news is, she's fine and had twins.'

'What's the bad news?' asked Jamie.

Rick said: 'Mine died.'

183 A woman with a baby was waiting in the doctor's examining room. After putting the baby on the scales, the doctor found him to be underweight. 'Is the baby breast or bottle fed?' he asked.

'Breast fed,' replied the woman.

'Right,' said the doctor. 'Please strip down to your waist.'

The woman took off her top, and the doctor pressed, kneaded, rolled, cupped, and pinched both of her breasts. Finally he said: 'No wonder the baby is under weight. You don't have any milk.'

'I know,' she said. 'I'm his grandmother. But I'm really pleased I brought him in!'

184 A gang member was holding his baby while his wife was in the kitchen fixing lunch. When the baby murmured 'Mother,' the guy got excited and yelled to his wife: 'Hey, the baby just said half a word!'

BANKERS

185 A guy went into a bank to ask for a loan. 'I have some black powder,' he told the manager. 'You sprinkle it on a woman's vagina and it makes it taste like a peach.'

'I'm sorry,' said the manager. 'I don't think we can give you a loan for that.'

A few months later the same guy entered the same bank pushing a wheelbarrow full of money.

The manager said: 'Congratulations. I guess that idea for black powder really paid off.'

'No, that didn't go anywhere. I made my money with this white powder.'

'Really?' said the manager. 'What does it do?'

The guy said: 'Give me a peach and I'll show you.'

186 Two accountants and a banker visited a lap dancing club. Keen to impress his friends, one of the accountants pulled out a $10 bill, licked it, and put it on the dancer's ass. Not to be outdone, the other accountant called the girl back over, pulled out a $50 bill, licked it, and put it on the girl's other cheek. As all eyes turned to the banker, he got out his ATM card, swiped it down her crack, grabbed the sixty bucks, and headed for the door.

BARTENDERS

187 A huge muscular guy walked into a bar and ordered a beer. The bartender couldn't help but notice that, in contrast to his bulging muscles, the guy had a head that was no bigger than an orange. As he served him his beer, the bartender said: 'If you don't mind me saying so, you've got a phenomenal physique, but one thing puzzles me: why is your head so small?'

The big guy pulled up a stool. He had obviously answered the same question many times before. 'OK,' he began. 'One day I was out hunting and got lost in the woods. I heard someone crying for help, so I followed the cries and they led me to a frog that was sitting beside a stream. So I picked up the frog and it said: "If you kiss me, I will turn into a beautiful woman and grant you three wishes." '

'No kidding?' said the bartender, captivated by the story.

'So,' continued the big guy, 'I gave the frog a kiss and, sure enough, it turned into a beautiful, voluptuous naked woman. And she said: "You now have three wishes." I looked down at my scrawny 115-pound body and said: "I want a body like Arnold Schwarzenegger." Then she snapped her fingers and suddenly there I was, so huge that my body ripped my clothes open and left me standing there naked!

'Then she said: "What will be your second wish?" I looked hungrily at her gorgeous body and replied: "I want to make passionate love with you here by this stream." She nodded, laid down on the ground and we made love right there by that stream for hours!'

'Go on,' begged the bartender.

'Afterwards,' continued the big guy, 'as we lay next to each other, sweating from our sensuous lovemaking, she whispered into my ear: "You know, you still have one more wish. What will it be?"

'I looked at her tenderly and said: "How 'bout a little head?"' '

188 A guy walked into a London bar and heard a voice coming from the cigarette machine. 'You're a waste of space,' said the voice. 'Your hair is a mess, you've got no dress sense, and your career's going nowhere. You're a total loser.'

Shaken, the guy went over to the bartender and told him what had happened. The bartender apologized for such behaviour and said: 'The cigarette machine is out of order.'

189 A man walked into a bar and said to the bartender: 'Beer for me, beer for you, and beer for everyone who is in the bar now.'

After finishing his beer, the man began to walk out of the bar.

'Hey,' shouted the bartender. 'You haven't paid for the drinks!'

'Sorry,' said the man, 'I haven't got any money.'

Furious at being duped, the bartender whacked him around the head and threw him out onto the street.

The same man returned to the same bar the following evening and said to the bartender: 'Beer for me, beer for you, and beer for everyone who is in the bar now.'

Thinking that nobody would be crazy enough to pull the same stunt twice, the bartender figured that the customer must have the money this time, so he handed out the beers. But as the man finished his drink, he headed for the door.

'Hey!' yelled the bartender. 'You haven't paid again!'

'Sorry,' said the customer, 'I've got no money.'

Red with rage, the bartender pummelled the man to the ground and hurled him out onto the street.

The next night, the same man was back in the same bar. He said to the bartender: 'Beer for me, and beer for everyone who is in the bar now.'

Disgusted, the bartender asked: 'What, no beer for me this time?'

'No,' said the man. 'You get violent when you drink.'

190 A woman walked into a bar and asked for a double entendre. So the bartender gave her one.

191 A woman walked into a bar and ordered two shots. She downed the first one, saying 'This is for the shame.' Then she downed the second one, saying 'This is for the glory.' Then she ordered two more shots and repeated the shame/glory routine.

She was about to order another two shots when the bartender asked her: 'What's all this about shame and glory?'

'You see,' she explained, 'I like to do my housework naked. But last week when I bent over to pick something up, my Great Dane dog mounted me from behind.'

'Ah, right,' said the bartender. 'That must be the shame.'

'No,' she said, 'that was the glory. The shame was when we got locked out and he dragged me around the front yard for half an hour.'

192 A popular bar installed a new robotic bartender that was programmed to strike up a conversation according to the customer's IQ. So when a guy came in for a drink, the robot asked him: 'What's your IQ?'

The man replied: '130.'

The robot then proceeded to make conversation about nuclear physics, astronomy and advanced math. The customer was impressed.

Then another guy came in for a drink and the robot asked him: 'What's your IQ?'

The man responded: '120.'

So the robot started talking about the Super Bowl, dirt bikes and hockey. The customer thought it was really cool.

Then a third guy came in to the bar and, as before, the robot asked him: 'What's your IQ?'

The man replied: '80.'

The robot said: 'So, how are things in Alabama these days?'

BED

193 A married couple were lying in bed at night. The wife had settled down ready to go to sleep, but the husband was reading a book by the light of his bedside lamp. As he was reading, he paused momentarily, reached over to his wife and started fondling her pussy before resuming reading his book.

Aroused by his touch, she got out of bed and slipped off her nightdress. The husband was mystified. 'What are you doing?' he asked.

'You were playing with my pussy,' replied the wife. 'I thought it was foreplay for something heavier.'

The husband exclaimed: 'Hell no! I was just wetting my fingers so I could turn the pages.'

194 What's soft and warm when you go to bed, but hard and stiff when you wake up? – Vomit.

195 A married couple slept in twin beds. One night just as they were settling down to sleep, he called across to her: 'My little honey bunch, I'm lonely.'

Taking the hint, she got out of her bed and crossed to his, but on the way she tripped on the rug and fell flat on her face. Concerned, he inquired: 'Oh, did my little honey-woney fall on her nosey-wosey?'

After they had passionate sex, she got up to return to her own bed, but on the way back she again tripped on the rug and fell flat on her face. He glanced at her and said: 'Clumsy bitch!'

BESTIALITY

196 A guy, a pig, and a dog were the only survivors of a terrible shipwreck, as a result of which they found themselves stranded on a desert island. After being there for a few weeks, they got into a ritual of going to the beach every evening to watch the sun go down.

One particular evening, the sky was red with beautiful cirrus clouds, and the breeze was warm and gentle. It was a perfect night for love. In such a romantic atmosphere, that pig gradually started looking better and better, and soon the guy rolled towards the pig and put his arm around it. The dog was not happy with this and growled fiercely at the guy until he removed his arm from the pig.

Over the ensuing weeks, the trio continued to enjoy the sunsets together, but there was no further cuddling. Then there was another shipwreck, and this time the sole survivor was a beautiful young woman. Slowly they nursed her back to health and she was eventually introduced to their evening beach ritual.

It was another beautiful evening, red sky, cirrus clouds, warm gentle breeze, perfect for romance, the four of them lying there. The guy started getting 'those' ideas again, so he leaned over towards the girl and said: 'Er, would you mind taking the dog for a walk?'

197 A man from the Internal Revenue Service knocked on the front door of a house. A small boy answered.

'Is your mom in?'

'She's in the backyard screwing the goat.'

The man was horrified. 'Son, it's not nice to make up stories like that!'

The boy said: 'I'm not making it up. If you don't believe me, come through and I'll show you.'

So the taxman followed the boy to the back of the house and, sure enough, through the window he could see a woman screwing a goat.

Disgusted, he turned to the boy and said: 'Doesn't that bother you?'

The boy replied: 'Naaaaaaaaah!'

198 Why did the pervert cross the road? – Because he was stuck in the chicken.

199 A farmer asked his vet how he could tell whether his pigs were pregnant.
'It's simple,' said the vet. 'If the pigs are standing up in the morning, they're not pregnant; but if they're rolling in the mud, they are pregnant.'

The following morning, the farmer looked out of the window to see all of his pigs standing up. So he loaded the pigs into the back of his pick-up truck, drove them to the woods and fucked them all once. He then brought them back to their pen before retiring to bed, tired from the effort.

The next morning he looked out again. The pigs were standing up, so he loaded them into the truck, drove them to the woods and fucked every pig twice. He then brought them back to the farm before flopping into bed, very tired.

When he woke up the next morning, the first thing he did was look out of the window. To his dismay, the pigs were all standing. So he loaded them into the truck, drove them to the woods and fucked them all three times. He then drove them back to the farm and crashed into bed, absolutely exhausted.

The following morning he was too tired to get out of bed, so he asked his wife whether the pigs were standing up or rolling around in the mud.

'Neither,' she said. 'They're all in the back of the truck, and one's lying on the horn.'

BIKERS

200 A biker and his wife were celebrating their fiftieth wedding anniversary. That night, she entered the bedroom wearing the same sexy little negligee that she had worn on their wedding night. She said: 'Honey, do you remember this?'

'Yeah,' he said. 'You were wearing that on the night we married.'

'That's right,' she smiled. 'And do you remember what you said to me that night?'

'Yeah, I said: "Baby, I'm going to suck the life out of those big tits and screw your brains out."'

She giggled and said: 'That's exactly what you said. So now it's fifty years later, and I'm in the same negligee I wore that night. What do you have to say tonight?'

He looked her up and down and said: 'Mission accomplished.'

201 Why do Hell's Angels wear leather? – Because chiffon wrinkles too easily.

202 What's the difference between a Harley and a Hoover? – The location of the dirtbag.

203 'Help! Send someone over quickly!' a middle-aged spinster yelled into the phone. 'Two naked bikers are climbing up towards my bedroom window.'
'This is the Fire Department, lady. I'll have to transfer you to the Police Department.'
'No, it's you I want,' insisted the woman. 'They need a longer ladder.'

204 What's the best thing about being an older biker chick? – You don't have to pull your shirt up so far to show your tits.

205 A guy riding a motorbike was wearing a leather jacket with a broken zip. After a mile or so, he stopped the bike and said to his pillion passenger: 'I can't ride any more with the wind hitting my chest. I'm gonna put my jacket on backwards to keep the cold out.'
A couple of miles further on, he took a bend too fast and smashed the bike into a tree. A farmer living nearby immediately called the police.
When the police officer arrived on the scene, he asked the farmer: 'Are either of them showing any signs of life?'
The farmer said: 'That first one was till I turned his head around the right way.'

206 Two bikers were talking at a bar.
'How's married life?' asked one.
'Fine,' said the other.
'And how's the sex?'
'No problem – and at least I don't have to wait in line any more!'

OSAMA BIN LADEN

207 A small boy came home from first grade and told his father that they learned about the history of Valentine's Day. 'Since Valentine's Day is for a Christian saint and we're Jewish, will God get mad at me for giving someone a Valentine?'

'I shouldn't think so,' said his father. 'Why? Who do you want to send a Valentine to?'

'Osama Bin Laden,' replied the boy.

'Why Osama Bin Laden?' asked his father, shocked.

'Well,' said the boy, 'I thought that if a little American Jewish boy could have enough love to send Osama a Valentine, he might start to think that maybe we're not all bad, and maybe start loving people a bit. And if other kids saw what I did and sent Valentines to Osama, he'd love everyone a lot. And then he'd start travelling the world, telling everyone how much he loved them and how he didn't hate anyone anymore.'

His father's heart swelled and he looked at the boy with newfound pride. 'Son,' he said, 'that's the most wonderful thing I've ever heard.'

'I know,' said the boy, 'and once that gets him out in the open, the Marines will be able to get a clear shot at him!'

208 Irish terrorist police have surrounded a Dublin department store. They heard Bed Linen was on the second floor.

209 A group of Osama Bin Laden's Taliban soldiers were marching down a track in Afghanistan when they heard an American voice call out from behind a sand dune: 'One Marine is better than ten Taliban!'

Bin Laden quickly despatched ten of his finest soldiers over the sand dune, whereupon there was a fierce gun battle, followed by silence. An American voice then called out: 'One Marine is better than 100 Taliban!'

The furious Bin Laden immediately sent his next best 100 troops over the dune. A battle raged for ten minutes, followed by silence. An American voice then called out: 'One Marine is better than 1,000 Taliban!'

Enraged, Bin Laden mustered 1,000 fighters and sent them over the dune. There was a huge battle, lasting for more than an hour, followed by silence. Eventually one wounded Taliban fighter crawled back over the dune and with his dying words told Bin Laden: 'Don't send any more. It's a trap. There's actually two of them.'

BIRDS

210 A man was in court charged with killing a tawny owl, an endangered and protected species. After listening to the evidence in what appeared to be an open and shut case, the judge asked the defendant if he had anything to say.

The defendant stood up and said: 'It was a life or death situation. I had broken my leg while out hiking and it was pouring with rain, so I took refuge in a barn. Days passed without seeing a single person. I was starving and needed to eat, so I killed the bird and ate it. I really had no choice.'

Impressed by the speech, the judge decided to grant him his freedom. Before the court adjourned, the judge asked out of curiosity what a tawny owl tasted like.

The man thought for a second and replied: 'A bit like golden eagle.'

211 If the dove is the bird of peace, what is the bird of true love? – The swallow.

212 A guy was horny as hell . . . but broke. He went to a New York whorehouse with five dollars and begged the madame to give him whatever she could for that price.

'I'm sorry,' she said, 'but five dollars will only cover the rent of a room for ten minutes. And none of my girls work for free.'

Nevertheless he paid up and was shown to the room, but there was nothing to screw. In desperation, he spotted a pigeon on the window ledge. He gently opened the window, grabbed the pigeon and fucked the hell out of it. Satisfied, he then went home.

The following week he returned to the whorehouse, this time with a wallet full of cash from payday. He said to the madame: 'I've got lots of money now, so give me a hooker.'

She said: 'All of my girls are busy right now. Why don't you go to the peep show and get yourself in the mood?'

So he went to the peepshow and was enjoying it so much that he turned to the guy next to him and said: 'These broads are really hot, huh?'

'Yeah, but you should've been here last week. There was this guy fucking a pigeon!'

213 After the Easter Sunday egg hunt, a farm boy played a prank by going to the chicken coop and replacing every egg with a brightly coloured one. A few minutes later, the rooster walked in, saw all the coloured eggs, then stormed outside and beat the hell out of the peacock.

214 An elderly woman said to her friend: 'Last week I bought two budgerigars – a male and a female – but the trouble is, I don't know which is which.'

'Can't you tell by the colour above their beak?' said the friend.

'No, not when they're young.'

'Well, why don't you wait until they're "doing the business", as it were, then put a collar on the bird on top, because that will be the male?'

'That's an excellent idea,' said the woman. So she waited for the birds to start mating and put a collar on the male budgerigar.

A week later, the vicar came round for tea. The budgie took one look at him and squawked: 'Caught you, too, did they, mate?'

215 A Mississippi woodpecker and a Texas woodpecker were in Mississippi arguing about which state had the toughest trees to peck. The Mississippi woodpecker said his state had a tree that no woodpecker had ever been able to peck, and challenged the Texas woodpecker to try it. To the amazement of the Mississippi woodpecker, the Texas woodpecker pecked a hole in the tree with no problem.

Now it was the Texas woodpecker's turn to try and prove that his state had the most impenetrable trees. He told the Mississippi woodpecker that in Texas was a tree with a bark so hard that no bird had managed to get his beak into it. The Mississippi woodpecker took up the challenge of driving his beak into the tree and, to the dismay of the Texas woodpecker, succeeded easily.

Both woodpeckers were puzzled as to why they were more successful with trees in states other than their own. In the end they concluded that your pecker is always harder when you're away from home.

BIRTH

216 It was the talk of the town when an eighty-year-old man married a twenty-year-old girl, particularly when a year later she went into hospital to give birth. The nurse came out to congratulate the proud father. 'This is amazing. How do you do it at your age?'

He answered: 'You've got to keep that old motor running.'

The following year his young wife gave birth again. The same nurse said: 'You really are amazing. How do you do it?'

He replied knowingly: 'You've got to keep that old motor running.'

The same thing happened the next year. The nurse said: 'You must be quite a man.'

He laughed: 'You've got to keep that old motor running.'

The nurse said: 'Well, you had better change the oil. This one's black.'

217 A farmer was helping one of his cows to give birth when he noticed his son watching wide-eyed. 'Oh, dear,' thought the farmer, 'I can see I'm going to have to explain the birds and bees.'

So when he finished, he asked the boy: 'Well, do you have any questions?'

'Just one,' gasped the boy. 'How fast was that calf going when it hit that cow?'

218 A nervous young man was pacing up and down the waiting room at a maternity hospital. Eventually he asked another guy, who seemed more experienced in these matters: 'How long after the baby is born can you have sex with the mother?'

The older guy said: 'It depends whether she's in a public ward or a private ward.'

219 A Catholic couple were becoming increasingly desperate for a baby. Eventually they asked their priest to pray for them.

The priest said: 'I'm going to Rome on a long sabbatical and, while I'm there, I'll light a candle for you at the altar of St Peter.'

When the priest returned to his parish ten months later, he discovered that the woman had given birth to sextuplets. 'It's a miracle!' exclaimed the priest. 'But I understand your husband has left the country?'

'So he has, Father. He's flown to Rome to blow your bloody candle out.'

220 A young teenager came home from school and asked her mother: 'Is it true what Sarah just told me? That babies come out of the same place where boys put their thingies?'

'Yes, dear,' replied her mother, pleased that the subject had finally come up and that she wouldn't have to explain it.

The girl looked mystified. 'But then when I have a baby, won't it knock my teeth out?'

221 A married couple had to rent their first two homes, so when they finally saved up enough money to be able to afford to buy a house, they were absolutely thrilled. So was the husband's brother, who bought them a bottle of champagne to mark the occasion.

In the hustle and bustle of settling into the first home that they actually owned, the gift was tucked away and temporarily forgotten. Then three months later, the couple held a Christening party for their third child. Champagne flowed in celebration until, running short, the wife remembered her brother-in-law's housewarming gift. In front of her guests, she opened the attached card and read it aloud: 'Bill, take good care of this one – it's yours!'

BIRTH CONTROL

222 Three women were discussing birth control.

The first said: 'We're Catholic, so we don't practise birth control.'

The second said: 'I am, too, but we use the rhythm method.'

The third said: 'We use the bucket and saucer method.'

'What's that?' asked the others.

'Well,' she said, 'I'm 5ft 11 in tall and my husband is 5ft 2in. We make love standing up, with him standing on a bucket, and when his eyes get as big as saucers, I kick the bucket out from under him.'

223 What's a diaphragm? – A trampoline for dickheads.

224 A bus driver was sitting in the canteen when an inspector asked him: 'What time did you pull out this morning?'

'I didn't,' said the driver. 'And it's been worrying me all day.'

225 Four young women spent the afternoon on a clothes-shopping spree but, as they made their way back to the car, one of them realized that she had forgotten to stop at the pharmacy for her contraceptive pills. So she ran to the nearest store, rushed in with a prescription and said to the pharmacist. 'Please fill this immediately. I've got people waiting in my car.'

226 What's the best form of birth control after fifty? – Nudity.

227 An old man complained to the doctor of feeling tired. The doctor asked him if he had done anything unusual lately.

The old man said: 'Wednesday night, I picked up a twenty-year-old secretary and nailed her three times. Thursday, I hit on a nineteen-year-old waitress; Friday, I made out with an eighteen-year-old friend of my granddaughter; and Saturday, I was lured to a motel by seventeen-year-old twins.'

The doctor said: 'I hope you took precautions.'

'Sure,' replied the old man. 'I gave 'em all phoney names.'

TONY BLAIR

228 Tony Blair gave the half-time team talk at a soccer match. But nobody believed him when he warned that the opponents could mount a serious attack in the next forty-five minutes.

229 Bill Clinton, George W. Bush and Tony Blair all died in a plane crash and went to heaven.

First, God asked Clinton about his beliefs. Clinton replied: 'I am a strong believer in freedom of choice for people.'

'Those are admirable principles,' said God. 'Come and sit at my right hand.'

Then God asked Bush for his views. Bush answered: 'I believe in freeing countries from tyrannical regimes.'

'Noble sentiments,' said God. 'Come and sit at my left hand.'

Finally God turned to Blair, who was staring at him indignantly. 'What's the matter, Tony?' asked God.

Blair replied: 'You're sitting in my bloody chair!'

BLINDNESS

230 Dave, an experienced skydiver, was getting ready for a jump one day when he spotted another man preparing to dive wearing dark glasses, carrying a white stick and holding a seeing-eye dog by the leash. Shocked that a blind man was also going to jump, Dave struck up conversation, expressing admiration for the man's bravery. Then puzzled, he asked: 'How do you know when the ground is getting close?'

'Easy,' replied the blind man. 'The leash goes slack.'

231 Children at a blind school set off on their annual day trip to the coast, and pulled into a motorway service station for lunch. So that the children could stretch their legs while their lunch orders were being taken, one of the teachers took out a special ball with a bell in it and suggested they had a game of soccer on a nearby strip of grass. The teachers started the game off, then went to collect the food.

While the teachers were waiting at the restaurant, the coach driver came running in. 'Quick!' he yelled. 'Your kids are kicking the shit out of a group of Morris dancers!'

232 What goes: CLICK – is that it? CLICK – is that it? CLICK – is that it? – A blind person with a Rubik's Cube.

233 A friend of Stevie Wonder's bought him a cheese grater for his birthday. A few weeks later, the friend met up with Stevie and asked him whether he liked his present.

'Hey, man!' replied Stevie. 'That was the most violent book I've ever read!'

234 Why are Stevie Wonder's legs always wet? – Because his dog is blind too.

235 What is the name of Stevie Wonder's favourite book? – *Around the Block in Eighty Days*.

236 A blind man was travelling in his private jet when he detected something was wrong. He made his way to the cockpit but got no response from the pilot. The blind guy then found the radio and started calling the tower: 'Help! Help!'

The tower came back and asked: 'What's the problem?'

The blind guy yelled: 'Help me! I'm blind. The pilot is dead, and we're flying upside down!'

The tower said: 'How do you know you're upside down?'

'Because the shit is running down my back!'

237 How do you recognize a blind man in a nudist colony? – It's not hard.

238 A little old lady was nearly blind. Her three sons doted on her and each wanted to prove that he was the kindest. The first son, who was very wealthy, bought her a mansion; the second son, who was fairly wealthy, bought her a Mercedes with a chauffeur; the third son, who was much poorer than the other two, spent all his savings on buying her a parrot, which, by virtue of fifteen years' dedicated training, could recite the entire Bible. Knowing that she was such a devoted churchgoer, he thought it would be an ideal and unique gift for her.

The old lady told the first son: 'The house is lovely, but it is too big for me, so I don't really want it.'

Then she told the second son: 'The car is beautiful, but I don't drive and I don't care for the driver, so please return the car.'

Turning to the third son, she said warmly: 'I just want to thank you for that most thoughtful gift. That chicken was delicious.'

239 Did you hear about the blind circumcisionist? – He got the sack.

240 A blind man was at the optician's with his guide dog. Man and dog were facing the eye chart on the wall. Then the optician took the guide dog away, replaced it with another guide dog and asked the man: 'There, is that better or worse?'

241 Stevie Wonder and Jack Nicklaus were in a bar. Jack turned to Stevie and asked: 'How is the singing career going?'

'Great,' said Stevie. 'The latest album has gone into the top ten, I'm setting off on a world tour next month, so, yeah, pretty good. How's the golf?'

'Not too bad,' replied Jack. 'I don't play as much as I used to, but I still make a bit of money. I had some problems with my swing, but I think I've got that sorted now.'

Stevie nodded. 'I always find that when my swing goes wrong, I need to stop playing for a while and think about it. Then the next time I play it seems to be all right.'

'You play golf?' said Jack, surprised.

'Yeah, I've been playing for years.'

'But I thought you were blind,' said Jack. 'How can you play golf if you're blind?'

'I've got a system,' explained Stevie. 'I get my caddie to stand in the middle of the fairway, and he calls to me. I listen for the sound of his voice and I play the ball towards him. Then when I get to where the ball lands, the caddie moves to the green or further down the fairway and again I play the ball towards his voice.'

'But how do you putt?' asked Jack.

'Well,' said Stevie, 'I get my caddie to lean down in front of the hole and call to me with his head on the ground, and I just play the ball to the sound of his voice.'

'What's your handicap?' asked Jack.

Stevie replied: 'I play off scratch.'

Jack was amazed and said to Stevie: 'We must play a game sometime.'

Stevie said: 'Well, people don't take me seriously, so I only play for money. And I never play for less than $100,000 a hole.'

Jack thought about it for a moment before saying: 'OK, I'm up for that. When would you like to play?'

Stevie said: 'I don't mind. Any night next week is OK with me.'

BLONDES

242 A blonde entered a store that sold curtains and told the salesman she wanted to buy a pair of pink curtains. He showed her several patterns but the blonde was struggling to make a choice. Eventually she selected a pink floral print.

'What size curtains do you need?' asked the salesman.

'Fifteen inches,' replied the blonde.

'That sounds very small. What room are they for?'

'They're not for a room,' said the blonde. 'They're for my computer monitor.'

The salesman was baffled. 'But, miss, computers do not need curtains!'

The blonde said: 'Helloooo! . . . I've got Windoooows!'

243 Ten blondes and a brunette were on a rock climbing expedition when some of the grappling hooks suddenly gave way, leaving the entire party clinging precariously to the rope two hundred feet above the ground. The situation was so desperate that as a group they decided that one of their number should let go to ease the weight on the rope. No one volunteered until eventually the brunette gave a truly moving speech saying that she would sacrifice her own life to save the lives of the others. All of the blondes applauded.

244 A blonde was speeding when a cop pulled her over. The officer, who also happened to be blonde, asked for her driver's licence.

The blonde driver searched in her purse, then said: 'What does a driver's licence look like?'

The blonde cop said: 'You dummy, it's got your picture on it!'

The blonde driver finally found a small rectangular mirror at the bottom of her purse. Holding it up to her face, she said, 'Aha, this must be my driver's licence,' and handed it to the blonde cop.

The blonde policewoman looked in the mirror, handed it back to the driver and said: 'You're free to go. And if I had known you were a police officer, too, we could have avoided all of this.'

245 Did you hear about the blonde who put lipstick on her forehead because she wanted to make up her mind?

246 Did you hear about the blonde who didn't like breast-feeding her children because it hurt when she boiled her nipples?

247 Did you hear about the blonde who, at the bottom of the application form where it said 'sign here', put 'Sagittarius'?

248 A blonde decided to redecorate her bedroom. She wasn't sure how many rolls of wallpaper she'd need but she knew her blonde friend Sharon from next door had recently done the same job and the two rooms were identical in size.

'Shaz,' she said, 'how many rolls of wallpaper did you buy for your bedroom?'

'Ten,' answered Sharon.

So the blonde bought ten rolls of wallpaper and did the job, but at the end she had two rolls left over.

'Shaz,' she said, 'I bought ten rolls of wallpaper for the bedroom, but I've got two left over.'

'Yeah,' said Sharon. 'So did I.'

249 One night a blonde nun was praying in her room when God appeared before her. 'My daughter,' said God, 'you have pleased me greatly. Your heart is full of love for your fellow creatures, and your actions and prayers are always for the benefit of others. I have come to you, not only to thank and commend you, but also to grant you anything you wish.'

'Dear Heavenly Father,' she replied, 'I am blissfully happy. I am a bride of Christ. I am doing what I love. I lack for nothing material since the Church supports me. I am content in all ways.'

'There must be something you would have of me?' asked God.

'Well, I suppose there is one thing,' she replied.

'Just name it,' said God.

'It's those blonde jokes,' she said. 'They are so demeaning to blondes everywhere, not just to me. I would wish for blonde jokes to stop.'

'Consider it done,' said God. 'Blonde jokes shall be stricken from the minds of humans everywhere. But there you go again, always thinking of others. Surely there is something that I can do just for you.'

'There is one thing,' she said hesitantly. 'But it's really small, and simply not worth your time.'

'Name it. Please,' said God.

'It's M&Ms,' she said. 'They're so hard to peel!'

250 What do a blonde and an instant lottery ticket have in common? – All you have to do is scratch the box to win.

251 What's the difference between a blonde and an inflatable doll? – About two cans of hair spray.

252 An executive interviewed a blonde for a job. Wanting to find out something about her personality, he asked her: 'If you could have a conversation with someone, living or dead, who would it be?'

The blonde gave the question careful consideration before answering: 'The living one.'

253 A blonde holding a baby walked into a drugstore and asked to use the store's baby scale.

'Sorry,' said the clerk, 'but our baby scale is broken. However, we can work out the baby's weight if we weigh mother and baby together on the adult scale, then weigh the mother alone, and subtract the second number from the first.'

'That won't work,' said the blonde.

'Why not?' asked the clerk, mystified.

'Because,' said the blonde, 'I'm not the mother – I'm the aunt.'

254 A blonde was making her first plane trip. Boarding the aircraft, she found herself a window seat in a non-smoking area and settled down. A few minutes later, however, a guy came over and insisted that she was in his seat. But the blonde flatly refused to move.

'OK, lady,' he stormed, 'if that's the way you want it, you fly the plane!'

255 Did you hear about the blonde who got a pair of water-skis? – She's still looking for a lake with a slope.

256 Why does it take longer to build a blond snowman? – Because you have to hollow out the head.

257 What did the blonde say when she got a book for her birthday? – Thanks, but I've got one already.

258 A blonde motorist pulled out sharply from a side road, causing a truck driver to slam on his brakes. The furious trucker stormed over to the blonde's car and ordered her out. Then he drew a circle on the roadside and told her: 'Lady, don't step out of that circle.'

Overflowing with road rage, he ripped off her wing mirrors, but as he did so, the blonde began laughing. This further infuriated him and, taking a sledgehammer from his truck, he proceeded to smash every window on her car. Still, the blonde roared with laughter. So he picked up the sledge-hammer again and, with a violent blow, punctured a gaping hole in her car's bodywork. Still she laughed hysterically.

With steam almost coming from his ears, he marched over to her and roared: 'Lady, I just wrecked your car. What's so funny?'

The blonde giggled: 'Every time you turned around, I stepped out of the circle!'

259 A blonde came home from her first day of commuting into the city. Her mother saw that she was looking tired and asked: 'Honey, are you feeling OK?'

'Not really,' replied the blonde. 'I'm nauseous from sitting backwards on the train.'

'Oh, you poor love,' said the mother. 'Why didn't you ask the person sitting opposite you to switch seats?'

'I couldn't,' said the blonde. 'There was no one there.'

260 Did you hear about the blonde who faked an orgasm with her vibrator?

261 A blonde went to a seafood restaurant and saw the tank where they kept the lobsters. Taking pity on them, she hid them in her handbag. Later she went to the woods and set the poor animals free.

262 As a trucker stopped for a red light, a blonde caught up with him. She jumped from her car, ran up to his truck and knocked on the door. When he wound down the window, she said: 'Hi, I'm Kelly. You're losing some of your load!' He ignored her and drove on.

At the next red light, the blonde caught up with him again. Jumping from her car, she ran to his truck and knocked on the door. As if she had never met him before, she trilled: 'Hi, I'm Kelly. You're losing some of your load!' He shook his head at her and drove off.

At the next red light, the blonde again jumped from her car, ran to the truck and knocked on the door. 'Hi, I'm Kelly,' she shouted. 'You're losing some of your load!' The trucker waved his arms at her angrily and drove off.

At the next red light, the trucker quickly jumped from his cab and ran back to the blonde's car. As she wound down the window, he said: 'Hi, I'm Clint, it's winter in Canada, and I'm driving the salt truck!'

263 A blonde in a headscarf decided to take up the accordion. So she went into a music shop and asked to see the accordions.

'They're over there,' said the shop owner.

'Right, I'll have the big red one in the corner.'

The shop owner looked at her quizzically. 'You're a blonde, aren't you?'

'Yes, how did you know?'

'That big red accordion is a radiator.'

264 A young businessman picked up a blonde in a bar and took her back to his place. When she saw the bedroom, she exclaimed: 'Wow! A water bed! I've never had sex on a water bed before!'

As they lay down on the bed, things soon got hot. She said: 'Before we go any further, don't you think we should put on some protection?'

'Good idea,' he said.

So the blonde jumped up from the water bed and went into the next room. When she returned she was wearing a lifejacket.

265 A blonde called the police to report that she had been assaulted.

'When did this happen?' asked the officer.

'Ten days ago.'

'Why did you wait until now to report it?'

'Well, I didn't know I was assaulted till the cheque bounced.'

266 A blonde went out of her house and checked her mailbox. Seeing nothing, she closed the mailbox and went back into the house. Ten minutes later, she came out again to check for mail, but, finding nothing, closed the mailbox and returned indoors. When she did this for a third time in quick succession, her nosey neighbour called out: 'You must be waiting for a very important letter?'

'No,' said the blonde. 'But I'm working on my computer and it keeps telling me, "You've Got Mail".'

267 Two blondes were strolling along Australia's Bondi Beach by moonlight. One turned to the other and said: 'Which do you think is closer? The moon or New York?'

The other blonde replied: 'Helloooo! Can you see New York?'

268 A blonde rang down to hotel reception to complain that she was trapped in her room. 'I can't get out!' she wailed.

'Why not?' asked the reception clerk. 'Have you tried the door?'

The blonde said: 'But there are only three doors in here. One is the bathroom, one is the closet, and one has a sign on it that says "Do Not Disturb".'

269 Desperate for money, a blonde decided to kidnap a small boy and hold him for ransom. Having snatched her victim, she wrote a note saying, 'I've kidnapped your son. Tomorrow evening put $100,000 in a bag and leave it by the fountain in the park.' And she signed it mysteriously 'A. Blonde.' She then pinned the note to the boy's jacket and sent him home.

The following evening, she went to the fountain in the park and found the boy standing there with the bagful of money. He handed the blonde a note that read: 'How could you do this to a fellow blonde?'

270 Why do blondes get confused in the ladies' room? – Because they have to pull their own pants down.

271 Did you hear about the blonde who thought Meow Mix was a CD for cats?

272 Did you hear about the blonde who thought Eartha Kitt was a set of garden tools?

273 A blonde riding in a taxi cab suddenly realized that she didn't have any money for the fare. So she said to the driver: 'You'd better stop. I can't pay you, and it's $10 already.'

The driver checked her out in the rear-view mirror and said: 'That's OK. I'll turn down the next dark street and I can get in the back seat and take off your bra.'

'You'd be cheating yourself,' said the blonde. 'This bra is only worth $5.'

274 A brunette, a redhead and a blonde escaped a burning building by climbing to the roof. On the street below, firemen were waiting, holding a blanket for them to jump into.

The firemen yelled to the brunette: 'Jump! Jump! It's your only chance of survival.'

The brunette jumped, but suddenly the firemen yanked the blanket away, and she slammed into the sidewalk like a tomato.

'Jump! Jump!' the firemen yelled to the redhead. 'You gotta jump!'

'No!' shouted the redhead. 'You're gonna pull the blanket away!'

'No,' replied the firemen. 'It's only brunettes we hate, we're OK with redheads.'

So the redhead jumped but halfway down the firemen whipped the blanket away, and she was flattened on the pavement like a pancake.

Finally the blonde stepped to the edge of the roof. Again the firemen yelled: 'Jump! You have to jump! It's your only hope!'

'No way!' shouted the blonde. 'You're just gonna pull the blanket away!'

'We promise we won't,' replied the firemen. 'You have to jump. We won't pull the blanket away this time.'

'Listen,' said the blonde. 'Nothing you can say will convince me that you're not gonna pull the blanket away! So what I want you to do is, put the blanket down, and back away from it . . .'

275 A young man wanted to get his beautiful blonde wife something nice for their first wedding anniversary. So he decided to buy her a mobile phone. After he had explained to her all the features on the phone, she was absolutely thrilled with the present.

The next day the blonde was out shopping when her phone rang. It was her husband. 'Hi, honey,' he said, 'how do you like your new phone?'

'I just love it,' she replied. 'It's so compact, and your voice is as clear as a bell. And I love all the different features. There's just one thing I don't understand though.'

'What's that, baby?' asked the husband.

'How did you know I was at Wal-Mart?'

276 Hired as a secretary at an office, a blonde's first job was to go out for coffee. Eager to impress on her first day, she grabbed a large thermos and hurried to a nearby coffee shop. She held up the thermos, and the coffee shop assistant quickly came over to take her order.

The blonde asked: 'Is this big enough to hold six cups of coffee?'

The assistant looked at the thermos for a few seconds before replying: 'Yeah. It looks like about six cups to me.'

'Oh, good!' sighed the blonde in relief. 'Then give me two regular, two black, and two decaf.'

277 Why do blondes wear underwear? – They make good ankle warmers.

278 How can you tell if a blonde has been in your refrigerator? – By the lipstick on the cucumber.

279 Did you hear about the blonde who was treated in the emergency room for concussion and serious head wounds? – She had tried to commit suicide by hanging herself with a bungee cord.

280 What can strike a blonde without her even knowing it? – A thought.

281 What can save a dying blonde? – Hair transplants.

282 Why do blondes have TGIF on their shirts? – Tits Go In Front.

283 A blonde went to a restaurant, bought a coffee, and sat down to drink it. She looked on the side of her cup and found a peel-off prize. Then she pulled off the tab and yelled excitedly: 'I won! I won! I won a motor home! I won a motor home!'

The waitress ran over and said: 'That's impossible. The biggest prize given away was a DVD player!'

The blonde insisted: 'No. I won a motor home, I won a motor home!'

Hearing the commotion, the manager made his way over to the table and said: 'You couldn't possibly have won a motor home because we didn't have that as a prize!'

Again the blonde said: 'There's no mistake. I won a motor home, I won a motor home! Look, here's the ticket if you don't believe me.'

She handed the prize ticket to the manager, and he read out loud: 'WIN A BAGEL.'

284 A blonde playing Trivial Pursuit threw the dice and landed on a Science and Nature question. The question was: 'If you are in a vacuum and someone calls your name, can you hear it?'

After a moment's thought, she asked: 'Is the vacuum on or off?'

285 A blonde was trying to sell her old car, but was having trouble attracting a buyer because the car had almost 250,000 miles on the clock. One day she was pouring out her problems to a brunette workmate who confided: 'There is a way of making the car easier to sell, but it's not legal.'

'I don't mind whether or not it's legal,' said the blonde. 'I just want to sell that damned car.'

'OK,' said the brunette. 'Here is the address of a friend of mine who owns a car repair shop. Tell him I sent you and he'll sort it out. After that, you shouldn't have any difficulty selling your car.'

The next day, the blonde went to see the mechanic. A few weeks later, she bumped into the brunette at work.

'Did you sell your car?' asked the brunette.

'No,' replied the blonde. 'Why should I? It only has 40,000 miles on the clock!'

286 What's the first thing a blonde learns when she takes driving lessons? – You can sit upright in a car.

287 What's the difference between a chorus line of blondes and a magician? – A magician has a cunning array of stunts.

288 When a surgeon came to see his blonde patient on the day after her operation, she asked him just how long it would be before she could resume her sex life.

'Uh, I hadn't really thought about it,' replied the surgeon. 'You're the first one ever to ask that after a tonsillectomy.'

289 Visiting a blonde's house, her friend asked: 'Why do you have that huge picture of yourself above the wash basin in the bathroom?'

The blonde said: 'My bathroom mirror broke, and I didn't want to buy a new one.'

290 A young blonde went to a gynaecologist and said that she and her husband were desperate to start a family. 'We've been trying for months and I just don't seem able to get pregnant,' she said.

'I'm sure we can solve your problem,' said the gynaecologist. 'If you'll just take off your underpants and get up on the examining table.'

'Well, all right,' said the blonde, blushing, 'but I'd rather have my husband's baby.'

291 When her husband came home from work, a blonde hugged him and told him excitedly: 'I'm pregnant. And it's twins!'

'How do you know it's twins?' asked the husband.

'Because,' she explained, 'I went to the pharmacy and bought the two-pack pregnancy test kit. And both tests came out positive.'

292 The boss asked his blonde secretary why she was late for work. She explained that on her journey to the office she had been first on the scene at a terrible car crash. 'It was just awful,' she said. 'The driver looked to have broken both legs, his passenger had suffered horrific head injuries, and there was blood everywhere. Thank goodness I took that first aid course. All my training came back to me in a flash.'

'What did you do?' asked the boss.

The blonde said: 'I sat down and put my head between my knees to stop myself from fainting.'

293 A furious farmer spotted three girls — a brunette, a redhead and a blonde — helping themselves to his apples and then sneaking into his barn where they hid in three sacks. Wielding a sharp pitchfork, the farmer began searching the barn for the culprits.

Soon he came to the three sacks. He prodded the first sack, and the brunette went, 'Miaow.' So he thought it was just a cat.

Then he prodded the second sack, and the redhead went, 'Woof, woof.' So the farmer thought the sack contained just a dog.

Finally he prodded the third sack, and the blonde went, 'Potatoes.'

294 A blonde walked into the doctor's office and said: 'Did I leave my panties here yesterday?'

'No,' said the doctor, taken aback. 'I don't think so.'

'Damn!' exclaimed the blonde. 'I must have left them at the dentist's.'

295 Two blondes were out walking in the park.

The first said: 'Look at that dog with one eye.'

The second covered one of her eyes and said: 'Where?'

296 What is the worst thing about sex with a blonde? – Bucket seats.

297 What do blondes use for protection during sex? – Bus shelters.

298 What do you call a blonde behind a steering wheel? – An air bag.

299 Why don't blondes have elevator jobs? – They can't remember the route.

300 A blonde working in a large company attended a fire safety demonstration in the car park. Issuing instructions on how to operate the extinguisher, the fire official said: 'Pull the pin like a hand grenade, then depress the trigger to release the foam.'

The blonde was then selected to demonstrate the procedure, but in her nervousness she forgot to pull the pin.

Offering a helpful hint, the official said: 'Like a hand grenade, remember?'

So she pulled the pin, and hurled the extinguisher at the blaze.

301 Two blondes and a brunette were walking on the beach when a seagull dropped poo on one of the blondes.

The brunette said: 'I'll go and get some toilet paper.'

When she left, one blonde said to the other: 'Boy, is she ever stupid! By the time she gets back, that seagull will be miles away.'

302 A blonde and two male friends decided to go away on a camping trip to Montana for the weekend. One of the guys was in charge of the tent and the sleeping bags, the other guy was in charge of all the provisions, and the blonde's only duty was to bring the box of matches for lighting the campfire.

When they arrived at the camping site, one guy set up the tent while the other prepared to cook supper. But he was having problems lighting the fire with the matches that the blonde had brought.

'I don't understand,' said the blonde. 'They should be fine. I tested them all before we left.'

303 Why can't blondes dial 911? – They can't find the 11 on the phone.

304 What do you call a blonde at university? – A visitor.

305 Why did God create blondes? – Because sheep can't fetch beer from the fridge.

306 How do blondes pierce their ears? – They put tacks in their shoulder pads.

307 How many blondes does it take to play hide and seek? – One.

308 Why didn't the blonde want a window seat on the plane? – She'd just blow dried her hair and didn't want it blown around too much.

309 How did the blonde break her leg raking leaves? – She fell out of the tree.

310 A police officer stopped a blonde for speeding and asked her politely if he could see her licence. She replied in a huff: 'I wish you guys would get your act together. Just yesterday you take away my licence and then today you expect me to show it to you!'

311 Two blondes were decorating a house. One was painting the ceiling while the other painted the walls.

After a while, the one painting the walls said: 'Have you got a good grip on your brush?'

'Sure.'

'Well, hold on tight. I'm taking away the ladder.'

312 On her first visit to Washington, DC, a blonde was keen to visit the Capitol building. Unable to find it, she asked a police officer for directions.

'Wait here at this bus stop for bus number 54,' he said. 'It'll take you right there.'

Three hours later, he saw her still waiting at the bus stop. 'I said to wait for bus number 54. That was three hours ago. Why are you still waiting?'

The blonde said: 'Don't worry, it won't be long now. The 47th bus just went by.'

313 The blondes at university were fed up with not fitting in. Tired of the other students assuming they were just stupid bimbos, they yearned for a place where they felt they actually belonged. So they pressured the administration to set up a new department especially for them. Eventually the university agreed, and established the Blonde Education Department.

The blondes were delighted to have a department of their own where they could meet without being ridiculed. They felt they really belonged now. To emphasize their new status to the other students and to prove that they weren't merely brainless bimbos, they even designed their own sweatshirts.

So now the blondes all proudly wear the official sweatshirt of the Blonde Education Department, which sports the words: 'I Belong in B.E.D.'

314 Why do blondes wear green lipstick? – Red means stop.

315 What's the difference between a blonde and a limousine? – Not everyone has been in a limousine.

316 What do you call a fly buzzing around a blonde's head? – A space invader.

317 A blonde bought a box of laundry detergent, which said on the box '20 uses'. The next day she phoned the laundry detergent company to complain.

'Listen,' she said, 'I bought your product and the box says '20 uses', but all it does is my laundry!'

318 Two blondes were playing golf on a foggy day. When they reached the green on a short par-3, they found that one ball was in the hole while the other was sitting about five feet from the flag. Since both were playing with the same make of ball, they couldn't work out whose ball was in the hole and whose was on the green, so they went to the club professional to ask for a ruling.

After hearing the blondes' story and congratulating them on such fine shots in adverse conditions, he said: 'OK. So which of you was playing with the red ball?'

319 A policeman was interrogating three blondes who were training to become detectives. To test their skills in recognising a suspect, he showed the first blonde a picture for five seconds. 'This is your suspect,' he said. 'How would you recognize him?'

The blonde answered; 'That's easy. We'll catch him real fast because he only has one eye.'

The policeman looked at her in disbelief. 'Er, that's because the picture showed his profile.'

Hoping for a more sensible reply, he then flashed the picture to the second blonde and said: 'This is your suspect. How would you recognize him?'

The second blonde giggled, flicked her hair and said: 'Ha! He'd be so easy to catch because he only has one ear.'

The policeman reacted angrily. 'What's the matter with you two? Of course only one eye and one ear *showing* because it's a picture of his profile! Is that the best answer you can come up with?'

Beyond frustration, he then showed the picture to the third blonde for five seconds and said testily: 'This is your suspect. How would you recognise him? And think hard before giving me a stupid answer.'

The blonde said: 'Hmmm. The suspect wears contact lenses.'

The policeman was taken aback by her answer, partly because he had no idea whether the suspect wore contact lenses or not. 'Well,' he said, 'that's certainly an interesting reply. Wait here a minute while I check his file to find out if you're right.'

After checking the suspect's file on the computer, he came back with a huge grin on his face. 'Wow! I can't believe it. It's true. The suspect does wear contact lenses. Great work! You've clearly got what it takes to become a detective. Tell me, how were you able to make such an astute observation?'

'It was obvious,' the blonde replied. 'He can't wear regular glasses because he only has one eye and one ear.'

320 What does a blonde say after multiple orgasms? – 'Way to go, team!'

321 What's the difference between a blonde and a roll of film? – A roll of film can be developed.

322 A blonde hairdresser told her psychiatrist: 'I'm on the road a lot, and my clients keep complaining that they can never reach me.'

'Don't you have a phone in your car?' asked the psychiatrist.

'It was too expensive to install,' said the blonde. 'So I did the next best thing. I put a mailbox in my car.'

The psychiatrist was baffled. 'Er . . . and how exactly does that work?'

'Actually,' said the blonde, 'I haven't received any letters yet.'

'And why do you think that is?' asked the psychiatrist.

'Well,' said the blonde, 'I figure it's because when I'm driving around, my zip code keeps changing.'

323 Three blondes bought a can of Pepsi One and were anxious to try it for the first time. The first blonde opened the can, and the second blonde poured it into three glasses. The third blonde eyed the glasses suspiciously and said: 'I wonder which one has the calorie?'

324 A virile, young Italian stallion met a spectacular blonde in a bar in Rome. Things progressed to the point where he invited her back to his apartment and, after some small talk, they retired to his bedroom and made love. Thirty minutes of passion later, he asked with a smile: 'So . . . you finish?'

She paused for a second, frowned and replied: 'No.'

Surprised, the young man resumed his love making with renewed vigour. This time she thrashed about wildly and screamed with ecstasy. Twenty minutes later, when she began to calm down, the young man smiled again and asked: 'You finish?'

Pulling him close, she whispered: 'No.'

Stunned, but damned if she was going to outlast him, he summoned his last few ounces of strength and began pumping away again. A few minutes later they climaxed simultaneously, screaming, bucking, clawing and ripping the bed sheets. Exhausted, he fell onto his back, gasping for air. Barely able to turn his head, he looked into her eyes, smiled proudly and asked again: 'You finish?'

Equally out of breath, she puffed in his ear: 'No! I Norwegian.'

325 Why do blondes always smile during lightning storms? – They think their picture is being taken.

326 How do you brainwash a blonde? – Give her a douche and shake her upside down.

327 What did the blonde say to the physicist? – Why, I just love nuclear fission! What do you use for bait?

328 Why can't blondes make ice cubes? – They forget the recipe.

329 How do you make a blonde's eyes light up? – Shine a torch into her ear.

330 Why did the blonde roast a chicken for three and a half days? – The instructions said 'cook it for half an hour per pound', and she weighed 125.

331 A blonde was enjoying a drink at her friend's house late one evening when it started to rain heavily. As the weather deteriorated further, the friend said to the blonde: 'Why don't you stay here for the night and go home in the morning?'

At this, the blonde rushed out the door, only to return an hour later, soaking wet and carrying a small bag.

'Where did you run off to?' asked the friend.

The blonde replied: 'I went home to get my pyjamas.'

332 Two blondes were waiting at a bus stop. A bus pulled up, and one of the blondes asked the driver: 'Will this bus take me to the train station?'
'No, sorry,' said the driver.
The other blonde smiled and said: 'Will it take me?'

333 'Did you hear what happened?' asked Jack when he met Phil in the corridor at work.
'No,' said Phil.
'The CEO died this morning.'
'My God! How?'
'Well, he was working through lunch when he had a heart attack. Everyone was gone except his secretary – you know the one.'
'Boy, do I! She's that young blonde babe.'
'Yeah, that's the one. Turns out that she isn't too smart, though.'
'How do you mean?'
'He kept yelling at her to "call 911". And she just stood there waiting for him to give her the rest of the phone number.'

334 A blonde went to the hospital to donate blood. The nurse asked. 'What type are you?'
The blonde replied: 'I'm an outgoing cat-lover.'

335 Did you hear about the blonde New Yorker who arranged to meet her friend at the corner of Walk and Don't Walk?

336 Did you hear about the blonde who thought Doris Day was a national holiday?

337 Three women – a blonde, a brunette and a redhead – worked in an office with the same female boss. Each day the boss left work early, so finally the three decided that they would do the same. The brunette was thrilled to leave early so that she could get home and play with her baby son. The redhead was thrilled to leave early so that she could go to the gym. And the blonde was thrilled to leave early so that she could get home and surprise her husband. But when she got home she heard muffled noises coming from her bedroom. Slowly she opened the door and was mortified to see her husband in bed with her boss. Gently she closed the door and crept back out of the house.
The next day at coffee break, the brunette and the redhead said they were

planning to leave early again and they asked the blonde whether she was going to do the same.

'No way,' replied the blonde. 'I almost got caught yesterday!'

338 A blonde walked into a bank to withdraw money. The bank clerk asked: 'Can you identify yourself?'

The blonde opened her handbag, looked in a mirror and said: 'Yes, it's definitely me.'

339 Two bowling teams – one all blondes, the other all brunettes – hired a double-decker bus for a weekend tournament in Denver. The brunette team rode on the bottom deck of the bus while the blondes travelled on the top level. The brunette team were having a great time, laughing and joking, until one of them realized that it was totally silent upstairs where the blondes were sitting. So she decided to go upstairs and investigate. There, she found all the blondes frozen in fear, staring straight ahead at the road, and gripping the seats in front of them with white knuckles.

'What the heck's going on up here?' asked the brunette. 'We're having a grand time downstairs.'

One of the blondes looked up and said: 'Yeah, but you've got a driver!'

340 A blonde was summoned to appear as a witness in a court case. The prosecutor asked her: 'Where were you on the night of April 9th?'

'Objection!' said the defence attorney. 'Irrelevant!'

'Oh, that's OK,' said the blonde from the witness stand. 'I don't mind answering the question.'

'I object!' said the defence again.

'No, really,' said the blonde. 'I'll answer.'

The judge ruled: 'If the witness insists on answering, there is no reason for the defence to object.'

'I demand an adjournment!' said the defence attorney.

'Very well,' said the judge wearily. 'The court will adjourn for fifteen minutes while I sort this matter out with the two attorneys.'

Fifteen minutes later, the court reconvened, and the judge began 'As I ruled earlier, if the witness is happy to answer the question, the defence has no right to object in law. So the prosecution may ask the question.'

'Thank you, your honour,' said the prosecutor. Turning to the witness stand, he asked once more: 'Where were you on the night of April 9th?'

The blonde replied brightly: 'I don't know.'

341 What's the difference between a blonde and a pair of sunglasses? – The sunglasses sit higher on your face.

342 Why did the blonde try to steal a police car? – She saw '911' and thought it was a Porsche.

343 What's the similarity between a blonde and dog poo? – The older they get, the easier they are to pick up.

344 What's the similarity between blondes and carpenters? – They both have saws in their boxes.

345 Why did the blonde stand in front of the mirror with her eyes closed? – She wanted to see what she looked like asleep.

346 What's blonde, brunette, blonde, brunette . . . ? – A blonde doing cart-wheels.

347 A young ventriloquist touring the clubs stopped to entertain at a small town bar. He was going through his usual routine of blonde jokes when a busty blonde woman in the fourth row stood on her chair and shouted out:

'OK, jerk, I've heard just about enough of your denigrating blonde jokes. What makes you think you can stereotype women that way? What do a person's physical attributes have to do with their worth as a human being? It's guys like you who prevent women like me from being respected at work and in my community, from reaching my full potential as a person, because you and your kind continue to discriminate against not only blondes but women as a whole . . . and all in the name of humour.'

Flustered, the ventriloquist began to apologize, but the blonde interrupted angrily: 'You stay out of this, mister, I'm talking to that little fucker on your knee!'

348 A brunette and her blonde sister inherited a farm. One day the brunette was attending a large agricultural show when she spotted the ideal bull for the farm. She just about had enough money to buy it but, because she hadn't brought the animal trailer and the dealer was unable to deliver, she faced a problem with transporting the beast home. The phone wasn't working, so she went to the telegraph office to send a message telling her sister to drive over with the trailer. However the telegraph office charged one dollar per word, and the brunette discovered that she only had one dollar left.

After thinking for a moment, she told the telegraph operator to send the message 'comfortable'.

'Just "comfortable"?' queried the operator. 'How's that going to tell your sister to hitch a trailer to her car and pick up a bull?'

The brunette replied: 'She's blonde. She'll read it slowly.'

349 What did the blonde say to her swimming instructor? – Will I really drown if you take your finger out?

350 Why is a blonde like a doorknob? – Because everyone gets a turn.

351 What job does a blonde have in an M&M factory? – Proofreading.

352 Why was the blonde fired from the M&M factory? – For throwing out the Ws.

353 Why do blondes use tampons with long strings? – So the crabs can go bungee jumping.

354 A blonde was driving along the highway when she was pulled over by a police patrol car. The officer stepped out of the car and said: 'You've been driving erratically, ma'am. I'm afraid I'm going to have to give you a breathalyser test to determine whether you're under the influence of alcohol.'

So she did the test and he studied the result. 'Hmm,' he said, 'it looks like you've had a couple of stiff ones.'

The blonde blushed. 'You mean it shows that too?'

355 A blonde arrived home to find that her house had been burgled. She immediately called the cops who sent the nearest patrol in the area, which happened to be a dog handler. Seeing the cop and his dog approach the house, the blonde suddenly burst into tears.

'What's up?' asked the cop.

The blonde sobbed: 'I come home to find all my possessions stolen, so I call the police for help, and what do they do? They send me a blind policeman!'

356 After stopping at a gas station, a blonde had just paid at the cash desk when she realized that she had locked her keys in the car. So she asked the attendant for a coat hanger in the hope of opening the car door that way. The attendant gave her a hanger and she took it outside. Ten minutes later, he went out to the car to see how she was doing. He found her crouched down by the door, carefully manoeuvring the hanger through a crack in the driver's window, while her blonde friend in the passenger seat was saying: 'A bit more to the left, down a little, a bit more to the right . . .'

357 A brunette, a blonde and a redhead are all in fifth grade. Who has the biggest tits? – The blonde, because she's 18.

358 A brunette said to a blonde, 'Look! A dead bird!' And the blonde looked up and said, 'Where?'

359 A blonde, a brunette and a redhead were about to be consigned either to heaven or hell. They had to walk up one hundred stairs but on each stair God told a joke, and if they laughed they went to hell. The brunette got as far as the 39th stair when she laughed and was sent straight to hell. The redhead reached the 81st stair when she, too, laughed and was sent to hell. The blonde got all the way to heaven but then she suddenly burst out laughing.
'Why are you laughing?' demanded God.
The blonde replied: 'I just got the first one!'

BLOW JOBS

360 A young guy dropped his girlfriend off at her home after their date. When they reached the front door, he leaned up against the house with one hand and said: 'How about a blow job?'
'No way!' she said.
'I'll be quick,' he promised.
'No, it's too public,' she insisted.
'Oh, come on,' he pleaded, 'I know you enjoy it as much as I do.'
'I said no.'
Suddenly the girl's younger sister appeared at the door, wearing her nightgown and rubbing her bleary eyes. She said: 'Dad says either you blow him, I blow him, or he'll come downstairs and blow the guy himself – but for God's sake tell your boyfriend to take his hand off the intercom!'

361 Why did God give women foreheads? – So you would have something to kiss after you blow in their mouth.

362 What's the similarity between walking a tightrope and getting a blow job from an eighty-year-old woman? – In both cases you don't really want to look down.

363 Back in the old days in Texas, three people were travelling in a stagecoach: a true red-blooded born-and-raised Texas gentleman, a tenderfoot city slicker from back east, and an elegant Texas lady. The city slicker kept eyeing the lady until he leaned forward and said, 'Lady, I'll give you three dollars for a blow job.'

The Texas gentleman looked appalled, pulled out his pistol and shot the city slicker dead. The lady gasped and said: 'Thank you, sir, for defendin' mah honour.'

Whereupon the Texan holstered his gun and said: 'To hell with your honour! No tenderfoot from back east is gonna raise the price of a woman in Texas!'

364 A guy went up to a hooker and asked: 'How much for a blow job?'

'$100,' said the hooker.

He tried to get her to lower her price, but she wouldn't budge, so he agreed to pay the full amount. Then he started jacking off.

'What are you doing that for?' she asked.

He said: 'For a hundred bucks, do you think I'm gonna give you the easy one?'

365 A redneck teenager was walking downtown when a girl whispered to him: 'Blow job, five dollars.' He gave her a strange look and kept walking. Soon another girl did the same thing. Confused, he kept walking. When he got home, he asked: 'Mom, what's a blow job?'

His mother replied: 'Five dollars, just like downtown.'

366 Returning from the men's room, a bar customer was shaking his head in despair.

'What's the problem?' asked the bartender.

'While I was in the washroom back there, I noticed among the scribblings on the wall, one that said: "Wendy give fabulous head – absolutely the greatest B.J. in the whole world!"'

'Aw, buddy, I wouldn't give it a second thought — we get jerks in here all the time.'

'I know. One of them has scratched out the phone number.'

367 What's the difference between oral sex and anal sex? — Oral sex makes your day, anal sex makes your hole weak.

368 What's the best thing about a blow job? — Ten minutes of silence.

369 What's the difference between an airship and 365 blow jobs? — One's a good year, the other's an excellent year.

370 A guy went into a whorehouse and said he wanted the best blow job money could buy. The madame said it would cost $150, and told him to go upstairs to a room. A few minutes later, the hooker came in and proceeded to suck him off. Afterwards, she reached under the bed, pulled out a jar and spat in it. The guy enjoyed the whole experience so much that he paid another $150 for a repeat performance.

The hooker happily gave him another blow job. Afterwards, she again pulled out the jar and spat in it. Intrigued, he asked her what the jar was for.

She said: 'I have a bet with the girl across the hall. Whoever fills up their jar first gets to drink them both.'

371 A guy was rushing home from the office late one night when he was accosted by a hooker. She said: 'How 'bout a blow job, honey? Only $50. You look as though you need it — you're all uptight.'

'No way,' he said. 'I'm married.'

'So?'

'My wife will do it for $35.'

372 What's the similarity between lobster thermidor and a blow job? — You only ever get them when you're away from home.

373 Two high school sweethearts promised to stay together forever but, when they went to different colleges hundreds of miles apart, her interest began to cool. When he phoned her, she was never around; if he wrote love letters to her, she would take weeks to reply; even his urgent e-mails did not warrant an immediate response. Eventually she confessed that she wanted to see other guys.

He took the news badly, and increased the number of calls, letters, and e-mails in an attempt to win her back. She felt harassed by this unwanted bombardment and, to convince him that it was time to move on, she took drastic action: she sent him a Polaroid of her giving her new boyfriend a blow job. Attached was a note that read: 'I found a new boyfriend, leave me alone.'

Although heartbroken, the guy was also livid. So he decided to mail the photo on to her parents with a note that read: 'Dear Mom and Dad, having a great time at college, please send more money! I'm getting pretty desperate!'

374 A salesman was on business in Las Vegas. One evening he got chatting to a woman in a bar and eventually realised that she was a hooker.

He said: 'I'll give you $200 for a mediocre blow job.'

'Honey,' she answered, 'for $200, I'll give you the blow job of a lifetime!'

'You don't understand,' he said. 'I'm not horny, just homesick.'

BOOKS

The World's Shortest Books:

375 • Lawyers' Code of Ethics
376 • The Australian Book of Foreplay
377 • The World Guide to Good American Beer
378 • The Canadian Book of Insults
379 • Mastering Inglish Grammer by George W. Bush
380 • Al Gore: The Wild Years
381 • Bill Clinton: A Portrait of Integrity
382 • Great Swedish Cuisine
383 • Donald Rumsfeld: My Quest for World Peace
384 • Princess Anne's Beauty Tips
385 • Great British Tennis Players
386 • Detroit: A Travel Guide
387 • The Amish Phone Directory
388 • The Art of Diplomacy by Prince Philip
389 • O.J. Simpson: My Plan to Find the Real Killers
390 • The Engineers' Guide to Fashion
391 • A History of German Humour

392 • Fun Days Out in Albania
393 • Proud to be Black by Michael Jackson
394 • How to Look Good at Sixty by Keith Richards
395 • Human Rights Advances in China
396 • Mike Tyson's Guide to Dating Etiquette
397 • Who's Who in Puerto Rico

398 Is a book on voyeurism a peeping tome?

BOSSES

399 The secretary walked into her boss's office and announced: 'I'm afraid I have some bad news for you.'

'Kelly,' said the boss, 'why do you always bring me bad news? Try to be more positive.'

'OK,' she said. 'The good news is you're not sterile.'

400 The boss told four of his employees: 'We made a heavy loss last quarter, and I'm afraid I'm going to have to let one of you go.'

The first, a black man, said: 'I'm a protected minority, you can't fire me.'

The second said: 'And I'm a woman. You can't get rid of me.'

The third, an old man, said: 'And if you fire me, I'll hit you with an age discrimination suit so fast it'll make your head spin!'

All eyes turned on the young, white, male employee who thought for a second before suggesting meekly: 'I think I might be gay . . .'

Things You Wouldn't Want Your Boss to Overhear:

401 • After he cut our pay, I'm the one that keyed his car.
402 • No, I only hack from my work computer.
403 • The combination is the same as his birthdate.
404 • Sure, I banged his wife at the Christmas party.
405 • I only forge his name on the important stuff.
406 • And then I said, 'My name's Kev, and I'm an alcoholic.'
407 • Don't worry, the cops will never find out who I really am.
408 • And so there I was, his daughter was on her knees . . .

BREASTS

409 Why is the space between a woman's breasts and her hips called a waist? – Because you could easily fit another pair of tits in there.

410 An old man was sitting on a beach when he spotted a beautiful young girl in a bikini. Walking over to her, he announced boldly: 'I want to feel your breasts.'

Disgusted by the suggestion, she told him: 'Go away, you dirty old man!'

But the old man repeated: 'I want to feel your breasts. I'll give you $20.'

'$20?' she exclaimed. 'Are you crazy? Get away from me before I call the police!'

The old man persisted. 'I want to feel your breasts. I'll give you $100.'

'What part of "get lost" don't you understand?' she snapped.

'OK,' said the old man. '$200.'

She paused momentarily to think about it before coming to her senses and answering: 'I told you, no. Go away NOW!'

The old man looked at her and said: 'I'll give you $500 if you let me feel your breasts.'

Against her better judgement, she had to admit that it was good money for a quick grope, and, besides, he was a harmless old man. 'All right,' she said, 'I'll let you feel my breasts for $500, but only for a few seconds.'

So she loosened her bikini top and he slid his hands underneath. As he caressed her breasts, he began moaning over and over again: 'Oh, my God! Oh, my God! Oh, my God!'

She said: 'Why do you keep going "Oh, my God!"?'

While continuing to feel her breasts, he answered: 'Oh, my God! Oh, my God! Oh, my God! Wherever am I going to find $500?'

411 What are the small bumps around women's nipples? – It's Braille for 'suck here'.

412 A flat-chested woman was delighted when her fairy godmother said her breasts would increase in size each time a man said 'Pardon' to her.

Walking down the street, the woman accidentally bumped into a man who said: 'Pardon me.' To her delight, her breasts immediately grew an inch. The next day, she bumped into a man in the grocery store, and when he begged her pardon, another inch was added to her breasts. She was in seventh heaven.

That evening, she walked into an Indian restaurant, and collided with a waiter who bowed and said: 'A thousand pardons for my clumsy behaviour.'

The headline in the following morning's paper read: 'Indian Waiter Crushed to Death.'

413 What did one saggy boob say to the other saggy boob? – If we don't get some support soon, people are going to think we're nuts.

414 A woman wanted to have surgery to make her breasts bigger. Her husband was all in favour of the idea, but baulked at the cost.

'Why don't you rub toilet paper between them instead?' he suggested.

'How will that make my breasts bigger?' she asked.

'I don't know,' he said. 'But it sure worked for your ass!'

415 What's worse than silicon tits? – A cardboard box.

416 A teenage girl came downstairs for her date wearing a see-through blouse and no bra. Her grandmother went mad.

'Loosen up,' said the teenager. 'These are modern times. You gotta let your rosebuds show!'

And with that she left for her date.

The next day the teenager came downstairs to find her granny sitting there with no top on. The sight of granny's wrinkled breasts made the girl want to die, particularly as she was expecting friends to call on her any minute.

'Loosen up,' said granny. 'If you can show off your rosebuds, then I can display my hanging baskets!'

417 How do you spot Dolly Parton's kids in the playground? – They're the ones with the stretch marks around their mouths.

418 A flat-chested woman went shopping for a new bra. She tried six shops in search of a size 28A bra, but couldn't find one anywhere. She was just about to give up when she stumbled across a small lingerie shop that was run by an elderly deaf lady.

'Have you got any bras in size 28A?' asked the woman.

'What did you say?' said the old lady.

'Have you got anything in size 28A?' repeated the woman, louder.

'Sorry, I didn't catch that, dear. What is it you want?'

In despair, the woman lifted up her T-shirt to reveal her breasts. 'Have you got anything for these?' she asked.

The old lady looked at the woman's breasts and said: 'Have you tried Clearasil?'

419 In the beginning God created Eve, and she had three breasts. After a few weeks, God called on her in the Garden of Eden to make sure that she was having a good time.

'So how's things?' asked God.

'Everything here is really lovely,' said Eve, 'apart from one problem. It's these three breasts. The middle one pushes the other two out, as a result of which I'm always knocking them with my arms or bumping into trees with them. I reckon two breasts would be enough. Is there anything you can do?'

'I see your point,' said God. And with that he removed Eve's middle breast and threw it into the bushes. 'There, is that better?'

'Much better,' said Eve. 'Thank you.'

A few weeks later, God visited Eve again to find out how she was adjusting to her new shape.

'Everything is wonderful,' enthused Eve, 'apart from just one thing. You see, all the animals in the garden have a mate, but I have nobody. Is there any chance that you can create a mate for me?'

'You're right,' said God. 'I knew there was something I'd forgotten. You do need a mate. I will create Man from a part of your body. Now, let me see . . . Where did I put that useless tit?'

GEORGE W. BUSH

420 While visiting England, George W. Bush was invited to tea with the Queen. He asked her what her leadership philosophy was and she said that it was to surround herself with intelligent people. He asked her how she tested intelligence.

'I ask them the right questions,' said the Queen. 'Allow me to demonstrate.'

So she phoned Tony Blair and said: 'Prime Minister, please answer this question: Your mother has a child, and your father has a child, and this child is not your brother or sister. Who is it?'

Blair replied: 'It's me, ma'am.'

'Correct,' said the Queen. She put down the phone and said: 'Did you get that, Mr Bush?'

'Yes, ma'am,' said Bush confidently. 'Thanks a lot. I'll definitely be using that.'

On returning to Washington, he decided to put Donald Rumsfeld to the test. He summoned him to the White House and said: 'Donald, I wonder if you can answer a question for me.'

'Of course, sir. What's on your mind?'

'Uh, your mother has a child, and your father has a child, and this child is not your brother or your sister. Who is it?'

Rumsfeld scratched his head until finally asking: 'Can I think about it and get back to you?' Bush agreed.

Rumsfeld immediately called a meeting of his senior advisers but, after poring over the puzzle for several hours, they were unable to come up with an answer. In desperation he rang Colin Powell and explained his problem.

'Now, look here, Colin Powell, your mother has a child, and your father has a child, and this child is not your brother or your sister. Who is it?' Powell answered straight away. 'It's me, of course, you dumb ass!'

A relieved Rumsfeld rushed back to the White House and told the President: 'I know the answer, sir! I know who it is! It's Colin Powell!'

And Bush replied in disgust: 'Wrong, you dumb ass! It's Tony Blair!'

421 George W. Bush was visiting a fourth grade class at an elementary school. The kids were in the middle of talking about words and their meanings, and the teacher asked the President if he would like to lead the class in a discussion of the word 'tragedy'. So Bush asked the class for an example of a 'tragedy'.

One little boy stood up and offered: 'If my best friend, who lives next door, is playing in the street and a car comes along and runs him over, that would be a tragedy.'

'No,' said Bush, 'that would be an accident.'

A little girl raised her hand. 'If a school bus carrying fifty children drove off a cliff, killing everyone on board, that would be a tragedy.'

'I'm afraid not,' explained the President. 'That's what we would call a "great loss".'

The room fell silent until Bush asked: 'Isn't there someone here who can give me an example of a tragedy?'

Finally a boy at the back named Johnny raised his hand and suggested: 'If

Air Force One, carrying you and Mrs Bush, was struck by a missile and blown to pieces, that would be a tragedy.'

'Correct,' said Bush. 'And can you tell me *why* that would be a tragedy?'

'Well,' said Johnny, 'because, like you just told us, it wouldn't be an accident, and it sure as hell wouldn't be a great loss.'

422 How did George W. Bush create 14 million new jobs? – 13 million of them are comedians.

423 George W. Bush was visiting famous Washington landmarks for inspiration. At the Washington monument he asked: 'What can I do to be a strong President?'

George Washington's spirit replied: 'Maintain a strong army and rule it wisely.'

At the Jefferson monument he asked: 'What can I do to be a strong ruler?'

Thomas Jefferson's spirit said: 'Maintain the constitution and listen to the people.'

At the Lincoln monument Bush asked: 'How can I best listen to the people? What do they really want?'

Abraham Lincoln's spirit answered: 'Visit the theatre.'

424 George W. Bush was waiting in an airport lobby when he noticed a man in a long white flowing robe with a long flowing white beard and flowing white hair. The man had a staff in one hand and some stone tablets under the other arm.

Bush approached the man and said: 'Aren't you Moses?'

The man ignored Bush and stared at the ceiling.

Bush persisted and said: 'It is Moses, isn't it?'

The man continued to peruse the ceiling.

Then Bush tugged at the man's sleeve and asked once again: 'You are Moses, aren't you?'

Finally the man broke his silence, replying irritably: 'Yes, I am.'

'So why have you been ignoring me?'

'Because,' explained Moses, 'the last time I spoke to a Bush, I had to spend forty years in the desert.'

425 Why does George W. Bush keep his fly open? – In case he needs to count to eleven.

426 A stranger walked into a cowboy bar and ordered a beer just as George W. Bush appeared on television. After a few sips, he looked up at the TV set and mumbled: 'Now, there's the biggest horse's ass I've ever seen.'

At this, a customer at the end of the bar stood up, walked over to the stranger and decked him.

A few minutes later, as the stranger was finishing his beer, Bush's wife also appeared on TV. 'She's a horse's ass, too,' muttered the stranger.

This time, a customer from the other end of the bar stood up, marched over to the stranger and shoved him off his stool.

'Damn it!' said the stranger, getting to his feet. 'This must be Bush country!'

'Nope,' said the bartender. 'Horse country!'

427 What were George W. Bush's three hardest years? – Second grade.

428 George W. Bush went to a primary school to talk about the war in Iraq. At the end of his talk, he asked whether there were any questions.

One little boy put up his hand.

'What is your name?' asked the President.

'Billy.'

'Right. What is your question, Billy?'

'I have three questions,' said the boy. 'First, why haven't you found weapons of mass destruction in Iraq? Second, why were you elected President when Al Gore got more votes? And third, whatever happened to Osama Bin Laden?'

Just then the bell rang for break. Bush informed the children that they would continue the session after the break. When they resumed, Bush said: 'OK, where were we? Oh, that's right, question time. Who has a question?'

A different little boy put up his hand, and the President asked his name.

'Bradley,' said the boy.

'Right, what is your question, Bradley?'

'I have five questions,' said Bradley. 'First, why haven't you found weapons of mass destruction in Iraq? Second, why were you elected President when Al Gore got more votes? Third, whatever happened to Osama Bin Laden? Fourth, why did the bell for break go twenty minutes early? Fifth, what happened to Billy?'

429 George W. Bush went to the doctor to get the results of his brain scan. The doctor said: 'Mr President, I have some bad news for you. First, we have discovered that your brain has two sides: the left side and the right side.'

Bush interrupted: 'But that's normal, isn't it? I thought everybody had two sides to their brain?'

'Yes, Mr President,' continued the doctor. 'But your brain is extremely unusual because on the left side there isn't anything right, while on the right side there isn't anything left.'

430 George W. Bush confided to Dick Cheney: 'You know, I really hate all those jokes people tell about me, making out that I'm stupid.'

'Don't worry,' said Cheney. 'Jokes can't hurt you. They are just made up by a bunch of stupid people. In fact, most of the people on this planet are incredibly stupid. Watch, and I'll show you what I mean.'

Cheney then stepped outside the White House, hailed a cab, handed the driver a note and said: 'Take me to this address and see if I'm home.'

Without querying the request, the cab driver took them to the address scribbled on the note. Cheney then got out, rang the doorbell, returned to the car and said to the driver: 'Damn! I guess I'm not at home! Take us back to where we started, please.'

Without a word, the cabbie did as he was told and dropped the pair back outside the White House. As they stepped out of the cab, Cheney said to Bush: 'See what I mean? People are idiots wherever you go! Don't pay any attention to their opinions.'

'Thanks, Dick,' said Bush. 'I feel a lot better. And boy, was that cabbie ever stupid! He picked us up right in front of a phone booth. He should have realized you could have called home instead.'

431 A woman bought a car with a voice-activated radio. When she said 'rock', it automatically switched to a rock music station; when she said 'classical', it automatically switched to a classical music station, and so on.

One day she was driving along when a van pulled out in front of her, causing her to brake sharply. 'Asshole,' she yelled. And the radio switched automatically to George W. Bush's press conference.

432 On the way to Air Force One, George W. Bush and his driver were passing a farm when a pig suddenly jumped out into the road. The driver tried to swerve, but couldn't help ploughing into the pig. He went to the farm to explain what had happened, and emerged five minutes later clutching a beer, a cigar and a stack of money.

Seeing this, Bush asked the driver: 'What on earth did you tell them?'

The driver replied: 'I told them I'm George W. Bush's driver and I just killed the pig.'

433 George W. Bush and Tony Blair were sitting in a bar when another guest arrived and asked them what they were talking about.

'We're planning for World War Three,' announced Bush.

'Oh, dear,' said the guest. 'What are you going to do?'

Bush replied: 'We are planning to kill 1,500,000 Muslims and one IS consultant.'

The guest was mystified. 'An IS consultant? Why in heaven's name are you going to kill an IS consultant?'

Bush patted Blair on the shoulder and exclaimed jubilantly: 'I told you! No one is going to ask about the Muslims.'

CALIFORNIA

You might be from Los Angeles if:

434 • You've inadvertently learned Spanish.

435 • Your pizza delivery guy is also on contract with Warner Bros.

436 • You have a gym membership because it's mandatory.

437 • Your favourite TV show is interrupted by a police chase.

438 • You drive to any destination more than five minutes away on foot.

439 • Your co-worker says she has eight body piercings . . . and none are visible.

440 • You know someone named Freedom, Rainbow or Destiny.

441 • You've been to more than one baby shower that has two mothers and a sperm donor.

442 • A really great parking space can move you to tears.

443 • Your best friends just named their twins after her acting coach and his personal trainer.

444 • You can't fall asleep without the lull of a helicopter flying overhead.

445 How many Los Angeles Police Department officers does it take to beat the hell out of a gang member? – None, he fell down.

446 What is an LA cop's favourite sandwich? – Truncheon meat.

447 An LA cop pulled over a car being driven by two black guys. No sooner had the driver wound down his window than the cop hit him across the face with his flashlight.

'Hey, what was that for?' asked the driver.

'I expect you to have your licence and registration ready when I come to your window. Got it?'

The driver produced his licence and registration and handed the documents to the cop. The officer checked the details before returning them to the driver. Just as the driver was about to wind up his window, the cop hit him again.

'Ow!' yelled the driver. 'What the hell was that for?'

'I expect you to say "thank you",' snarled the cop.

The shaken driver quickly said 'thank you', and wound up his window. The cop then walked around to the passenger side and tapped on the window. When the passenger rolled down his window, the cop hit him over the head.

'Why did you do that?' shouted the passenger.

'I was making your wish come true,' said the cop.

'What do you mean?'

The cop sneered: 'A hundred yards down the road you'd have turned to your buddy and said: "I wish that son-of-a-bitch had tried that shit with me.'

448 How do you know when a relationship gets serious in California? – They take you to meet their Tarot Card reader.

449 Two little girls – Chelsea and Harley – were in the lunchroom of a Beverly Hills elementary school.

'Guess what?' said Chelsea. 'My mommy's getting married again, so I'm going to have a new daddy.'

'Who's she marrying?' asked Harley.

'Karl Wilkinson,' said Chelsea. 'He's a famous Hollywood actor.'

'Oh, you'll like him,' said Harley. 'He was my daddy last year.'

450 Why don't blondes wear miniskirts in San Francisco? – Because their balls hang down below their hemlines.

451 A Californian tourist asked the guide: 'Can you tell me why so many famous Civil War battles were fought on National Park sites?'

452 A Californian tourist visited England and joined a group on an excursion to Runnymede. The guide explained: 'This is the spot where the barons forced King John to sign the Magna Carta.'

'When did that happen?' asked the Californian.

'1215,' answered the guide.

The Californian looked at his watch and sighed: 'Damn! Just missed it by half an hour!'

453 Two black guys were walking down a street in Los Angeles when they were hit by a police car driven by a drunken cop. One guy was thrown through the windscreen and his buddy was sent hurtling down an embankment. The first was charged with breaking and entering, and the second was charged with leaving the scene of an accident.

CAMELS

454 A guy was riding through the desert on a camel. He had been travelling so long that he felt an urgent need to have sex. Since there were no women in the desert, he turned to his camel and tried to position himself to have sex with the animal, but the camel ran off. The man ran as fast as he could in the blistering heat to catch the camel, climbed back on and they set off on their journey again.

Soon the urge to have sex returned, so again he turned to his camel but the horrified beast ran off once more. He managed to catch it and together they continued their trek through the desert. Finally at the end of the vast wilderness, they came to a road and there in a broken down car were three beautiful, busty young blondes.

The sex-starved man went over and asked the women if they needed any help. The hottest girl said: 'If you fix our car, we will do anything you want.'

Luckily he knew a fair bit about cars and quickly fixed it. When he finished, the three girls asked: 'How can we ever repay you?'

The man thought for a moment, then said: 'Could you hold my camel?'

455 What's invisible and smells like camels? – Camel farts.

456 An American tourist in Egypt got chatting to a man in a bar.

'What do you do for a living?' asked the tourist.

'I'm a camel castrator.'

'Wow!' exclaimed the tourist. 'How do you castrate a camel?'

The man explained: 'You go behind him and spread his legs. Then you take a big rock in each hand and smack his testicles between the rocks.'

'That must really hurt,' winced the tourist.

'Not if you keep your thumbs out of the way.'

CANADIANS

457 Two guys who were best friends had both recently got divorced and the experience had left them so bitter that they vowed never to have anything to do with women again. To start a new life away from women, they decided to move up to the far north of Canada. There, they went into a trader's store and said: 'Give us enough supplies to last two men for a year.'

The trader assembled the gear and on top of each one's supplies he laid a board with a fur-lined hole in it.

'What's the board for?' asked the guys.

The trader said: 'Well, where you're going, there are no women and you might need this.'

'No way!' they chorused. 'We've sworn off women for life!'

The trader said: 'Well, take the boards with you anyway, and if you don't use them, I'll refund your money next year.'

The guys agreed and off they went.

A year later one of them entered the same store and said: 'Give me enough supplies to last one man for a year.'

The trader said: 'Weren't you in here last year with a partner?'

'Yeah,' said the guy.

'Where is he?' asked the trader.

'I killed him – I caught him in bed with my board.'

458 Why don't Canadians have group sex? – Too many thank-you letters to write afterwards.

459 Two Canadian men were sitting around the house bored. Then one suggested: 'Why don't we play Twenty Questions? I'll think of the first subject.'

He thought for a few seconds and came up with the subject 'moose cock'.

'OK,' he said, 'Ask me the first question.'

His friend began: 'Is it something you can eat?'
'I guess you could eat it.'
'Is it a moose cock?'

Signs That You Might Be Canadian:

460 • You design your Hallowe'en costume to fit over a snowsuit.
461 • You know that the four seasons mean: almost winter, winter, still winter, and road work.
462 • You own five pairs of hockey skates and only one pair of shoes.
463 • You say 'no big deal' to a sidewalk cyclist who's just knocked you down.
464 • You think sexy lingerie is tube-socks and a flannel nightdress with only eight buttons.
465 • You dismiss all beers under six per cent as 'for children and the elderly'.
466 • You get excited whenever a US TV show mentions Canada.
467 • You find Kentucky Fried Chicken 'a bit too spicy'.
468 • You think driving is better in winter because the potholes are filled with snow.
469 • You have ten favourite recipes for moose meat.
470 • You say, 'Sure it's 33 below, but it's a dry cold.'

471 Why do Canadians screw doggie-style? – So both can watch the hockey game.

472 A guy was driving along the highway towards Edmonton when he spotted a pretty girl standing by the side of the road. As the driver slowed down to offer her a lift, a huge Canadian suddenly stepped out into the middle of the road and dragged him from the car. Before the driver could make sense of what was happening, the burly Canadian had issued a grim order:
'Have a wank or I'll kill you.'
The driver realized he had no choice and, using the pretty girl as his inspiration, managed to jerk himself off quickly. But just as he thought this bizarre ordeal would be over, the Canadian barked:
'Have another wank or I'll kill you.'
Even with the pretty hitch-hiker in his line of vision, it was tough going a second time, but he managed it and afterwards headed for the car. But

before he could reach the door, the mountainous Canadian had grabbed him again and demanded:

'Have another wank or I'll kill you.'

The driver tried to protest but the menacing look on the Canadian's face told him that reason was pointless. So for the third time the guy set about jerking himself off. He could just see the pretty girl beyond the car, but it took him twenty-five minutes to come, at the end of which he collapsed exhausted into the dirt.

The Canadian immediately hauled him to his feet. 'Right,' he rasped. 'Now you can give my daughter a lift to Edmonton.'

473 Why does a Canadian cross the road? – To get to the middle.

474 A young couple headed up to the wilds of Canada for a romantic weekend. The guy went off to chop wood but returned after twenty minutes, complaining that his hands were cold.

'That's OK,' said his girlfriend. 'You can warm them between my thighs.'

So he slipped his icy hands between her warm thighs before going back to his wood chopping. A few minutes later he was back again, complaining that his hands were cold. Once more, she let him warm them between her thighs before he resumed his work in the forest. Five minutes later, he returned again.

'My hands are so cold,' he said. 'Can I warm them between your thighs?'

His girlfriend glared at him: 'Don't your ears ever get cold?'

475 In Canada there are only two seasons – six months of winter and six months of poor snowmobiling.

476 What's the definition of a Canadian? – A disarmed American with health care.

477 Seeing two dogs mating, an embarrassed Canadian teacher tried to explain it to her young students.

'You see,' she said, 'the dog on top hurt his paw, and the one underneath is taking him to the doctor.'

'Oh, I get it,' said one student. 'Just like in the US: try to help somebody and they screw you every time!'

478 When a Canadian thinks of hell, he wonders what the heating bill must be.

479 A girl sat sobbing in a police station. 'I was raped by a Canadian,' she wailed.

'How do you know it was a Canadian?' asked the officer.

'Because I had to help him.'

480 What do you call a Canadian who moves to America and becomes an international celebrity through movies, music or sport? – An American.

CANNIBALS

481 At the site of a plane crash deep in a wooded valley, the lone survivor sat chewing on a bone. As he tossed it onto a huge pile of bones, the rescue team arrived.

'Thank heavens!' he cried out in relief. 'I am saved!'

The rescue team did not respond. Instead their eyes were fixed in horror at the pile of human bones beside this solitary survivor. It was clear that he had eaten all his fellow passengers.

Seeing the stunned expressions on the rescuers' faces, the survivor hung his head in shame. 'You can't judge me for this,' he insisted. 'What else was I supposed to do? I had to eat. Is it so wrong to want to live?'

The leader of the rescue team stepped forward, shaking his head in disbelief, and said: 'I won't judge you for doing what was necessary to survive, but good heavens, man, your plane only went down yesterday!'

482 When do cannibals leave the table? – When everyone's eaten.

483 Why do cannibals like Jehovah's Witnesses? – They're free delivery.

484 Did you hear about the cannibal who passed his sister in the street?

485 Did you hear about the cannibal who went on a diet? – He only ate midgets.

486 Did you hear about the cannibal policeman who was arrested? – He was caught grilling his suspects.

487 Did you hear about the cannibal who ate his mother-in-law? – She still didn't agree with him.

488 Three cannibals were given jobs with an international corporation, but only on condition that they didn't eat any of the other staff. For six months there were no problems, but then their boss called them into his office and told them that an office cleaner had gone missing. As obvious suspects, the cannibals were sacked on the spot.

As they collected their things, the cannibal leader asked the other two: 'Which of you fools ate the cleaner?'

One raised his hand sheepishly.

'You idiot!' said the leader. 'For months we've been feasting on project managers, team leaders and human resources staff, then you go and eat someone they'll actually miss!'

489 Did you hear about the cannibal who loved fast food? – He ordered a pizza with everybody on it.

490 Did you hear about the cannibal who was expelled from school for buttering up his teacher?

491 Two missionaries were captured by a tribe of cannibals who put them in a large pot of water, lit a huge fire beneath it, and left them to boil. After a few minutes, one of the missionaries began to laugh uncontrollably.

'What's wrong with you?' asked his colleague angrily. 'We're being boiled alive! They're gonna eat us! What could possibly be funny at a time like this?'

The other missionary said: 'I've just crapped in the soup!'

CATS

492 You are putting up shelves.

The dog thinks: 'Master, I don't know what you're doing but it looks fantastic and I love you.'

The cat thinks: 'Wanker. He's not read the instructions, he's using allen keys instead of the self-tapping screws, and that hinge is upside down.'

493 What do you do if a cat spits at you? – Turn the grill down.

CHICAGO

494 Told that he was being transferred to Chicago, a Seattle office worker said he would rather quit his job than move there.

'What's the problem?' asked his boss. 'You'll be getting a big salary increase and much improved benefits. I thought you'd jump at the chance.'

'It's the crime rate,' explained the worker. 'I just wouldn't feel safe taking my wife and kids to such a violent city.'

'That's nonsense,' said the boss. 'Chicago is a fantastic city, steeped in history, with great museums, excellent public transport, and it's close to Canada. I myself worked in Chicago for ten years, and in all that time I never had a problem with crime.'

'What did you do there?'

'I was tail-gunner on a bread truck.'

495 A woman from Chicago attended a party in New York where the hostess was determined to make her mid-west guest feel cheap and unimportant.

'My dear,' said the New York matron snobbishly, 'here in the east we think breeding is everything.'

'Oh, I don't know,' said the Chicago woman. 'Where I come from we think it's fun, too, but we try to have a few outside interests as well.'

496 A guy was knocking back the drinks in a Chicago bar so fast that the man on the next barstool asked him what the problem was.

The first guy said: 'I'm drinking to the memory of my wife. She was a saint on earth. She went to church every single morning, spent her days reading and quoting the scriptures, sang hymns and psalms all evening, filled our house with religious statues and paintings, and invited priests and nuns to dinner three times a week.'

'She sounds like an angel,' said the second man. 'I suppose the good Lord took her early to Himself.'

'No,' said the first guy. 'I strangled her.'

CHILDREN

497 Little Jenny came home from playing at Dean's house and called out: 'Hey, mom, guess what! Dean's got a penis like a peanut!'

Her mother was understandably confused for a second, then queried: 'What, you mean it's shaped like a peanut?'

'No, silly . . . it tastes salty!'

498 Finding her young son scooping ice cream in the kitchen, a mother raged: 'Dinner is going to be ready soon. Put that ice cream away, and go and play.'

'But, mom,' wailed the child, 'there's no one to play with.'

'OK,' said the mother wearily. 'I'll play with you. What do you want to play?'

'Let's play mommy and daddy. You go upstairs and lie on the bed.'

So the mother went upstairs and lay on the bed. The boy put on his father's fishing hat, lit up one of his cigars, went upstairs and opened the bedroom door.

Seeing him standing there, the mother asked: 'Now what do I do?'

The boy answered: 'Get your ass out of bed, you whore, and fix that kid some fucking ice cream!'

499 How do you stop kids from bed-wetting? – Give them an electric blanket.

500 Two poor kids went to a birthday party at a rich kid's house. The birthday boy was so rich that he had his own swimming pool and all the kids went in. As they were changing afterwards, one of the poor kids said to the other one: 'Did you notice how small the rich kid's penis was?'

'Yeah,' said his mate. 'It's probably because he's got toys to play with.'

501 A young boy came home from school with a sofa slung across his back and carrying two armchairs. His father said crossly: 'I told you not to accept suites from strangers.'

502 One day, two very loving parents got into a huge fight, in the course of which the man called the woman a 'bitch', and she called him a 'bastard'. Their young son walked in at the height of the row and asked: 'What do bitch and bastard mean?'

Embarrassed by their appalling behaviour, the parents explained: 'It means "ladies and gentlemen".'

By the next day the parents had made up, and decided to have sex. The woman said 'feel my titties' and the man said 'feel my dick'. When their son walked in and asked what titties and dick meant, they replied: 'Hats and coats.'

On Thanksgiving the Dad was shaving when he cut himself. 'Shit!' he exclaimed. When the kid came in and asked what 'shit' meant, the father covered up his bad language by saying it was the brand of shaving cream he was using.

Meanwhile downstairs the mother, while preparing the turkey, also cut herself. 'Fuck!' she exclaimed. Once again the kid asked what the word meant, and the mother pretended that it was her word for stuffing the turkey.

Moments later, the doorbell rang. The kid answered the door to his relatives and announced loudly: 'All right, you bitches and bastards, put your titties and dicks in the closet, my Dad is upstairs wiping the shit off his face, and Mom is in the kitchen fucking the turkey.'

503 A woman saw a small boy leaning against a wall smoking a cigarette and taking swigs from a bottle of scotch.

'Shouldn't you be at school?' she asked.

'School?' said the boy. 'No way. I'm only four!'

504 A five-year-old boy came crying to his mother because his little sister pulled his hair.

'Don't be angry,' said the mother. 'Your baby sister doesn't realize that pulling hair hurts.'

A few minutes later, there was more crying, and the mother went to investigate. This time the baby was crying, and her brother said: 'Don't worry, mom, she knows now.'

505 Why do little boys whine? — Because they're practising to be men.

506 A little girl came running into the house in tears.

'Mummy, I need a glass of cider. Quick!'

'Why?' asked her mother.

'Because I cut my hand on a thorn and I want the pain to go away.'

The mother reached for the bottle, but was still puzzled by the request. 'What makes you think this will work?' she said.

'Because I overheard my big sister saying that whenever she gets a prick in her hand, she can't wait to get it in cider.'

507 On a visit to his sister, who was married to a poor farmer, a young man had to share a room with his six-year-old nephew. When the young man entered the bedroom, he saw the little boy kneeling at the side of the bed with his head bowed. Thinking he was in prayer, he decided to follow his example and knelt at the other side of the bed with his head bowed.

The boy asked: 'What are you doing?'

'The same as you,' replied the young man.

'Well, ma's gonna be mad. The pot's on this side.'

CHINESE JOKES

508 A Chinese man arranged for a hooker to come to his room for the evening. After sex, he suddenly ran to the window, took a deep breath, dived under the bed, climbed out the other side and started screwing her again. This happened four times. During the fifth encore, the hooker was so impressed by his stamina that she decided to try his routine for herself. So when he had finished, she ran to the window, took a deep breath, dived under the bed . . . and found four Chinese men.

509 A garbage collector was going along the street emptying the wheelie bins. At one house the bin hadn't been left out, so he knocked on the door. Eventually a Chinese man answered the door breathlessly.

'Where's ya bin?' asked the garbage collector.

'I bin on toiret,' said the Chinese man, bemused.

'No, mate,' said the collector, 'you don't understand. Where's ya dustbin?'

'I told you,' replied the Chinese man, 'I dust bin on toiret.'

'No, listen,' said the collector, trying to explain: 'Where's ya wheelie bin?'

'OK,' said the Chinese guy. 'I wheelie bin having wank.'

510 What do you get when you cross a Mexican and a Chinese man? — A car thief who can't drive.

511 A Chinese man had three daughters. He asked the eldest daughter what kind of man she wanted to marry. She said: 'I would like to marry a man with three dragons on his chest.'

Then he asked his second daughter the same question. She replied: 'I would like to marry a man with two dragons on his chest.'

Finally he asked the same question to his youngest daughter. She answered: 'I would like to marry a man with one draggin' on the ground.'

512 After an evening of drinking, a guy and his Chinese girlfriend ended up in his bedroom.

'What do you want to do?' she asked. 'I'm up for anything.'

'Well, in that case,' he whispered, 'what I'd really like is a 69.'

'Forget it,' she said. 'There's no way I'm cooking chicken chow mein at this time of night!'

513 A beautiful PA to a leading New York banker was given the task of entertaining an important Chinese client on his visit to the Big Apple. The evening went so well that at the end of it, much to her surprise, the client asked her to marry him.

Remembering what her boss had told her about not hurting the client's feelings at any cost, she decided not to reject him outright. So she tried to think of a way of dissuading the little man from wanting to marry her. After a few moments' thought, she announced: 'I will only agree to marry you on three conditions. First, I want my engagement ring to have a huge diamond with a matching diamond tiara.'

The Chinese man nodded his head enthusiastically. 'No problem. I buy. I buy.'

Realizing that her first condition was too easy, she then said: 'Second, I want you to build me a 100-room mansion in New York. And as a vacation home, I want a chateau built in the middle of champagne country in France.'

The Chinese man paused to think for a while. Then he whipped out his mobile phone, called brokers in New York and France before nodding to the woman: 'OK. I build. I build.'

Aware that she had just one condition left, the PA knew she had better make it a really tough one. So she said: 'Since I simply adore to have sex, I want the man I marry to have a twelve-inch penis.'

The little Chinese man looked distraught, and sank to his knees, all the while muttering to himself in his native tongue. Finally, shaking his head in despair, he said to the woman. 'All right. I cut. I cut.'

514 A Spanish guy, a Russian guy and a Chinese guy were all working for the same construction company. At the start of the day the boss came out and said to the Spanish guy: 'You're in charge of the cement.' Then he said to the Russian guy: 'You're in charge of the dirt.' Then he said to the Chinese guy:

'You're in charge of supplies.' Finally he said: 'I'm gonna be back at the end of the day to check your work. It better be good or you're fired.' So they all went off to get their work done.

At the end of the day, the boss returned to check on their work. He looked at the big pile of cement and said to the Spanish guy: 'Good work.'

Then he looked at the big pile of dirt and said to the Russian guy: 'Good work.'

But he couldn't find the Chinese guy, so he asked: 'Where the heck is he?'

Just then the Chinese guy jumped out from behind the big pile of dirt and yelled: 'SUPPLIES!'

CHRISTMAS

515 Like all pilots, Santa Claus receives regular visits from the Federal Aviation Administration to ensure that all of his equipment is in proper working order for the festive season. In preparation for the FAA examiner's inspection last month, Santa got the elves to wash the sleigh and bathe all the reindeer. Santa then went through his books to make sure they were right up to date, for he knew that the examiner would be extremely thorough.

On arrival, the examiner walked slowly around the sleigh. He checked the reindeer harnesses, the landing gear, and Rudolph's nose. He painstakingly reviewed Santa's weight and balance calculations for the sleigh's enormous load.

Finally they were ready for the test ride, in which Santa's flying skills would come under intense scrutiny. Santa got in to the sleigh, fastened his seat belt and shoulder harness, and checked the compass. All the reindeer were in position. Then the examiner hopped in, carrying, to Santa's surprise, a shotgun.

'What's that for?' asked Santa nervously.

The examiner winked and confided: 'I'm not supposed to tell you this ahead of time, but you're gonna lose an engine on takeoff.'

516 Why is Santa's sack so big? – Because he only comes once a year.

517 A boy was sitting on Santa's lap. Santa put his finger on the boy's nose and, tapping out the letters, said: 'I bet your name is J-i-m-m-y.'

The little boy's eyes lit up. Then Santa put his finger on the boy's nose again and, tapping out the letters, said: 'I bet you want a b-i-k-e.'

'How did you know that?' asked the boy.

'Because I'm Santa, and I know everything.'

The little boy thought for a moment and said: 'I bet you like g-i-r-l-s?'

'Well, yes,' said Santa. 'How did you know that?'

The boy replied. 'Because your finger smells like p-u-s-s-y!'

THE CHURCH

518 On his deathbed, an ageing preacher sent a message for his banker and his lawyer, both of whom were church members, to come to his home. When they arrived, they were ushered up to his bedroom. As they entered the room, the preacher held out his hands and motioned for them to sit on either side of the bed. The preacher gripped their hands, sighed contentedly, smiled, and stared silently at the ceiling.

Both the banker and the lawyer were touched and flattered that the preacher should ask them to be with him during his final moments. But they were also puzzled. For the preacher had never previously given any indication that he particularly liked either of them. Indeed they remembered how his many long sermons about greed made them squirm uncomfortably in their seats.

Finally the banker broke the silence by saying: 'Preacher, why did you ask us to come?'

The preacher replied: 'Jesus died between two thieves, and that's how I want to go.'

519 What's Catholic Alzheimer's Disease? – It's when you forget everything but the guilt.

520 A man attended a service at a small church in the Deep South one Sunday morning and was so moved by the preacher's sermon that at the end, he stopped to shake the clergyman's hand.

'Reverend, that was the best damn sermon I ever did hear!'

The preacher replied: 'Why, thank you, sir, but please, I'd appreciate it if you didn't use profanity in the Lord's house.'

'I'm sorry, Reverend,' the man continued, 'but I can't help myself. It was such a damn fine sermon!'

The Reverend replied: 'Sir, please! I cannot have you behaving this way in church.'

'OK, Reverend, but I just wanted you to know that I thought it was so damn fine, I put $5,000 in the collection plate.'

The Reverend's eyes widened as he said: 'No shit!'

521　Did you hear about the guy who told jokes about religion? – He was put on the Sects Offenders List.

522　A man was hit by a bus in a busy street in New York City. As he lay dying on the sidewalk, a crowd of onlookers gathered around.

'A priest,' he gasped. 'Somebody get me a priest.'

A police officer checked the crowd but there was no clergyman present.

'A priest, please!' spluttered the dying man again.

Then out of the crowd stepped an elderly man. 'Sir,' he said to the policeman, 'I'm not a priest, in fact I'm not even a Catholic. But for the past forty-eight years I've lived behind St Mary's Catholic Church on Twelfth. Avenue, and every night I listen to the Catholic litany. So maybe I can be of some comfort to this man.'

The police officer thought this a good idea and beckoned the old man over. The old man knelt down, leaned over the dying man and said solemnly: 'On its own, number six; legs, eleven; two fat ladies, eighty-eight; four and six, forty-six . . .'

Why Beer is Better Than Religion:

523　● If you have a beer, you don't go around door to door trying to give it to someone else.

524　● Nobody has ever been hanged, tortured, or burned at the stake over his particular brand of beer.

525　● You don't have to wait over 2,000 years for a second beer.

526　● No one will kill you for not drinking beer.

527　● Beer does not tell you when or how to have sex.

528　● You can prove you have a beer.

529　● There are laws saying beer labels can't lie to you.

530　● There have been virtually no major wars fought over beer.

531　● They don't force beer on minors who can't think for themselves.

532　● You can switch your brand of beer whenever you want without losing your beer-drinking friends.

533　● If you have devoted your entire life to beer, there are groups you can join to help you stop.

534 Did you hear they're coming out with a new Catholic version of *Playboy*? – It has the same centrefold as the regular edition, but you have to pull it out at just the right moment.

535 A Southern Baptist minister was addressing his congregation. 'Today I am a sad man. And I'm gonna tell you why I am a sad man. I am a sad man because a member of this church has been spreading the word that I am a member of the Ku Klux Klan. That person has not had the courage to speak this falsehood to my face, so I call upon them to stand up now before you all and tell me why they have been peddling such malicious lies.'

An attractive blonde woman stood up nervously.

'You?' said the minister, shocked. 'My own sister-in-law? How could you say such things about me?'

'I didn't mean any harm,' said the woman. 'It was all a terrible misunderstanding. All I did was tell my friend you were a wizard beneath the sheets!'

536 Two Irishmen were sitting in a bar, watching the entrance to the brothel across the street. A Baptist minister went in, and one of the Irishmen said: 'Ah, 'tis a shame to see a man of the cloth goin' bad.' Then a rabbi went in, and the Irishman shook his head sadly and remarked: ''Tis a shame to see that the Jews are fallin' victim to temptation.' A few minutes later, a Catholic priest went in. 'Ah, what a terrible shame,' said the Irishman. 'One of the girls must be very ill.'

537 A minister decided to do something a little different for his Sunday morning service. 'Today, congregation,' he announced, 'I am going to say a single word and you are going to help me preach. Whatever word I say, I want you to sing whatever hymn comes into your head.'

First, the pastor yelled out, 'Cross!' Immediately the congregation started singing 'The Old Rugged Cross'. Then the pastor yelled out, 'Grace!' And the congregation began to sing 'Amazing Grace'. Next the pastor shouted out, 'Sex!' The congregation fell in total silence. Everyone was in shock. They all shifted uncomfortably in their seats, glancing at each other, afraid to say anything. Then suddenly, from the very back of the church, a little ninety-year-old grandmother stood up and began to sing, 'Precious memories . . .'

BILL CLINTON

538 Bill Clinton died and went straight to hell. When he arrived there, the Devil greeted him and offered him three ways to spend eternity. At the first door the Devil showed him Newt Gingrich, hanging from the ceiling with fire raging beneath him.

'No, thank you,' said Clinton. 'That's not how I want to spend all eternity.'

They went to the second door where Rush Limbaugh was chained to the wall being tortured.

'That's not for me, either,' said Clinton.

So they moved on to the third door. Behind it was Ken Starr, chained to the wall with Monica Lewinsky on her knees giving him a blow job.

Clinton's face lit up. 'Yeah, looks OK to me. I'll take it.'

The Devil said: 'Good. Hey, Monica, you've been replaced.'

539 The wives of three world leaders were talking about what a penis is called in their country.

Tony Blair's wife said: 'In England people call it a gentleman, because it stands up when women are entering.'

The wife of Jacques Chirac said: 'In France we call it a curtain, because it goes down after the act.'

Bill Clinton's wife said: 'In the US we call it a rumour, because it goes from mouth to mouth.'

540 Did you hear that Monica Lewinsky turned Republican? – The Democrats left a bad taste in her mouth.

541 In an ambassadorial role, former President Clinton met the Pope for an international summit. Their meeting was supposed to last for an hour, but instead it went on for two days.

Finally an exhausted but smiling Clinton emerged and revealed to the world's media that the summit had been a resounding success. 'I am pleased to announce that the Pope and myself have reached agreement on 80 per cent of the matters we discussed.'

But when the Pope appeared a few minutes later, he had a different story to tell. Looking tired and dismayed, he declared that the meeting with the former President had been a failure.

Confused, one reporter asked: 'But your Holiness, former President Clinton just announced that the summit was a great success and that you agreed on 80 per cent of the things you discussed.'

'That is true,' replied the Pope wearily. 'But we were talking about the Ten Commandments.'

542 What's green and smells like Monica Lewinsky? – The pool table in the oval office.

543 Bill Clinton, Al Gore and George W. Bush died and found themselves standing on the other side of the River Jordan, looking across at the Promised Land. The Archangel standing on the opposite bank yelled across to the three Americans: 'Each of you will have to wade across the river to reach the Promised Land. But don't worry. You will sink only in accordance with your sins on Earth. The more you have sinned, the deeper into the water you will sink.'

Bush decided to go first, and the water was soon up to his waist. Fearing that his sins were catching up with him, he inched precariously across the river but, against all the odds, he managed to reach the other side. As he did so, he turned around to see how the others were doing. To his amazement, he saw that the water was only up to Al Gore's ankles.

Bush protested to the Archangel: 'I have known Al Gore for many years, and he has sinned much more than that.'

Before the Archangel could reply, Gore shouted out: 'I'm standing on Clinton's shoulders!'

544 What is Monica Lewinsky's favourite musical instrument? – She's good at the piano, but she sucks at the organ.

545 When Bill and Hillary first got married, Bill said: 'I am putting a box under our bed. You must promise never to look in it.'

In all their years of marriage, Hillary never looked until, on their thirtieth wedding anniversary, curiosity got the better of her and she lifted the lid and peeked inside. In the box were three empty beer cans and $1,943.58 in cash.

Hillary intended keeping quiet about her discovery, but eventually she came clean and confessed to looking in the box. 'I truly am sorry,' she said. 'I just couldn't hold back any longer. After thirty years of living in suspense, I simply had to know what was in the box. But tell me, Bill, why do you keep empty beer cans in there?'

Bill gave the matter careful consideration before replying: 'I guess after all these years you deserve to know the truth. Whenever I was unfaithful to you, I put an empty beer can in the box under the bed to remind myself not to do it again.'

Hillary took stock of his reply and said: 'I admit to being very disappointed and saddened, but I guess after so many years away from home on the road, temptation does happen. And I guess three times is not that bad considering the number of years we've been together.'

They hugged and made their peace. Then five minutes later, Hillary asked Bill: 'So why do you have all that money in the box?'

Bill said: 'Well, whenever the box filled up with empty cans, I took them to the recycling centre and redeemed them for cash.'

546 What did Clinton say to Hillary when he felt like making love? – 'I'll be back in an hour.'

547 A little boy and a little girl were sitting on their porch.

The girl said: 'Do you want to get undressed and we can play doctor?'

The boy said: 'That's too old-fashioned. Spit out your gum – I want to play President.'

548 During a staff meeting in Heaven, God, Moses and St Peter concluded that the behaviour of former President Clinton had necessitated the creation of an eleventh commandment. The three worked long and hard in a brainstorming session to try to settle on the wording of the new commandment because they were aware that it should have the same majesty and dignity as the other ten. After many revisions, they finally agreed that the eleventh commandment should be: 'Thou shalt not comfort thy rod with thy staff.'

549 What did it say under Monica Lewinsky's picture in her high school yearbook? – Most Likely to Suck Seed.

550 Hillary Clinton went to a fortune-teller who revealed: 'I have some bad news. Bill is going to die a horrible death.'

Hillary said: 'Can you tell me one thing? Will I be acquitted?'

551 In the year 2025, Bill Clinton died and approached the Pearly Gates of Heaven.

'And who might you be?' inquired St Peter.

'It's me, Bill Clinton, formerly the President of the United States and Leader of the Free World.'

'How can I help you?' asked St Peter.

'Well, I'd like to come in,' said Clinton.

'OK,' said St Peter, 'but first you have to confess your sins. What bad things have you done in your life?'

Clinton shifted uncomfortably and answered: 'Well, I tried marijuana, but you can't call it "dope-smoking" because I didn't inhale. There were inappropriate extramarital relationships, but you can't call it "adultery" because I didn't have full "sexual relations". And I made some statements that were misleading, but legally accurate, but you can't call it "bearing false witness" because, as far as I know, it didn't meet the legal standard for perjury.'

Having listened to Clinton's pleas of mitigation, St Peter briefly consulted the Book of Life before announcing: 'Right, here's the deal. We'll send you somewhere hot, but we won't call it "hell". You'll be there indefinitely, but we won't call it "eternity". And when you enter, you don't have to abandon all hope, just hold your breath waiting for it to freeze over.'

552 How will everyone remember Bill Clinton in history? – The President after Bush.

CLOTHES

553 The doctor said: 'Tom, the good news is I can cure headaches. The bad news is it will require castration. You have a very rare condition, which causes your testicles to press on your spine, and the pressure creates one hell of a headache. The only way to relieve the pressure is to remove the testicles.'

Tom was shocked and depressed, but rather than dwell on his misfortune too long, he decided to undergo the necessary surgery as quickly as possible.

When he left the hospital after the operation, it was the first time in twenty years that he didn't have a headache. Although only too aware that an important part of himself was missing, he resolved to make a fresh start and, spotting a clothes shop, decided to go in.

Entering the shop, he told the elderly tailor: 'I'd like a new suit.'

The tailor eyed him briefly and said: 'Let's see . . . size 44 long.'

Tom laughed. 'That's right, how did you know?'

'Been in the business sixty years,' smiled the tailor.

Tom tried on the suit. It fitted perfectly.

As Tom admired himself in the mirror, the tailor asked: 'How about a new shirt?'

'Sure. Why not?' said Tom.

The tailor eyed him before announcing: '34 inch sleeve and 16 neck.'

'Incredible!' said Tom. 'You're right again. How did you know?'

'Been in the business sixty years,' smiled the tailor.

Tom tried on the shirt and it fitted perfectly. As he adjusted the collar in the mirror, the tailor, sensing he was on a roll, asked: 'How about new shoes?'

'Sure,' said Tom.

The tailor glanced at Tom's feet. 'Hmm, 9½ E, I think.'

'That's right!' exclaimed Tom. 'How did you know?'

'Been in the business sixty years,' said the tailor.

Tom tried on the shoes and they fitted perfectly. As Tom walked comfortably around the shop, the tailor, keen for another sale, asked: 'How about some new underwear?'

Tom thought for a second and said: 'Sure.'

The tailor stepped back, eyed Tom's waist and said: 'Let's see . . . size 36.'

Tom laughed. 'Ah! I got you! I've worn size 34 since I was eighteen years old.'

The tailor shook his head. 'You can't wear a size 34. A size 34 underwear would press your testicles up against the base of your spine and give you one hell of a headache.'

554 With a strong wind gusting down the street, a police officer noticed an old woman standing on a corner holding on tightly to her hat while her skirt blew up to her waist.

The cop said: 'Hey, lady, while you're holding on to your precious hat, everybody's getting a good look at everything you have.'

'Listen, sonny,' replied the old woman, 'what they're looking at is eighty-five years old. But this hat is brand new!'

555 Why do ballerinas wear tights? — So that when they do the splits they don't stick to the ground.

556 Called to testify before the IRS, a man asked his accountant for advice on what to wear. The accountant said: 'Wear your scruffiest clothes. Let them think you're a pauper.'

Then the man asked his lawyer the same question, only to receive conflicting advice. For the lawyer suggested: 'Wear your best suit. Don't let them intimidate you.'

Confused, the man consulted a rabbi who told him a story. 'A woman, about to be married, asked her mother what to wear on her wedding night. The mother said: "Wear a heavy, long flannel nightgown that goes right up to your neck." But the bride's best friend said: "Wear your sexiest negligee."'

The man looked baffled. 'What has this got to do with my problems with the IRS?'

The rabbi said: 'No matter what you wear, you are going to get screwed.'

557 Why was the two-piece bikini invented? – To separate the meat section from the dairy section.

558 An attractive woman was browsing in an exclusive New York shoe store when a pair of boots caught her eye. She immediately fell in love with them, but was put off by the $950 price tag. Seeing her dilemma, the store owner came over and whispered in her ear: 'If you let me have sex with you, I'll let you have the boots for free.'

The woman considered the proposition for a moment before answering: 'Well, OK. But don't expect me to enjoy it.'

The owner gave her the boots and took her home. Up in the bedroom, he dropped his pants, took off the woman's underwear, pushed her back on the bed, and yanked her legs over his shoulders. As he screwed her frantically, the woman began shouting: 'Oh my God, yes! Fantastic! Absolutely fantastic . . .'

'Yeah?' gasped the owner, still thrusting away. 'I thought you said you wouldn't enjoy having sex with me?'

'I'm not,' said the woman. 'I'm admiring my new boots.'

559 An elegant young woman wearing a long fur coat was accosted by an animal rights activist who yelled: 'And what poor creature had to die so that you could have that fur coat?'

The woman replied simply: 'My mother-in-law.'

560 On holiday in Morocco, a couple were accosted by a street trader selling footwear. When the husband began admiring a pair of sandals, the trader unleashed his full sales pitch, telling the man that he would become a sex god if he wore them.

Naturally the man was sceptical. 'What are you talking about?' he said. 'How can wearing a pair of sandals possibly turn me into a sex god?'

'Try them on, try them on,' insisted the trader.

'Well, it wouldn't do any harm,' smiled the customer's wife.

So the man put on the sandals, and was immediately overcome with intense feelings of sexual desire. But instead of lusting after women, he suddenly fancied the Moroccan and, with a wild look in his eyes, rushed at the startled trader.

The Moroccan screamed: 'You've got them on the wrong feet!'

561 'I'd like to buy some gloves for my girlfriend,' said the young man, eyeing the pretty salesgirl, 'but I don't know her size.'

'Will this help?' she said sweetly, placing her hand in his.

'Yes,' he said. 'Her hands are just slightly smaller than yours. Thank you.'

'My pleasure,' she said. 'Will there be anything else?'

'Now that you mention it, she also needs a bra and panties . . .'

562 Two guys were chatting in a bar. 'I like your new suit,' said one.

'Thanks,' said the other. 'It was a surprise present from my wife. I came home early last night and found it hanging over a chair in the bedroom.'

563 A young man bought a new pair of boots, of which he was very proud. He decided to show them off at his favourite nightclub.

After dancing with one girl for a few minutes, he said: 'I bet you I can guess the colour of your panties.'

'OK,' she said. 'What colour do you think they are?'

'Blue,' he replied.

'How did you know that?' she asked.

'I saw the reflection in my shiny new boots,' he said.

'Here,' she said, 'dance with my sister and tell me what colour she was on.'

After dancing a while, the young man started rubbing the toes of his boots on the legs of his jeans. Then he danced again. But a few minutes later, he asked the new girl: 'What colour panties do you have on? I can't seem to make them out.'

She replied: 'I'm not wearing panties.'

'Good,' said the young man, breathing a huge sigh of relief. 'For a minute I thought I had a crack in my new boots.'

COLLEGE

564 On vacation in Alabama, a US senator from a northern state went on a sightseeing trip to the Mississippi Sound. While there, he was horrified to see a man wearing an Auburn University jersey struggling to free himself from the jaws of a twelve-foot long shark. At that precise moment, a boat containing three men wearing University of Alabama T-shirts roared into view.

Without hesitation, one of the men took aim and fired a harpoon into the shark's ribs, immobilizing it instantly. The other two reached out and pulled the Auburn fan from the water and, using long clubs, the three beat the shark to death. They then bundled the bleeding, semi-conscious man into the boat along with the dead shark and ferried them to their waiting truck. As they made the transfer to dry land, they heard the senator shouting to them.

The senator heaped lavish praise upon the rescuers. He said: 'I had always been led to believe that there was bitter hatred between supporters of Auburn University and those of the University of Alabama, but now I have seen with my own eyes that this is not true. I can see now that your state is an enlightened example of true harmony and could serve as a role model for others with internal feuds.' He then promised to call the governor and congratulate these fine young men. With that, they drove off in a cloud of dust.

Inside the truck, the harpoonist asked one of his buddies: 'Who the heck was that?'

'Darned if I know,' answered his friend. 'Just some Yankee who knows nothing about shark hunting. How's the bait holding up or do we need to get another one?'

565 How do you get a Harvard graduate off your front porch? – Pay him for the pizza.

566 Six college students fell out of a city bar and crowded into a Jeep for the ride back to campus. One threw the vehicle keys to a guy leaning precariously against a lamppost and said: 'Henry, you drive. You're too drunk to sing.'

567 Did you hear about the transvestite from Harvard? – He spent the year a broad.

568 A college professor said there would be no excuses for handing in an assignment late.

'What about extreme sexual exhaustion?' asked one student cheekily.

The professor replied: 'I guess you'll just have to write with your other hand.'

569 What's the difference between a camel and a medical student? – A camel can go five days without drinking.

570 A Harvard graduate died and went to hell. The Devil showed him around, leading him through corridors of fire until they reached a door marked 'Graduates'. Inside, guys were being buggered senseless by men in masks while other acts of depravity were taking place in dark corners. And everyone was wearing Harvard colours.

The newcomer said to the Devil: 'How come there are no Yale graduates in hell?'

The Devil replied: 'We used to have them till we realized this was their idea of heaven!'

571 A Daughter's Letter Home:

Dear Mom and Dad,

It has been three months since I left for college. I have been remiss in writing and I am very sorry for my thoughtlessness. I will bring you up to date now, but before you read on, please sit down. You are not to read any further unless you are sitting down. OK?

Well, I am getting along fine now. The skull fracture and the concussion I got when I jumped out of the window of my dormitory when it caught fire shortly after my arrival are pretty much healed now. I only spent ten days in intensive care, and now I can see almost normally and I only got the nauseous headaches once a week.

Fortunately the fire in the dorm and my jump were witnessed by an attendant at the gas station near the dorm and he was the one who called the fire department and the ambulance. He also visited me in hospital and since I had nowhere to live because of the burnt-out dorm, he kindly invited me to share his apartment. It's really a basement room but it's kind of cute and though it's in the red-light quarter, it's near to the train station. Anyway he is a fine boy, and we have fallen deeply in love and are planning to get married. We haven't exactly set a date yet, but it will be before my pregnancy begins to show.

Yes, Mom and Dad, I am pregnant. I know how you are looking forward to being grandparents and I know you will welcome the baby and give it the same love, devotion and tender care you gave me as a child. The reason for the delay in our marriage is that my boyfriend has some minor infection which prevents us from passing our premarital blood tests and carelessly I caught it from him. This will soon clear up with the penicillin injections I am taking daily.

I know you will welcome him into the family with open arms. He is kind and although not well-educated, has ambitions. His family background is good, too, for I hear that his father is an important gun-bearer in the African village from which he comes.

Now that I have brought you up to date, I want to tell you that there was no dormitory fire. I do not have concussion or a skull fracture, I was not in hospital, I am not pregnant, I am not engaged, I do not have syphilis and there is no coloured man in my life. However I am getting a 'D' in history and an 'E' in geography, and I wanted you to see these marks in their proper perspective.

Your loving daughter,
Carla

COMPUTERS

572 Can anyone help with this software problem?

Eighteen months ago a man upgraded to Girlfriend 1.0 from Drinking Mates 4.2, which he had used for years without any trouble. However, apparently there are conflicts between these two products and the only solution was to try and run Girlfriend 1.0 with the sound turned off.

To make matters worse, Girlfriend 1.0 is also incompatible with several other applications, such as Lads Night Out 3.1, Football 2, and Playboy 6.1. Successive versions of Girlfriend proved no better. A shareware beta-program, Party Girl 2.1, had many bugs and left a virus in his system, forcing him to shut down completely for several weeks. Eventually he tried to run Girlfriend 1.2 and Girlfriend 1.0 at the same time, only to discover that when these two systems detected each other, they caused severe damage to all his hardware.

Sensing a way out, he upgraded to Fiancée 1.0, only to discover that this product has to be upgraded to Wife 1.0. He did this largely because, whilst Wife 1.0 uses up all available resources, it does come packaged with FreeSex Plus and Cleanhouse 2002. However he discovered that Wife 1.0 can be very unstable and costly to run. For example, any mistakes he made were automatically stored in Wife 1.0's memory and could not be deleted. They then resurfaced months later. Wife 1.0 also has an automatic Diary Explorer and e-mail porn filter, and can, without warning, launch Photostrop and Whingezip. These latter products have no helpfiles and he has to try and guess the problem himself.

Additional costly problems are that the Wife 1.0 package that came with the original system needs updating regularly, requiring Shoe Shop Browser Pro for new attachments. Also, Hairstyle Express needs to be reinstalled every other week. It also conflicted with some of the new games he wanted to try, stating that they are an illegal operation. When Wife 1.0 attaches itself to his Audi TT program, it often crashes or runs the system dry. Wife 1.0 also has a rather annoying pop-up called Mother-in-Law, which cannot be turned off.

Recently, he's been tempted to try Mistress 2005, but there could be problems. If Wife 1.0 detects the presence of Mistress 2005, it will delete all MS Money files before un-installing itself.

So does anyone have any suggestions?

573 Chris and Derek were regular users of an Internet chat room. After months of virtual sex, they finally agreed to meet up in a New York bar. Derek, a short, fat man in his mid-fifties, arrived first and sat alone at the far end of the bar, as arranged.

A few minutes later Chris walked up to him and said: 'Are you Derek?'
'Yes, I'm Derek.'

Chris's jaw dropped. 'But you told me you were tall, dark, handsome and thirty-five!'

'How do you think I feel?' said Derek. 'You told me you were slim, blonde and female!'

Celebrity Computer Viruses:

574   • Mike Tyson virus – quits after one byte
575   • Lorena Bobbit virus – turns your hard disk into a 3.5-inch floppy
576   • Saddam Hussein virus – won't let you into any of your
       programs

577 • Monica Lewinsky virus – sucks all the memory out of your computer

578 • Ellen DeGeneres virus – your IBM suddenly claims it's a MAC

579 • Oprah Winfrey virus – your 200MB hard drive suddenly shrinks to 80MB and then slowly expands back to 200MB

580 • Titanic virus – makes your whole computer go down

581 • Disney virus – everything in the computer goes Goofy

582 • Ronald Reagan virus – saves your data, but forgets where it's stored

583 • Dr Jack Kevorkian virus – deletes your old files

CONDOMS

584 A deaf mute walked into a pharmacy to buy some condoms, but he had trouble communicating with the pharmacist and couldn't see any condoms on the shelf. Frustrated, he eventually unzipped his pants, placed his dick on the counter, and put down a five-dollar bill next to it.

The pharmacist looked puzzled for a second but then he unzipped his pants, placed his dick on the counter, put down a five-dollar bill next to it, picked up both bills and stuffed them in his pocket.

Exasperated, the deaf mute cursed the pharmacist in sign language.

'Look,' said the pharmacist, 'if you can't afford to lose, you shouldn't bet.'

585 George W. Bush called Canadian Prime Minister Paul Martin with a pressing emergency. 'Our biggest condom factory has exploded!' cried the US President. 'My people's favourite form of birth control has been virtually destroyed. This is a national emergency. So I need your help. Could you possibly send us one million condoms to tide us over?'

'Certainly,' said the Canadian PM. 'I'll get onto it straight away.'

'Thanks,' said Bush. 'And there's one more thing: could the condoms be red, white and blue, and at least ten inches long and four inches in diameter?'

'No problem,' said Martin.

With that, Martin called the head of Trojan. 'I need a favour,' he said. 'I need one million condoms straight away, and I need them to be sent to America.'

'Consider it done,' said the head of Trojan.

'And listen,' continued Martin. 'They have to be red, white and blue in colour, ten inches long and four inches in diameter.'

'That's easily done. Anything else?'

'Yes,' added Martin. 'Print on them: Made in Canada, size Medium.'

586 What did the cock say to the condom? — Cover me, I'm going in.

587 A male and a female duck were feeling randy on the pond. But when he told her he wanted to mate, she came over all shy and said there was no way she was doing it in public: instead she wanted to be treated like a lady and taken to a hotel.

So he booked them both into a smart hotel for the day. She liked the room, but just as he was preening his feathers ready for action, she announced that there would be no sex unless he wore a condom.

'Where am I going to get a condom?' he demanded.

'Have you no class?' she said. 'Ring down for room service. And while you're at it, you can order a round of smoked salmon sandwiches and a pot of Earl Grey.'

So the male duck phoned room service. Fifteen minutes later, there was a knock on the door. The male duck answered it to find the room service man standing there with a tray of orders.

'Here are your sandwiches, sir,' he said, 'and your tea, oh, and your condom. Shall I put it on your bill?'

'Certainly not,' said the duck. 'What do you think I am, a pervert?'

588 A big Indian chief went to his local pharmacy and told the clerk: 'Last night me fuck squaw. Left nut go oomph, right nut go oomph, dick go oomph, condom go BOOM!'

The clerk was quite impressed by this sexual feat, so he grabbed a packet of extra-strength condoms from the shelf, gave them to the chief and told him to report back on how they worked.

The next day the chief returned to the pharmacy, and told the clerk gruffly: 'Last night me fuck squaw. Left nut go oomph, right nut go oomph, dick go oomph, condom go BOOM!'

Since the chief's powerful ejaculation had already blown off two different makes of condom, the clerk didn't know what to suggest. Then he remembered a box of prototype condoms that were kept in a locked box. The label on the box read: 'This is a joint effort between Goodyear and Michelin. This condom is steel belted and should only be used in extreme circumstances.' So the clerk handed one of the condoms to the chief, and asked him to report back on whether it worked.

The next day the chief limped in to the pharmacy on crutches with a shotgun under his arm, and stormed up to the clerk. 'Shit!' thought the clerk. 'That super-strong condom obviously didn't hold him either!'

The chief yelled: 'Last night me fuck squaw. Left nut go oomph, right nut go oomph, dick go oomph, condom go oomph . . . left nut go BOOM!'

589 Two condoms were walking down the street when they came to a gay bar. One condom said to the other: 'What do you say we go in and get shit-faced tonight!'

590 An old couple were on honeymoon. While she slipped into bed in her skimpiest nightdress, he went into the bathroom. After he had been in there for fifteen minutes, she thought she had better see what he was doing. She found him struggling to put on a condom.

'Why are you putting on a condom?' she asked. 'I'm eighty-two. I can't get pregnant!'

'Yes,' he said, 'but you know how dampness affects my arthritis.'

591 The sergeant major of a Scottish army regiment went into a pharmacist's and placed a battered old condom on the counter. Pointing to at least half a dozen minor tears, he said: 'How much would it cost to repair this condom?'

The pharmacist looked at him in disbelief. 'There's no point in repairing it. For a start, it needs a thorough wash, and to patch up all the holes would take best part of a day. Why don't you just buy a new one?'

The sergeant major said he would think about it.

He returned to the shop the next day and said: 'I'd like to buy one of your condoms.'

'Ah, so you've decided to take my advice?' said the pharmacist.

'Aye. I had a word with the lads, and they reckon a new one would be a sound investment.'

592 A guy had reached the supermarket checkout when he remembered he had to forgotten to buy a packet of condoms.

'Could I buy a packet of condoms?' he asked the checkout girl.

'Sure. Do you know what size you are?'

'No, sorry.'

'OK,' she said. 'Drop your pants and I'll tell you your size.'

Being a confident sort of guy, he dropped his pants, she had a feel and said into the microphone: 'One packet of large condoms to aisle three, please.'

He then pulled up his pants, paid for the condoms and went on his way.

The guy behind in the checkout line decided he liked the idea of being fondled by the girl, so he too asked for a packet of condoms. After asking him to drop his pants, the girl felt his dick and said in the microphone: 'One packet of medium condoms to aisle three, please.'

The guy pulled up his pants, paid for the condoms and left the supermarket with a smile on his face.

Watching all this with mounting excitement was a sixteen-year-old boy. So when it was his turn in the line, he breathlessly asked the girl for a packet of condoms. She asked him to drop his pants, then she felt his dick and said quickly into the microphone: 'Oops, mop and bucket to aisle three, please.'

593 A teenage girl walked into a drugstore and asked for condoms.

'What size?' asked the shop assistant.

'Oh, just mix them up,' said the girl. 'I'm not going steady with anyone right now.'

594 A refined gentleman began going into the neighbourhood drug store every week to purchase two dozen boxes of condoms. After six months of this, the clerk felt he had to say something. 'Excuse me,' he said, 'but you must have the stamina of a bull. How do you get through so many condoms in a week?'

The gentleman looked at him in disgust and said: 'I beg your pardon, but I find the whole idea of sex repulsive!'

'So what do you do with all those condoms?' asked the clerk.

'If you must know, I feed them to my poodle, and now she poops in little plastic bags.'

595 A man bought a new range of Olympic condoms. 'There are three colours,' he told his wife. 'Gold, silver and bronze.'

'What colour are you going to wear tonight?' she asked.

'Gold, of course,' he replied proudly.

'Why don't you wear silver?' she said. 'It would be nice if you came second for a change!'

596 An Alabama farmer walked into a drugstore and said to the pharmacist. 'I want one of them thar condoms with pesticide on it. Where do I find them?'

The pharmacist replied: 'Sir, I think you mean the condoms with spermicide, not pesticide. They're on aisle two.'

'No,' insisted the farmer, 'I want them thar condoms with pesticide on them.'

'Sir,' said the pharmacist, becoming exasperated, 'pesticide is for killing insects, spermicide is for killing sperm. I'm sure that you mean spermicide rather than pesticide.'

'Listen,' growled the farmer, 'my wife's got a bug up her ass and I'm goin' a huntin' for it. Like I said, I want one of them thar condoms with pesticide on it!'

597 A New Yorker met a southern gal and brought her to the big city for the first time. Lying on the bed in their seedy hotel room, she saw a discarded condom near the waste bin.

'Yuk!' she squealed. 'What a revolting sight! I've never seen anything so disgusting!'

'What's the matter?' he asked. 'Don't they use those things where you come from?'

'Yeah,' she said. 'But we don't skin 'em!'

598 Have you heard about the new super-sensitive condoms? — They hang around after the man leaves and talk to the woman.

599 Little Johnny walked into his dad's bedroom one day and caught him sitting on the side of the bed sliding on a condom. The father, in an attempt to hide his full erection with a condom on it, swiftly bent over as if to look under the bed.

'What ya doing, dad?'

Thinking quickly, the father said: 'I thought I saw a rat go underneath the bed.'

Little Johnny said: 'What ya gonna do, fuck him?'

Possible Slogans for National Condom Week:

600   • Cover your stump before you hump.
601   • Before you attack her, wrap your whacker.
602   • You can't go wrong if you shield your dong.
603   • If you think she's spunky, cover your monkey.
604   • It will be sweeter if you wrap your peter.
605   • Don't be silly, protect your willy.

606 • When in doubt, shroud your spout.
607 • Don't be a loner, cover your boner.
608 • Wrap it in foil before checking her oil.
609 • If you go in heat, package your meat.
610 • She won't get sick if you wrap your dick.
611 • Especially in December, gift wrap your member.
612 • Never, never deck her with an unwrapped pecker.
613 • If you're not going to sack it, go home and whack it.
614 • If you're gonna have it off, have it on.

CONSTIPATION

615 A construction worker went to the doctor and said: 'Doctor, I'm constipated.'
    The doctor examined him and told him to bend over the table. Then he whacked the patient on the ass with a baseball bat. There was a cracking sound and the doctor sent him to the bathroom.
    The guy emerged a few minutes later and smiled: 'Doctor, I feel great. What should I do to prevent constipation?'
    The doctor said: 'Stop wiping with cement bags.'

616 Two guys were in a locker room taking a shower after a game of squash when one noticed that the other had a huge cork stuck in his butt.
    'That looks really uncomfortable. Why don't you take it out?'
    'I can't. It's stuck there permanently.'
    'How in hell did it happen?'
    'Well, I was walking along the beach, and I tripped over an oil lamp. There was a puff of smoke, and a genie appeared and said he could grant me a wish. Unfortunately my immediate reaction was, "No shit!"'

617 A farmer told the vet that his horse was constipated. The vet handed him a bottle of pills and a length of tube, and said: 'Insert the tube in the horse's anus, put a pill into the other end of the tube, and then blow the pill up into its rectum.'
    The farmer returned the following day looking decidedly ill.
    'What happened?' asked the vet.
    'It was that pill,' said the farmer. 'I did what you said, but the darned horse blew first!'

618 An old woman went to the doctor about her constipation. 'I haven't moved my bowels for ten days,' she said.

'Have you done anything about it?' asked the doctor.

'Well, I sit in the bathroom for half an hour in the morning and again at night.'

'No, I mean, do you take anything?'

'Oh, I see,' said the woman. 'Yes, I take a book.'

619 Sister Bernadette lived in a convent, a few hundred yards from Wayne's liquor store. One day she asked Wayne for a bottle of brandy.

He said: 'I'm sorry, Sister Bernadette, I can't sell brandy to a nun.'

'But it's for the Mother Superior,' she explained. 'It helps with her constipation.'

Hearing this, Wayne relented and sold her the brandy. But on his way home that night, he saw Sister Bernadette staggering drunkenly along the road.

'Sister Bernadette!' he exclaimed. 'Shame on you! You told me the brandy was for the Mother Superior's constipation.'

'And so it is,' said Sister Bernadette. 'When she sees the state of me, she's going to shit herself!'

COWBOYS

620 Why did the cowboy get shit in his moustache? – Looking for love in all the wrong places.

621 A young man wanted to be the best gunfighter in the Wild West. One night in a saloon he spotted a celebrated old gunfighter and asked him for a few tips.

'Tie the bottom of your holster lower onto your leg,' advised the old guy.

'Will that make me a better gunfighter?' asked the youngster.

'Definitely.'

So he took the advice, drew his gun, and shot the bow tie off the piano player. 'Wow! That really helped. Got any more suggestions?'

'Yeah,' said the old timer. 'If you cut a notch in the top of your holster where the hammer hits, the gun will come out smoother.'

'Will that make me a better gunfighter?'

'Sure will.'

So he followed the advice, drew his gun, and shot a cufflink off the sleeve of the piano player. 'This is really helping. Any other ideas?'

'Yeah,' said the old guy. 'Get that can of axle grease over there and rub it all over your gun – the whole gun, handle and everything.'

'Will that make me a better gunfighter?'

'Nope. But when Wyatt Earp gets done playing that piano, he's going to shove that gun of yours right up your ass, and this way at least it won't hurt so much.'

622 Why are cowgirls bowlegged? – Because cowboys like to eat with their hats on.

623 A city slicker named Brad was staying with friends in Texas. His hosts decided to show him some good ole southern hospitality by taking him to the local rodeo. The star attraction was the greatest bucking bronco of all time, Iron Duke, a beast so fearsome that the organizers were offering a $10,000 prize to anyone who could ride him for just ten seconds.

All the local cowboys tried their luck, but all failed dismally. As soon as they got on Iron Duke, he hurled them to the ground. None lasted longer than three seconds. To keep the interest going, the organizers asked if anyone in the crowd wanted a try. To roars of laughter, Brad stepped forward.

Everybody thought he would hit the dirt in an instant but he stayed on for five seconds . . . ten seconds . . . a minute . . . five minutes. By then, Iron Duke was so exhausted that Brad was able to ride him around the ring like a party pony. The crowd were stunned.

As Brad collected his cash, one of his friends asked him: 'You've never even sat on a horse before, so how come you managed to stay on so long?'

Brad replied: 'My wife's an epileptic.'

624 Two cowboys, Bart and Matt, were having a beer in a saloon when they saw a guy walk in with an Indian's head under his arm. The guy handed the head to the bartender who in return gave him a fistful of dollars.

'I hate Indians,' explained the bartender. 'They burned my barn to the ground and killed my wife and five kids. Anybody who brings me the head of an Indian, I'll give them a thousand bucks.'

Bart and Matt knocked back their drinks and went off to hunt Indians. Soon they found one and Bart hurled a rock, hitting the Indian on the head and sending him tumbling from his horse and rolling eighty feet down a ravine. The two cowboys raced down the ravine in hot pursuit and Bart pulled out his knife ready to claim his trophy. But just as he was about to slice off the Indian's head, Matt said: 'Bart, take a look at this.'

'Not now,' said Bart, 'I'm busy.'

'I really think you should have a look,' persisted Matt.

'Can't you see I'm busy?' snapped Bart. 'I've got a thousand dollars in my hand here.'

Matt said: 'Please, Bart, take a look.'

Bart knew Matt would keep on, so he did as his friend said and looked up at the top of the ravine. Standing there were five thousand Indians.

'Jesus!' said Bart. 'We're gonna be millionaires!'

CRIME AND PUNISHMENT

625 While on a trip to Saudi Arabia, three Americans accidentally stumbled into a harem filled with more than a hundred beautiful women. Just as they started getting friendly with the women, the Sheik burst in and roared: 'I am the master of all these women. No one else may touch them except me. You three men must pay for what you have done today, and you will be punished according to your profession.'

The Sheik turned to the first man and demanded to know what he did for a living.

'I'm a cop,' replied the man.

'Then we will shoot your penis off,' announced the Sheik.

Then the Sheik turned to the second man and asked him what he did for a living.

'I'm a fireman,' came the reply.

'Then we will burn your penis off!' declared the Sheik.

Finally the Sheik asked the third man what he did for a living.

Barely suppressing a smile, the man answered: 'I'm a lollipop salesman.'

626 A little old lady walked up to a police officer and said: 'Officer, I was sexually assaulted. It happened in the park and it went on for half an hour.'

'When did this happen?' asked the officer.

'Twenty-four years ago.'

'What are you telling me now for?'

She smiled: 'I just like to talk about it once in a while.'

627 Travelling by horse and wagon across the Wild West to start a new life in California with his wife, daughter and $8,000 in cash, a gold prospector was held up by an outlaw. After searching the wagon thoroughly, the bandit rode off with it.

'Damn!' said the stranded prospector. 'There goes my $8,000!'

'No, Pa,' said his daughter. 'Look, I managed to hide the money in my fanny!'

The prospector sighed: 'If only your mother had thought of that, we could have saved the horse and wagon too!'

628 A man was in court charged with theft. His lawyer told the crusty old judge: 'My lord, my client has produced receipts for, firstly, the high-speed modem . . .'

'What is a high-speed modem?' asked the judge, peering over his spectacles.

The lawyer answered: 'My lord, a high-speed modem allows computers to communicate over vast distances at high speeds. It allows e-mail and something called cybersex in Internet chat rooms.'

'Cybersex?' queried the judge. 'Sex through a computer? What is the world coming to? The morals of modern society appal me! Sex should be a wholesome, natural act.'

'Secondly, my lord,' continued the lawyer, 'my client can produce a receipt for the twelve-speed CD-ROM . . .'

'Twelve-speed CD-ROM?' interjected the judge.

'Yes, my lord, it enables millions of bits of information to be read off a small disk.'

'And I suppose most of this "information" is cybersex related?' said the judge. 'Frankly, I'm disgusted at what technology is doing to morality.'

'Thirdly, my lord,' continued the lawyer, 'my client can produce a receipt for the super deluxe inflatable milk maid, whatever that is . . .'

The judge said: 'That's the one with the silicone breasts and real hair.'

629 A missionary was walking through the jungle with the chief of the tribe he was teaching. On their way, they came across a couple making love.

'What is going on here?' asked the chief.

Embarrassed, the missionary said: 'Uh, well chief, he is riding a bicycle.'

The chief grunted, pulled out his blowgun, and shot a poisoned dart into the man's back.

The shocked missionary said: 'Chief, you shouldn't have killed him! It was a perfectly natural act they were performing. Why did you have to kill him?'

The chief answered: 'He was riding my bicycle!'

630 A woman was walking home through Central Park when a guy grabbed her and dragged her into bushes.

'Help!' she screamed. 'I'm being robbed!'

'You ain't being robbed, lady,' growled her assailant 'You're gonna get screwed!'

The woman looked down at her attacker as he unzipped his jeans and sneered: 'If you're screwing me with that, I *am* being robbed!'

DATING

631 A girl went out on a date with a racing-car driver and was so impressed by his style that they ended up in bed. After sex, they fell asleep, only for him to be rudely awakened when she slapped him in the face.

'What's the matter?' he groaned. 'Didn't I satisfy you when we screwed?'

'It was after you fell asleep that you got into trouble,' said the girl angrily. 'In your sleep, you felt my tits and mumbled, "What perfect headlights." Then you felt my thighs and murmured, "What a smooth finish." '

'What's wrong with that?' he asked.

'Nothing, but then you felt my pussy and yelled, "Who the hell left the garage door open?" '

632 'I'm telling you, Lisa, I've never been happier,' said Victoria. 'I have two boyfriends. One is just fabulous. He's handsome, sensitive, caring, and considerate.'

'So what do you need the second one for?' asked Lisa.

'The second one is straight.'

633 A mother and her teenage daughter were sitting down to afternoon tea. The mother wanted to show her daughter that she was a hip parent and tried to get her to talk about dating boys. 'So now you've started dating,' she asked, 'how are you dealing about getting intimate with young men?'

The daughter replied shyly: 'Oh, you know how it is, boys are always insensitive and never care if intimacy isn't working for me.'

'In what way?' persisted the mother.

'Oh . . . stuff.'

'It's OK, darling. You can trust me. I think it's important for mothers and daughters to talk about these things.'

'I don't know . . .'

'Don't forget, I was a teenager once and I can remember what dating boys was like.'

'Really?'

'Yes. Really.'

'OK, for starters, how did you get their come out of your hair?'

634 Two girls were chatting about their weekends.

One said: 'My boyfriend came round last night.'

The other said: 'I didn't even know he'd been in a coma.'

635 Searching for a suitable bride, a handsome blond man chanced upon a farmer who had three beautiful blonde daughters. Unable to decide which one he liked best, he took each of the three girls out on separate dates.

After the first date, the farmer asked him what he thought. 'Well,' said the man, 'she's just a wee bit, not that you could hardly tell, bow-legged.'

So the man took out the second daughter, after which the farmer once again sought his opinion. 'Well,' said the man, 'she's just a wee bit, not that you could hardly tell, boss-eyed.'

Finally the man took out the third daughter. The next day he told the farmer excitedly: 'She's absolutely perfect – definitely the girl I want to marry.'

The man duly married the farmer's daughter but six months later his new bride gave birth to an ugly, red-haired baby. The man was distraught and asked the farmer how such a thing could have happened.

'Well,' explained the farmer, 'when you met her, she was just a wee bit, not that you could hardly tell, pregnant.'

636 A student guy picked up his date and took her to a fancy restaurant. To his dismay, she ordered the most expensive items on the menu.

He asked: 'Does your mother feed you like this at home?'

'No,' said the girl, 'but my mother's not looking to get laid.'

637 What should you do if your girlfriend starts smoking? – Slow down and use a lubricant.

638 Patrolling a local lovers' lane, a policeman noticed a young couple sitting in their car with the interior light on. The young man was sitting in the driver's seat reading a magazine while the girl was sitting in the back seat doing her nails. Mystified, the officer tapped on the window and asked the driver: 'What's going on?'

The driver wound down the window and answered: 'What does it look like? I'm reading this magazine.'

The officer gestured towards the girl in the back and asked: 'And what is she doing?'

The young man glanced over his shoulder and replied: 'What does it look like? She's doing her nails.'

'How old are you?' the officer asked the young man.

'I'm nineteen.'

'And how old is she?' continued the officer.

The young man looked at his watch and said: 'In about eleven minutes, she'll be sixteen.'

639 A guy said to his new girlfriend: 'How about us spending a romantic weekend in a nice quiet hotel?'

She said: 'I'm afraid that my awareness of your proclivities in the esoteric aspects of sexual behaviour precludes you from such erotic confrontation.'

'Er . . . sorry . . . I don't get it.'

'Exactly!'

640 How can you tell if your date really likes oral sex? – She hikes up her skirt every time you yawn.

641 A girl brought her boyfriend home late one night. With her parents being asleep in bed, she asked him to be quiet. So when he said he was desperate to use the bathroom, rather than send him upstairs and risk him waking her parents, she told him to use the kitchen sink instead.

A few minutes later, he popped his head around the door.

'Have you finished?' she whispered.

'Yeah,' he said. 'Have you got any paper?'

642 A guy told his mom that he had met the girl of his dreams. His mother said:
'Why don't you send her flowers, and on the card invite her to your place for
a home-cooked meal?'
'That's a great idea,' he said. 'Thanks, Mom.'
But the day after the date he rang his mother to say that it had been a disaster.
'Why? What went wrong?' asked his mother. 'Didn't she show up?'
'Yes, but she refused to cook!'

643 Rick and Don were chatting at the bar. Rick was complaining about his live-in
girlfriend. 'I tell you, I've just about had it with her. I'm gonna dump her. She
keeps bringing her work home, night after night.'
Don said: 'Just because she wants to pursue a career, is that any reason
to end the relationship? Is it so bad to bring work home?'
Rick replied: 'It is if your girlfriend's a hooker!'

644 What did Jack the Ripper's mother say to him? – No wonder you're still
single; you never go out with the same girl twice.

645 Three girls all had boyfriends with the same name, so in order to avoid
confusion, they decided to give the boys nicknames.
The first girl said: 'I call my man 7-Up.'
'Why do you call him that?' asked her friends.
'Because he's seven inches long and is always up.'
The second girl said: 'I call my man Mountain Dew.'
'Why do you call him that?' said the other two.
'Because he likes to mount me and do me!'
The third girl said: 'I call my man Jack Daniels.'
The others look at her in bewilderment and say: 'Why do you call your man
that? Jack Daniels is a hard liquor.'
'Exactly.'

646 What's the best part of having a homeless girlfriend? – At the end of a date,
you can drop her off wherever you want.

Things Not to Say on a First Date:

647 • I used to have a real bad bedwetting problem, but the last
couple of weeks I seem to have got it under control.

648 • I know we just met and this might seem a little sudden, but
could you lend me $500?

649 • I don't see my ex-girlfriend that much . . . thanks to the restraining order.

650 • There's $10 riding on me bedding you tonight.

651 • Do you wanna see my collection of Ted Bundy memorabilia?

652 • You could be a real babe if you lost a couple of stone.

653 • What are your feelings about whips and manacles?

654 • I won't be a minute, but I have to phone my mom if I'm out after ten o'clock.

655 • I can't stay out too late; I have to start work at the abattoir at seven.

656 • Sorry, I can't see you tomorrow – I'm on day release.

657 • Would you like a lift home in my Skoda?

658 • Wait till my wife hears about this!

DEAFNESS

659 A guy drove past an isolated farm and was horrified to see an old woman yanking on her boobs while an old man was jerking off. The driver was so freaked out by this that he stopped at the next house.

'What's up with your neighbours?' He asked.

'Oh, that's the Harts, they're both deaf. She's telling him to go milk the cow and he's telling her to go fuck herself!'

660 An old man was wondering if his wife had a hearing problem. So one evening, while they were sitting in their armchairs, he called over to her: 'Can you hear me?' There was no response.

A few seconds later he asked her again, this time a little louder. 'Can you hear me?' There was still no response.

So he tried for a third time, louder still. 'Can you hear me?'

She answered impatiently: 'For the third time, yes!'

661 Two deaf people got married but struggled to communicate in the bedroom after turning the lights off because they couldn't see each other using sign language. Following several nights of fumbling and misunderstandings, the wife came up with a solution.

'Honey,' she signed, 'Why don't we agree on some simple signals? For instance, at night if you want to have sex with me, reach over and squeeze my left breast one time. If you don't want to have sex, reach over and squeeze my right breast one time.'

The husband thought this was a great idea and signed back to his wife: 'OK. Now if you want to have sex with me, reach over and pull on my penis one time. If you don't want to have sex, reach over and pull on my penis fifty times.'

662 Three deaf old men were walking along the street on a March day.

One said: 'Windy, ain't it?'

'No,' said the second, 'it's Thursday.'

The third man said: 'So am I. Let's have a beer.'

663 An Englishman, a Canadian and an American were due to give speeches to the Deaf Society. Each was keen to make an impression on the audience.

The Englishman went first and, to the surprise of his colleagues, he began by rubbing first his chest and then his groin. After he had completed his speech, the Canadian and the American asked him what he had been doing. The Englishman explained: 'By rubbing my chest, I indicated breasts and thus Ladies. And by rubbing my groin, I indicated balls and thus Gentlemen. So my speech started "Ladies and Gentlemen".'

On his way up to the podium the Canadian thought he would go one better, so he started his speech by making an antler symbol with his fingers above his head before also rubbing his chest and groin. Afterwards, when his colleagues asked what he had been doing, he replied: 'By imitating antlers and then rubbing my chest and groin, I was starting my speech by saying "Deer Ladies and Gentlemen."'

On his way up to the podium, the competitive American was determined to outdo the Englishman and the Canadian. So he started his speech by making an antler symbol above his head, rubbing his chest and groin, and then masturbating furiously. When he had finished his speech, the other two asked him what on earth he had been doing. He explained: 'By imitating antlers, rubbing my chest and groin, and then masturbating, I was starting my speech with the words "Deer Ladies and Gentlemen, it gives me great pleasure . . ."'

664 Two deaf men were talking about being out late the night before. The first signed: 'My wife was asleep when I got home, so I was able to sneak into bed and not get into trouble.'

The second deaf man signed: 'You were lucky. My wife was wide awake, waiting for me in bed, and she started swearing, and giving me hell for being out so late.'

'What did you do?'

'I turned out the light.'

665 A woman was driving carefully along the highway. She frequently checked her speed to make sure that she was not exceeding the limit but, to her dismay, she saw in her rear mirror that a police car was following her, lights flashing.

She thought to herself: 'What have I done wrong? I'm not speeding, I haven't been drinking, I've got my seat belt on, my licence is up to date.' As she pulled to a halt, she rolled down the window and waited for the inevitable ticket, even though she didn't deserve one.

The police officer walked up to the window and spoke to her. The woman pointed to her ear and shook her head, indicating that she was deaf.

The policeman smiled and signed back: 'I know. I'm here to tell you that your horn is stuck!'

666 A ninety-one-year-old man went to the doctor for a physical. A few days later the doctor saw him walking down the street with a gorgeous young lady on his arm.

At his follow-up visit, the doctor said to the old man: 'You're really doing great, aren't you?'

'I'm only doing what you said, doctor – "Get a hot mamma and be cheerful."'

The doctor replied: 'I didn't say that. I said you got a heart murmur. Be careful.'

DEATH

667 An old man was lying on his deathbed. With only hours to live, he suddenly smelt chocolate chip cookies wafting up from the kitchen. Driven on by his favourite smell, he somehow managed to pull himself out of bed, across the floor to the stairs, and slowly down the stairs to the kitchen. There, the old man's wife was baking chocolate chip cookies. With his last ounce of energy, he reached for a cookie, only for his wife to slap him across the hand and say: 'They're for the funeral!'

668 A woman was shaking out a rug on the balcony of her seventeenth-floor apartment when a sudden gust of wind blew her over the railing. As she plummeted towards certain death, a man standing on his fourteenth-floor balcony reached out and caught her in his arms. As she looked at him in gratitude, he asked: 'Do you suck?'

'No,' she snapped indignantly, so he dropped her.

As she hurtled down past the twelfth floor, another man reached out and caught her.

'Do you screw?' he demanded.

'No, I do not,' she replied, so he dropped her.

With the ground drawing ever nearer, the desperate woman prayed to God for one more chance. As luck would have it, she was caught by a man on the seventh floor. No way was she going to waste this opportunity.

'I suck! I screw!' she screamed.

'Slut!' said the man, and dropped her.

669 'But my elderly aunt was considered a highly respectable spinster,' protested the society lady to the cop. 'Can't you find some way to cover up the shocking fact that she died in bed while being simultaneously serviced by two paid studs?'

'Leave it to me, ma'am,' said the officer reassuringly. 'I'll just put it in my report that she died at the stroke of two.'

670 A man was so distraught following the death of his wife that he broke down in tears at the funeral. Afterwards a friend took him to one side and tried to comfort him.

'Listen,' said the friend, 'I know it's tough at the moment but time really is a great healer. Eventually you will get over it. Who knows, in four or five months, you might even meet somebody else.'

'Four or five months?' wailed the man. 'What am I going to do tonight?'

671 A mortician was working late one night, examining bodies before sending them to be buried or cremated. As he examined the body of Mr Schafer, he noticed that he had the longest private part he had ever seen. It was of such record-breaking proportions that the mortician decided he would have to save it for posterity.

'I'm sorry, Mr Schafer,' he said to the corpse, 'but I simply have to do this.'

And with that he sliced off the giant penis, put it in his briefcase and took it home to show his wife.

'Honey,' he said. 'You'll never believe what I've got in my case.'

Then he opened the case to reveal the mighty member.

'Oh, my God!' screamed the wife. 'Schafer is dead!'

672　At the end of a funeral service, the pallbearers were carrying the casket when they accidentally bumped into a wall. The jolt produced a faint moan from inside the casket, and when the lid was raised, the woman inside was found to be still alive.

She went on to live for another ten years, and when she eventually died her husband arranged for the funeral ceremony to be held at the same place. At the end, as the pallbearers carried out the casket and the mourners dabbed their eyes, he suddenly called out: 'Watch the wall!'

673　Becky was on her deathbed with her husband Jake at her side. He held her cold hand, and tears silently streamed down his face.

Her pale lips moved. 'Jake . . .' she whispered.

'Hush,' he quickly interrupted. 'Don't talk.'

But she insisted. 'Jake,' she gasped. 'I have to talk. I have to confess my sins.'

'There is nothing to confess,' sobbed Jake. 'It's all right. Everything is all right.'

'No, you don't understand,' said Becky. 'I must die in peace. I must confess, Jake, or I will rot in hell. I have to tell you the truth finally. You see, Jake, my dearest, I have been unfaithful to you.'

Jake stroked her hand tenderly. 'Now, Becky, don't be concerned. I know all about it.'

'You do?' she groaned weakly.

'Of course,' he said. 'Why else would I poison you?'

674　There were two Miami brothers named Don and Doug. Don was married and Doug was single. Doug was the proud owner of a dilapidated boat and it so happened that Doug's boat sank on the same day that Don's wife died.

A few days later a kindly old lady met Doug in the street and, mistaking him for Don, said: 'I heard about your loss. I am so sorry. You must feel terrible.'

Doug replied: 'Well, I'm not sorry. She was a rotten old thing from the start. Her bottom was all chewed up, and she smelled of old fish. The first time I got into her she made water faster than anything I ever saw. She had a crack and a pretty big hole in front that kept getting bigger and bigger every time I used her. It got so I could handle her all right, but when someone else was using her she leaked like anything. This is what finished her off: Four guys from the other side of town came down looking for a good time. They asked if I could rent her to them. I warned them that she wasn't so hot, but the crazy fools all tried to get into her at the same time. It was just too much for her and she cracked right up the middle!'

At that, the old lady fainted.

DENTISTS

675 A dentist was preparing to clean an elderly lady's teeth. Noticing that she appeared a little nervous, he began telling her a story as he was putting on his surgical gloves.

'Do you know how they make these rubber gloves?' he asked.

'No,' she replied.

'Well,' he spoofed, 'down in Mexico they have this big building that houses a large tank of latex, and the workers are all chosen according to hand size. Each individual walks up to the tank, dips his or her hands in, and then walks around for a bit while the latex sets and dries onto the hands. Then they peel off the gloves, throw them into a finished goods crate, and start the process all over again.'

The story didn't even raise a smile. But five minutes later, the dentist had to stop scraping the woman's teeth because she suddenly burst out laughing. She blushed and exclaimed: 'I just suddenly thought how they must make condoms!'

676 Murphy told O'Reilly: 'I went to the dentist this morning.'

O'Reilly asked: 'Does your tooth still hurt?'

'I don't know,' said Murphy. 'The dentist kept it.'

677 An attractive young woman told her friend she had fallen in love with her middle-aged dentist.

'But why?' asked her friend. 'You could have your pick of the boys. Why go for your dentist?'

'Because he's the first man that's ever said to me, "Spit, don't swallow." '

678   A guy went to the dentist to get a tooth pulled.
'I'll give you a shot to numb your jaw,' said the dentist.
'No, you can't. I'm afraid of needles.'
'OK, I'll give you gas to put you to sleep.'
'No, I'm allergic to gas.'
So the dentist searched his medicine cabinet for something suitable. Eventually he came up with a packet of pills and said: 'Here, take two of these, then.'
'What are they?' asked the patient.
'Viagra.'
'What? Why the hell are you giving me Viagra?'
'They won't help the pain, but they'll give you something to hang on to while I pull your tooth.'

Signs that Your Dentist Loves to Inflict Pain:

679   • He says afterwards, 'We usually sedate people for that.'
680   • His drill is by Black and Decker.
681   • The dentist's chair is located in a soundproof room.
682   • The hygienist wears skintight leather and carries a whip.
683   • Rather than take X-rays, he takes core samples.
684   • While you scream, he giggles.
685   • Just before you go under, you see him bring out a stun gun.
686   • The windows are blacked out.
687   • He advises you to gargle with Coke.
688   • The dentist's chair has restraining straps.
689   • There are blood spots on the ceiling.
690   • You have to sign a form in advance promising not to press charges.

PRINCESS DIANA

691   Prince Harry and Prince Charles were at Diana's funeral. Prince Harry asked:
'Daddy, why are there so many people?'
Prince Charles said: 'It's always this crowded when Elton John plays.'

DIARRHOEA

692 Gathered around the fire at a lodge one evening, the members of a hunting club regaled each other with heroic tales from the African bush. All, that is, except the oldest member – a ninety-one-year-old man who slept peacefully in his chair.

Eventually the old man woke up and instantly launched into a story of his own. His audience was captivated.

'I'll never forget my first visit to Africa,' he began. 'It was back in 1939, and I was travelling south of Nairobi. There were four of us in the party, but somehow I had become separated from the others. Trying to find my way back to the jeep, I headed down this overgrown track. I had only gone a few yards when I heard a rustling noise in the bushes. Then suddenly the biggest lion I had ever seen jumped out of the bushes at me like this. ROOAAARRRR! I tell you, I just messed my pants.'

'I don't blame you,' said one of the younger members. 'I would have messed my pants too if a lion jumped out at me.'

The old man said: 'No, not then, just now when I went ROOAAARRRR!'

693 Did you hear about the giant with diarrhoea? – You didn't? It's all over town!

694 A drugstore clerk was a hopeless salesman. He could never find the item the customer wanted, and it reached the point where the owner warned him that the next sale he missed would be his last.

Just then a man came in coughing and asked the clerk for some cough syrup. Despite searching everywhere, the clerk couldn't find any but, remembering the owner's threat, he sold the customer a box of Ex-Lax and told him to take it all at once.

The owner, who had been watching from the back of the shop, asked the clerk what had happened.

'He wanted something for his cough,' explained the clerk, 'but I couldn't find the cough syrup. So I substituted Ex-Lax and told him to take it all at once.'

'Ex-Lax won't cure a cough,' shouted the owner angrily.

'Sure it will,' said the clerk, pointing to the man leaning outside on a lamppost. 'Look at him. He's afraid to cough.'

695 Serving tea in the lounge of an old people's home, the nurse caught a whiff of something unpleasant. 'OK,' she said. 'Who's messed in their pants?'

Nobody answered, so she patrolled the room to trace the origin of the stench. Finally she found the culprit, an old man sitting in the corner.

'Why didn't you answer when I asked who had messed in their pants?' she demanded.

'Oh,' he said. 'I thought you meant today.'

696 A man phoned a pharmacist and asked urgently: 'Do you sell incontinence pants?'

'Yes,' replied the pharmacist. 'Can I ask where you're ringing from?'

The man replied: 'From the waist down.'

697 When her husband died, his widow put the usual death notice in the paper, but added that he had died of gonorrhoea. On reading the notice, a family friend complained: 'You know very well that he died of diarrhoea, not gonorrhoea.'

The widow said: 'I know, but I figured it would be better for him to be remembered as a great lover rather than the big shit he really was.'

DISABILITY

698 One day a man with no arms and no legs was on a beach sunning himself when he noticed three beautiful women approaching him.

The first woman bent down and said: 'Have you ever been hugged before?'

'No,' he replied.

And she hugged him warmly.

The second woman bent down and said: 'Have you ever been kissed before?'

'No,' he said.

And she kissed him tenderly.

Then the third woman bent down and said: 'Have you ever been fucked before?'

'No,' he gasped excitedly.

'Well, you are now. The tide's coming in!'

699 Two strangers in the street approached each other from opposite directions, each dragging their left legs.

Glancing down at his leg, one man said: 'Vietnam, 1969.'

The other said: 'Dog doo, about a block ago.'

700 A man hobbled into church on crutches. Stopping in front of the holy water, he splashed some on both legs, then threw his crutches away. An altar boy, who had witnessed the incident, ran to tell the priest.

'My son,' said the priest, 'you have just witnessed a miracle. Tell me, where is this man now?'

The boy replied: 'Lying on his back by the font.'

701 A woman gave birth to a baby that was just a head – no arms or legs, not even a torso. But the couple loved it dearly and indulged it. After twenty years, they finally found time to take a vacation in Europe where they met a Swiss doctor who had recently pioneered a major medical breakthrough. He told the couple: 'I can attach a body, arms and legs to your child, to make him whole.'

The couple cut their trip short, rushed home excitedly and into the room where the head lay in its crib, and said: 'Honey, Mom and Dad have the most wonderful surprise for you!'

The voice from the crib said: 'Not another fucking hat!'

702 A guy with a bad stutter walked into a bar and said: 'B-b-b-bartender, g-g-g-gimme a b-b-b-beer.' The bartender, who had a hunched back, served him and said: 'That'll be $2.50 please.'

The guy was shocked at the price and said: 'D-d-d-damn! Th-th-th-that's h-h-h-high!'

The bartender said: 'Sorry, those are our prices.'

The guy paid him and ten minutes later said: 'B-b-b-bartender, g-g-g-gimme a w-w-w-whiskey.'

The bartender served him a shot of whiskey and said: 'That'll be $5.00 please.'

Once again the guy was horrified by the price. 'D-d-d-damn! Th-th-th-that's h-h-h-high!'

The bartender apologized again. 'Sorry,' he said. 'Those are our prices.'

The guy paid him, drank his whiskey and before leaving, said: 'B-b-b-bartender, th-th-th-thanks f-f-f-for n-n-n-not m-m-m-making f-f-f-fun of my s-s-s-stuttering w-w-w-while I was in h-h-h-here.'

The bartender said: 'Oh, that's OK. I want to thank you for not making fun of my hunched back while you were here.'

The guy said: 'A-actually, e-everything else in th-this p-place w-was s-so h-high, I th-thought it w-was y-your ass!'

703 A man said to his neighbour: 'Did you go to the Paralympics?'

'No,' said the neighbour, 'we had to turn around and come home. We couldn't get a parking space anywhere near the place.'

704 A guy called round to visit his disabled friend who lived in a large bungalow. After talking for a while, the wheelchair-bound man said: 'My feet are cold. Would you be so kind as to get my sneakers from the main bedroom?'

The guest obliged and went through to the bedroom where he bumped into his friend's two teenage daughters, both of whom were extremely attractive. Thinking on his feet, he said: 'Hi, ladies! Your daddy sent me here to have sex with you.'

The girls stared at him and said: 'That can't be!'

'OK,' he replied. 'Let's check.'

So he shouted through to his friend: 'Both of them?'

Back came the reply: 'Yes, both of them.'

705 What do you call a woman with no arms and no legs who gives good head? — Partially disabled.

706 What do you call a woman with no arms and no legs who's lying on a grill? — Patty.

707 A man with no arms walked into a bar and asked for a beer. The bartender pushed the foaming glass in front of him.

'I'm sorry,' said the customer, 'but I've got no arms. Would you mind holding the glass up to my mouth?'

'Sure,' said the bartender, and he did.

'Now,' said the customer, 'I wonder if you'd be so kind as to pull my handkerchief out of my pocket and wipe the foam off my mouth?'

'Certainly,' said the bartender. And it was done.

'If,' continued the armless man, 'you'd reach in my right hand pants pocket, you'll find the money for the beer.'

The bartender got it.

'You've been very kind,' said the customer. 'Just one thing more: where is the men's room?'

'Out the door,' said the bartender, 'turn left, walk two blocks, and there's one in a filling station on the corner.'

708 Quasimodo arrived home to find Esmerelda holding a wok and a laundry basket.

'Great,' said Quasimodo. 'Are you cooking Chinese tonight?'

'No,' said Esmerelda, 'I'm ironing your shirt.'

709 What do you call a man with no arms and no legs standing on a stage? – Mike.

710 What do you call a man with no arms and no legs holding a drill bit in his teeth? – Chuck.

711 What do you call a man with no arms and no legs in a stream? – Eddy.

712 Three guys entered a disabled swimming contest. The first had no arms, the second had no legs, and the third had no body, just a head. The guy with no legs took the lead, closely followed by the guy with no arms while the head sank straight to the bottom of the pool. Four lengths later, the guy with no legs came home first and, because he could still see bubbles coming from the bottom of the pool, he decided he ought to dive down and rescue the head. So he plunged down, collected the head and brought it back up to the surface. He then placed it by the side of the pool.

The head began coughing and spluttering violently. 'I've spent two years learning to swim with my ears,' shouted the head, 'and then thirty seconds before the start some asshole puts a swimming cap on me!'

713 A guy with a wooden leg wanted to insure it against fire damage. The first company he approached was unsure how to categorize a wooden leg but quoted him an annual premium of $750. However he thought that was a bit high so he tried another firm who quoted him a yearly payment of just $75.

'How come your charges for insuring my wooden leg are so low?' he asked.

The insurance agent drew the man's attention to the fire policy ratings table and said: 'It's all here in black and white. The object is a wooden structure with an upper sprinkler.'

714 Quasimodo was running along the street being chased by a pack of kids. He stopped, turned around, and shouted: 'Get lost, all of you! I haven't got your bloody ball!'

715 A guy started talking to Siamese twins in a bar, and they ended up back at his apartment. While making love to one, he started to work on the other. Realizing that the first one might get bored watching, he asked her what she'd like to do.

She said: 'Is that a trombone in the corner? I'd love to play your trombone.'

So she played the trombone while the guy screwed her sister.

A few weeks later the girls were walking past the guy's apartment building. One said: 'Let's stop and see that guy.'

The other said: 'Gee . . . do you think he'll remember us?'

DISEASE

716 The Mother Superior called the nuns together and said to them: 'I have something to tell you. We have a case of gonorrhoea in the convent.'

'Thank God,' said an elderly nun at the back of the room, 'I'm so tired of Chardonnay.'

717 How can you get AIDS from a toilet seat? – By sitting down before the last guy gets up.

718 At the cinema a man noticed a young woman sitting alone. He was excited to see that she had both hands up her skirt and was fingering herself furiously. Increasingly aroused, he moved to the seat next to her and offered to help. To his delight, she welcomed the gesture, so he began fingering her like crazy. When he eventually tired and withdrew his hand, he was surprised to see her go back to work on herself with both hands.

'Wasn't I good enough?' he asked sheepishly.

'You were great,' she said, 'but these crabs are still itching!'

719 What's yellow and green and eats nuts? – Gonorrhoea.

720 There was this woman who was desperate to meet a man. She went to single bars, singles dances and went on singles holidays but she could never meet anyone willing to go on a date with her. Eventually in desperation, she went to a sex doctor by the name of Dr Chang.

'Please, doctor,' she began, 'help me find out what's wrong with me.'

'Take off all yur cwothes,' he ordered.

So she did.

Then he said: 'Now get on yur hands and knees and crawl real fass away from me, then crawl real fass back to me.'

So she did.

Then he sat down behind his desk and said: 'You got real bad case of Zachary disease.'

'What's that,' she asked.

Dr Chang replied: 'That's when yur face look zachary like yur ass.'

721 What do you call a man with Parkinson's disease who shaves? – Nick.

722 A jelly baby went to the doctor. After examining him, the doctor said: 'You've picked up a sexually transmitted disease.'

'Is that it?'

'You don't sound very surprised, jelly baby.'

'I'm not. I've been sleeping with allsorts.'

723 A guy was dying of cancer. Realizing it might be his last chance to say goodbye, he summoned his friends to the local bar. There, he told everyone that he had AIDS.

His son took him to one side and whispered: 'I thought you said you are dying from cancer? Yet you just told your friends you are dying from AIDS!'

'That's because I don't want any of those bastards shagging your mother after I'm dead.'

724 The doctor informed his patient that he had a nasty case of Hags.

'What the hell is Hags?' asked the patient.

'It's a combination of herpes, AIDS, gonorrhoea and syphilis,' explained the doctor. 'The only cure is total isolation and a diet of pancakes and bacon.'

'Why pancakes and bacon?' inquired the patient.

The doctor said: 'It's the only food we can slide under the door.'

725 A guy had $10 left in his pocket, and decided to spend it on a cheap hooker. After a night of hardcore sex in a dirty hotel room, he woke in the morning to find that he had got crabs. So he went searching for the hooker. When he found her on a street corner, he yelled: 'Hey, bitch, you gave me crabs!'

She said: 'What did you expect for $10? Lobsters?'

726 A guy was using a public urinal when a man with no arms came up to him and asked: 'Can you give me a hand?'

He reluctantly agreed to help, unzipped the stranger's pants and gingerly took out his penis. To his horror, it was green and mouldy. Nevertheless, taking a deep breath, he continued to hold it while the stranger urinated before giving it a shake and zipping it back in his pants.

'Thanks,' said the stranger. 'I owe you.'

'That's OK. But tell me, what the hell is wrong with your dick?'

The stranger pulled his arms out into his sleeves and said: 'Dunno, but there's no way I'm going to touch it!'

727 What's the first sign of AIDS? – A pounding sensation in the ass.

728 How did the tugboat get AIDS? – It was rear-ended by a ferry.

729 An old man sighed: 'Arthritis is the cruellest disease.'

'Crueller than cancer?' queried his friend.

'You bet. It makes every single one of your joints stiff, except the right one.'

730 Seamus hired a hooker for the night but, when she turned up at his hotel room, they realized that neither of them had any condoms. Since the girl didn't want to miss out on her money and Seamus had no objections, they had unprotected sex.

Afterwards Seamus turned to the girl and said: 'My God, I've just had an awful thought. You haven't got AIDS, have you?'

'No,' said the girl.

'Thank heavens for that,' sighed Seamus. 'I'd hate to catch it twice.'

731 A guy said to his friend: 'Are you still seeing that girl?'

'No, she bled to death from gonorrhoea.'

'You don't bleed to death from gonorrhoea.'

The friend said: 'You do if you give it to me.'

DIVORCE

732 A divorced guy was delighted when his daughter reached her 18th birthday because it would be his final child support payment. Month after month, year after year he had paid, and now at last he would be free of the financial burden.

So he called his daughter over to his house and said: 'I want you to take this last cheque to your mother's house. You tell her this is the last cheque she's ever going to get from me. Then I want you to come back here and tell me the expression she had on her face.'

The girl took the cheque and returned a couple of hours later. 'Well,' said the father gleefully, 'what did she have to say?'

The girl replied: 'She told me to tell you that you ain't my dad.'

733 What's the definition of irreconcilable differences? – When she's melting down her wedding ring to cast it into a bullet.

734 Addressing a middle-aged woman, the judge said: 'Tell me, on what grounds do you wish to divorce your husband?'

'Adultery,' she replied.

'And what evidence do you have to support this claim?' asked the judge.

The woman said: 'I'm certain he's not the father of my sixth child.'

DOCTORS

735 'Doc,' said Joe, 'I want to be castrated.'

'Why?' asked the doctor, amazed.

'It's something I've been thinking about for a long time and I want to have it done.'

The doctor frowned. 'Have you thought it through properly? It's a very serious operation and, once it's done, there's no going back. It will change your life for ever.'

'I know all that, but I've made my decision. I want to be castrated and if you won't refer me to a surgeon, I'll go to another doctor.'

'OK,' sighed the doctor, 'but it's against my better judgement.'

Joe went ahead with it and the day after the operation he was walking painfully along the hospital corridor, legs apart, with his drip stand. Heading towards him was another patient walking exactly the same way.

'Hi,' said Joe, 'looks like you've had the same operation as me.'

'Well,' said the other patient, 'I finally decided that after thirty-seven years of life I would like to be circumcized.'

Joe stared at him in horror. 'Shit! *That's* the word!'

736 A few days before his proctological examination, a one-eyed man accidentally swallowed his glass eye. Since he appeared to suffer no ill effects, he forgot all about it.

So he kept his appointment and, once inside the doctor's office, he undressed and bent over as requested. The first thing the proctologist saw when he looked up the man's ass was that eye staring right back at him.

The doctor said: 'You know, you really have to learn to trust me.'

737 A woman went to the doctor for a check-up. The doctor was concerned about a series of bruises on the outside of her thighs and when he asked her how she had got them, she said it was from having sex.

He advised: 'You'll have to change positions until the bruises heal.'

'Oh, doctor, I can't,' she said. 'My dog's breath is awful!'

738 A man asked the doctor: 'Are you sure I'm suffering from pneumonia, because I heard once about a doctor treating someone for pneumonia and finally he died of tuberculosis?'

'Don't worry,' said the doctor. 'It won't happen with me. If I treat someone for pneumonia, he will die of pneumonia.'

739 A woman said to her doctor: 'Kiss me, kiss me, you handsome brute!'

The doctor replied: 'I can't. It wouldn't be ethical. To be honest, I shouldn't be screwing you at all!'

740 A man went to the doctor's and asked for a new penis.

The doctor said: 'OK, we have a five-incher, a seven-incher, and a ten-incher. Which would you like?'

'Oh, the ten-incher, please.'

The doctor reached into the fridge for it. The man looked at it for a few seconds, then said: 'Does it come in white?'

741 During her annual check-up, a pretty young woman was asked to disrobe and climb onto the examining table.

'Doctor,' she said shyly, 'I can't undress in front of you.'

'That's OK,' he said. 'I'll flick off the lights. You get undressed and tell me when you're through.'

A few minutes later, her voice rang out in the darkness: 'Doctor, I've undressed. What should I do with my clothes?'

'Just put them over here, on top of mine . . .'

742 A man went to the doctor's surgery and told the receptionist: 'There's something wrong with my dick.'

'Excuse me, sir!' she said icily. 'I will not allow patients to use such language in a crowded surgery. Now, will you please go out, come back in and say there's something wrong with your ear or whatever.'

So the man went out, came back in and told the receptionist: 'There's something wrong with my ear.'

The receptionist smiled and said: 'And what is wrong with your ear, sir?'

The man said: 'I can't piss out of it!'

743 'How did it happen?' the doctor asked the middle-aged farmhand as he set the man's broken leg.

'Well, doc, twenty-five years ago . . .'

'Never mind the past,' interrupted the doctor. 'Tell me how you broke your leg this morning.'

'Like I was saying,' continued the farmhand. 'Twenty-five years ago, when I first started working on the farm, that night, right after I'd gone to bed, the farmer's beautiful daughter came into my room. She asked me if there was anything I wanted. I said: 'No, everything is fine.'

' "Are you sure?" she asked.

' "I'm sure," I said.

' "Isn't there anything at all I can do for you?" she persisted.

' "I reckon not," I replied.

'Excuse me,' said the doctor, 'but what does this story have to do with your leg?'

'Well, this morning,' the farmhand explained, 'when it dawned on me what she meant, I fell off the roof!'

744 A guy went to the doctor and said: 'I got a mole on the end of my penis.'

'Drop your pants and show me,' said the doctor who then proceeded to examine the area.

'Yes,' continued the doctor,' 'I can get rid of the mole, but I'm going to have to report you to the animal welfare people.'

745 A man went to the doctor's because his arm was covered in sores.

'What do you do for a living?' asked the doctor.

'I work in a circus – my job is to give enemas to the elephants. I have to shove my arm right up their backsides and clean them out.'

'Dear me!' said the doctor. 'No wonder your arm's in such a state. Have you ever thought of looking for another job?'

'What?' said the man. 'And give up show business?'

746 A man phoned the doctor and said in a panic: 'A mouse ran up my wife's honeypot.'

'Right,' said the doctor, 'I'll be over in ten minutes. In the meantime, try waving a piece of cheese between her legs to lure it out.'

When the doctor arrived, the husband was waving an open can of tuna over the wife's opening.

'What are you doing?' exclaimed the doctor. 'I said to use cheese!'

'I know,' said the husband, 'but I've got to get the cat out first!'

DOGS

747 A man with a terrier walked into a bar and ordered a drink. From his change, he gave the dog a fifty-dollar note and told it to go across the street for a pack of cigarettes.

The bartender was amazed. 'Does your dog always run errands for you?' he asked.

'My dog can do anything,' boasted the man. 'He does the weekly shopping, cleans the house from top to bottom, and even cooks the dinner. I wouldn't swap him for anyone.'

But just as he was listing his dog's talents, he was cut short by the screeching of tyres. He rushed outside to see that a car had swerved to avoid his dog humping another terrier in the middle of the street.

'What's going on?' shouted the man to his dog. 'You've never done anything like this before.'

The dog said: 'I've never had fifty bucks before.'

748 Joe and Jack were out walking their dogs in the park when Joe started bragging about how his dog could count. Jack challenged him to prove it.

So Joe said to his dog. 'OK, Rex, go count the ducks in the pond.' The dog ran off, returned a minute later and barked four times. Joe said: 'That means there's four ducks in the pond.'

When Jack went down to the pond, sure enough there were four ducks. But Jack thought it was a fluke and when he met up with Joe, he said: 'Let's see him do it again!'

So Joe said to his dog: 'Do it again, boy.' The dog ran down to the pond and on his return, barked nine times. Jack went down to the pond once more and, sure enough, there were nine ducks.

But Jack still refused to concede that Joe's dog could count, and challenged him to do it a third time. So Joe despatched Rex to the pond again. Moments later, the dog returned and started vigorously screwing Joe's leg. Then the dog picked up a stick and began shaking it furiously. 'See,' said Jack, gloating, 'that dog can't count! He's gone mental!'

Joe said: 'No, you don't understand him. He's saying, 'There's more fucking ducks down there than you can shake a stick at!''

749 What's a shiatsu? – A zoo with no animals.

750 An eight-year-old boy went into a grocery store and picked out a large box of laundry detergent. The grocer walked over and asked him if he had a lot of laundry to do.

'Oh, no laundry,' said the boy, 'I'm going to wash my dog.'

'You shouldn't use this stuff on your dog,' advised the grocer. 'It's very powerful. If you wash your dog in this, he'll get sick. In fact, it might even kill him.'

But the boy wouldn't listen and carried the detergent to the checkout where he paid for it.

A week later, the boy was back in the store to buy some biscuits. The grocer asked him how his dog was doing.

'Oh, he died,' said the boy.

'I'm real sorry to hear that,' said the grocer, 'but I did try to warn you about using that detergent on your dog.'

'I don't think it was the detergent that killed him,' said the boy.

'Oh,' said the grocer. 'What was it, then?'

'I think it was the spin cycle.'

751 If you're being chased by a police dog, try not to go through a tunnel, then on to a little seesaw, then jump through a hoop of fire. They're trained for that.

752 Late at night an old lady rang her vet and asked what she should do to separate two mating dogs. 'Throw some water over them,' advised the vet.

A few minutes later, the old lady rang back to say that the water treatment hadn't worked. 'Have you any other suggestions?' she asked.

'Oh, I don't know,' he said. 'Try prising them apart with a stick or something.'

A few minutes later, she rang back again to say that the stick hadn't worked either. 'What else can I try?' she asked.

Irritated, the vet said: 'Go and tell one of the dogs that it's wanted on the phone.'

'Will that work?' she said.

The vet replied: 'Well, it's already worked three times with me!'

753 In theory, housetraining your puppy may seem like a sensible idea, but it doesn't look good on paper.

754 A drunk took his dog for a midday walk. When he reached his favourite bar, he tied the dog to a lamppost out front and went in for a beer.

An hour later, a police officer came in to the bar and asked: 'Whose dog is that tied up out front?'

'Mine,' said the drunk, nearly falling off his stool.

'She's in heat,' said the officer, who clearly knew a thing or two about dogs.

'It's OK,' slurred the drunk. 'It's shady out there.'

'That's not what I mean,' persisted the cop. 'Your dog wants to mate.'

'Go ahead, officer,' said the drunk. 'I've always wanted a police dog.'

755 Did you hear about the Irish wolfhound? – It got caught in a trap, chewed off three legs and was still trapped.

756 A man was bitten by a stray dog. Half an hour later, as he waited for an ambulance to take him to hospital, his wife saw him writing frantically.

'It's OK,' she said. 'You probably haven't got rabies, and in any case it can be cured. There's no need to worry about writing a will just yet.'

'Will?' he said. 'What will? I'm making a list of the people I want to bite.'

757 A southern preacher was standing outside church when a sweet little girl walked by with her dog.

'What's your name, little girl?' asked the preacher.

'My name is Petal,' she replied.

'My, what a lovely name! Why did your parents name you Petal?'

The little girl explained: 'When I was growing in my mommy's tummy, one day mommy and daddy went on a picnic and a rose petal drifted down to land on mommy's tummy, and daddy said if we have a girl we'll call her Petal.'

'That's a lovely story,' smiled the preacher. 'And tell me, what is your little dog called?'

'Porky.'

'I suppose that's because of his inky-winky curly tail?'

'No, it's because he fucks pigs.'

758 How do you know if you've got kinky dogs? – They do it in the missionary position.

759 Before catching the plane home at the end of an out-of-town business trip, a man bought a small puppy as a present for his son. Since he didn't have time to complete the necessary paperwork for taking the puppy on board, he slid it down the front of his pants and sneaked it on board the airplane. About half an hour into the trip, the steward noticed the man shaking and quivering.

'Are you OK, sir?' he asked.

'Yes, I'm fine,' said the man.

Twenty minutes later, the steward could not help noticing the man moaning and shaking again.

'Are you sire you're all right, sir?'

'Yes,' said the man, 'but I do have a confession to make. I didn't have time to get the paperwork to bring a puppy on board, so I hid him down the front of my pants.'

'What's wrong?' asked the steward. 'Isn't he house trained?'

'It's not that,' said the man. 'The problem is he's not weaned yet!'

760 A woman looked out the window and saw that the neighbour's dog was humping hers. So she rushed outside to try and pull them apart. She tried hitting the male dog, she tried throwing a bucket of water over them, but nothing worked. Just then a small boy walked past and the woman said: 'I'll give you five dollars if you can get that dog off mine.'

While the woman went back indoors, the boy walked up to the dogs, wet his finger, lifted the male's tail, and stuck his finger in its ass. The dog backed off immediately, and the boy knocked on the door of the house to collect his money.

'How did you manage to get him off?' asked the woman.

'Well, lady,' said the boy, 'he can dish it out but he can't take it!'

761 A woman had her dog neutered because she was told it would curb the animal's aggression. But the next day it savaged the postman.

'I'm so sorry,' she said, rushing to the man's aid. 'I was told he'd stop attacking people if I had him neutered.'

'Lady,' said the postman, picking himself off the ground, 'you should have had his teeth pulled. I knew when he came out the door he wasn't going to screw me!'

Reasons why Men Envy Dogs:

762 • When a dog puts his head between girls' legs, they pet him.

763 • He can lick his own balls.

764 • He can stick his head out the car window without being yelled at.

765 • It's OK to drool a bit.

766 • It's easier to find a good bitch.

767 • He can hump hot chicks' legs without going to jail.

768 • He doesn't care where he scratches or who's watching.

769 • He licks his own butt but his breath is still fresher than most men's.

770 • He has a full head of beautiful hair.

771 • He can eye other dogs without being yelled at.

772 • He's too dumb to know when he's bored.

DRUGS

773 Two young men were picked up by the cops for smoking dope and appeared in court on Friday. The judge told them: 'You seem like basically decent young men, so I'd like to give you a second chance rather than send you to jail. So I want you to go out this weekend and try to persuade others of the evils of drugs, and, if possible, to get them to give up drugs for ever. I'll see you back in court on Monday.'

Come the Monday and the pair were back in court. Addressing the first one, the judge said: 'How did your anti-drugs crusade go over the weekend?'

'Very well, your honour. I managed to persuade twenty-two people to give up drugs forever.'

'Twenty-two?' echoed the judge. 'That's very impressive. Tell me, how did you persuade them of the error of their ways?'

'I used a diagram, your honour. I drew two circles, one large and one small. I told them the big circle is your brain before drugs and the small circle is your brain after drugs.'

'That's admirable,' enthused the judge.

Then he turned to the second youth. 'And how did you do over the weekend?'

'Well, your honour,' he said, 'I managed to persuade 143 people to give up drugs forever.'

'143 people! That's amazing!' said the judge. 'How did you do it?'

'I used a similar approach, one large circle and one small circle. I pointed to the small circle and said: "This is your asshole before prison . . ."'

774 A little rabbit was running through the woods when he came across a giraffe rolling a joint. He ran up to the giraffe and said: 'Hey, giraffe, you shouldn't do that. Think of your health. You should come running in the woods instead.' The giraffe looked at him, looked at the spliff, shrugged his shoulders, tossed the joint away and ran off through the woods with the little rabbit.

After a while the rabbit and the giraffe came across an elephant about to do a line of coke. The rabbit said: 'Hey, elephant, you shouldn't do that. Think of your health. You should come running in the woods instead.' The elephant looked at him, looked at the line of cocaine, shrugged his shoulders, then ran off through the woods with the rabbit and the giraffe.

Soon the three animals stumbled across a bear about to shoot up heroin. The rabbit ran up to him and said: 'Hey, bear, you shouldn't do that. Think of your health. You should come running in the woods instead.' The bear looked at him, looked at the syringe, shrugged his shoulders, threw the syringe away and ran off through the woods with the rabbit, the giraffe and the elephant.

A few minutes later they met a tiger drinking his way through a six pack of beer. The rabbit ran up to the tiger and said: 'Hey, tiger, you shouldn't do that. Think of your health. You should come running in the woods instead.' The tiger immediately jumped up and start beating the hell out of the rabbit. The giraffe grabbed the tiger and managed to pull him off the rabbit.

'What do you think you're doing, man?' asked the giraffe.

The tiger replied: 'Ah, that little fucker really pisses me off: he always makes me run round the bloody woods when he's on Ecstasy!'

775 Why is sex like pot? – The quality depends on the pusher.

776 A monkey was sitting in a tree in the jungle, smoking a joint, when a lizard walked past, looked up, and said: 'What are you doing?'

'I'm smokin' a joint,' said the monkey. 'Come on up and have some.'

So the lizard climbed the tree and smoked a joint, but after half an hour his mouth was dry. 'I'm going to get a drink of water from the river,' he told the monkey. So he climbed back down the tree and found a bush over-hanging the water. But when he leaned over, he was so stoned that he toppled off his branch and fell into the river.

A crocodile saw this and asked the lizard what had happened. The lizard explained: 'I was up in a tree smoking a joint with a monkey, and then I came down for a drink. But I'm so drugged up, I leaned over too far and fell in.'

The crocodile decided to check out the lizard's story, and ambled off into the jungle. Eventually he found the tree where the monkey was sitting finishing a joint.

The crocodile yelled: 'Hey!'

The monkey looked down and said: 'Bugger me! How much water did you drink?'

777 Up in heaven, Jesus convened all the apostles and disciples to an emergency meeting to discuss the spiralling world drug consumption. Following a lengthy debate, they decided that they should try the different types of drugs themselves before settling on a course of action to ensure the salvation of mankind. It was therefore decided that a select commission should return to Earth to acquire various drugs. Two days later the appointed disciples began to return to heaven.

'Who is it?' asked Jesus as the first caller arrived.

'It's Paul.'

Jesus opened the door.

'What did you bring, Paul?'

'Hashish from Morocco.'

'Very well, Paul. Come in.'

A few minutes later, there was a second visitor. 'Who is it?' asked Jesus.

'It's Mark.'

Jesus opened the door.

'What did you bring, Mark?'

'Marijuana from Colombia.'

'Very well, Mark. Come in.'

Soon there was another knock. 'Who is it?' asked Jesus.

'It's Luke.'

Jesus opened the door.

'What did you bring, Luke?'

'Speed from Amsterdam.'

'Very well, Luke. Come in.'

Five minutes later, there was another caller. 'Who is it?' asked Jesus.

'It's Matthew.'

Jesus opened the door.

'What did you bring, Matthew?'

'Cocaine from Colombia.'

'Very well, Matthew. Come in.'

A few minutes later, another caller turned up. 'Who is it?' asked Jesus.

'It's John.'

Jesus opened the door.

'What did you bring, John?'

'Crack from New York.'

'Very well, John. Come in.'

Ten minutes later, there was another knock on the door. 'Who is it?' asked Jesus.

'It's Judas.'

Jesus opened the door.

'What did you bring, Judas?'

'The FBI. OK, you mother fuckers! Everybody up against the wall!'

DRUNKS

778 Two drunks were sitting at a bar when one smelt something foul. He turned to the other and said, 'Hey, man, did you just shit yourself?'

'Yeah,' said the second drunk.

'Get out of here! Why don't you go clean yourself up?'

'I ain't through yet.'

779 Three lads were drinking in a bar when a guy, clearly the worse for wear, came over to them, pointed at the one in the middle and said, in a drunken slur: 'I've shagged your mom.'

The bewildered lads ignored him and he went back to drinking at the bar.

Ten minutes later he came over again and announced: 'Your mom has sucked my cock.'

Again the lads ignored him and he staggered back to the bar.

After another ten minutes he came back and shouted: 'I've had your mom up the arse.'

By now the lads had heard enough and one in the middle stood up and said: 'Look, Dad, you're pissed. Now fuck off home.'

780 A young man was staggering about drunk with a key in his hand.

'What's going on?' inquired a passing cop.

'They stole my car!' said the man.

'Where did you last see it?'

'On the end of this key!'

The cop looked him over and said: 'Are you aware, sir, that your penis is hanging out of your trousers?'

'Holy shit!' exclaimed the man. 'They got my girlfriend too!'

781 A drunk staggered out of a bar and began walking down the street, one foot on the kerb, the other foot on the street.

Seeing this, a policeman went over to him and said: 'You're drunk.'

'Thank God for that!' said the drunk. 'I thought I was crippled.'

782 Two drunks were sitting at a bar. One said: 'What's this thing they call a breathalyser?'

'It's a bag that can tell how much you drink.'

'Oh, I married one of those years ago.'

783 A belligerent drunk walked into a bar and hollered: 'I can lick any man in this place!'

The nearest customer looked him up and down and said: 'Crude, but direct. Tell me, is this your first time in a gay bar?'

784 A man went into a bar and saw a drunk playing with a ball of gloop. The drunk kept muttering to himself: 'It looks like plastic, but it feels like rubber.'

Intrigued, the man peered over the drunk's shoulder in order to get a better view of the mysterious substance. Meanwhile the drunk was still saying: 'It looks like plastic, but it feels like rubber.'

Eventually the man said: 'Listen, I'm a chemist, so perhaps I can tell you what it is.'

So the drunk handed him the gloop. Carefully rolling it between his fingers, the chemist pronounced: 'You're right. It does look like plastic but feel like rubber. Do you know where it came from?'

'Sure,' said the drunk. 'It just fell out of my nose.'

785 A Highway Patrolman waited outside a popular bar, waiting for a bust. At closing time, everyone came out and he spotted his potential quarry. The man was so obviously inebriated that he could barely walk. He stumbled around the parking lot for a few minutes, looking for his car and, after trying his keys on five other vehicles, he finally found his own car. He sat in the car for a good ten minutes while the other patrons left. He turned his lights on, then off, wipers on, then off. He started to pull forward onto the grass, but then stopped. Finally, when every other car had gone, he pulled out onto the road and started to drive away.

The patrolman, waiting for this, turned on his lights and pulled the man over. He administered the breathalyser test, but to his surprise, the man registered a zero. He wasn't drunk at all!

The patrolman was dumbfounded. 'The equipment must be broken!' he exclaimed.

'No, it isn't,' smiled the driver. 'I'm the designated decoy.'

786 A drunk was staggering around the car park of a bar, feeling the roofs of the various cars.

'What are you doing?' asked a fellow customer.

'I'm looking for my car,' said the drunk, swaying unsteadily on his feet, 'and I can't find it.'

'How does feeling the roof help you?'

'Because,' said the drunk, barely able to stand, 'my car has two blue lights and a siren on the roof.'

787 A drunk was walking unsteadily along a riverside path one Sunday afternoon when he stumbled across a baptism. Intrigued by what was going on, he proceeded to walk down into the water and stand next to the preacher. After a minute or so, the minister became aware of the drunk and asked: 'Are you ready to find Jesus?'

The drunk replied: 'Yesh, preacher, I sure am.'

So the minister dunked him under the water and pulled him straight back up. 'Have you found Jesus?' asked the minister.

'Noo,' said the drunk.

So the preacher dunked him under for a little longer before bringing him back up. 'Now, brother, have you found Jesus?'

'Nooo,' answered the drunk.

In disgust, the preacher held the man's head under for at least half a minute, then brought him back up and demanded impatiently: 'Have you found Jesus yet?'

The drunk wiped his eyes and said to the preacher: 'Are you sure this is where he fell in?'

788 A drunk was weaving down the road when he saw a man fiddling under a car bonnet.

'What's up?' shouted the drunk.

'Piston broke,' replied the man.

'Me too,' said the drunk, and he continued on his way.

789 A drunk got on a bus and swayed down the centre gangway. Suddenly he started yelling that everybody to the right of the gangway was an asshole and that everybody to the left was a son of a bitch.

A passenger to the right immediately jumped up and said angrily: 'Hang on! I'm not an asshole!'

The drunk said: 'So move to the other side then.'

790 As it was a beautiful day, a woman decided to stretch out on a park bench and soak up the sun. After ten minutes, a down-and-out wino came over to her and said: 'Hi, gorgeous. How about you and me getting together?'

'How dare you?' replied the woman. 'I'm not one of your cheap pick-ups!'

'No?' said the wino. 'Then what are you doing in my bed?'

791 In the course of a heavy drinking session, the right-hand pocket of a drunk's jeans somehow became ripped out. Having slept in his clothes all night, he finally began to take stock of the situation when he sobered up in the morning.

Rising uneasily to his feet, he felt in his jacket pocket and found a set of keys and some chewing gum. 'Ah, that's what happened to my keys,' he said, relieved. Next he reached into the left pocket of his jeans and pulled out the contents – some loose change. 'Oh, at least I didn't spend it all,' he mused. Then he reached down into the right pocket of his jeans, felt around a bit and said to himself: 'Prunes . . . Why on earth did I buy prunes?'

792 A drunk staggered down to hotel reception and demanded a change of room.

'But you have the best room in the hotel,' said the receptionist.

'I want another room,' insisted the drunk.

'Very well, sir,' said the receptionist. 'But may I ask what it is that you don't like about your room?'

'Well,' said the drunk, 'for one thing, it's on fire.'

793 A drunk was peeing in the fountain in the town square when a cop yelled: 'Hey, stop that! Put it away!'

The drunk shoved his dick into his pants and did up the zip. As the cop turned to go, the drunk started laughing.

'What's so funny?' demanded the cop.

'Fooled you!' shouted the drunk. 'I put it away, but I didn't stop!'

Signs That You're Drunk:

794 • You have to hold on to the lawn to stop falling off Earth.

795 • The back of your head keeps getting hit by the toilet seat.

796 • You can focus better with one eye closed.

797 • Mosquitoes get a buzz after attacking you.

798 • The shrubbery's drunk too from frequent watering.

799 • Roseanne looks good.

800 • You lose arguments with inanimate objects.

801 • Your job interferes with your drinking.

802 • Your doctor finds traces of blood in your alcohol stream.

803 During a wild party at a Long Island country house, Shelley had way too much to drink and staggered outside for some air. Reaching a grassy field, she lay down to watch the stars. She was almost asleep when a cow, searching for clover, carefully stepped over her. Groggily, she raised her head and said: 'One at a time boys, one at a time.'

804 A shy man was in hospital for a series of tests which included filling him with laxatives. One evening, unable to get to the bathroom in time, he accidentally messed his bed sheet. He was so embarrassed by the thought of the nurses discovering what had happened that he bunched the sheet together and threw it out of the window.

It just so happened that a drunk was shambling along the street below when the sheet landed on him. The drunk immediately began cursing and yelling and, with flailing arms, left the sheet in a heap on the sidewalk. Hearing the commotion, a police officer asked: 'What's going on here?'

Staring down at the soiled sheet, the drunk replied: 'I just beat the crap out of a ghost.'

805 Two drunks were sitting at the bar, staring into their drinks. One said: 'Hey, you ever seen an ice cube with a hole in it before?'

The other said: 'Sure. I've been married to one for eighteen years.'

806 With only a dollar in change between them, two drunks were trying to figure out how to get some alcohol for free. Then one had an idea. They went to a hot dog stand, bought a hot dog and threw away the bun. 'Now we'll go into a bar and order drinks, and when the bartender asks for money, I'll unzip my fly and pull out the hot dog. You drop to your knees and pretend to suck me off.'

The second man agreed to the plan, and they headed for their first bar. When they arrived, they sat down and drank their beers. The bartenders told them: 'That will be three dollars.'

As arranged, the first man stood up and unzipped his fly whereupon the second man sank to his knees and began sucking on the hot dog.

'You dirty faggots!' screamed the bartender. 'Get the hell out of here!'

They immediately ran out of the bar, delighted to have got away without paying. They tried the same ruse at the next bar. They downed their drinks and when the bartender asked for payment, the first man unzipped his fly and the second man dropped to his knees. The bartender then threw them out.

After the sixth bar, the second man complained to his fellow drunk: 'This isn't working so well. My knees are killing me.'

'You think you've had it bad,' said the first drunk. 'I lost the hot dog four bars ago!'

807 A guy had been propping up the bar for six hours when he happened to mention that his girlfriend was outside in the car. As it was a bitterly cold day, the bartender thought he had better make sure that she was all right. But when he peered into the car, he saw the drunk's buddy Kyle screwing the girlfriend on the back seat.

Unsure how to handle the situation, the bartender went back in and simply told the drunk that it might be an idea to check on his girlfriend. So the drunk staggered outside into the car park, saw Kyle and the girl entwined, then walked back into the bar laughing.

'What's so funny?' asked the bartender.

'The drunk said: 'That idiot Kyle — he's so bloody drunk, he thinks he's me!'

808 A guy staggered out of the bar one night, hopelessly drunk. As he stumbled out the door, he saw a nun walking on the sidewalk. He went straight up to her and punched her in the face. Then he punched her again, even harder. As she fell to the ground, he kicked her in the butt, then picked her up and threw her into a wall.

By now the poor nun could hardly move. Swaying on the spot, the drunk jeered: 'Not very strong tonight, are you, Batman?'

809 A drunk was staggering along through the park when he saw a man doing push-ups. He yelled: 'I think you ought to know, pal — your girlfriend has gone home!'

810 A paralytic drunk was staggering around a fairground when he spotted a rifle range and decided to try his luck. To the horror of the showman, he somehow scored three bullseyes. The star prize was a set of glassware but, reckoning that the drunk would never know what he had scored, the showman palmed him off with the consolation prize, a turtle.

Twenty minutes later, the drunk came back for another go. Once again, he scored three bulls and the showman managed to get away with giving him a turtle.

Ten minutes later, the drunk was back for a third go, and yet again he scored three bulls. The showman was just about to reach for another turtle when an onlooker said: 'Hasn't he scored three bulls?'

Curing his luck, the showman turned to the drunk and said: 'Congratulations, you have won this magnificent eighty-two-piece set of glassware.'

'I don't want any glasses,' slurred the drunk. 'Just give me another of those delicious crusty meat pies.'

DWARFS

811 Two dwarfs went on vacation to Las Vegas. There, they met two beautiful women and took them back to their adjoining hotel rooms. Alas, the first dwarf was so intimidated by the girl's beauty that he simply couldn't get aroused. To make matters worse, all he could hear from the next room were cries of 'One, two, three . . . oh!' all night long.

The next morning the second dwarf said: 'How did it go?'

His friend said: 'It was so embarrassing. I couldn't get an erection.'

'You think that was embarrassing?' said the second dwarf. 'I couldn't even get on the bed!'

812 The Seven Dwarfs came home tired from a long, hard day's work and decided to relax in the hot-tub. They put on their swimming trunks, grabbed some beers and hopped in. Soon they started to feel happy. So Happy left.

813 A guy was standing in the toilet having a pee when he noticed to his left a dwarf whose head was shaking incessantly.

'Excuse me,' asked the guy, 'but why does your head shake all the time?'

'I used to be a human cannonball in a circus,' explained the dwarf. 'The vibration from the cannon has left me like this.'

Just then the dwarf left, and to his right the guy then noticed another dwarf who was also shaking his head vigorously. 'Were you in the circus too?' asked the guy.

'No,' said the dwarf angrily. 'When you were busy talking to that other bloke, you were pissing in my ear!'

814 A guy walked into a bar and said: 'Bartender, give me two shots – one for me and one for my buddy here.'

The bartender said: 'Do you want both drinks now or do you want me to wait till your buddy arrives to pour his?'

'No, it's OK,' said the guy, 'I've got my best buddy in my pocket here.' With that, he pulled out a little three-inch man from his pocket.

'That's amazing,' said the bartender. 'Can he walk?'

The guy flicked a coin down to the end of the bar and said to his tiny friend: 'Hey, Mikey, go and get that coin.'

Mikey duly ran along the bar, fetched the coin and brought it back to the guy.

The bartender was impressed. 'What else can he do? Can he talk?'

'Talk?' said the guy. 'Sure he talks. Hey, Mikey, tell him about that time we were on safari in Africa and you pissed off that witch doctor.'

815 What does a dwarf get if he runs through a woman's legs? – A clit around the ear and a flap across the face.

816 A tall, willowy blonde met a midget at a party and, although the midget was barely three feet tall, there was a definite chemistry between them. After a few drinks, they went back to the woman's apartment.

'I can't imagine what it will be like making love to a midget,' she said, 'especially with the size difference.'

The midget said: 'Just take off your clothes, lie back on the bed, spread your legs apart and close your eyes.'

The woman did as she was told and soon she felt the biggest thing she'd ever experienced inside her. Within a few minutes she had climaxed seven times.

'If you think that was good,' said the midget, 'just wait till I get *both* legs in there!'

DYSLEXIA

817 An old man was standing outside a supermarket with a collection box reading: 'Please help my dailysex.' His wife came up to him and said: 'Arthur, you've misspelled dyslexia again!'

818 Did you hear about the dyslexic pimp who bought a warehouse?

819 A man who filled in a job application form was told by his prospective employer: 'Your spelling is very wayward. Are you sure you haven't got dyslexia?'

'Have it?' said the applicant. 'I can't even smell it!'

ENGLAND AND THE ENGLISH

820 Three aristocratic Englishmen in a bar spotted an Irishman having a quiet drink. One of the Englishmen walked over to the Irishman, tapped him on the shoulder and said: 'I say, I hear your St Patrick was a faggot!'

'Oh, really?' muttered the Irishman. 'I didn't know that.'

Disappointed by the lack of reaction, the Englishman walked back to his friends and said: 'I told him St Patrick was a faggot, and he simply didn't care.'

The second Englishman said: 'Tarquin, you just don't know how to get him going. Watch and learn.' So he walked over to the Irishman, tapped him on the shoulder and said: 'I say, I hear your St Patrick was a transvestite faggot!'

'Oh, really?' muttered the Irishman. 'I didn't know that.'

Shocked, the Englishman went back to his friends and said: 'You're right. He's unshakeable.'

The third Englishman said: 'Tristram, dear boy, you simply don't have the knack. Fear not, I'll show you how to wind him up.' So he walked over to the Irishman, tapped him on the shoulder and brayed: 'I say, I hear your St Patrick was an Englishman!'

'Yeah,' muttered the Irishman. 'That's what your friends were trying to tell me.'

821 An Irish priest was openly hostile towards the English. He would regularly tell his congregation: 'If you do not lead a better life, you will all go to hell along with the English.' When news of these rants reached the bishop's ears, he warned the priest that he would be transferred or even defrocked if he did not mend his ways. The priest promised to be more diplomatic in future.

For his next sermon, the priest told the story of the betrayal of Jesus. 'And Jesus looked at all of the apostles one at a time and said, "Tonight, one of you will betray me." Peter said, "It is not I, master." Jesus looked at Judas. Feeling the steady gaze of the Lord upon him, Judas said, "Blimey, guv'nor, ya don't fink it's me, do ya?"'

822 An Essex girl was involved in a bad car crash, which left her trapped in the wreckage and bleeding.

Paramedics arrived on the scene and asked her: 'What's your name?'

'Sharon,' she replied.
'OK, Sharon, where are you bleeding from?'
'Romford.'

823 What do you call three Mancunians in a filing cabinet? – Sorted!

824 What is the difference between a walrus and an Essex girl? – One is wet, has a moustache and smells of fish; the other is a walrus.

825 How do you know when an Essex girl has had an orgasm? – She drops her bag of chips.

826 What does the label in an Essex girl's panties say? – NEXT.

827 What's the difference between an Essex man and an Essex girl? – The Essex girl has a higher sperm count.

828 An Essex girl and her boyfriend were spending the evening at home. Bored, she suggested. 'Let's play a game.'
'What sort of game?' he said wearily.
'Hide and seek. And I'll tell you what, if you can find me, I'll give you a blow job.'
'What if I can't find you?'
She said: 'I'll be behind the piano.'

829 What do you call a Scouser in a detached house? – A burglar.

830 An old man was strolling through the French countryside in the 1950s, admiring a glorious spring day, when over a hedgerow he spotted a young couple making love in a field. Overcoming his initial shock, he thought to himself: 'Ah young love, ze springtime, ze air, ze flowers. *C'est magnifique*!' He continued to watch for a couple of minutes before suddenly recoiling in horror. 'Mais sacre bleu!' he exclaimed. 'Ze woman, she is dead!'
He immediately hurried back to town to tell the police chief. 'Jean, Jean,' he gasped, 'zere is zis man, zis woman, naked in farmer Gaston's field, making love.'
The chief smiled and said: 'Come, come, Henri, you are not so old. Remember ze young love, ze springtime, ze air, ze flowers. Zis is OK.'
'*Mais non*,' persisted the old man, 'you do not understand. She is dead!'

The police chief jumped on his bicycle and went to investigate for himself. After watching the couple in the field for a few minutes, he rode straight back into town and informed the doctor. 'Pierre, Pierre, you must come. I was in Gaston's field. Zere is a young couple naked 'aving sex.'

The doctor said calmly: 'Jean, you are not so old. Remember ze young love, ze springtime, ze air, ze flowers. *L'amour*, it is very natural.'

The police chief said: 'No, you do not understand: ze woman, she is dead.'

The doctor grabbed his bag and rushed down to the field, but after carefully examining the participants he drove back to the police station where the old man and the police chief were waiting.

'*Mes amis*, do not worry,' said the doctor. 'Ze woman, she is not dead, she is English!'

EXCREMENT

831 A woman was walking through the woods when a little white duck covered in shit crossed her path. Feeling sorry for it, she took a Kleenex from her purse and cleaned the duck up.

A few yards further on, another little white duck waddled out of the woods covered in shit. So she took a Kleenex from her purse and cleaned it up.

Moments later, a third white duck emerged from the bushes, covered in shit. Once again, she pulled out a Kleenex and wiped the duck's feathers. Just as she finished doing so, she heard a male voice call out from the bushes.

'Hey, lady,' said the voice, in some distress, 'do you have any Kleenex?'

'Not any more, no.'

'Too bad, I'll have to use another duck.'

832 Two male flies were buzzing around in search of good-looking females. Then one spotted a real cutie sitting on a pile of cow shit and dived down towards her. 'Pardon me,' he asked with his best manners, 'but is this stool taken?'

833 Why did the husband stop having anal sex with his wife? – Because every night it was the same old shit.

834 What do you do if a bird craps on your car? – Don't ask her out again.

835 Stranded in the desert for two weeks with no prospect of imminent rescue, a platoon of soldiers became desperate for food. So the sergeant sent two men out to look for supplies. They returned a day later and announced: 'There is good news and bad news.'

'What's the bad news?' asked the sergeant.

'All we found to eat is camel shit,' replied one of the soldiers.

'I see,' said the sergeant gloomily. 'And what's the good news?'

The soldier said: 'We found tons of the stuff.'

836 An old lady took her dog to the vet. He said: 'I can tell there is something seriously wrong with your dog just by looking at his stools.'

'Is it because they're a strange colour?' she asked.

'No,' said the vet. 'It's because they're coming out of his ears.'

837 The town fathers were looking for a way to increase attendance and participation at their regular meetings. One member suggested bringing in a hypnotist, and the idea was adopted.

A month later, following extensive publicity for the event, the meeting hall was packed. The townspeople sat fascinated as the hypnotist produced a pocket watch and began chanting: 'Watch the watch, watch the watch, watch the watch . . .'

The crowd became mesmerized as the watch swayed back and forth, light gleaming off its polished surface. Hundreds of pairs of eyes followed the swaying watch's every move until suddenly the hypnotist's fingers slipped and the watch fell to the floor.

'Shit!' exclaimed the hypnotist.

It took three weeks to clean up the town hall.

838 Two rats were living in a sewer. One turned to the other and said: 'I'm sick of this.'

'Sick of what?'

'Sick of shit for breakfast, shit for lunch, shit for dinner, shit for tea – shit all day long. I'm just sick of it.'

'I know what'll cheer you up,' said the other rat. 'Tonight we'll go on the piss.'

839 One day, all the human body parts started arguing about who was on top.

The mouth said: 'I should be on top because, without me, you wouldn't be able to eat.'

The stomach disagreed. 'I should be on top because if it weren't for me, you wouldn't be able to digest and transfer all the minerals and vitamins throughout the body.'

Then the heart said: 'I should be on top because I'm the one who circulates the blood. Without me, the whole body would die.'

But the brain insisted: 'Without me, you wouldn't be able to move, eat, digest, or allow circulation of blood. So I should be on top.'

Listening to all this, the asshole was becoming increasingly annoyed. Finally it said: 'You know, I should be on top because if I shut my hole, shit will accumulate and block the digestive system and screw the lot of you.'

As the argument continued to rage, the asshole had a hissy fit. 'That's it. I'm fed up. I'm shutting my hole.'

For the next few days, the body couldn't shit, the brain had trouble thinking, the stomach couldn't digest, the mouth could barely eat, and the heart was struggling to keep the blood flow going. They all begged the asshole to open up again for business.

The brain said: 'Please open up, you've made your point.'

The asshole smiled: 'So everyone agrees that I'm on top?'

'Yes,' they all shouted.

So the asshole opened up, allowing the body to shit once more.

And the moral of the story is, you have to be an asshole to be on top . . .

FAIRY TALES

840 Once upon a time a princess was walking along a woodland path when she came across a really ugly frog. In fact, it was the most hideous frog she had ever seen.

The princess did not mince her words. 'My, you're ugly!' she said to the frog.

'I know,' said the frog. 'I got a really bad spell put on me by a particularly evil witch.'

'I've seen frogs with spells before, but never one as repulsive as you.'

'OK, there's no need to go on about it. I can't help it.'

'Even so, if I kiss you, will you turn into a handsome prince?'

'I think a spell this bad will probably need a blow job.'

841 One evening Snow White said she was sleepy and told the Seven Dwarfs she was going to bed early. After the protracted 'Goodnights', she retired to her room, whereupon all seven dwarfs dashed outside and stood on each other's shoulders so that one of them could see through the window into Snow White's bedroom. It was Happy's turn to be on top and to relay news to the other dwarfs below.

'She's taking off her blouse,' said Happy. And each of the dwarfs told the one below, 'She's taking off her blouse.'

Next Happy said: 'She's taking off her skirt.' And the others went, 'She's taking off her skirt . . . She's taking off her skirt,' all the way down to Bashful at the bottom.

Then Happy said: 'She's taking off her bra.' The news was passed down the chain: 'She's taking off her bra . . . She's taking off her bra.'

Then Happy gasped: 'She's taking off her panties. Oh, someone's coming.' The other dwarfs said: 'Me too . . . Me too . . . Me too . . . Me too . . . Me too . . . Me too.'

842 Little Red Riding Hood was getting ready to visit her grandmother in the forest. But her mother warned: 'You'd better not go out tonight, Little Red Riding Hood, because the Big Bad Wolf's out and you know what he'll do: he'll lift up your little red dress, pull down your little red panties, and fuck your little red socks off.'

However Little Red Riding Hood pulled out a shotgun and said: 'Don't worry, Mother, I've got it covered.'

Walking through the forest, Little Red Riding Hood came across the Three Little Pigs. One of them ran out of the brick house and said: 'You shouldn't be out tonight, Little Red Riding Hood, because the Big Bad Wolf's out and you know what he'll do if he catches you: he'll lift up your little red dress, pull down your little red panties, and fuck your little red socks off.'

'Don't worry, boys,' said Little Red Riding Hood. 'Got it covered.'

Little Red Riding Hood continued on her way and further into the forest she met the Big Bad Wolf. He said: 'You shouldn't have come out tonight, Little Red Riding Hood, because you know what I'm going to do: I'm going to lift up your little red dress, pull down your little red panties, and fuck your little red socks off.'

At this, Little Red Riding Hood lifted up her little red dress, pulled down her little red panties, lay down on her back with her legs apart, pointed the shotgun at the wolf and said: 'No! You're going to eat me like the book says . . .'

843 Once upon a time in a land far away, a beautiful, independent, self-assured princess happened upon a frog as she sat contemplating ecological issues on the banks of an unpolluted pond in a verdant meadow near her castle.

The frog hopped onto the princess's lap and said: 'Elegant lady, I was once a handsome prince until an evil witch cast a spell upon me. One kiss from you, however, and I will turn back into the dapper young prince that I am, and then, my sweet, we can marry and set up housekeeping with my mother in your castle where you can prepare my meals, clean my clothes, bear my children, and feel forever grateful doing so.'

That night, as the princess dined sumptuously on a repast of lightly sautéed frogs' legs seasoned in a white wine and cream sauce, she smiled to herself: 'I don't fucking think so.'

844 Little Red Riding Hood was walking through the woods when she saw the wolf hiding behind a tree. So she crept up behind him, tapped him on the shoulder and said teasingly: 'My, what big eyes you have, Mr Wolf!'

The wolf immediately ran off and hid behind another tree. Little Red Riding Hood followed him and tapped him on the shoulder again. 'My, what a big nose you have, Mr Wolf!' she said mockingly.

The wolf let out a yelp and ran off to hide behind another tree. But Little Red Riding Hood sneaked up on him again, tapped him on the shoulder and said: 'My, what big teeth you have, Mr Wolf!'

The wolf turned on her and snarled: 'Do you mind? I'm trying to have a crap!'

FAMILIES

845 A weedy little guy got into an argument with a big, burly bouncer outside a nightclub. The little guy was pushing his luck to the point that it looked as though they were going to come to blows.

'You've got a lot of nerve for such a shrimp!' snarled the bouncer.

'Listen, you fat jerk,' barked the little guy, 'I'm not scared of anybody, or anything! I come from a long line of jumpers. My great-grandfather jumped out of a balloon with no parachute. My grandfather jumped out of a biplane without a 'chute. My mother and father both jumped from a jet. My brother and sister jumped from planes. And tomorrow, I'm gonna jump from a rocket.'

'You're crazy, you little twerp,' said the bouncer. 'You could get killed!'
'So what? I have no family!'

846 A small boy ran down the street in search of a cop. Eventually finding one, he begged: 'Please come back to the bar with me. My dad is in a fight!'

The officer accompanied him back to the bar where he found three men involved in a violent fistfight. 'OK, son,' said the cop, 'which one is your father?'

'I don't know,' said the boy. 'That's what they're fighting about!'

847 A modern mother was explaining to her little girl about pictures in the family photo album. 'This is the geneticist with your surrogate mother, and here's your sperm donor and your father's clone. And this is me holding you when you were just a frozen embryo.'

'Mommy,' asked the little girl, 'who is that lady with the worried look on her face?'

'Oh, that's your Aunt Erica. She's the family genealogist.'

848 What's the ideal weight for a mother-in-law? – About 2.3lb, including the urn.

849 A newlywed farmer and his wife were visited by her mother who immediately demanded an inspection of the place to make sure that it met with her approval. While they were walking through the barn, the farmer's mule suddenly reared up and kicked the mother-in-law in the head, killing her instantly.

At the funeral a few days later, the farmer stood near the casket and greeted the mourners as they filed by. The pastor noticed that whenever a woman whispered something to the farmer, he would nod his head 'yes' and say something. But whenever a man whispered something to the farmer, he would shake his head 'no' and mumble a reply.

Curious, the pastor later asked the farmer what that was all about. The farmer explained: 'The women would say, "What a terrible tragedy", and I would nod my head and say, "Yes, it was." The men would ask, "You wanna sell that mule?" and I would shake my head and say, "Can't. It's all booked up for a year." '

850 What's the difference between in-laws and outlaws? – Outlaws are wanted.

851 Phil was sitting in the bar looking dejected. His friend Mike asked him: 'What's wrong?'

'It's my mother-in-law,' replied Phil. 'I have a real problem with her.'

'Cheer up,' said Mike. 'Everyone has problems with their mother-in-law.'

'Yeah, but I got mine pregnant.'

FANTASIES

852 A guy had been working for years in a pickle factory and had long harboured a secret fantasy about putting his penis in a pickle slicer. The urge became so great that he even went to therapy, but after a dozen sessions, the therapist admitted defeat and said: 'OK, if you really want to put your penis in a pickle slicer, go ahead, do it. That's the only way you're going to get this fantasy out of your system.'

So the guy said that he was going to do it.

The next day he came home early from work. His wife was puzzled. He explained for the first time that he'd had this yearning desire to put his penis in a pickle slicer and that he'd finally done it but had been fired as a result.

His wife gasped in horror, and quickly pulled down his pants and briefs, only to see his penis perfectly intact.

'I don't understand,' she said. 'What happened to the pickle slicer?'

He replied: 'I think she got fired too.'

853 Why do men like women in leather? – Because they smell like new cars.

854 A couple that had been married for thirty-five years had just celebrated their sixtieth birthdays. To mark the occasion, a fairy appeared and granted them a wish.

The wife said: 'I'd like to spend six months in a hot country.'

And POOF! She was given two tickets to Australia.

Then it was the husband's turn. Somewhat hesitantly, he said: 'I'd like to have a woman thirty years younger than me.'

And POOF! He was ninety.

855 Two young women were chatting over lunch. One confided: 'My last boyfriend used to fantasize about making love to two girls at once.'

'Really?' said her friend. 'What did you tell him?'

'I said, "If you can't satisfy one woman, why would you want to piss off another one?"'

856 Jack was walking along the road when he spotted a ladder leading up to the clouds. Being curious, he began climbing it.

On the first cloud he found an ugly, naked woman who said: 'Fuck me now or climb the ladder to success.'

This was no contest, so Jack climbed up to the next cloud where a fairly pretty, naked woman was waiting. 'Take me now,' she said, 'or climb the ladder to success.'

Jack decided to carry on climbing and on the next cloud he met a very attractive, naked woman. 'Have sex with me,' she purred, 'or climb the ladder to success.'

Jack was sorely tempted, but he reasoned: 'These women have been getting better and better, so the next one should be absolutely gorgeous.'

Thus Jack climbed onwards and upwards to the next cloud and the end of the ladder. But waiting there, to his horror, was a fat, ugly man.

'Who the hell are you?' asked Jack.

'Hi, I'm Cess!'

857 *Husband*: I fancy kinky sex. How about I come in your ear?

Wife: No, I might go deaf.

Husband: I've been coming in your mouth for twenty years, and you're still bloody talking!

858 Stumbling across a magic lamp, a man was granted one wish by the genie. Embarrassed about his wish, he whispered it in the genie's ear. The genie looked surprised but shrugged his shoulders and said: 'Very well, if that's what you definitely want. Your wish will be granted at midnight.'

As the clock struck twelve that night, the man heard a knock at the door. He opened it to find two slaughterhouse men standing outside holding a rope. 'Right,' said one. 'Are you the guy who wants to be hung like a donkey?'

FARMERS

859 A farmer gave his son a duck for his sixteenth birthday and said: 'Go into town and see what you can get with this.'

The boy went off in search of the best deal he could find and soon ran into a hooker who offered: 'I'll have sex with you if you give me the duck.' He agreed, and afterwards she was so impressed by the boy's virility that she said: 'If you do it again, I'll give you the duck back.'

He went along with her idea and, since he had now got the duck back, he carried on through town in search of a good trade. But then as he walked down the main street, the duck suddenly flew out of his arms and into an incoming truck. The driver was so distraught at having killed the duck that he gave the boy a dollar.

When the boy arrived home, his dad asked him what he had received for the duck. The boy said: 'Well, I got a fuck for a duck, a duck for a fuck, and a buck for a fucked-up duck.'

860 A farmer was giving his wife last-minute instructions before going into town on business. 'That fellow will be along this afternoon to impregnate one of the cows,' he said. 'I've hung a nail by the correct stall so you'll know which one I want him to impregnate.'

Satisfied that his wife understood, the farmer left for town.

That afternoon, the inseminator arrived, and the wife, who knew next to nothing about farming, dutifully led him out to the barn and directly to the stall with the nail.

'This is the cow right here,' she said.

'What's the nail for?' asked the inseminator.

She shrugged and replied: 'I guess it's to hang up your pants.'

861 A farmer lived with a tame bear, but one day the bear had misbehaved, so the farmer put him in the barn. That evening, a travelling businessman knocked on the door, saying that his car had become trapped by the rising river. The farmer allowed him to stay the night in the barn, but pointed that there was no lighting in there. 'And don't worry about the bear,' said the farmer. 'He's tame.'

Half an hour later, another businessman knocked on the door, saying that he, too, had become stranded in the floodwater. The farmer told him he could stay in the barn for the night, and mentioned the presence of the other salesman and the tame bear, as well as the absence of lighting.

An hour later, a New York broad in a tight skirt knocked on the door, desperate for somewhere to stay overnight. The farmer said she could stay in the barn and told her about the two businessmen. 'I don't mind sharing with two guys,' she said. 'It might be kinda fun!' And she headed straight for the barn before the farmer had a chance to mention either the lighting or the bear.

Two hours later, the woman staggered into the farmhouse, her clothes ripped and torn.

'What happened to you?' asked the farmer.

The woman replied: 'The first guy gave me $40, the second guy gave me $50, but the cheap bastard in the fur coat never even said thanks!'

862 A farmer had a French farmhand working with him to help castrate his sheep. As the farmer castrated the sheep, the French farmhand took the parts and was about to throw them in the trashcan when the farmer said: 'Don't throw them away. My wife fries them for supper. We call them sheep fries.'

At the end of a hard day, the farmhand asked the farmer's wife what was for supper.

'Sheep fries,' she replied.

He wasn't too keen on the idea but, having tasted frogs' legs in his native France, he was willing to experiment. So he gave them a try and, to his surprise, he found them quite tasty.

For the next two nights, he had sheep fries for supper but then on the fourth night, he was nowhere to be seen. The farmer asked his wife where the farmhand had gone.

'It's odd,' she said. 'When he came in and asked what was for supper, I told him French fries, and he ran like hell!'

863 A hitch-hiker was passing through a small country town when he decided to rest for the night. A local farmer was willing to put him up overnight, but on condition that the guest kept away from his teenage daughter. The hitch-hiker agreed but, just to make sure there was no hanky-panky, the farmer secretly placed three fresh eggs above the daughter's bedroom door. Any attempt to open the door in the course of the night would produce a telltale sign of smashed eggs.

Despite the warning, the hitch-hiker couldn't resist the beautiful daughter, and sneaked into her room for sex. In doing so, he broke all the eggs. Consequently he and the girl spent the rest of the night patiently gluing the shells back together and putting them back on top of the bedroom door in the hope that her father wouldn't notice that they had been smashed.

The next morning the farmer checked the eggs and was relieved to see that they were still in place. As a reward for the guest's restraint, he decided to cook him breakfast with the eggs he had used. The farmer cracked open the first egg . . . but there was nothing inside. And it was the same story with the other two.

The farmer thought to himself: 'I'm no fool!' And with that he stormed outside onto the porch.

'Right!' he yelled. 'I wanna know the truth! Which of you roosters is wearing a condom?'

864 Three hookers were comparing notes about their customers from the night before.

'I entertained a cowboy last night,' said the first.

'How did you know he was a cowboy?' asked the others.

'Well, he wore a cowboy hat, cowboy boots, and kept both the hat and the boots on all the time we were together.'

'Sounds like a cowboy, all right,' agreed the others.

'I entertained a lawyer,' announced the second. 'I could tell because he wore a three-piece suit and packed a briefcase. He wore the vest of the suit and hung on to the briefcase all the time.'

The others agreed he sounded like a lawyer.

'I had a farmer for a client,' said the third.

'How do you know he was a farmer?' asked the others.

'First he complained it was too dry, then he whined that it was too wet, then he asked if he could pay me in the fall.'

865 A salesman was talking to a farmer when he glanced over and noticed a rooster wearing pants, a shirt and suspenders. 'What's all that about?' he asked.

The farmer said: 'We had a fire in the chicken coop and all his feathers got singed off, so the wife made him some clothes to keep him warm. There ain't nothin' funnier than watching him try to hold down a hen with one foot and get his pants down with the other!'

866 Finishing the day's harvesting early, a farmer became suspicious when he noticed the curtains drawn in his wife's bedroom. Grabbing his shotgun, he crept up the stairs and then threw the bedroom door open to find his wife in bed with his neighbour.

'I'm gonna blow your balls off!' yelled the farmer.

The neighbour jumped out of bed stark naked and pleaded: 'Don't shoot me! Give me a chance!'

'OK,' said the farmer, taking aim with the shotgun, 'I'll give you a chance: now swing 'em!'

867 A female reporter was interviewing a farmer about Mad Cow Disease. 'Mr Brown,' she began. 'Do you know the causes of this terrible disease?'

'Sure,' said the farmer. 'Do you know that the bulls only screw the cows once a year . . . ?'

'That's interesting, but what has this got to do with the origins of Mad Cow Disease?'

'. . . And do you know we milk the cows twice a day?'

'Mr Brown, what exactly is your point?'

'Well, lady, if I played with your tits twice a day but only screwed you once a year, wouldn't you go mad?'

868 A salesman stopped at an isolated farmhouse to ask for a room for the night. The farmer said there wasn't a vacancy but suggested: 'I could let you sleep with my daughter if you promise not to bother her.'

The salesman agreed, undressed in the dark, slipped into bed and felt the farmer's daughter at his side. The next morning he asked the farmer for his bill.

'It'll be just two dollars,' said the farmer, 'since you had to share the bed.'

'Your daughter was very cold in that bed,' said the salesman.

'Yes, I know,' said the farmer. 'We're going to bury her today.'

869 Did you hear about the farmer who couldn't keep his hands off his young wife? — So he fired them.

870 A clergyman watched while a young farmer struggled to load a pile of manure back onto the cart after it had fallen off. Seeing him toiling in the hot son, the clergyman said: 'Why don't you rest a moment?'

'No,' mumbled the young man, 'my father wouldn't like it.'

'But surely everyone is entitled to a break.'

'My father wouldn't like it.'

'He must be a real slave driver,' said the clergyman. 'Tell me where he is, and I'll give him a piece of my mind!'

'He's under the pile of manure.'

871 A farmer went to market to buy a cow, but found that the only animal he could afford was a female zebra being sold off cheap by the local zoo. Thinking he might be able to use her around the farm, he bought the zebra and took her home. The zebra was eager to earn her keep and asked the other farm animals how they kept busy.

'I peck corn all day,' said the chicken.

'I'm afraid I can't do that,' said the zebra.

'I pull the plough all day,' said the horse.

'That looks too heavy for me,' said the zebra.

Eventually the zebra asked the bull what he did all day. 'It's difficult to explain,' said the bull, 'but if you take your pyjamas off, I'd be happy to show you.'

872 A man moved from New York to a farm in the country. In the first week of his new life, he realized he was out of chicken feed so he made the two-hour drive to the nearest store. However, the clerk refused to sell him any unless he could prove that he actually kept chickens.

'It's a health thing,' explained the clerk. 'We don't want people eating chicken feed or they could get sick and sue us. So I need proof that you have chickens.'

Exasperated, the guy drove all the way home, fetched one of his chickens and drove all the way back to the store. The clerk happily sold him some chicken feed.

The next day the guy ran out of dog food and drove to the store. Again the clerk refused to sell him any unless he could prove that he owned a dog. Furious, the guy drove all the way home, loaded his dog into the truck and drove all the way back to the store. Seeing the dog, the clerk happily sold him the dog food.

The following day the guy went to the store again. This time he was carrying a shoebox with a lid on it that had a hole in the top. He said to the clerk: 'Put your finger in this hole, take it out and smell it.'

'Urgh! That smells like shit!' said the clerk.

'Yup. I'd like to buy some toilet paper.'

873 A high-tech milking machine arrived when the farmer's wife was away for a month visiting her sick mother, so, in her absence, the farmer decided to try it out on himself. He inserted his penis into the equipment, turned on the switch and found that it provided him with as much pleasure as his wife. But when he had finished, he couldn't manage to take the instrument off.

He read through the manual and pressed every possible button. He discovered buttons that made the equipment contract, shake, or suck harder, but none that removed it.

Starting to panic, he called the supplier's customer help line. 'Hello,' he said, 'I just bought a milking machine from your company. It worked fantastic. But how do I take it off the cow's udder?'

The voice at the other end replied: 'Don't worry. The machine is programmed to release automatically after collecting about two litres of milk.'

874 A farmer had more than 200 hens, but no rooster. Desperate for chicks, he called on his neighbour to ask whether he could sell him a rooster.

'Sure,' said the neighbour, 'I've got this great rooster named Randy; he'll service every chicken you've got. No problem.'

Randy didn't come cheap but the farmer figured he would be worth it. So after concluding the deal, he took the bird home, set him down in the barnyard and gave him a pep talk.

'Now listen, Randy,' he began, 'I want you to pace yourself. You've got a lot of chickens to service here and you cost me a lot of money, and I need you to do a good job. So by all means have fun but take your time.'

Randy seemed to understand, so the farmer pointed towards the hen house. Randy immediately took off like a rooster possessed, nailing every hen in sight three, sometimes even four, times. The farmer could hardly believe his eyes. But Randy wasn't finished yet. He raced straight from the hen house to turn his amorous attention to a flock of geese down by the lake. After servicing every goose, he broke into the pigpen. Then he started on the cows. Within two hours of his arrival, Randy had jumped on every animal in the farm. The farmer was distraught, worried that his expensive rooster wouldn't even last the day.

Sure enough, the following morning the farmer woke to see Randy lying dead in the middle of the yard. Buzzards were circling overhead. Saddened, the farmer walked over to him and, shaking his head, said: 'Oh, Randy, I told you to pace yourself. I tried to get you to slow down. Now look what you've done to yourself.'

Randy opened one eye, nodded towards the sky and whispered: 'Sshh! They're getting closer . . .'

FARTING

875 An old woman was riding in an elevator in a smart New York City building when a beautiful young woman stepped in, smelling of expensive perfume. She turned to the old woman and said arrogantly: 'Romance by Ralph Lauren, $150 an ounce.'

On the next floor, another beautiful young woman got into the elevator, also smelling of expensive perfume. She, too, turned to the old woman and sniffed: 'Chanel No. 5, $200 an ounce.'

Three floors later, the old woman reached her destination. As she was about to leave the elevator, she looked at the two beautiful young things, bent over, farted and announced: 'Broccoli, 49 cents a pound.'

876 Two flies were sitting on a piece of shit when one farted. The other said: 'Please, I'm trying to eat here.'

877 An old man and his wife were lying in bed. After a few minutes, he let out an almighty fart and shouted, 'Seven points.'

His wife rolled over and said: 'What in the world was that?'

The old man said: 'Touchdown, I'm ahead 7–0.'

A few minutes later, the wife, entering into the spirit, let one go and declared: 'Touchdown, tie score.'

But ten minutes later, the old man farted again and announced: 'Touchdown, I'm ahead 14–7.'

Not to be outdone, the wife quickly farted again and said: 'Touchdown, tie score.'

Desperate to regain the lead, the old man strained really hard, but he just couldn't force out a fart. He gave it everything he had and in the end he strained so hard that he pooped in the bed.

The wife asked: 'Now what in the world was that?'

The old man replied: 'Half-time, switch sides.'

878 What did the maxi pad say to the fart? – You are the wind beneath my wings.

879 A woman in a restaurant farted loudly just as the waiter was approaching her table. Knowing that everyone in the place must have heard the noise, she desperately tried to save face by telling the waiter. 'Stop that!'

The waiter said: 'Sure, lady. Which way is it headed?'

880 Two old ladies were comparing the merits of stockings and tights.

'I prefer stockings,' said one.

'Me too,' said the other. 'I think they're more refined and elegant, don't you?'

'Definitely. Besides, if I fart wearing tights I usually blow my slippers off!'

881 What happens when you eat baked beans and peanut butter? – You get a fart that sticks to the roof of your ass.

882 A tramp walked into a bar and ordered a drink. The bartender said: 'I'll have to see your money first.'

'I'm broke,' admitted the tramp, 'but if you give me a little bottle of whiskey, I'll get up on that stage and fart "Dixie".'

Thinking that this had to be worth seeing, the bartender agreed. The tramp drank the bottle of whiskey, staggered on stage, and the audience applauded. Next he dropped his pants, and the audience cheered wildly. But then he crapped all over the stage, and the audience walked out in disgust.

The bartender yelled: 'You said you were gonna fart "Dixie", not crap all over my stage!'

'Hey,' said the tramp. 'Even Frank Sinatra had to clear his throat before he sang!'

883 A woman went into an exclusive store to buy a rug but as she bent down to inspect it, she farted loudly. 'I'm terribly sorry,' she told the salesman. 'It just slipped out.'

The salesman said: 'Lady, if you farted just touching it, you're gonna crap your pants when you see what the price is!'

884 Alone in an elevator, an Avon lady could no longer hold in a fart. Immediately after letting it go, she reached into her bag and sprayed the air with deodorizer.

Two floors later, a man got in and began to sniff.

'Can you smell something?' asked the Avon lady.

'Yes, I can,' said the man.

'What does it smell like?'

'Mmm,' he mused. 'It smells like someone crapped in a pine tree.'

People Who Fart:

885 ● The vain person – one who loves the smell of his own farts.

886 ● The amiable person – one who loves the smell of other people's farts.

887 ● The proud person – one who thinks his farts are exceptionally fine.

888 ● The shy person – one who releases silent farts, then blushes.

889 • The imprudent person – one who boldly farts out loud, and then laughs.

890 • The unfortunate person – one who tries hard to fart, but shits instead.

891 • The nervous person – one who stops in the middle of a fart.

892 • The honest person – one who admits he farted, but offers a plausible medical reason.

893 • The dishonest person – one who farts but blames the dog.

894 • The thrifty person – one who always holds several farts in reserve.

895 • The unsociable person – one who excuses himself and farts in private.

896 • The strategic person – one who conceals his farts with loud coughing.

897 • The sadistic person – one who farts in bed and then fluffs the covers over his bedmate.

898 • The intelligent person – one who can determine, from the smell of his neighbour's fart, exactly what he has eaten recently.

FISHING

899 Three guys – a German, an Englishman and a Nigerian – went fishing at a lake. The German took out his dick, dipped it in the water, waited a few moments and told the others: 'I can feel the temperature of the water. It's 18 degrees Celsius.'

His two companions were amazed. 'Let me try,' said the Englishman. So he put his organ in the water, waited and announced: 'To be more precise, the temperature is 18.4 degrees Celsius.'

Then the Nigerian man said: 'Let me have a try.' So he took his dick, dipped it in the lake, waited a moment and said: 'I've no idea about the temperature, but the water is 2ft 7in deep!'

900 A Boston couple went away on vacation to Canada. The husband loved to fish, but the wife was happy reading. One morning the husband set off early to finish and when he returned to their cabin, he decided to take a nap. While he slept, the wife took the boat out to enjoy the beautiful scenery. Unfamiliar with the geography of the lake, she rowed out to the middle, dropped anchor and began reading her book.

A few minutes later, another boat pulled alongside. It was the game warden.

'Do you mind if I ask what you're doing, ma'am?'

'Reading my book,' she replied.

'Well, I'm afraid this is a restricted fishing area, and you're not allowed to be here.'

'But I'm not fishing,' she protested.

He glanced at the boat. 'But you have all this equipment. I'm sorry, but I'm gonna have to report you.'

'If you do,' she argued, 'I'll charge you with rape.'

'But I didn't touch you!'

'No, but you have all the equipment!'

901 A man and his grandson went fishing. After an hour on the riverbank, the man lit a cigarette.

'Grandpa,' asked the boy, 'can I try some of your cigarette?'

'Can you touch your asshole with your penis?' asked the grandfather.

'No,' said the boy.

'Then you're not old enough for cigarettes.'

Half an hour later, the grandfather opened a can of beer.

'Grandpa, can I try some of your beer?'

The old man looked at him. 'Can you touch your asshole with your penis?'

'No,' said the boy solemnly.

'Then you're not old enough for beer.'

Ten minutes later, the boy took some cookies from his lunchbox.

'They look good,' said his grandfather. 'Can I have one of your cookies?'

The boy said: 'Can you touch your asshole with your penis?'

'I sure can,' replied the old man.

'Then go fuck yourself,' said the boy. 'These are *my* cookies!'

FLIGHT ATTENDANTS

902 One winter, two little fleas headed for the sunny beaches of California to escape the cold. The first flea arrived and started rubbing suntan lotion on his little flea arms and legs. Just then the second flea turned up, shivering and shaking.

'What happened to you?' inquired the first flea.

The second flea said: 'I just rode out here on a biker's moustache, and I'm so very cold.'

The first flea shook his head. 'Don't you know the special trick to getting here? First you go to the airport, go straight to the ladies' toilet, wait for a pretty young stewardess to come along, and when she sits down you climb right up in there where it's nice and warm.'

The second flea thought it sounded a great idea and promised to try it.

The following winter it was time for the two fleas to head for the sun once more. The first flea arrived in California and started putting on his suntan cream. Just then the second flea showed up, shivering and shaking and complaining about how cold he was.

'Didn't you learn anything I taught you about getting here nice and warm?' asked the first flea.

The second flea replied: 'I did just as you said. I waited in the ladies' toilet at the airport and this pretty stewardess came in and sat down, and I climbed right up in there and it was so very warm. Next thing I knew we stopped at a bar and I fell asleep. All of a sudden I woke and there I was, right back on that biker's moustache!'

903 There was a long queue for the toilet on a flight from Washington to Boston. But everything was perfectly orderly until a self-important businessman tried to push in and created a scene that required the intervention of one of the female flight attendants.

'I'm sorry, sir,' she explained politely, 'but the queue starts back there.'

'I haven't got time to get in line,' he blustered. 'I've got important business to conduct on my laptop. I'll be wasting twenty precious minutes just standing here.'

The flight attendant stood firm. 'I cannot allow you to barge your way in, sir,' she said. 'You'll have to get in line like everyone else.'

The businessman lost his temper and yelled: 'Fuck you!'

Still smiling sweetly, the flight attendant responded: 'I'm sorry, sir, but you'll have to stand in line for that, too!'

904 Three men were trying to guess the professions of their respective dates of the previous evening, based on their bedroom performance and conversation.

The first reckoned that his date was a nurse because she said: 'Lie back and relax. This won't hurt a bit.'

The second concluded that his must have been a schoolteacher because she had said: 'Do it over and over until you get it right.'

The third figured that his date must have been a flight attendant because all she had said was: 'Put this over your mouth and nose and continue to breathe normally.'

905   A plane was coming in to land at Kennedy Airport. The pilot came over the intercom and announced: 'We're now on our final descent into Kennedy Airport. On behalf of myself and the cabin crew, I hope you have had a pleasant flight and that you enjoy your stay in New York.' However at the end of his message, he forgot to switch off the intercom, so all of the passengers and crew heard his private conversation with his co-pilot.

'What are you going to do in New York?' asked the co-pilot.

'Well,' said the pilot, 'first I'm gonna check into the hotel and take a crap. Then I'm gonna take that new stewardess out for supper – you know, the one with the big boobs. I'm gonna wine her and dine her, take her back to my room, then 69 her.'

By now, everyone on the plane was staring at the new stewardess. She was so embarrassed that she rushed up the aisle towards the cockpit, but half-way down, she tripped over an old lady's bag and fell over. As the stewardess picked herself up, the old lady whispered: 'No need to rush, dear, he's gotta take a crap first!'

906   A plane was flying over the ocean when an armed hijacker suddenly burst into the cockpit. Holding a gun to the pilot's head, he snarled: 'Take this plane to Iraq or I'm gonna spill your brains all over the place!'

The pilot calmly pushed the gun aside and said: 'Look buddy, if you shoot me this plane will crash right into the sea and you'll die along with the rest of us.'

The hijacker thought about this for a moment, and then pointed the gun at the co-pilot's head. 'Take this plane to Iraq or I'm gonna spill your brains all over the place!'

The co-pilot calmly pushed the gun aside and said: 'Listen, my friend, the pilot's got a bad heart, and he could keel over at the sight of me being killed. So if you shoot me, the plane will still crash right into the sea and you'll die along with the rest of us.'

The hijacker thought for a moment and then pointed the gun at the head of the navigator. 'Take this plane to Iraq or I'm gonna spill your brains all over the place!'

The navigator calmly pushed the gun aside and said: 'I wouldn't do that if I were you. These two guys have absolutely no sense of direction. Without me, they'll never find their way to Iraq. They won't even be able to keep the plane airborne. If you shoot me, this plane will crash right into the sea and you'll die along with the rest of us.'

The hijacker pondered for a moment, then pointed the gun at the head of the flight attendant. She responded by whispering in his ear whereupon the hijacker turned bright red, dropped his gun, and fled the cockpit in panic.

'What did you say to scare him?' asked the pilot.

The flight attendant replied: 'I told him if he killed me, he'd be the one who'd have to give you guys your blow jobs.'

FLORIDA

907 A man from Helena, Montana, decided to write a book about churches around the United States. He started by flying to Sacramento, and then planned to work his way east from there.

At a big church in Sacramento, he spotted a golden telephone on a wall with a sign that read: 'Calls $5,000 a minute.' Intrigued, he asked the pastor for an explanation. The pastor revealed that the golden phone was a direct line to Heaven, and that for $5,000 the caller could talk directly to God.

As he continued on his travels – via Phoenix, Denver, St Louis, Chicago, Detroit, New York and Washington – the man found more phones with the same sign. From each pastor, he received the same explanation.

Finally he arrived in the south-east of the United States, and, upon entering a church, he found yet another golden telephone, but this time the sign read: 'Calls 35 cents a minute.'

He sought out the pastor and said: 'Reverend, I have been in cities all across the country and in each church I have found this very same golden telephone. Each time I have been told that it is a direct line to Heaven and that the caller can talk to God. However in the other churches, the cost was $5,000 a minute. Yet your sign says that it's just 35 cents a minute to talk to God. Why is that?'

Smiling benignly, the pastor replied: 'My son, you're in Florida now. It's a local call.'

908 A Miami Beach women's group arranged a trip to a dairy farm out in the country. For most of them, having lived their entire life in the city, it was a new experience. On arrival, they were greeted by the farmer who gave them a tour of the premises before asking if there were any questions.

One blue-rinsed matron by the name of Sylvia raised her hand and asked: 'Can you tell me why the cow in this stable doesn't have any horns?'

The farmer cocked his head for a moment, before answering: 'Well, ma'am, cattle can do a heck of a lot of damage with horns. Sometimes we keep 'em trimmed with a hacksaw. Other times we can fix up the young 'uns by puttin' a couple of drops of acid where their horns would grow, and that stops 'em cold. And there are some breeds of cattle that never grow horns. But the reason this cow don't have no horns, ma'am, is 'cause it's a horse.'

FOOD

909 At work a guy eagerly opened his packed lunch that his wife had prepared for him that morning. But he took one bite and spat it out.

He immediately phoned his wife: 'What was in that sandwich you gave me?'

'Why?'

'Because it was disgusting. What was in it?'

'Crab paste.'

'Well, I've never tasted anything that awful in my life. Where did you get it from?'

'The pharmacy.'

910 What's the difference between bogeys and Brussels sprouts? – Kids will eat bogeys.

911 Two Korean tourists arrived in New York and were amazed to see a street vendor selling hot dogs. 'I never knew Americans also ate dogs,' said one. 'Let's see what they're like.'

So they ordered hot dogs and sat down on a bench to eat them. The first Korean opened his bun and looked inside. 'Yuk!' he exclaimed to his friend. 'I'm not eating mine! What part of the dog did you get?'

912 What can you make from baked beans and an onion? – Tear gas.

913 Realizing to her horror that she hadn't got anything in for her husband's dinner, an elderly woman raided the pantry in search of something suitable. But all she could find was a tin of cat food, an onion and a potato. So she mixed the onion in with the cat food, heated it up, served it with chips, and watched her unsuspecting husband devour it. Afterwards, he said it was the best thing she had cooked him in ages and he wanted to know when he was going to have it again. So for the rest of the week, she gave him cat food and chips for dinner.

When she told a friend about her husband's unusual tastes, the friend warned: 'You can't keep serving him cat food. You'll kill him.'

Sure enough, the following week the husband died.

'I told you all that cat food would kill him,' said the friend.

'It was nothing to do with the cat food,' said the wife. 'He died when he fell off the fence.'

'What was he doing up there?' asked the friend.

'Trying to lick his ass.'

914 A husband came home with half a gallon of ice cream and asked his wife if she wanted some.

'How hard is it?' she asked.

'About as hard as my dick,' he replied.

'Pour me some.'

915 Once upon a time there were three guys who didn't have any money for food. They had managed to steal food for a couple of days, but still needed more. Eventually one of them said: 'Wouldn't it be better to ask for food instead of stealing it?'

They all agreed that was a better idea, so later that day they went up to a house and rang the doorbell. A wizened old lady answered. They asked her for food, but she said she would only give them some if they slept with her. The first guy refused and so did the second, but the third guy was so hungry that he reluctantly agreed.

She led him into the barn and told him to get started. Saying that he felt nervous about her looking at him, he asked if he could blindfold her. She was that desperate for sex that she agreed. Once blindfolded, he took a piece of corn and began fucking her with that. She had gone without sex for so long that she was none the wiser. When he had exhausted that piece of corn, he threw it out the barn window, and then took another piece of corn and began fucking her with that. He then threw that piece of corn out the barn window before finishing her off with a third piece. Afterwards, she fed him as promised, and then he left.

When he met up with the other two guys, they said they couldn't believe he had done that for food, especially as they had found free corn around the side of the barn.

916 A wife asked her husband to buy some organic vegetables. He went to the supermarket, but couldn't find any on the shelves. So he asked an elderly male employee: 'These vegetables are for my wife. Have they been sprayed with poisonous chemicals?'

The employee said: 'No. You'll have to do that yourself.'

917 Did you hear about the guy who ordered a thin and crispy Supreme from his local pizza shop? – They sent him Diana Ross.

918 A teenage boy met an old man who was carrying a bag. 'What's in the bag?' asked the boy.

'Magic apples,' said the old man.

'Prove it,' said the youngster.

'Well, beside apples, what are your favourite two fruits?'

'Watermelon and peaches,' said the boy.

The old man handed him an apple and told him to taste it. The boy took a bite and said it tasted like watermelon.

'OK, turn it over,' said the old man.

The boy did, and took another bite. This tasted like peach. Nevertheless the boy remained unconvinced that the apples were magic, so the old man told him to name something else that he liked to eat.

'I like to eat pussy,' grinned the boy mischievously.

The old man handed him another apple and told him to try it. The boy took a big bite, but spat it out immediately. Wiping his mouth, he exclaimed: 'That tasted like shit!'

The old man smiled and said: 'Turn it over.'

FOREPLAY

919 A guy was on his first date with the easiest girl in town. After they parked the car, she wasted no time in climbing on to the back seat and encouraging him to put his hand inside her panties. The petting grew heavier and she began moaning with pleasure until she suddenly cried: 'Ow! That ring is hurting me!'

He said: 'That's no ring – that's my watch!'

920 As things started hotting up, a girl said to her boyfriend: 'Slow down, baby. Foreplay is an art.'

'Well, you'd better get your canvas ready soon,' he panted, 'because I'm about to spill my paint!'

921 What's an Australian's idea of foreplay? – 'Brace yourself, Sheila.'

922 What's a redneck's idea of foreplay? – 'Are you awake yet, sis?'

923 A guy picked up an attractive girl sitting alone at a bar and to his delight, she asked him back to her place. They were both about to get undressed in her bedroom when he decided he fancied a cigarette. Unable to find his lighter, he asked her if she had one, and she suggested there might be a box of matches in the top drawer of the bedside table. Opening the drawer, he found the matches . . . sitting on top of a framed photo of another man. He immediately started to worry.

'Is this your husband?' he inquired nervously.

'No, silly,' she replied, nibbling his ear.

'Your boyfriend then?'

'No, don't be silly,' she said, working her tongue into his mouth.

'Who is he then?'

Calmly the girl replied: 'That's me before the operation.'

924 Two flowers were wafting gently in the breeze. One said to the other: 'I love you, darling.'

The other said: 'I love you too.'

'I want you so much.'

'And I want you too.'

'I really want you now! Where are the fuck are those darned bees?'

THE FRENCH

925 Once upon a time in the Kingdom of Heaven, God went missing for six days. Eventually the Archangel Gabriel found him resting on the seventh day.

He said to God: 'Where have you been?'

God sighed a deep sigh of satisfaction and proudly pointed downwards through the clouds. 'Look, Gabriel. Look what I've made.'

Gabriel looked puzzled and asked: 'What is it?'

'It's a planet,' said God, 'and I've put life on it. I'm going to call it Earth, and it's going to be a great place of balance.'

'Balance?' queried Gabriel, still none the wiser.

God explained what he meant by pointing to different parts of Earth. 'For example,' he said, 'North America will be an area of great opportunity and wealth while South America is going to be poor. Over here, I've placed a continent of white people and over there is a continent of black people. This land will be extremely hot and arid while this one will be very cold and covered in ice.'

Impressed by God's work, Gabriel pointed to a small land mass and said: 'What's that one?'

'Ah,' said God. 'That's Britain, the most glorious place on Earth. There are beautiful lakes, rivers, streams and hills. The people from Britain are going to be modest, intelligent and humorous and they're going to travel the world. They'll be extremely sociable, hard-working and high-achieving and they will be known throughout the world as diplomats and carriers of peace.'

Gabriel gasped in wonder and admiration, but then proclaimed: 'What about balance, God? You said there would be balance!'

God replied wisely: 'Wait until you see the wankers I'm putting next to them in France . . .'

926 What do you call 100,000 Frenchmen with their hands up? – The French Army.

927 Why don't they have fireworks at Euro Disney? – Because every time they set them off, the French try to surrender.

928 How can you recognize a French veteran? – Sunburned armpits.

929 Why are there so many tree-lined boulevards in France? – Because Germans like to march in the shade.

930 What do you call a Frenchman advancing on Baghdad? – A salesman.

931 Why didn't France want to bomb Saddam Hussein? – He hates America, he loves mistresses, and he wears a beret. He is French.

932 Why did the Americans want France on their side in the war in Iraq? – To show the Iraqis how to surrender.

933 Why do the French call their fighter plane the Mirage? – Because it's never been seen in a combat zone.

934 How do you confuse a French soldier? – Give him a rifle and ask him to fire it.

935 George W. Bush and the French ambassador to the United Nations were debating the Iraq crisis. Through an interpreter, Bush said that he believed the conflict with Saddam Hussein could turn into a bloodbath.
    The French ambassador did not understand. Then an aide explained to Bush: 'There is no word for "bath" in French.'

936 Where is the best place to hide anything from a French woman? – Under the soap.

937 What do you call a Frenchman who wears sandals? – Philippe Philoppe.

938 A Frenchman walked into a bar with a toad on his head.
    'What the heck is that?' asked the bartender.
    'I don't know,' said the toad. 'It started as a wart on my ass and grew.'

GAMBLING

939 After an evening's drinking, Jake said to his girlfriend Julie just as she was about to go home: 'I'll bet you two dollars that I can screw you for twenty-five minutes without coming inside you.'
    'You're crazy,' said Julie. 'You never keep going that long. Here's two dollars that says you can't.'
    The four dollars were placed on the table, and they took off their clothes.

Jake then began screwing her passionately. A minute later, she cried: 'But you've come!'

Jake climbed off her, shrugged and said: 'So I lose . . .'

940 A guy was strolling down a city street when he came across an old lamp. He picked it up, rubbed it vigorously, and out popped a genie. The genie offered to grant him one wish, to which the guy replied: 'I've always wanted to be lucky.'

The genie granted his wish, and the guy strolled off, wondering how it would change his life. Less than fifty yards down the street, he noticed a $10 bill lying on the sidewalk. Not a bad start, he thought.

As he picked it up, he spotted a betting shop across the road. He wandered over, studied the racing pages and put the ten dollars on a horse called Genie's Wish. It romped in at 100–1.

Feeling on a roll, he headed for the roulette table at the casino and put the entire $1010 on number 7. His number came up. He was seriously rich.

To celebrate, he went to the local brothel. As he entered, he was showered with streamers and handed a glass of champagne by the Madame, who explained that he was their 1,000th customer and as such could have his way with any girl on their books for the entire evening absolutely free of charge.

The guy said that he had always wanted to have sex with an Indian girl, so he was ushered into a room where he was joined shortly afterwards by a beautiful Indian girl. After they had enjoyed fantastic sex, he turned to her and said: 'I cannot believe my luck, making love to such a fabulously attractive woman. I don't mean to offend you, but there is just one thing I don't like about Indian women: I don't like that red spot you all have on your forehead.'

The Indian girl looked him in the eye and replied: 'Sir, I am here to please you and to agree to your every desire. If you wish to see it gone, then please scratch off my caste mark.'

He proceeded to remove the mark with his fingernail. Suddenly he leaned back and began laughing. 'You're never going to believe this,' he said. 'I've just won a car!'

941 What is the only game in which the more you lose, the more you have to show for it? – Strip poker.

942 Having just begun a round of golf, a man was approached by a stranger who asked whether he could join him. Although the first man preferred to play alone, he thought he would make an exception on this occasion and accepted the offer. After a couple of holes, the second guy said: 'We seem pretty evenly matched. What do you say we play for five bucks a hole?'

Against his better judgement, the first man agreed to the bet, whereupon the stranger won the remaining sixteen holes and pocketed $80. As they walked off the 18th green, he confessed that he was really the professional at a neighbouring course and that he liked to pick on suckers.

The first man then revealed that he was the priest at the local church, at which the professional felt hugely embarrassed and offered to return all of his winnings.

The priest said: 'No, you won fair and square. I was foolish to bet with you. You keep your winnings.'

The pro said: 'Well, is there anything I can do to make it up to you?'

The priest said: 'You could come to Mass on Sunday and make a donation. Then, if you bring your mother and father by after Mass, I'll marry them for you.'

943 It was Little Johnny's first day at school, and his father warned his teacher that the boy was an avid gambler. He said that Johnny might win lunch money from the other children if he was not watched closely. The teacher was not unduly worried by this news and insisted that she was perfectly capable of monitoring Johnny's gambling urges.

Shortly after lunch on that first day, Johnny's father called the teacher to ask how things were going.

'Everything is just fine,' she said, 'and as a matter of fact, I think I may have cured Johnny of his gambling habit.'

'How have you managed that?' asked the father.

'Well,' explained the teacher, 'the little monkey absolutely insisted on betting me ten dollars that I had a mole on my rear. Finally I agreed to the bet and took him to the staff room so that I could show him that there was no mole. Now that he's lost the money, I don't think he'll be gambling again.'

'Damn!' said the father. 'He bet me fifty dollars this morning that he would see the teacher's ass before the day was over.'

944 A husband arrived home early from work to find his wife in the arms of another man. He yelled at the interloper: 'What right do you have to be making love to my wife?'

The lover replied: 'You may as well know that I am in love with Ethel and I would like to marry her. I understand you're a gambler? Why don't you be a sport and sit down and play a game of gin rummy with me? If I lose, I'll never see her again; if you lose, you must agree to divorce her. OK?'

'All right,' said the husband. 'But just to make it a little more interesting, why don't we play for a dollar a point?'

BILL GATES

945 Bill Gates died and went to heaven, where St Peter showed him to his new home – a beautiful fifteen-room house with swimming pool and tennis court. Bill was delighted with it, and thoroughly enjoyed his stay in heaven until one day he bumped into a fellow resident who was wearing a fine tailored suit.

Admiring the garment, Bill said: 'That's a nice suit. Where did you get it?'

'As a matter of fact,' the man replied, 'I was given fifty of these when I got here. They've really looked after me. I've got a thirty-room mansion set in a hundred acres, and it's got three pools, half a dozen tennis courts, a private golf course, health club and croquet lawn. They've also given me a fleet of Rolls-Royces.'

'What were you?' asked Bill. 'A Pope, or a doctor healing the sick?'

'Neither,' said the man. 'Actually I was the captain of the *Titanic*.'

Bill was so angry at hearing this that he immediately sought out St Peter to complain. 'How come you've given me a modest house, yet you've given expensive suits, new cars, and a splendid mansion to the captain of the *Titanic*? I invented the Windows operating system! Why does he deserve better?'

'Yes, but we use Windows,' replied St Peter, 'and the *Titanic* only crashed once.'

946 How did Bill Gates accumulate all his wealth? – By never spending more than three dollars on a haircut.

947 Tony Blair was invited for an audience with the Pope but found that it clashed with a meeting he had already arranged with Bill Gates.

Blair asked his private secretary: 'Which one do you think I should go to?'

'Definitely the Pope,' replied the secretary. 'He'll only expect you to kiss his hand.'

948 God summoned a meeting of George W. Bush, Tony Blair and Bill Gates. God was not happy. He told the three: 'I've given you all the tools needed to create a better world, but you have failed miserably. Consequently I'm going to end the world one month from today.'

Bush went straight on TV to relay the news to the American people. 'I have good news and bad news,' he said. 'The good news is that God definitely exists. The bad news is that the world will end in a month.'

Blair told a news conference: 'I have bad news and really bad news. The bad news is that God is terribly angry. The really bad news is that he's so angry he's going to destroy us all.'

Meanwhile Bill Gates called his workforce together and said: 'I have good news and great news. The good news is that God thinks I'm one of the three most powerful men in the world. The great news is we don't have to fix the bugs in the new Windows package.'

GAYS

949 On a visit to a tattoo artist, a gay guy spotted a picture of Evander Holyfield on the wall. 'He's my favourite boxer,' he told the artist. 'Could I have a tattoo of him on the left cheek of my ass?' Then on his way out, he spotted a picture of Mike Tyson. 'Ooh, can you put Iron Mike on the other cheek? I adore him.'

When he got home, he was keen to show his new tattoos to his boyfriend. But the boyfriend took one look and gasped: 'I think our relationship is over! There's no way I'm getting in the ring with those two!'

950 A gay guy fell hopelessly in love with his young male doctor. Looking for any excuse to meet him, he went to the doctor's office and said he had an obstruction. The doctor put his hand up the guy's ass but couldn't find anything. However when he saw that the patient had an erection, he ordered him out of the office.

The next day the gay guy called the doctor to report another obstruction. The doctor didn't believe him but when the patient insisted that he was in great pain, the doctor relented and agreed to examine him. So the doctor stuck his hand up the guy's ass.

'Good God!' exclaimed the doctor. 'No wonder you're in pain! There are two dozen red roses shoved up your ass!'

The gay guy turned around excitedly and said: 'Read the card! Read the card!'

951 Two gay men decided they would like to have a baby, but they didn't want to adopt because they wanted the baby to be as close to their own as possible. So they both masturbated into a cup and had a doctor use their sperm to impregnate a female friend.

Nine months later the pair were looking adoringly at their baby in the hospital nursery. All the other babies were crying and screaming but theirs was a picture of contentment.

'Look,' said one of the men, 'our baby is the best behaved one in here.'

Hearing this, a passing nurse remarked: 'Now he's quiet, but wait till we take the pacifier out of his ass.'

952 A young gay guy came running downstairs in floods of tears because his boyfriend had just dropped him. Thinking sex was at the root of the split, his liberal mother proceeded to tell him all about the birds and the bees.

'No, mom!' he sobbed. 'It's got nothing to do with sex. I can fuck and suck with the best of them, but he says I can't cook!'

953 How can you tell if you're watching a gay Western? – All the good guys are hung.

954 How do you know you've walked into a gay church service? – Only half the congregation are kneeling.

955 How do you know if you're at a gay picnic? – The hot dogs all taste like shit.

956 Did you hear about the two gay guys who had an argument in the bar? – They went outside to exchange blows.

957 Did you hear about the gay guy who's using the patch? – He's down to four butts a day.

958 How can you tell if you're in a gay amusement park? – They issue gerbils at the tunnel of love.

959 Two construction workers were becoming increasingly frustrated playing golf behind two gay men. The problem was that the gay pair were so slow, agonizing over every shot and making sure that their stance looked just right. With the light beginning to fade, the workers feared that they might not finish their round, so they decided to hurry the gay pair along by playing up close to them. Unfortunately an over-hit shot struck one of the gays on the head, knocking him out cold.

The other gay panicked. 'Jonty! Jonty! Get up! Get up!' he shrieked. With his friend still lying there, he turned on the construction workers. 'You bad men!' he shouted. 'Look what you've done. We're going to sue you!'

The workers were hacked off by his hysteria and one of them yelled back menacingly: 'There's no way I'm gonna let you sue us. I'd just as soon suck your dick!'

'Jonty! Jonty!' the gay squealed. 'Get up! Hurry! They want to settle out of court!'

960 Did you hear about the two gay judges? – They tried each other.

961 Did you hear about the gay truckers? – They exchanged loads.

962 Did you hear about the gay bank robber? – He tied up the safe and blew the guard.

963 Two gay men were talking. One said: 'You know, my mother made me a homosexual.'

'Ooh,' said the other. 'If I bought enough wool, do you think she'd make me one as well?'

964 When a gay guy went to heaven, St Peter was waiting for him at the Pearly Gates. After reviewing his records, St Peter let him in and said, 'Follow me.'

As they walked through heaven, St Peter accidentally dropped his keys. He bent over to pick them up, but the sight proved irresistible to the gay guy who immediately shafted him feverishly.

St Peter was furious. 'If you do that again,' he warned. 'You'll go straight to hell.'

Continuing their journey, St Peter dropped his keys again and, despite the warning, the gay guy jumped on him as soon as he bent over to pick them up. St Peter was fuming, but decided to give him one last chance.

Nearing the end of their journey, St Peter clumsily dropped his keys for a third time, and bent over to pick them up. Having no self-control, the gay guy jumped on him again. This was the final straw, and St Peter sent him straight to hell.

A few weeks later, St Peter visited hell for a routine inspection, but this time something was amiss. Hell was freezing, there was no fire, no lava, and in a corner, he found the Devil lying shivering under a pile of blankets.

'Why is it so cold down here?' asked St Peter.

The Devil replied: 'Well, you just try bending down for firewood!'

965 Have you heard about the two poor gays who wanted to be buried together? – After they died, the mortician cremated them and put them in a fruit jar.

966 What are the rules of gay poker? – Queens are wild and straights don't count.

967 Did you hear about the new gay sitcom? – *Leave it, it's Beaver.*

968 A priest and a rabbi walked into a bar. After they had sat down with their drinks, it suddenly dawned on them that there were no women present. The priest said: 'I think we're in a gay bar.'

A few minutes later, a guy came over and tried to flirt with the priest. The priest was dumbfounded, and didn't know what to do. Then the rabbi leaned over and whispered something in the man's ear, after which the man nodded and walked off.

'Thank you,' said the relieved priest. 'What did you tell him?'

The rabbi replied: 'I just told him we're on our honeymoon.'

969 A gay guy walked into a delicatessen and asked the shopkeeper for a large knob of salami.

'Would you like it sliced, sir?' asked the shopkeeper politely.

'What do you think I am? A slot machine?'

970 Two gay men were discussing AIDS, and concluded that the only way to be safe was to abstain from sex. But both found abstention easier said than done. When the pair met up again a few weeks later, they compared notes.

'How's it going?' asked one.

'Wonderful!' said the other. 'I've made this fantastic discovery that's changed my life. Come with me into the men's room and I'll show you.'

So they went into a cubicle, and the second guy unzipped his fly to reveal his penis, on the end of which was a nicotine patch.

'What on earth is that?' asked the first guy.

'It's a nicotine patch, like smokers use.'

'Does it work?'

'Sure does. I haven't had a butt in five days.'

971 What happened when three gay guys attacked a woman? – Two held her down while the third did her hair.

972 Two gay men – Alan and Tony – went to a fairground. Tony said he wanted to go on the Ferris wheel but Alan had a sore bum so he declined. The wheel went round and round, but then suddenly the cart Tony was sitting in crashed to the ground, landing near Alan's feet.

'Are you hurt?' asked Alan, rushing over to his friend.

'Of course I am,' snapped Tony. 'Three times I went round and you didn't wave once.'

973 How many gay men does it take to put in a light bulb? – Only one . . . but it takes an entire Emergency Room to get it out.

974 What's the definition of tender love? – Two gays with haemorrhoids.

975 What do you call haemorrhoids on a gay guy? – Speed bumps.

976 Why was the gay guy fired from the sperm bank? – He was caught drinking on the job.

977 Why did the gay guy put his ass in the fridge? – So that his boyfriend would have something cool to slip into when he came home.

978 A truck driver pulled over to the side of the highway and picked up two homosexuals who were hitchhiking. A few miles down the road, one of the gay guys said: 'Excuse me, but I have to fart.' He held his breath and let a low hissing sound.

Five minutes later the second gay guy announced: 'Excuse me, but I have to fart.' And he too let out a low hiss.

The truck driver roared with laughter. 'Jesus Christ!' he exclaimed. 'You fairies can't even fart like men! Listen to this.' And he let out a rapid burst of machine gun fire from his ass.

'Oooh!' trilled one fag to the other. 'You know what we've got here, Clive? A real virgin!'

979 Three gay guys were fantasizing about what sport they would most like to play.

The first nominated football 'because of all those gorgeous guys bending over in their tight pants'.

'Definitely wrestling,' sighed the second guy. 'Those skimpy little costumes, and think of the holds.'

'No, it would be baseball for me,' insisted the third guy. 'You wanna know why? Well, I'd be pitching with the bases loaded, the batter would hit a line drive right to me, I'd catch it, and I'd just stand there while the other guys rounded the bases. Meanwhile the crowd would be going crazy, screaming: "Throw the ball, you cocksucker!" And that's what I like – the recognition!'

980 A gay guy and a straight guy were in a strip club that catered for all tastes. The straight guy was sitting directly in front of the gay guy. First on stage was a big black man. 'Oh, yeah, oh, yeah!' shrieked the gay guy as the black man started stripping.

'Hey,' said the straight guy, turning round. 'Shut up, will you.'

Next on stage was a well-built white man. 'Oh, yeah! Jesus, yeah!' screamed the gay guy as the white man stripped off. Once again the straight guy turned round and told him to be quiet.

Next an Asian guy dressed in leather came on stage and began stripping. The gay guy fell silent. The straight guy said to him: 'Hey, where's all your excitement now?'

The gay guy replied: 'All over your back!'

GERMANS

981 A Polish soldier was asked whom he would shoot first if he ran into a Russian soldier and a German soldier. 'The Russian soldier,' replied the Pole. 'Always business before pleasure.'

982 Why are so many Germans born by Caesarean section? – Ever try to get a square head through a round hole?

983 Why do Germans have huge heads? – Otherwise their mouths wouldn't fit in.

984 How do you make German chocolate cake? – First, you occupy the kitchen.

985 Why didn't Hitler drink vodka? – It made him mean.

986 Hitler went to a psychic to find out what day he would die. After looking into her crystal ball, the psychic said: 'Mein Führer, you will die on a Jewish holiday.'

Hitler was shocked. 'Well which holiday is it?' he demanded.

The psychic replied: 'Fuhrer, the day that you die will always be a Jewish holiday.'

987 What did the German bisexual do? – She went down on her Hans and niece.

GIFTS

988 Before agreeing to marry her boyfriend, a girl insisted on being bought a special present.

'Anything,' he said. 'Just name it. A new wardrobe, a diamond necklace, even a car.'

'None of those,' she answered. 'What I want is a solid gold Boy Scout knife.'

Although taken aback by her demand, the young guy was determined to follow it through. He scoured the whole city for a solid gold Boy Scout knife and eventually had to have one specially made. After collecting it, he placed it in a box, wrapped it neatly with a little bow, and presented it to the girl he loved.

She was delighted with the present and immediately agreed to marry him. Then she put the gold Boy Scout knife in a drawer where her fiancé noticed there were already half a dozen similar knives.

'What's all this about?' he asked. 'Why do you collect these gold knives?'

She explained: 'Someday I will be older. My hair will be grey, my skin will be wrinkled, my looks will have faded. Who will want me then? But do you know what a Boy Scout would do for one of these knives . . . ?'

Greeting Cards Rejected by Hallmark:

989 1. I heard you had herpes . . . and I feel terrible . . . I'd say 'Get well soon' . . . but I know it's incurable.

990 2. Our love will never . . . become cold and hollow . . . unless, one day . . . you refuse to swallow.

991 3. Heard your wife left you . . . how upset you must be . . . don't fret about your wife though . . . she's moving in with me.

992 4. Happy vasectomy! . . . hope you feel zippy . . . cause when I got one . . . I got real snippy.

993 5. You've announced that you're gay . . . won't that be a laugh . . . when they find out you're . . . one of the Joint Chiefs of Staff.

994 6. This feels so good . . . it feels so right . . . I just wish it wasn't . . . $250 a night.

995 7. You are the girl . . . I long to be near . . . so I hope you get over . . . this bout of diarrhoea.

996 8. So your daughter's a hooker . . . and it spoiled your day . . . look on the bright side . . . she's a really good lay.

997 9. So you lost your job . . . it's one of those hardships in life . . . next time, work harder . . . and don't shag the boss's wife.

998 10. I bought this Valentine's card at the store . . . in the hope that, later . . . you'd be my whore.

999 11. If you think that hickey . . . looks like a blister . . . check out the one . . . I gave to your sister.

1000 12. My tyre was thumping . . . I thought it was flat . . . when I looked at the tyre . . . I found your cat . . . Sorry!

1001 A man asked his wife what she would like for her birthday. After thinking for a moment, she sighed wistfully: 'What I'd really love is to be eight again.'

So on her birthday he told her: 'Honey, we're going for a little drive.'

'Where to?' she asked.

'You'll see . . .'

With that, he loaded her into the car and set off down the highway. Two hours later, they arrived in Disneyland. He took her on over a dozen rides, fed her candyfloss and ice cream, and won her a Donald Duck stuffed toy. That evening, after eating at McDonald's, they went to the cinema where they watched a two-hour non-stop cartoon carnival.

At the end of the day, both were feeling exhausted and queasy. As they lay in bed, he turned to her and said: 'So what was it like being eight again?'

She said: 'You idiot! I meant my dress size!'

1002 A little kid sat on Santa's lap, and Santa asked: 'What would you like for Christmas?'

'A fucking swingset for the backyard,' said the kid.

Santa told him: 'You'll have to ask more politely than that if you want Santa to bring you any presents. Now let's try again. What else would you like?'

The kid said: 'A fucking sandbox for the side yard.'

Santa warned him: 'That's no way to talk to Santa. One more time. What else would you like for Christmas?'

The boy thought for a moment, and then said: 'I want a fucking trampoline in the front yard.'

Santa lifted the boy off his lap and went to talk to the kid's parents. He told them about the child's swearing, and said: 'I know how to put a stop to it. Don't get him anything for Christmas except dog doo. Put a pile of dog doo in the backyard where he wants the swingset, put another pile in the side yard where he wants the sandbox, and another pile in the front yard where he wants the trampoline. That should make him change his attitude.'

Come Christmas morning, the kid went downstairs to open his presents, but there weren't any. He ran out the back door, looked around, and came back in. Then he ran out the side door, looked around, and came back in. Finally he ran out the front door, looked around, and came back in, shaking his head.

His father said: 'What's wrong, son?'

The kid said: 'Santa bought me a fucking dog, but I can't find it.'

GOD

1003 While a little boy was away at school, his cat died. His mother was worried about how he would take the news, so when he came home she comforted him and told him: 'Don't worry, Snowy is in heaven with God now.'

The kid said: 'What's God gonna do with a dead cat?'

1004 Why did God invent football? – So that married men could have some form of physical contact in their lives.

1005 God was planning a holiday but couldn't decide where to go.
'Why don't you visit Mercury?' suggested an angel.
'No, too hot,' said God.
'How about Mars?' said the angel.
'No, too dry and dusty,' said God.
'Then what about Earth?' said the angel.
'No way,' said God. 'I went there two thousand years ago, knocked up some bird, and they're still going on about it!'

1006 A deeply religious man lived next door to an atheist. The religious man prayed three times a day without fail and was regularly on his knees in communion with the Lord, but the atheist never went anywhere near a church. Yet while the atheist enjoyed a prosperous life with a well-paid job and a loving family, the pious man was poorly paid and had to put up with a cheating wife and three tearaway kids.

One day, reeling at the injustice of it all, the believer looked up to heaven and said: 'God, I honour you every day and confess to you my every sin, yet you have chosen to make my life thoroughly miserable. But my neighbour, who does not believe, has been granted every possible happiness. Why is this so, Lord? Why am I not blessed?'

And God replied: 'Because you're a bloody pest!'

1007 Why did God create Eve? – To iron Adam's leaf.

1008 A jungle explorer woke up one morning to find himself surrounded by hundreds of natives wielding bows and arrows. He said to himself: 'Oh, God, I'm fucked!'

All of a sudden he heard a voice from above booming down. 'No, you're not,' said the voice. 'This is God. Go ye unto the man at the front there with the paint on his face, drive your knife through his heart, and he shall die.'

So the explorer ran up, stabbed the guy at the front, and, sure enough, he died. 'Now what, God?' asked the explorer.

'That was their revered chief,' said God. '*Now* you're fucked!'

1009 God had just about finished creating the universe but he had two extra items left in his bag of goodies. So he decided to divide them between Adam and Eve.

'Right,' said God, 'the first thing I have to give away is the ability to stand up while urinating.'

Adam put his hand up straight away. 'Oh, please, God, let me have it. Please, please, please! It would make me so happy if I could pee standing up. I could go just about anywhere. Life would be wonderful. Sheer bliss. It's something I've always dreamed of being able to do. Please, God, grant me the ability to urinate standing up. I promise to be good.'

God said to Eve: 'Have you any objections if I grant this facility to Adam?'

'No,' shrugged Eve. 'Whatever makes him happy.'

'OK, Adam, it's yours,' said God.

Adam was thrilled, and danced around excitedly before displaying his newfound talent all over the bark of a tree.

'Now,' said God to Eve, looking into his bag. 'What's left here? Ah, yes, multiple orgasms.'

GOLF

1010 A guy arrived home to find the following ransom note slipped under his front door: 'If you ever want to see your wife alive again, bring $50,000 to the 17th green at your golf club tomorrow at 11 a.m.'

But it was after 2 p.m by the time he arrived at the designated meeting place. As he did so, a masked man stepped out from behind some bushes and demanded, 'You're over three hours late. What took you so long?'

'Give me a break!' said the husband, pointing to his scorecard. 'I'm a 27 handicap.'

1011 Three guys – a father, a son and a grandfather – went off to play a round of golf. They were waiting on the first tee when a gorgeous young woman walked up, carrying her clubs.

'My playing partner hasn't shown up,' she said. 'Could I possibly join you?'

Their eyes nearly popped out of their heads at the prospect of spending the next four hours with this beautiful creature, and they readily agreed.

'There's just one thing,' she said. 'I don't mind you swearing or smoking but, whatever you do, just don't try to coach me on my game.'

The guys were happy to do whatever she asked. They let her tee off first. All eyes were on her ass as her short, tight skirt rode up it while she bent over to place the ball. She then proceeded to hammer the ball straight down the middle. It was the same story, hole after hole. None of the guys could compete with her.

On the 18th, she was left with a 12ft putt for a level-par round of 72. She turned to them and said: 'You guys have done a great job at not trying to coach me on my game. I have never shot a round of level par before and it is so important to me that I'm going to ask each of you for your opinion on this crucial putt. And if any of those opinions help me to make this putt, I'll give you all a blow job that you will never forget.'

The guys were in dreamland. The son walked over to her ball, studied the putt for a couple of minutes and said: 'Lady, aim that putt three inches to the right of the hole and it will break to the left and drop in the middle of the cup.'

The father walked over and said: 'Don't listen to the boy, ma'am. Aim six inches to the left and it will break right and drop in the middle of the hole.'

The grandfather looked at both of them in disgust, walked over, picked up the ball and said: 'Never mind the putt, that's a gimme.'

1012 How did the gay golfer break his leg at the course? — He fell off the ball washer.

1013 'How was your golf game today?' asked Bill's wife Tammy.

'I was hitting the ball pretty well,' he replied, 'but my eyesight is so bad now that I couldn't see where the ball went.'

'Bill, you're seventy-five years old!' admonished his wife. 'Of course your eyesight isn't as good as it used to be. Look, why don't you take my brother Dan along?'

'But Dan is eighty-four and doesn't even play golf any more,' protested Bill.

Tammy said: 'I know he no longer has all his faculties, but he has got perfect eyesight. At least he could watch your ball.'

Bill agreed to give it a go, and the next day he teed off with Dan looking on. Bill swung and the ball disappeared down the middle of the fairway.

'Did you see it?' asked Bill.

'Yup,' replied Dan.

'Well, where is it?' yelled Bill, heading down the fairway and peering into the distance.

Dan said: 'I forget.'

1014   A man and his wife had an argument in bed, after which he slept downstairs. The next day she felt guilty and decided to buy him a present. As he was a keen golfer, she went to the pro shop. The pro suggested a putter and showed her one of the best in stock.

'How much?' she asked.

'$150,' said the pro.

'That's a bit expensive.'

'But it comes with an inscription.'

'What kind of inscription?'

'Whatever you like, but one of the old golfers' favourites is NEVER UP, NEVER IN.'

'Oh, that will do,' said the wife. 'After all, that's what started the argument in the first place.'

1015   An American businessman was in Japan. He hired a local hooker and was going at it all night with her. She kept screaming 'Fujifoo! Fujifoo!', which the guy took to be pleasurable.

The next day he was playing golf with his Japanese counterparts and he got a hole-in-one. Wanting to impress the clients, he said: 'Fujifoo!'

The Japanese clients looked confused and said: 'No, you got the right hole.'

1016   A golfer drove his new Toyota into a country gas station. As the young attendant filled the car up, he spotted a handful of tees on the passenger seat.

'What are those for?' he asked.

'They're called tees,' replied the golfer. 'They're for resting my balls on when I drive.'

'Jesus!' exclaimed the attendant. 'Those Japanese have thought of everything!'

1017   Two guys were playing golf on a Saturday afternoon, just as they had every week for the past six years. The first guy was about to tee off when a woman in a wedding dress ran up to him screaming: 'You bastard! You stinking bastard! You promised!'

Stepping back from the ball, he replied calmly: 'Honey, I said only if it rains today . . .'

Rules of Bedroom Golf:

1018   1. Each player shall furnish his own equipment for play, normally one club and two balls.

1019   2. Play on the course must be approved by the owner of the hole.

1020   3. Unlike outdoor golf, the object is to get the club in the hole and keep the balls out.

1021   4. For most effective play, the club should have a firm shaft. Course owners are permitted to check shaft stiffness before play begins.

1022   5. Course owners reserve the right to restrict club length to avoid damage to the hole.

1023   6. The object of the game is to take as many strokes as necessary until the owner is satisfied that play is complete. Failure to do so may result in being denied permission to play again.

1024   7. It is considered bad form to begin playing the hole immediately upon arrival. Experienced players will normally take time to admire the entire course, paying special attention to well-formed mounds and bunkers.

1025   8. Players are cautioned not to mention other courses they have played or are currently playing to the owner of the course being played. Upset owners have been known to damage a player's equipment for this reason.

1026   9. Players are encouraged to have proper rain gear, just in case.

1027 10. Players should not assume that the course is in shape to play at all times. Players may be embarrassed if they find the course temporarily under repair. Players are advised to be extremely tactful in this situation. More advanced players will find alternate means of play when this is the case.

1028 11. Players should assume their match has been properly scheduled particularly when playing a new course for the first time. Previous players have been known to become irate if they discover someone else is playing what they considered a private course.

1029 12. The owner of the course is responsible for the pruning of any bushes that may reduce the visibility of the hole.

1030 13. Players are strongly advised to get the owner's permission before playing the backside.

1031   14. Slow play is encouraged, but players should be prepared to proceed at a quicker pace at the owner's request.

1032   15. It is considered an outstanding performance, time permitting, to play the same hole several times in one match.

1033   A guy was playing a golf course for the first time and was struggling to find his way around. So he asked a woman who was playing up ahead which hole he was on.

'I'm on the sixth,' she said, 'and you're a hole behind me, so you must be on the fifth.'

He thanked her for her help, but then became disorientated once more on the back nine. Again, he called out to her and asked her which hole he was playing.

'I'm on the fourteenth,' she said, 'and you're a hole behind me, so you must be on the thirteenth.'

At the end of his round, he bumped into the woman in the clubhouse and bought her a drink in return for her assistance. As they got chatting, he asked her what line of work she was in.

'You'll laugh when I tell you,' she said, 'but I sell Tampax.'

'Ha,' he replied, 'I sell toilet paper. So I guess that still makes me a hole behind you!'

1034   A guy was brought into hospital with a golf club wrapped around his neck. The doctors asked him to tell them everything he remembered.

'I was teaching my wife to play golf,' he began. 'Naturally I'd won every hole but on the short 18th she finally managed to sink a putt. I reached into the cup to retrieve her ball and I said: "Looks like your hole, dear." And that was the last thing I remember.'

1035   A passer-by came across four golfers in a bunker. One was lying face down in the sand while the other three were arguing furiously.

'What's going on?' asked the passer-by.

One of the golfers turned and said: 'It's these guys – they'll do anything to win. My partner's just had a stroke and they want to add it to our score!'

1036   After finishing his round of golf, Roger headed straight for the bar where he bumped into his friend Barney. Looking down at Roger's trousers, Barney asked him: 'Why are your trousers so wet at the front?'

Roger called him to one side and explained quietly: 'Today is the first time

I've played golf wearing bifocals. Throughout my round, I could see two sizes for everything. There was a big club and a little club, a big ball and a little ball, and so on. So I hit the little ball with the big club, and it worked a treat. And when I got to the green, I putted the little ball into the big cup. I played the best golf of my life.'

'I understand all that,' said Barney, 'but how did you get so wet?'

'Well,' said Roger, 'when I got to the 15th, I was desperate for a pee. I knew I couldn't wait until I got back to the clubhouse. So I sneaked into the woods and unzipped my fly. When I looked down there were two of them – a big one and a little one. Well, I knew the big one wasn't mine, so I put it back.'

1037 Two women were playing golf when one sliced her shot into a men's foursome, causing one man to collapse in agony with both hands in his crotch. Rushing to his aid, the culprit apologized profusely, explained that she was a physical therapist and offered to help ease the pain.

'No, it's OK,' winced the man, his hands still between his legs. 'I'll be fine in a few minutes.'

'No, I insist,' she said as she undid the zip on his jeans and began massaging his genitals. 'There, does that feel better?'

'Yes, it feels great,' said the man. 'But my thumb still hurts like hell!'

1038 A husband and wife were playing on the tenth green when she collapsed from a heart attack.

'Please, dear, I need help,' she gasped.

The husband ran off, promising: 'I'll fetch some help.'

Five minutes later, he returned, picked up his putter and began to line up his putt.

His wife, lying on the ground, raised her head and said: 'I may be dying and you're putting?'

'Don't worry, honey,' he said. 'I found a doctor on the third hole who said he'd come and help you.'

'The third hole?' she groaned, clutching her chest. 'When the hell is he coming?'

'Hey! I told you not to worry,' said the husband, practising his putt. 'Everyone's already agreed to let him play through.'

GREEKS

1039 How do Greeks separate the men from the boys? – With a crowbar.

1040 What's the Greek army motto? – 'Never leave your buddy's behind.'

1041 What's long and hard that a Greek bride gets on her wedding night? – A new last name.

1042 An Englishman, an American and a Greek were called upon to test a lie detector.

The Englishman said: 'I think I can drink twelve bottles of beer . . .' BUZZZ, the lie detector went off. 'OK, eight bottles.' The machine remained silent.

The American said: 'I think I can eat fifteen hamburgers . . .' BUZZZ. 'All right, seven hamburgers.' The machine was silent.

The Greek said: 'I think . . .' BUZZZ.

1043 How does every ethnic joke start? – By looking over your shoulder.

GYNAECOLOGISTS

1044 A mother asked the gynaecologist to examine her teenage daughter. 'She has been having some strange symptoms,' explained the mother, 'and I'm a little worried about her.'

The gynaecologist examined the girl before announcing: 'Madam, I believe your daughter is pregnant.'

'That's nonsense!' exclaimed the mother. 'My little girl has nothing whatsoever to do with boys. Do you, darling?'

'No, mumsy,' replied the daughter innocently. 'You know that I have never so much as kissed a boy!'

The gynaecologist looked at them both. Then silently he stood up and walked over to the window, staring out.

He continued staring out the window until the mother felt compelled to ask. 'Doctor, is there something out there?'

'No, madam,' he replied. 'It's just that the last time anything like this happened, a star appeared in the East, and I was looking to see if another one was going to show up.'

1045 What do a gynaecologist and a pizza delivery boy have in common? – They can both smell it, but can't eat it.

1046 A young woman was making her first visit to a gynaecologist and was understandably nervous. The gynaecologist sensed this.

'You're very nervous, aren't you?' he said.

'Yes,' she admitted.

'Would you like me to numb you down there?'

'Please.'

He stuck his head between her legs and went, 'Num, num, num . . .'

1047 Why do women prefer elderly gynaecologists? – Their shaky hands.

1048 What's the difference between a bandleader and a gynaecologist? – A gynaecologist sucks his fingers . . .

1049 Bored with his job, a gynaecologist decided to switch careers and become a car mechanic. So he went to training classes, at the end of which was a final exam where students had to strip a car engine completely and reassemble it in perfect working order. When the results came through, he got top marks – 150 per cent.

The former gynaecologist was amazed. 'How come I scored 150 per cent?' he asked. 'I thought that was impossible.'

The instructor explained: 'I gave you fifty per cent for taking the engine apart, fifty per cent for reassembling it, and I gave you a fifty per cent bonus for doing it all through the exhaust pipe!'

HAIR

1050 A woman had just had a baby when the doctor came in and said: 'There's good news and bad news.'

'What's the bad news?' she asked.

'Your baby is ginger.'

'And what's the good news?'

'It's dead.'

1051 Why are brunettes so proud of their hair? – It matches their moustache.

1052 A man went to a barbershop for a shave. He said: 'I have real trouble getting a close shave around the cheeks. Do you have any suggestions?'

'Certainly, sir,' replied the barber. 'I have the very thing.' He took a wooden ball from a drawer and said: 'Place this between your cheek and gum.'

So the customer put the ball in his mouth and experienced his closest shave ever. After a minute or so, he spluttered: 'What if I swallow it?'

'No problem, sir. Just bring it back tomorrow like everyone else does.'

1053 What do you call a good-looking man with a redhead? – A hostage.

1054 'You look different today, Jenny,' said her friend Martha. 'Your hair is extra curly, and you have this wide-eyed look. What did you use – special curlers and some dramatic eye makeup?'

'No,' said Jenny. 'My vibrator shorted out this morning.'

1055 Why did the bald man cut holes in his jeans pockets? – So he could run his fingers through his hair.

1056 On a visit to the barber, a male customer asked for any suggestions to cure baldness.

'It might sound strange, but the best thing I've found is female juices,' confided the barber.

'But you're balder than I am!' said the customer.

'But you must admit I've got a great moustache . . .'

HALITOSIS

1057 A surgeon told his patient: 'This is Nurse Smithers. She has a severe case of halitosis and she will be French-kissing you before your operation.'

'Why?' asked the patient.

The surgeon said: 'Because we've run out of anaesthetic.'

1058 What good is a mouthwash that kills germs? Who wants a mouth full of dead germs?

1059 Did you hear about the guy who spent years trying to find a cure for his halitosis and acne, only to find that people didn't like him anyway?

HALLOWE'EN

1060 A man with a bald head and a wooden leg was invited to a Hallowe'en party. Unsure of what costume to wear to hide his head and leg, he wrote to a fancy dress company asking for suggestions. A few days later he received a parcel with a note which read: 'Please find enclosed a pirate's costume. The spotted handkerchief will cover your bald head and, with your wooden leg, you will make an ideal pirate.'

The man was angry because the outfit emphasized his wooden leg, so he wrote a letter of complaint to the company. A week later he received another parcel with a note that read: 'Sorry about the pirate's costume, and please find enclosed a monk's habit. The long robe will cover your wooden leg and with your bald head, you will really look the part.'

The man was furious because this outfit emphasized his bald head, so he wrote another letter to the company. The next day he received a parcel with a note which read: 'Please find enclosed a jar of caramel. Pour the caramel over your bald head, stick your wooden leg up your ass and go as a toffee apple!'

1061 A guy went to a Hallowe'en party stark naked except for a jam jar on his cock.

A woman asked: 'What are you dressed as?'

'A fireman.'

'I don't understand,' she said.

He explained: 'You break the glass, pull the knob, and I'll come as fast as I can!'

1062 A young black boy and his sister were out trick or treating. They went to the first house in the street and rang the bell. The house owner opened the front door and asked: 'What are you two dressed as?'

'Jack and Jill,' they replied.

'You can't be Jack and Jill, they're white,' said the owner.

Nevertheless he gave them some candy and they moved on to the next house. There they rang the bell and the owner answered the door.

'What are you two dressed as?' he inquired.

'Hansel and Gretel,' they answered.

'You can't be Hansel and Gretel, they're white,' said the owner.

Even so, he gave them some candy and they moved on. Before reaching the third house, the boy had an idea and suggested that he and his sister take off all their clothes. Naked, they then walked up to the door and rang the bell. As the owner opened the door, the boy said: 'We're dressed as Hershey bars, one with nuts, one without nuts!'

HANGOVERS

1063 A guy woke in the morning with a massive hangover, unable to remember a thing he did the previous night. He picked up his bath robe from the floor and put it on, but found there was something in one of the pockets. It was a bra. 'Bloody hell,' he thought. 'What happened last night?' As he walked towards the bathroom, he found a pair of knickers in the other pocket. 'How did these get here?' he said to himself. 'I can't remember a thing. It must have been a wild party.' He went into the bathroom and when he looked in the mirror, he saw a little string hanging from his mouth. He said a silent prayer: 'Please, if there's a God, let this be a teabag!'

1064 Following a drunken night out, the teenage daughter of a millionaire was woken in the morning by the family butler.

'What happened?' she groaned. 'I've got a throat like sandpaper and my head feels like a bag of cement. I don't even remember getting into bed last night.'

'I carried you upstairs, miss,' said the butler.

'And where's my dress?' she asked.

'There was a red wine stain on it. Therefore I took the liberty of removing it so that it could be cleaned.'

'Thanks, Jenkins. But I appear to have lost my underwear too.'

'It looked as if it was interfering with your circulation,' said the butler, 'so I slipped it off.'

'You're so considerate, Jenkins. That was quite a night. I must have been really tight.'

'Only the first time,' said the butler.

1065 Sobering up from the night before, a man found the Sunday sermon heavy going and, still feeling hung over and tired, he eventually nodded off partway through. The preacher watched this with disgust and at the end of the sermon, decided to make an example of the man.

So the preacher said to his congregation: 'All those wishing to have a place in heaven, please stand.'

The whole church stood up . . . except for the sleeping man.

Then the preacher announced loudly: 'All those who would like a place in hell, please STAND UP!'

Only catching the last part, the hung over man rose groggily to his feet. Confused and embarrassed to see that the rest of the congregation were seated, he said: 'I don't know what we're voting on here, Reverend, but it seems like you and me are the only ones in favour!'

1066 A cowboy rode into town on payday and proceeded to get hopelessly drunk. Seeing the state he was in, a couple of his pals played a trick on him by popping outside and turning his horse around. Then they went back in and joined him for several more drinks.

The next morning, the cowboy could barely move. His wife hurled a bucket of cold water over him but even that failed to get him out of bed. Reminding him that he had to go to work, she began shaking him by the shoulders.

'Oh, leave me alone,' he groaned. 'I can't face hitting the trail today. I'm too beat.'

'Get the hell up!' she screamed. 'I've seen you this hung over a hundred times!'

'No, last night was different,' he wailed. 'Some son-of-a-bitch cut my horse's head off, and I had to pull him all the way home with my finger in his windpipe.'

HEALTH

1067 After enjoying sex three times a day on their honeymoon, a young couple had to adjust their lovemaking when they returned to work. Both always arrived home from the office at six o'clock, and so every day at 6.15, regular as clockwork, they would go to bed.

This daily sex schedule continued for months – sex every day at 6.15 – until the wife went down with flu and went to the doctor to get a flu shot.

The shot killed every germ inside her except for three. These three germs were huddled together inside her body, discussing their survival plans.

One germ said: 'I am going to hide between two toes on her right foot. I don't think the antibiotics will find me there.'

The second germ said: 'I am going to hide behind her left ear. I don't think they'll find me there.'

The last germ said: 'I don't know about you guys, but when that 6.15 pulls out tonight, I'm gonna be on it!'

1068 A country woman took her three sons to the doctor for their first-ever physicals. The doctor examined the boys and advised her to give them iron supplements. Not knowing what he meant by iron supplements, she went to the hardware store and bought some ball bearings, which she then mixed into their food.

A few days later the youngest son complained that he was pissing ball bearings, but the mother told him that it was normal because she had put them in his food. Then the middle son told her that he was crapping ball bearings. Again, she said it was normal because she had put them in his food.

That night the eldest son came in, extremely upset. 'Ma,' he said, 'you won't believe what happened!'

She said: 'I know, you're passing ball bearings.'

'No,' he said, 'I was out behind the barn jacking off and I shot the dog.'

1069 What's the best thing about schizophrenia? – It turns a wank into an orgy.

1070 A female worker told her boss that she was going home early because she didn't feel well. Since the boss himself was just recovering from illness, he wished her well and said he hoped it wasn't something he'd given her.

'So do I,' she said. 'I've got morning sickness.'

1071 When a man complained to his wife that he was suffering from stomach ache, she suggested he try the tablets that the doctor had given her for a similar pain. After taking the wife's tablets for a week, the pain disappeared but he developed two tender lumps, one behind each ear. He showed the doctor the lumps and explained what had happened.

'You idiot!' raged the doctor. 'I was treating your wife for a fallen womb. God knows how I'm going to get your balls back down!'

1072 A brown paper bag went to the doctor and complained of feeling unwell. The doctor conducted a series of tests and asked the bag to come back the following week.

When the bag returned, the doctor said: 'I'm afraid I have some bad news. We discovered from your blood tests that you have haemophilia.'

'How the hell can I have haemophilia? I'm a brown paper bag.'

'Yes,' replied the doctor, 'but it seems your mother was a carrier.'

1073 A woman with cerebral palsy was talking to her friend at a party. She said: 'Do you know what the toughest thing is for a woman with cerebral palsy?'

'Sex?' ventured the friend.

'No, it's plucking your eyebrows.'

'Really?'

'Yeah, that's how I originally got pierced ears!'

1074 Why didn't the epileptics order Coke at a restaurant? – They had shakes.

1075 A guy walked into his doctor's office, complaining that he thought he might have a tapeworm. The doctor carried out a thorough examination, at the end of which he concurred with the patient's diagnosis. 'Right,' said the doctor, 'I want you to come back tomorrow to start your treatment. And I want you to bring a banana and a cookie.'

The patient went along with the odd request and returned the next day with a banana and a cookie. The doctor said: 'OK, now drop your pants and bend over the table. This is going to hurt a bit.'

So the bemused patient dropped his pants and bent over. The doctor peeled the banana and swiftly rammed it up the patient's ass. While the doctor consulted his watch, the patient danced around the room in agony.

'Right,' continued the doctor, 'one minute is up and we must complete the second part of the treatment if we are going to get rid of that tapeworm.' He asked the guy to bend over again. Reluctantly, the patient complied and this time the doctor rammed the cookie up his ass. The man winced. Then the doctor asked him to return the same time next day with another banana and another cookie.

The routine was repeated the following day. The doctor rammed in the banana, waited exactly one minute, then thrust in the cookie. What's more, he carried on the same treatment day after day: up went the banana, a minute's wait, and then up went the cookie.

After a week of this, the doctor said: 'You'll be pleased to know that tomorrow is the final day of your tapeworm treatment. This time, I want you to bring in a banana and a hammer.'

'Not a cookie?' asked the patient nervously.

'No, a hammer,' confirmed the doctor.

So the guy returned for his final day of treatment. The doctor said: 'OK, you know the routine.' The patient dropped his pants and bent over. The doctor shoved the banana up the man's ass, looked at his watch and picked up the hammer. One minute passed. Then two minutes, three minutes, four.

Finally a little head poked out of the patient's ass: 'Where's my cookie?'

WHACK!

1076 An asthmatic received an obscene phone call in the middle of an asthma attack. The caller paused halfway through and said: 'Did I call you, or did you call me?'

HEAVEN AND HELL

1077 God summoned St Peter and said: 'Peter, we have a problem. Heaven is full. However we have a number of high-profile celebrities waiting at the Gates. We should let one in.'

When St Peter checked, he found Freddie Mercury, Gianni Versace and Princess Diana waiting at the Gates. St Peter explained: 'Heaven is really overflowing at the moment, but I have been instructed by God to admit one of you, so you will each have to come up with a reason why you should be allowed in to heaven.'

Freddie Mercury said: 'I was one of the world's greatest rock singers, responsible for some classic numbers, and if I am admitted, heaven will resound to my great singing voice. I will write tunes that will touch the hearts of angels.'

Gianni Versace said: 'I was Earth's greatest designer. If I am admitted, I will dress the cherubs and angels in the latest fashions. Heaven will never have looked better.'

'Now, Princess Diana,' said St Peter, 'what do you have to say?'

But Diana said nothing. Instead she just blushed shyly.

Then St Peter announced his decision – he was going to admit Princess Diana to heaven. Freddie and Gianni were furious and protested vigorously.

'Sorry, guys,' said St Peter, 'but a royal flush beats a pair of queens any day.'

In Heaven:

1078 The cooks are French,
1079 The policemen are English,
1080 The mechanics are German,
1081 The lovers are Italian,
1082 The bankers are Swiss.

In Hell:

1083 The cooks are English,
1084 The policemen are German,
1085 The mechanics are French,
1086 The lovers are Swiss,
1087 The bankers are Italian.

1088 Two identical twin brothers died at around the same time. One was happily married, did charitable works and generally led a blameless life; the other was a drunken womanizer, a serial liar and cheat. The bad twin went to hell and the good twin went to heaven, from where he was able to look down on his brother.

The good twin was dismayed that hell was not as bad as he had hoped. Indeed his brother seemed to be having the time of his life, drinking, partying and enjoying the company of a beautiful woman. Eventually the good twin complained to St Peter: 'Heaven is very nice and peaceful, but my brother appears to be having plenty of fun in hell. He has his own beer keg and just look at that gorgeous woman he has been given.'

St. Peter said: 'Fear not, my son. All is not as it seems. The keg has a hole in it; the woman doesn't.'

1089 Father O'Flynn walked into a pub in rural Ireland and said to the first man he met: 'Do you want to go to heaven?'

'I do, Father,' said the man.

The priest said: 'Then stand over there against the wall.'

Then the priest asked a second man: 'Do you want to go to heaven?'

'Certainly, Father,' came the reply.

'Then stand over there against the wall,' said the priest.

Then Father O'Flynn walked up to Mick Murphy and said: 'Do you want to go to heaven?'

Murphy said: 'No, I don't, Father.'

'I don't believe this!' exclaimed the priest. 'You mean to tell me that when you die, you don't want to go to heaven?'

Murphy said: 'Oh, when I die, yes. I thought you were getting a group together to go right now.'

1090 Hearing a knock at the Pearly Gates, St Peter looked out and saw a man waiting to enter. But before St Peter could conduct his interview, the man had disappeared. A puzzled St Peter returned to his duties, only to be disturbed a couple of minutes later by the same man knocking on the Gates. However once again the man vanished before speaking. Lo and behold, less than two minutes later, the man appeared at the Gates for a third time.

St Peter said: 'Are you playing games with me?'

'No,' said the man. 'They're trying to resuscitate me.'

1091 Fidel Castro died and went to heaven, but St Peter said he wasn't on the list and had to go to hell instead. So Castro went to hell where the Devil gave him a warm welcome. But then Castro realized he had left his luggage in heaven. 'No problem,' said Satan, 'I'll send a couple of my little devils up to fetch it.'

When the little devils arrived in heaven, they found that the Gates were locked and St Peter was at lunch. So they decided to climb the wall and get the luggage but as they did so, they were spotted by two angels.

One angel said to the other. 'Look at that! Castro hasn't been in hell five minutes and we're already getting refugees!'

1092 An American, a Scotsman and a Canadian were involved in a serious road smash. They were taken to the same emergency room, but all died before they arrived. Just as the staff were about to put the toe tag on the American, he suddenly stirred and opened his eyes. The astonished doctors asked him what happened.

'I remember the crash,' said the American, 'and then there was a beautiful light, and the Canadian, the Scotsman and myself were standing at the gates of heaven. St Peter approached us and said we were all too young to die and that for a donation of $100 we could return to Earth. So I pulled out my wallet, gave him the $100 and, the next thing I knew, I was back here.'

'That's amazing,' said one of the doctors. 'But tell me, what happened to the other two?'

The American said: 'The last time I saw them, the Scotsman was haggling over the price and the Canadian was waiting for the government to pay for his.'

1093 With heaven full to capacity, God decided to restrict admission. In future, applicants would have to prove that they had suffered a really bad day immediately prior to their death. So when the first person under the new regime arrived at the Pearly Gates, St Peter was waiting with his revised questionnaire.

'Before I can let you in,' said St Peter, 'I need you to tell me about the day you died.'

The man replied: 'For some time now, I've been convinced that my wife has been having an affair. I believed that each day on her lunch hour, she'd bring her lover home to our 25th-storey apartment and have sex with him. So today, I planned to come home and catch them. I got there and found my wife half-naked, but even though I searched the entire apartment, there was no sign of her lover. Just as I was about to give up, I glanced out onto the balcony and spotted a man hanging off the edge by his fingertips. The nerve of that guy to think he could hide from me! So I stamped on his fingers until he fell to the ground but, would you believe it, some bushes broke his fall. I was in a blind rage now and went back inside for something to throw at him. The first thing I could grab was the refrigerator. I unplugged it, pushed it out onto the balcony, and heaved it over the side. It plummeted twenty-five storeys and crushed him. But the strain on my heart had proved so great that I immediately collapsed and died.'

After listening to the tale, St Peter concluded that the guy did indeed have a bad day, and so he admitted him to heaven.

A few seconds later, another man came up to the Pearly Gates. St Peter explained that he needed details of his day of death and the man duly obliged. 'You're not gonna believe this,' he began. 'I was out on the balcony of my 26th-storey apartment, doing my daily exercises, when I slipped and fell over the side. Luckily I managed to hang on by my fingertips to the balcony beneath mine. Then suddenly this crazy guy came running out of his apartment and started cussing, and stamping on my fingers. Naturally I fell, but I hit some bushes on the way down, which broke my fall. So I was lying there in agony, unable to move, when I looked up and saw this same maniac hurl a refrigerator over the ledge. It fell right on top of me and killed me.'

St Peter smiled to himself on hearing the story and admitted the man to heaven.

A few seconds later, a third man arrived at the Gates. 'Tell me about the day you died,' said St. Peter.

'OK. Picture this,' said the man. 'I'm naked inside a refrigerator . . .'

1094 An alcoholic, a miser, and a gay guy were waiting to enter heaven. But St Peter said: 'With the lives you've led, you'll need to be tested first.'

So they were sent off to prove that they could resist temptation. The first stop was a bar where the alcoholic ordered a beer and, having failed the test, was immediately turned to ashes. The other two saw a $10 bill lying on the floor. The gay guy said to the miser: 'If you bend over now, we're both goners!'

1095 A woman died and when she got to heaven, she asked St Peter. 'Would it be possible for me to get together with my dear departed husband? He died seventeen years ago.'

'What's his name?' asked St Peter.

'John Smith,' replied the woman.

St Peter was not optimistic. 'That's a very common name, but sometimes we can identify people by their last words. Do you remember what they were?'

She answered: 'He said that if I ever slept with another man after he was gone, he would turn in his grave.'

'Oh,' said St Peter, 'you mean Spinning John Smith!'

1096 An Asian shopkeeper was very unhappy at having to go along with an arranged marriage. 'I've never even met the girl,' he complained to one of his white customers. 'How can I know whether I want to marry her? But my family say I must, according to my religion.'

The customer advised him to change religion, but on his way to the church the Asian guy was run over by a car and killed. He went straight up to heaven where St Peter was waiting at the Gates.

'What do you want?' asked St. Peter

'I have come for Jesus.'

St Peter looked round and called out: 'Jesus, your taxi's here!'

HOLLYWOOD

1097 Once there was a great Hollywood actor who could no longer remember his lines. His career had gone into terminal decline until, after years of unemployment, he finally found a theatre where they were prepared to give him another chance. The director explained: 'Even though you only have one line, your part is essential to the entire play. You come on at the start of Act One and walk on to the stage carrying a rose. You hold the rose to your nose with just one finger and thumb, sniff the rose deeply and then say the line: "Ah, the sweet aroma of my mistress." '

All day long the actor rehearsed his solitary line. Finally it was curtain up and he walked on to the stage and with great passion delivered the line: 'Ah, the sweet aroma of my mistress.' But the audience roared with laughter.

The director was livid. 'You bloody fool!' he screamed. 'You have ruined me!'

The actor was bewildered. 'What happened? Did I forget my line?'

'No,' yelled the director. 'You forgot the rose!'

1098 Did you hear about the actress who auditioned for *The Vagina Monologues*? – She dried.

1099 A Hollywood agent was trying to convince a nightclub owner to book a young dancer on his books. 'She's got the most amazing figure,' enthused the agent. '92–24–36.'

'And what sort of dance does she do?' asked the owner.

'Well, to be honest, it's not exactly a dance,' admitted the agent. 'She crawls on stage and tries to stand up.'

1100 Sean Connery had fallen on hard times. His work had completely dried up. Then one day out of the blue his agent rang and said: 'Sean, I've got a job for you. Starts tomorrow, but you've got to get there early, for 10ish.'

Sean frowned: '10ish? But I haven't even got a racket!'

1101 An aspiring Hollywood actress managed to acquire an invitation to a Tinseltown cocktail party where the rich and famous were gathered. She asked the hostess: 'Who's the most powerful guy in the room?'

'Jerry over there,' came the reply. 'He's a major league producer.'

So the girl sidled up to him and whispered: 'Jerry, I'm gonna take you outside, unzip your fly, take out your cock, and give you the best blow job you've ever had!'

'Well, OK,' he replied. 'But what's in it for me?'

1102 Once upon a time, a handsome young man walked into the office of a Hollywood agent. With him, he brought an impressive portfolio, including still photos from a wide variety of acclaimed productions, excellent critical notices, and a comprehensive CV. The agent had no doubt that this guy had the potential to go all the way to the top, but there was just one snag: his name was Penis Van Lesbian.

The agent didn't mince his words. 'I'd love to take you on, son, because I really think you've got what it takes, but you'll have to change your name. Who's ever heard of a movie star called Penis Van Lesbian? It's a joke! The public will never wear it.'

'But the name has been in my family for generations,' explained the actor.

'Listen,' said the agent, puffing on a cigar, 'everyone changes their name in Hollywood. Look at John Wayne and Tony Curtis! Would they ever have made it as Marion Morrison and Bernie Schwarz? The hell they wouldn't! So you see, it's no big deal, changing your name.'

'No,' insisted the actor. 'I want to keep Penis Van Lesbian.'

'Well,' sighed the agent, 'in which case I'm afraid there's no way I can take you onto my books.'

'I'm sorry, too,' said the actor, rising to his feet. 'But I just can't do it. I won't change my name from Penis Van Lesbian, not even for Hollywood.'

'OK,' said the agent, 'but let me know if you change your mind.'

And with that Penis Van Lesbian left the office.

Five years later, the agent received a cheque for $50,000. Attached to it was a letter, which read: 'Dear sir, several years ago I came to your office hoping to become a Hollywood actor. You said you would not represent me unless I changed my name. I refused at the time but later realized you were right. And eventually I did change my name and I am now a famous actor. So I figure I owe you, as you played a part in my fame. Yours, Dick Van Dyke.'

HOMICIDE

1103 The judge told a double-homicide defendant: 'You're charged with beating your wife to death with a hammer.'

A voice at the back of the courtroom yelled out; 'You bastard!'

The judge continued: 'You're also charged with beating your mother-in-law to death with a hammer.'

The voice at the back yelled out: 'You God-damned bastard!'

The judge stopped and told the man at the back: 'Sir, I understand your anger and frustration at this crime, but any more outbursts and I shall charge you with contempt. Do you understand?'

The man at the back stood up and snarled: 'For fifteen years, I've lived next door to that bastard, and every time I asked to borrow a hammer, he said he didn't have one.'

1104 Fred West was being interviewed by the police. 'How many people have you murdered?' asked the detective.

'Five,' answered West.

'You're lying,' said the detective. 'We've pulled up the floorboards in your house and dug up your garden, and found twelve bodies already.'

'Be fair,' said West. 'I'm a builder. It was only an estimate.'

1105 Did you hear the FBI was investigating Jeffrey Dahmer? – They think he might have been selling arms to Iraq.

1106 Two brothers – Eric and Abel – were national yodelling champions. One night their car broke down in the middle of nowhere, forcing them to seek refuge at a nearby farmhouse. The farmer agreed to let them stay the night, but only on condition that they did not try anything with his beautiful daughter.

The brothers had a way of communicating over several miles by yodelling to each other. One particular yodel (ay-la-de-o-la-te-tu) signalled trouble, and meant for the other brother to run.

Anyway, the next morning the farmer was up at the crack of dawn and caught his daughter in bed with Eric. He grabbed his shotgun and shouted that he would start counting, adding that if Eric wasn't out of his sight by the count of five, he would shoot him. Eric leaped out of bed, sprinted downstairs, and had just cleared the farm gate when the farmer reached a count of four. He yodelled the tune to warn his brother, but immediately the farmer shot Eric.

Abel came running from his room. 'What happened?' he screamed.

The farmer said: 'I caught your brother sleeping with my daughter and, although I gave him a fair chance, before he was out of sight he yelled, "I laid the old lady too." So I shot him.'

HONEYMOON

1107 A newlywed couple woke up on the first morning of their Caribbean honeymoon and decided to take a stroll down to the beach. On their way they passed a shanty house where, sitting on the front porch, was an overweight woman, stark naked, legs wide apart, eating a slice of watermelon. Seeing this, the husband liked the idea of his new wife exhibiting her body in public and so he asked her whether she would do the same. The wife looked at him in disgust and refused.

The next morning they passed the shanty house again and, sure enough, the big woman was sitting on the porch, stark naked, legs wide apart, eating another slice of watermelon. Undeterred by his wife's earlier refusal, the husband suggested: 'Why don't you go over and ask that woman what it feels like to sit there naked, letting the air waft over your pussy?' Once again the wife was appalled at the idea and flatly refused to consider it.

This continued every morning for two weeks until it was the final day of their honeymoon. Each morning they would pass by the woman, the husband would try to persuade his wife to copy her, and each morning the wife would refuse. On that last morning, the husband decided to give it one more try and asked his wife: 'Why don't you go over and ask that woman what it feels like to sit there naked, letting the air waft over your pussy?'

To his delight, the wife relented, opened the gate of the shanty house and walked up to the big woman on the front porch. Hesitantly, she asked: 'What does it feel like to sit there naked, letting the air waft over your pussy?'

'I don't rightly know,' replied the woman, 'but it sure keeps the flies off my watermelon.'

1108 An eighty-five-year-old man married a twenty-five-year-old woman and, because of his age, she decided that on their wedding night they should have separate suites in case he overdid things.

Nevertheless she expected some form of sexual activity and, sure enough, after a few minutes there was a knock on her door. Her new husband came in, they had sex, and then he said goodnight and retired to his suite across the corridor.

Ten minutes later, he was back again. She was surprised but happily consented to more sex, after which he bade her goodnight and returned to his suite.

Fifteen minutes later, just as she was settling down for the night, there was another knock on her door. Once again, it was her husband, wanting yet more sex. Stunned by his voracious appetite, she gladly gave in, and afterwards told him: 'I'm really impressed that a guy your age has enough juice to go for it three times.'

The old man looked puzzled and said: 'Was I here before?'

1109 A guy slipped out of the hotel room on the first night of his honeymoon in Florida to buy his new bride a single red rose. He returned to find her naked on the bed, screwing one of the bellhops for all she was worth. Another bellhop was shagging her ass and she was sucking off the desk clerk and jerking off two waiters.

'What the heck's going on?' screamed the groom.

'Well,' replied his bride, 'you always knew I was a flirt.'

1110 An elderly couple got married. On the first night of their honeymoon, they cautiously began to undress in front of each other.

She removed her false teeth and put them in a glass. Then she removed her prosthetic leg and rested it against the wall. And all the while he watched her intently. Then she removed her bra, which contained false inserts, and took out her glass eye, which she put in a box on the bedside table. Still he gazed at her longingly. But as she took off her wig, she realized that he had suddenly stopped undressing.

'What are you waiting for?' she asked.

'You know what I want,' he said. 'Take it off and throw it over here.'

1111 A young woman wanted to get rich quick, so she set her sights on a seventy-nine-year-old sugar daddy, whom she planned to screw to death on their wedding night. Despite the age gap, the wedding and reception passed off smoothly and then they left for a romantic honeymoon in Hawaii. While he got ready in the hotel bathroom, she stripped off ready to put her evil scheme into practice. Then to her amazement he emerged from the bathroom wearing nothing but a condom over his twelve-inch erection, and ear plugs and nose plugs.

'What's going on?' she asked.

Rubbing his hands together in anticipation, he replied: 'There are two things I can't stand: the sound of a woman screaming and the smell of burning rubber!'

HOOKERS

1112 There were three hookers living together — a daughter, a mother, and a grandmother. One night the daughter came home looking thoroughly dejected.

'How did you get on tonight?' asked her mother.

'Not so good,' replied the daughter. 'I only got $20 for a blow job.'

'You don't know how lucky you are!' said the mother. 'In my day, we gave a blow job for fifty cents!'

'Huh!' said the grandmother scornfully. 'In my day we were just glad to get something warm in our stomachs!'

1113 A hooker went to the doctor and told him: 'If I get the tiniest cut, it seems to bleed for hours. Do you think I might be a haemophiliac?'

'It is possible,' said the doctor. 'Tell me, how much do you lose when you have a period?'

The hooker thought for a moment and said: 'About $900, I guess.'

1114 What do a bungee jump and a hooker have in common? — They're both cheap, fast, and if the rubber breaks, you're dead.

1115 A guy went to Las Vegas and won $75,000 at one of the casinos. So he booked into a luxury suite at a top hotel. Needing someone with whom to celebrate his good fortune, he phoned down to reception and asked the clerk to send up one of the highest-priced call girls in town.

Half an hour later, there was a knock on the door of the hotel room. The guy opened it to find the most gorgeous girl he had ever seen: long blonde hair, short red dress, and spiked heels. After pouring a drink for himself and the hooker, he said: 'Now, down to business. How much for a hand job?'

'Honey,' said the hooker, 'a hand job is $500.'

'That's outrageous!' said the guy.

'Come over here,' she said, walking towards one of the windows. 'See that strip mall over there? I own the last two stores on the end. I was able to buy those stores with the money I earned from giving hand jobs. So I must be pretty damned good.'

'All right,' sighed the man. 'Screw it, money is no object. Give me a hand job.'

Thirty minutes after she had finished, the guy was sitting on the couch, basking in sheer ecstasy. Pouring two more drinks, he said: 'I have to admit, that was the best hand job I've ever had. How much for a blow job?'

'Honey,' she replied, 'a blow job is $5,000.'

'That's outrageous!' he exclaimed.

'Come over here,' she said, walking towards another of the windows. 'See that hotel and casino over there on the corner? I own that I was able to buy it with the money I earned from giving blow jobs. I must be pretty damned good.'

'Oh, all right,' he said. 'Screw it, money is no object. Give me a blow job.'

An hour after she had finished, he was lying on the couch, his eyes rolled up inside his head. Barely able to stand, he staggered over to the bar, mixed two more drinks, and said: 'My God, that was the best blow job I have ever had. I've gotta know, how much for some pussy?'

The hooker looked at him and replied: 'Honey, if I had a pussy, I would own the whole city!'

1116 What do peanut butter and hookers have in common? – Both spread for bread.

1117 Two drunks were standing at a whorehouse door. The first drunk said: 'I heard these broads have the clap and that none of them would think twice about stealing every penny we've got.'

The second drunk said: 'Not so loud, or they won't let us in.'

1118 Having been working in the desert for six months, a guy was desperate for sex. So when he finally got a weekend off he headed straight for the town brothel. But there was only one girl left and she was having a period and was also suffering from a terrible case of mouth sores. Seeing how desperate he was, however, she offered to take out her glass eye and let him fuck the socket.

It was the best sex he'd ever had, and afterwards he promised he'd be back the next time he had a weekend off.

'OK,' she said, 'I'll keep an eye out for you.'

1119 A guy went to a brothel, chose a girl and paid his $200 up front. The girl had just taken the money and slipped into a sexy blue negligee when the fire alarm sounded. As flames began to spread through the building, the pair fled into the street where the guy lost sight of her in the thick smoke.

He asked one of the firemen: 'Did you see a blonde in a sheer blue negligee, with $200 in her hand?'

'No,' said the fireman.

The guy said. 'Well, if you do, screw her. It's paid for.'

1120 A hooker went to file her taxes, and for occupation put 'prostitute'. But the tax collector said: 'You can't put that – prostitution is an illegal occupation.'

So she said she would go away and ring back with a more acceptable occupation. An hour later she phoned back and said: 'I've got it – I'm a chicken farmer.'

'How do you get chicken farmer out of prostitution?' asked the taxman.

'Well,' she said, 'I raised over a thousand cocks last year.'

1121 Three guys visited a prostitute. As it was a slow night, she told them they could pay by the inch. When the first guy came out, the others asked him he much he had paid. '$75,' he replied. Then the second guy went in and when he came out, he told them he had paid $80. Finally the third guy came out.

'How much did you pay?' asked his two mates.

'$20,' he said.

'Only $20? How come?'

'I ain't stupid,' he said. 'I paid on the way out instead of on the way in!'

1122 An old guy knocked on the door of a brothel. 'I want a girl,' he said.

'That'll be $150,' said the Madame.

'$150! You're putting me on!'

'No, that'll cost an extra $10.'

1123 On a bitterly cold night, a young man called in at the town brothel.

The Madame said: 'You'll have to wait.'

'But there are lots of girls who aren't busy right now,' said the guy.

'Yes, but several of the rooms are closed for repairs,' she explained.

'Listen,' he persisted, 'I'm really desperate. I don't need a room, I'll do it anywhere.'

So she took his money and he went upstairs with one of the girls. Looking for a place to go, they decided to do it on the roof. But it was such a cold night that they froze to death halfway through having sex and fell to the sidewalk below. A passing drunk looked them over, staggered to the brothel door, and knocked.

'Go away!' said the Madame. 'We don't allow drunks in here.'

'I don't want to come in,' said the drunk. 'I just wanted to tell you that your sign fell down.'

1124 Did you hear about the hooker who was into bondage? – She was strapped for cash.

1125 Two hookers were talking. The first said: 'Last night I made $500 and I feel like a bottle of champagne.'

The other one said: 'Last night I made $5,000 and I feel like a pot of glue.'

1126 A guy went into a Midwest whorehouse and told the Madame: 'I want something different.'

'Well,' she said, 'we've got one girl that loves to take it up the ass.'

'No,' said the guy. 'That's too common. I want something really different.'

'OK, have you ever tried a Hurricane Ellie?'

'No, can't say I have,' replied the punter. 'I'll go for that.'

So he paid his money and was taken through to a room out back where he undressed. A few minutes later, an Amazonian woman came in and began puffing out her cheeks furiously, whipping up a veritable gale.

'What on earth are you doing?' he asked.

'I'm Hurricane Ellie,' she replied, 'and that is the wind coming from the hurricane.'

Then she started beating him over the head with her enormous breasts.

'What the hell are you doing?' he asked.

'Those are the coconuts falling from the trees and hitting you on the head. It's all part of the hurricane.'

Then she began pissing all over him, explaining: 'These are the warm rains coming from the hurricane.'

Suddenly he got up and began putting his clothes on.

'Where are you going?' she said.

'I'm leaving. Who can shag in this weather?'

1127 An eighty-eight-year-old man went to Hollywood to pick up a prostitute and get some action. He noticed one hooker and began flirting with her, but the woman got annoyed and said: 'Get lost, old man! You're ruining business!'

'Sure would like to get some action tonight,' he persisted.

'You've got to be kidding!' sneered the hooker. 'You're too old! You're all finished.'

'What did you say?'

'You heard me — you're all finished.'

'Oh,' replied the old man, 'how much do I owe you?'

1128 A salesman in a strange city was feeling horny and asked a bartender for the address of the nearest whorehouse. The bartender told him to go to 341 West 28th Street but by mistake he went to number 314, the office of a chiropodist.

Being met by a beautiful woman in a crisp white uniform surprised but intrigued him. She directed him to an examining room, told him to uncover and promised that someone would be with him soon. He loved the thought of the table and the reclining chair and was getting really aroused because of the strange and different approach this house offered. Finally the doctor's assistant, a gorgeous redhead, entered and found him sitting in the chair with his generous member in his hand.

'My goodness!' she exclaimed. 'I was expecting to see a foot.'

'Well,' said the salesman, 'if you're going to complain about an inch then I'll take my business elsewhere.'

1129 A New York hooker mistook a Salvation Army man for a soldier and propositioned him.

The man said: 'Ma'am, you may be forgiven as a victim of circumstances. Tell me, are you familiar with the concept of "original sin"?'

The hooker answered: 'Well, maybe and maybe not. But if it's really original, it'll cost you an extra twenty bucks.'

1130 Two hookers were standing on a New York street corner. One said: 'It's gonna be a good night. I smell cock in the air.'

The other one said: 'No, I just burped.'

1131 A guy was walking along the road in a smart neighbourhood when he approached a large house. To his horror, he spotted a naked couple having sex out on the lawn. Then he noticed another couple behind a tree, and a third couple screwing behind some bushes. So he walked up to the door of the house, and knocked. A well-dressed woman answered the door.

'What kind of place is this?' he demanded.

'This is a brothel,' she replied.

'Well, what's all this out on the lawn?'

'Oh, we're having a yard sale today.'

1132 A horny guy went to a whorehouse but only had five dollars. He was thrown out of the first two places he tried, so he visited a third.

'I need a blow job,' he told the Madame. 'But I've only got five dollars.'

'OK,' she said. 'That's not much, but for five dollars we can give you a penguin.'

'What's a penguin?' he asked.

'You'll see.'

So he paid his five dollars, went upstairs and waited for his penguin. A few minutes later a young woman came in and gave him a blow job. But just as he was about to come, she suddenly stopped and walked away. Frustrated beyond belief, he waddled after her with his pants around his ankles, screaming: 'What's a penguin?'

1133 A guy was walking down the street late at night when a hooker emerged from the shadows and asked: 'Wanna have a good time?'

'Sure,' he said, and they headed off to the nearest hotel.

As she took off her clothes, he just stared at her.

She said: 'What's the matter? Is this the first pussy you've seen since you crawled out of one?'

'No,' he replied. 'Just the first one I've seen big enough to crawl back into.'

1134 A guy staying at a Los Angeles hotel removed a card offering sexual services from a nearby phone box. Back in his hotel room he rang the number, and a woman with a silky soft voice asked whether she could be of assistance.

'Yes,' he said. 'I'd like a doggie in bondage gear, leather, PVC, whips, the lot. And then some hardcore spanking, rounded off with a blow job. What do you think?'

The woman said: 'That sounds really good and I'd like to oblige, but if you press 9 first, you'll get an outside line . . .'

1135 The police rounded up a group of hookers and made them line up in the street for questioning. Among those busted was a young call girl who didn't want her grandma to know what she did for a living. So when the old lady passed by and spotted her granddaughter, the girl explained her presence by saying that some people were passing out free oranges and she was queuing up for some.

Grandma wanted oranges too, so she went to the back of the line. Meanwhile a cop was going down the line, asking for information about the hookers. When he got to grandma, he was bewildered and said: 'You're so old! How do you do it?'

'Oh, it's easy,' said grandma. 'I just take out my dentures and suck them dry.'

1136 Emma was a new recruit to the streets of New Orleans. After performing her first trick, she described the experience to the other girls.

'He was a big, muscular marine,' she said.

'What did he want to do?' asked the others.

'I told him a straight shag was $100, but he said he didn't have that much. So I told him a blow job would be $75, but he didn't have that much either. He said he only had $25, so I told him that all he could have for $25 was a hand job. He agreed, so I pulled it out. I put one hand on it. Then I put the other hand above that one.' Raising her eyebrows and smiling, she continued, 'Then I put the first hand above the second hand . . .'

'My God!' exclaimed the others. 'It must have been huge! Then what did you do?'

'I loaned him $75!'

1137 Bill and Olivia decided to celebrate their twenty-fifth wedding anniversary with a trip to Las Vegas. As they registered at the hotel, 'Mimi', a young woman in a short skirt, became very friendly, but Bill brushed her aside.

'That was extremely rude of you,' said Olivia.

'What do you mean?' replied Bill. 'She was a prostitute.'

'That sweet young thing? I don't believe you.'

'OK, let's go up to our room and I'll prove it to you.'

From the room Bill called down to the desk and asked for 'Mimi' to come to room 1198. He then told his wife to hide in the bathroom. A few minutes later there was a knock on the door and in walked 'Mimi', clearly ready to do business.

'How much do you charge?' asked Bill.

'$125 basic rate, $100 tips for special services.'

Bill was taken aback. 'I was thinking more like $25.'

'You must really be a hick if you think you can buy sex for that price,' sneered 'Mimi' and, when it became obvious that Bill was not willing to meet her price, she left.

An hour later, Bill and Olivia were enjoying a cocktail in the hotel bar. 'Mimi' wandered over to them and, pointing at Olivia, remarked icily: 'See what you get for $25!'

1138 Tom met a hooker with an unusual speciality. He told his pal Steve: 'I had the most amazing experience last night. This girl wedged my dick into a hot-dog bun, added cheese, cucumber, pickles, and ketchup, then grabbed it with both hands and slowly ate her way down from the tip to the balls.'

'Wow!' said Steve. 'I hope you kept her number. I fancy some of that!'

Tom gave him her number but when the two guys met up again the next day, Steve looked really sad.

'What's up, mate?' asked Tom. 'Couldn't you find her?'

'I found her all right,' said Steve. 'But this time she tried something different. She put my dick between two wafer biscuits, covered it with strawberry ice cream and pineapple chunks, put a succulent fresh strawberry on top, and covered it with chocolate sauce.'

'My God!' exclaimed Tom. 'That sounds even better than I got from her. So why the long face?'

'Well,' said Steve, 'it looked so good, I ate it myself.'

HOSPITALS

1139 A woman had been in a coma for three months. There seemed little hope until one day, while a male nurse was giving her a sponge bath, he noticed that there was a response on the monitor when he washed her 'private area'. The nurse told the husband what had happened and suggested: 'Crazy as this sounds, maybe a little oral sex will do the trick and bring her out of the coma.'

The husband was sceptical, but the hospital staff promised to close the curtains to allow him total privacy. Besides, they said, anything was worth a try. So the husband finally agreed and went into his wife's room. But after a few minutes the woman's monitor flat-lined. There was no pulse, no heart rate. The nurses dashed into the room. The husband stood there, pulling up his pants, and said sadly: 'I think she choked.'

1140 What's grey, sits at the bed and takes the piss? — A kidney dialysis machine.

1141 A gorgeous young woman was lying on a trolley in a hospital corridor prior to being taken down to the operating theatre. A young man in a white coat came over, lifted up the sheet and looked at the girl's naked body before discussing his findings with two other men in white coats. Then the second man lifted up the sheet to examine her. But when the third man came over and lifted the sheet, the young woman lost her temper.
'Are these examinations absolutely necessary?' she demanded.
'I've no idea,' said the man. 'We're here to paint the ceiling.'

1142 Two kids were trying to figure out what game to play. Eventually one said: 'Let's play doctor.'
'Good idea,' said the other. 'You operate, and I'll sue.'

1143 How can you tell a head nurse? — She's the one with the dirty knees.

1144 A man was lying in a hospital bed, covered in bandages from head to toe. The guy in the next bed asked: 'What do you do for a living?'
'I'm a former window cleaner.'
'Oh, when did you give it up?'
'Halfway down.'

1145 A disturbing pattern began to emerge in the intensive care unit of a major city hospital. Every Monday for ten successive weeks at 7 a.m. precisely, the patient in bed number twelve died suddenly. All manner of theories were advanced, but with no satisfactory explanation forthcoming, the medical staff decided to observe the bed in secret. As they waited for the fateful hour, some clutched crosses and prayer books to ward off evil influences while the less superstitious carried a video recorder to capture every moment on tape.
At the stroke of seven o'clock, the door to the ward opened slowly, then a cleaner came in, disconnected the life support and plugged in a vacuum cleaner.

1146   An old man in hospital complained to the nurse: 'My dick died.'

Later, when the doctor made his rounds, the old man told him: 'My dick died.'

And when Sister came around that evening, the old man announced: 'My dick died.'

Next day the doctor saw him walking down the corridor, exposing himself. The doctor told him: 'Your penis is hanging out of your pyjamas.'

The old man said: 'Well, I told you my dick died.'

'So . . . ?'

'Well, today's the viewing.'

HUNTING

1147   Two hunters were out in the woods when one of them collapsed. He didn't seem to be breathing and his eyes were glazed. His companion took out his phone and called the emergency services.

'My friend is dead,' he gasped. 'What can I do?'

The operator said: 'Calm down, I can help. First, let's make sure he's dead.'

There was a silence, then the sound of a gunshot.

The guy returned to the phone and said: 'OK, now what?'

1148   A guy was out hunting when his shotgun went off accidentally, shooting him right in the penis. When he woke up from surgery, he found that the doctor had removed the pellets and appeared to have done a wonderful job repairing it. As he prepared to be discharged, the doctor handed him a business card.

'This is my brother's card,' said the doctor. 'I'll make an appointment for you to see him.'

The patient said: 'Is your brother a doctor?'

'No, he plays the flute. He'll show you where to put your fingers so you don't piss in your eye.'

1149   A group of friends went deer hunting and split up in pairs for the day. That night one hunter returned alone, staggering under the weight of an 8lb buck.

'Where's Martin?' asked the others.

'Martin had a stroke of some kind. He's a couple of miles back up the trail.'

The others were stunned. 'You left Martin lying out there and carried the deer back?'

'It was a tough call, but I figured no one is going to steal Martin.'

1150 A British explorer in Africa came across a pygmy standing next to a dead elephant.

'Did you kill this elephant?' asked the explorer.

'Yes,' answered the pygmy.

'What did you use?'

'A big club,' replied the pygmy.

'That must have been an enormous club,' said the explorer.

'Yes, it is,' said the pygmy. 'There are about 500 of us.'

1151 A hunter was giving a fellow hunter a tour of his home. Occupying pride of place in the living room was a stuffed lion.

'Hey,' enthused the visitor hunter, 'when did you bag him?'

'About three years ago, when I went hunting with my wife.'

'And what's he stuffed with?'

'My wife.'

1152 A guy went deer hunting in North Carolina. After shooting a deer, he was dragging it back to his truck when he was stopped by a game warden who asked to see his hunting licence. The hunter showed him the licence and was just about to leave when the warden shouted out: 'Hey, not so fast! I need to inspect the deer.'

The warden reached down, inserted his finger up the deer's butt, pulled it out, then sniffed his finger. 'This ain't no North Carolina deer,' he snarled. 'This here is a Virginia deer. You need to have a Virginia hunting licence to hunt this deer. You got one?'

It so happened that the guy had been hunting in Virginia the week before and was able to produce a valid licence. Reluctantly, the warden let him go.

The next week the guy was out hunting again. He shot another deer and was dragging it back to his truck when the same game warden pounced. 'Just a minute,' yelled the warden. 'I need to inspect that deer.'

The warden reached down, stuck his finger up the deer's butt, pulled it out, sniffed his finger and announced triumphantly: 'This here is a South Carolina deer! You got a South Carolina hunting licence?'

'Sure,' said the hunter, fetching the necessary document from his truck. Thwarted again, the warden had no option but to let him go.

This battle went on for the next three weeks. Each week the hunter shot a deer – one from Georgia, one from Tennessee, and one from West Virginia. Each time the game warden did the finger test, only for the hunter to produce a correct licence.

The West Virginia deer was the last straw for the exasperated warden. He raged: 'You seem to have got a hunting licence for every damn state in the south! Where the hell are you from anyway?'

The hunter dropped his pants, bent over and said: 'You tell me!'

1153 An African village was troubled by a man-eating lion. So its leaders sent a message to the great white hunter, Cholmondley-Smythe, to come and kill the beast. For several nights the hunter lay in wait for the lion, but it never showed. Fearing that he was too visible, he told the chief to kill a cow and give him its hide. Draping the skin over his shoulders, Cholmondley-Smythe then went to the pasture and, with his cunning camouflage, waited for the lion.

In the middle of the night, the villagers were woken by blood-curdling screams coming from the pasture. They arrived to find Cholmondley-Smythe writhing in agony. 'What happened?' asked the chief. 'Where is the lion?'

'Damn the lion!' said the hunter. 'Which of you idiots let the bull loose?'

1154 A young man from the city went to visit his uncle in the country but after a few days he became bored. The uncle tried to think of something for the city slicker to do and eventually suggested: 'Why don't you grab a gun, take the dogs, and go shooting?'

The nephew cheered up immediately and off he went with the dogs in tow. He returned a few hours later.

'How did you enjoy that?' asked uncle.

'It was great!' exclaimed the nephew. 'Got any more dogs?'

SADDAM HUSSEIN

1155 The eight Saddam Hussein body doubles were summoned to a bunker in downtown Baghdad. The deputy Prime Minister, Tariq Aziz, entered and said: 'I have some good news and some bad news.'

'What is the good news?' they asked.

'The good news,' said Aziz, 'is that Saddam is still alive, so you all still have jobs.'

'And the bad news?'

'He's lost an arm.'

1156 What did Saddam Hussein say when he came out of his hole? – Did I beat David Blaine?

1157 Saddam Hussein, his vice-president and his head of security were relaxing on the balcony of one of Saddam's palaces when a flock of geese flew overhead.

'Quick,' said Saddam to his vice-president. 'Shoot the geese.'

The vice-president picked up a rifle, took aim at the geese, but missed completely. Saddam shook his head in despair.

'You try,' Saddam said to his head of security, who promptly took aim with the rifle but also failed to hit a single goose.

Saddam was unimpressed. 'You're both useless,' he snapped. 'Why is it I have to everything around here myself?'

With that, he picked up the rifle, took careful aim and fired five rounds into the air. Not one bird fell. An awkward silence descended upon his two colleagues until the head of security pointed at the flock and said: 'My God, would you look at that! Dead birds flying!'

1158 Good News
Saddam Hussein is facing the death penalty.

1159 Bad News
David Beckham is taking it.

1160 Saddam Hussein called George W. Bush and said: 'George, I had a wonderful dream last night. I could see America, the whole country, and on each house I saw a banner.'

'What did it say on the banners?' asked Bush.

'Long Live Saddam Hussein!'

Bush said: 'You know, Saddam, I'm really happy you called because last night I had a similar dream. I could see all of Baghdad, and it was more beautiful than ever. It had been completely rebuilt and on each house flew an enormous banner.'

'What did the banners say?'

'I don't know,' said Bush. 'I can't read Hebrew!'

1161 Why is Saddam Hussein afraid to have sex with a girl? – Because when he opens her legs he'll see Bush.

1162 Saddam Hussein was sitting in his Baghdad palace planning his next military campaign when his telephone rang.

'Hello, Mr Hussein,' said the voice on the other end of the phone. 'This is Paddy from County Donegal in Ireland. I am ringing to inform you that we are officially declaring war on you.'

'Well, Paddy,' replied Saddam, 'this is indeed important news. Tell me, how big is your army?'

'At this moment in time,' said Paddy after a moment's calculation, 'there is myself, my cousin Sean, my next door neighbour Michael, and the dominoes team from the pub – that makes eight in all.'

Saddam sighed. 'I must tell you, Paddy, that I have one million men in my army waiting to move on my command.'

Paddy fell silent, then said sombrely: 'I'll have to ring you back.'

Sure enough, the next day Paddy rang back. 'Right, Mr Hussein,' he said. 'The war is still on. We have managed to acquire some equipment.'

'And what equipment would that be, Paddy?' asked Saddam.

'Well, we have two combine harvesters, a bulldozer and Murphy's tractor.'

Once more Saddam sighed. 'I must tell you, Paddy, that I have 18,000 tanks, 13,000 armoured personnel carriers, and my army has increased to one and a half million since we last spoke.'

'Really?' said Paddy, crestfallen. 'I'll have to ring you back.'

Sure enough, Paddy rang again the next day. 'Right, Mr Hussein, the war is still on. We have managed to get ourselves airborne. We've modified Gerry's glider with a couple of rifles in the cockpit, and the bridge team has joined us as well!'

Saddam was silent for a minute, then sighed. 'I must tell you, Paddy, that I have 11,000 bombers, 20,000 MiG attack planes, my military complex is surrounded by laser-guided surface-to-air missile sites, and since we last spoke, my army has increased to two million.'

'Is that so?' said Paddy quietly. 'I'll have to ring you back.'

Sure enough, Paddy called again the next day. 'Right, Mr Hussein, I am sorry to tell you that we have had to call off the war.'

'I'm sorry to hear that,' said Saddam. 'Why the sudden change of heart?'

'Well,' replied Paddy, 'we had a chat about it, and there's no way we can feed two million prisoners.'

HYGIENE

1163 Two American guys were chatting over a beer. Then one said: 'Do you like women with bad body odour and bad breath?'
'No way,' replied his friend.
'Do you like pussies you could hide a watermelon in?'
'No way.'
'Then what the hell are you doing messing around with my wife?'

1164 Why do men take showers instead of baths? — Because pissing in the bath is disgusting.

Signs That You Don't Take Enough Baths:

1165 • The dirt on your body can be seen from 100 yards away.

1166 • The manager at a sewage plant greets you with the words, 'What's that smell?'

1167 • On Christmas morning you find several bars of soap in your stocking.

1168 • You stick to everything.

1169 • Two or more people have choked to death in your presence.

1170 • Whenever you walk down the street, it seems like it's raining flies.

1171 • Old people are offended by your odour.

1172 • Jehovah's Witnesses call at every house except yours.

1173 A man went into a pharmacy and asked for an anal deodorant.
'We don't stock anal deodorants,' said the pharmacist.
'Yes you do,' insisted the man. 'I bought one from this store only last month.'
The pharmacist was puzzled. 'Well, OK, then, if you bring in the old container, I'll do my best to match it up.'
The next day the man returned and handed the old can of deodorant to the pharmacist. The words on the label read: 'To use, push up bottom.'

HYPOCHONDRIA

1174 Mrs Peabody was an incorrigible hypochondriac who pestered her doctor for years with imaginary ailments. He simply used to prescribe her aspirin under a different name to keep her happy. One day she came to him complaining of chest pains, and he prescribed her the usual tablets. But this time her condition was genuine and she died two days later of a heart attack. The doctor was so distraught to hear of her death that he dropped dead from shock.

It so happened that Mrs Peabody and the doctor were buried in adjoining plots. The day after his burial, the doctor heard a tapping sound on his coffin. A muffled voice called out: 'Doctor, this is Mrs Peabody. Do you have anything for worms?'

IMPOTENCE

1175 Having being informed that the husband was infertile, a childless couple decided to try artificial insemination. When the woman arrived at the clinic, she was told to undress, climb on the table and place her feet in the stirrups. She was feeling very uncomfortable about the whole situation and when the doctor started dropping his pants, she freaked.

'Wait a second! What the hell is going on here?' she yelled.

'Don't you want to get pregnant?' demanded the doctor.

'Well, yes, but . . .'

'Then lie back and spread 'em,' ordered the doctor. 'We're out of the bottled stuff, so you'll have to make do with what's on tap.'

1176 No longer able to obtain an erection, a guy consulted a doctor about the problem. The doctor said that because of serious muscle damage to the base of the penis, the only hope was for radical experimental surgery in the form of inserting the muscles of a baby elephant's trunk into the base of the patient's penis. Even then, the doctor warned, it was a long shot. The guy admitted it sounded a daunting prospect but decided that it was worth the risk just to have the chance of having sex again.

The doctor performed the surgery and a couple of months later he gave the patient permission to try out his new equipment. By way of celebration, he took his girlfriend out to dinner, but while in the restaurant he suddenly began to feel unbearable pressure in his pants. Finally he could stand it no longer and secretly unzipped his pants in a bid to relieve the pain. No sooner had he done so than his penis rose out of his pants, reached across the table, grabbed a dinner roll and disappeared back into his pants.

His girlfriend was mightily impressed. 'Hey, that was cool. Can you do it again?'

By now the guy's eyes were watering with the pain. 'Probably,' he gasped, 'but I don't know if I can fit another dinner roll up my ass!'

1177 A man had problems getting an erection. So he went to a doctor who, after a thorough examination, said: 'There's nothing wrong with you physically. You're suffering from "performance anxiety". My advice is to wait until your wife is asleep and then reach down between her legs, get a little of her love juice on your finger and rub it under your nose. This will stimulate your brain and should result in an erection. With your wife asleep, there will be no performance anxiety. Once the desired effect is achieved, wake her up and make love to her.'

That night, the man went home and eagerly followed the doctor's instructions. He reached down between his wife's legs, got her love juice rubbed it on his upper lip right beneath his nose. After a couple of minutes, he began to feel a tingling sensation between his legs, so he grabbed more juice and rubbed it under his nose. Soon he had a full erection.

Excitedly he woke his wife and said: 'Look, honey! Look what I have!'

She moaned: 'You wake me up at two o'clock in the morning to show me you have a bloody nose?'

1178 An elderly man went to see a urologist who shared an office with several other doctors. The waiting room was full. The receptionist was a large, imposing woman, who said to him in a very loud voice: 'You want to see the doctor about impotence, right?'

All of the other patients' heads turned. Hugely embarrassed, the old man recovered his composure to reply in an equally loud voice: 'No, I've come to inquire about a sex change operation – and I'd like the same doctor that did yours!'

1179 A guy who suffered from impotence went to see a doctor who gave him a monkey gland implant. The treatment worked perfectly and, nine months and two weeks later, his wife had a baby.

When the nurse came out of the delivery room to break the news, the husband asked eagerly: 'Is it a boy or a girl?'

The nurse said: 'We won't know until it comes down off the chandelier.'

INCEST

1180 Jack and Jenny were twins who couldn't find dates to the prom. So Jenny asked Jack to go with her, but Jack wasn't too keen on the idea.

'No, you're my sister,' he said. 'That's gross.' But, as the day of the prom drew nearer and he still hadn't found another date, he reluctantly agreed to take Jenny.

As they stood by the punch bowl at the prom, Jenny asked Jack to dance. 'No,' said Jack. 'You're my sister. That's gross.' But Jenny persuaded him and they had fun.

After the dance Jenny asked Jack to drive her to Makeout Hill. 'No,' said Jack. 'You're my sister. It would be gross.'

Jenny promised that they would just talk, so Jack relented. They were at Makeout Hill talking when Jenny moved to the back seat and said: 'Come on, Jack, take me.'

This time, Jack didn't argue. When he moved on top of Jenny, she murmured: 'You're a lot lighter than Dad.'

Jack said: 'I know. Mom told me last night.'

1181 A young girl from the Deep South said to her father: 'Dad I really want to see that new Brad Pitt movie. Please can I go?'

The father replied: 'Only if you suck my dick.'

The girl was repulsed by the idea, but the father remained adamant. She was so desperate to see the movie that eventually she gave in and put his member in her mouth. As soon as she did, she leaped back and screamed. 'Yuk, it tastes like shit!'

'Yeah,' said the father. 'Your brother wanted to go to the movies too.'

INSANITY

1182 A farmer was pulling a cart load of horse manure past an asylum.

A mental patient peered over the fence and inquired: 'What are you going to do with all that?'

'I'm going to put it on my strawberries,' replied the farmer.

'You must be mad,' said the patient. 'We put cream and sugar on ours.'

1183 A man walked into a dentist's surgery and said: 'Excuse me, can you help me? I think I'm a moth.'

'You don't need a dentist. You need a psychiatrist!'

'Yes, I know.'

'So why did you come in here?'

'The light was on.'

1184 A man went to a psychiatrist and said: 'I think my wife should be put in a mental home. Last week she bought 20lbs of wire wool.'

'Well,' agreed the psychiatrist, 'that is certainly an abnormally large amount, but it doesn't mean that she's certifiable.'

'Oh, no?' said the man. 'But then she started knitting an electric fire!'

1185 A man who had been in a mental home for a number of years seemed to have improved to the point where he thought he might be released. But the head of the institution, exercising caution, wanted to interview him first.

'Tell me,' he said, 'if we release you, what do you intend doing with your life?'

The inmate said: 'I can't wait to get back to normality. I was a nuclear physicist, you know, and it was the stress of my work in weapons research that helped put me here in the first place. So if I am released, I shall confine my work to pure theory where I hope the situation will be less stressful.'

'That sounds admirable,' said the head of the institution.

'Alternatively,' continued the inmate, 'I might teach. There is a great deal to be said for spending one's life in encouraging a new generation of scientists.'

'I couldn't agree more,' said the head.

'Or then again I might write,' mused the inmate. 'There is considerable need for books on science to which the general public can relate. Or, who knows, I might even write a novel based on my experiences in this splendid institution.'

'That would be an interesting possibility,' agreed the head.

'And if all else fails,' added the inmate, 'I can always continue my life as a teapot.'

IRAQ

1186 On returning from service in Iraq, three US soldiers were asked to report to their commander who announced that, because of their gallantry, the army would be paying each of them $100 per inch on their bodies from one point to another of their choice. The commander asked the first soldier, a special forces commando, how he could measure him up.

'I'll have the top of my head to the tips of my toes, sahr!'

'Sure,' said the commander, measuring him. 'That's 70 inches, so here's $7,000.'

Next he asked the second man, a marine, who answered: 'I'll have from the tips of both arms outstretched, sahr!'

'OK,' said the commander, measuring the marine's outstretched arms. 'That's 75 inches, so here's $7,500.'

Finally he asked the third soldier, an explosives expert, who said: 'I'll have from the tip of my dick to the end of my balls, sahr!'

The commander was slightly taken aback by the request but agreed and began to measure the private's privates. After a few seconds, he suddenly stood up and demanded: 'Where are your balls, soldier?'

The soldier said: 'Baghdad, sahr!'

1187 Why is it twice as easy to train Iraqi fighter pilots? – You only have to teach them to take off.

1188 Morale was low among a US platoon stationed just outside Baghdad. In a desperate attempt to revive flagging spirits, the sergeant announced: 'Good news, men. We may not be getting the new weapons we've been promised, but at least we're going to have a change of underwear.'

The men visibly brightened. The sergeant continued: 'Right. Anderson, you change with Winters. Winters, you change with Kanchelsky . . .'

1189 What's the difference between Iraq and Vietnam? – Bush had an escape plan for Vietnam.

1190 News reports state that US forces have swooped on an Iraqi primary school and removed a ruler, a set square, a protractor, and a calculator. George W. Bush said this was clear and overwhelming evidence that Iraq did indeed possess weapons of maths instruction.

IRISH JOKES

1191 Paddy and Mick were walking home after a drunken night on the town. They had no money for a taxi and were staggering around aimlessly when they found themselves outside the bus depot. Suddenly Paddy had a brainwave and said to Mick: 'Get in there and steal a bus so we can drive home. I'll wait out here and keep a lookout for the police.'

So Mick went in, but twenty minutes later there was still no sign of him. Mystified as to what was going on, Paddy poked his head around the door and saw Mick running from bus to bus, looking extremely worried.

'What the hell are you doing?' asked Paddy. 'Get a move on!'

'I can't find a number 7 anywhere, Paddy.'

Paddy threw up his hands in disbelief. 'Just how stupid are you, Mick? For Christ's sake steal a number 9, and we'll get off at the roundabout and walk the rest of the way!'

1192 An Irishman went for a job on a construction site.

The foreman said: 'Can you brew tea?'

The Irishman said: 'Yes.'

'Good,' said the foreman. 'Can you drive a fork lift?'

'Why?' asked the Irishman. 'Just how big is the teapot?'

1193 Did you hear about the Irish loan shark who lent out all his money and then skipped town?

1194 A German, a Scotsman and an Irishman were enjoying their pints of beer until three flies suddenly buzzed into the bar and landed in each of their drinks. The German was disgusted and pushed his pint away. The Scotsman pulled the insect out of his pint and continued drinking. The Irishman was furious. He pulled the fly out by the wings, held it over his pint and yelled: 'Spit it out, ya bastard! Spit it out!'

1195 Why did the Irishman buy a plate with four corners? – So that he could have a square meal.

1196 Two Irish construction workers – Liam and Barry – were toiling away while their boss just sat around drinking tea. After a while Liam got so fed up that he turned to Barry and said: 'How come we do all the work while he drinks tea and gets all the money?'

'I don't know,' said Barry. 'Why don't you ask him?'

So Liam went over to his boss and said: 'How come we do all the work while you drink tea and get all the money?'

The boss replied simply: 'Intelligence.'

'What do you mean, intelligence?' said Liam.

The boss said: 'I'll show you.' He then put his hand on a tree and told Liam: 'Hit my hand as hard as you can.'

Liam wound up his most powerful punch but just as he was about to land it, the boss pulled his hand away and Liam's fist thudded into the tree.

Nursing his wounds, Liam went back to Barry. 'Well,' asked Barry, 'what did he say?'

Smiling to himself, Liam promised to explain. He looked around for a tree but couldn't find one. So he put his hand on his face and said to Barry: 'Hit my hand as hard as you can . . .'

1197 How can you spot the Irish Jew at the Wailing Wall? – He's the one with the harpoon.

1198 Murphy and O'Reilly were driving their truck down a country lane when they spotted a sign saying, 'Low bridge ahead. 11ft Clearance.'

'Damn,' said Murphy. 'This truck is 12ft high.'

O'Reilly leaned out the window to check up and down the lane. 'What do you say we go for it?' he said. 'There's nobody around to report us.'

1199 Paddy and Danny got in the car for the journey home and said their goodbyes
to their friend Mick.

'Thanks for putting us up for the weekend,' said Paddy. 'The food was
great, the booze was great, and I really enjoyed screwing your wife!'

On the way home, Danny turned to Paddy and said: 'I hope you weren't
serious about enjoying screwing his wife?'

'No,' said Paddy, 'I can't say that I enjoyed it, but I didn't want to hurt
Mick's feelings.'

1200 A motorist stopped at a country ford and asked an Irishman sitting nearby
how deep the water was.

'A couple of inches,' replied the Irishman.

So the motorist drove into the ford and his car promptly disappeared
beneath the surface in a cauldron of bubbles.

'That's odd,' thought the Irishman. 'The water only goes halfway up on
those ducks.'

1201 Paddy's wife went to the doctor's for a checkup. Afterwards the doctor told
her: 'I must inform you that you have a fissure in your uterus, and if you ever
have a baby it will be a miracle.'

When she got home, she told Paddy: 'Sure, you're not going to believe
this. I went to the doctor and he said: "You have a fish in your uterus, and if
you have a baby it will be a mackerel."'

1202 A penguin walked into an Irish bar in Antarctica and said: 'Have you seen my
brother?'

The bartender said: 'What does he look like?'

1203 How do you confuse an Irishman? – Give him two spades and tell him to take
his pick.

1204 Murphy walked into work with both of his ears bandaged up. The boss said:
'What happened to your ears?'

Murphy said: 'Yesterday I was ironing a shirt when the phone rang and I
accidentally answered the iron.'

The boss said: 'Well, that explains one ear, but what happened to your
other ear?'

'Jeez,' said Murphy, 'I had to call the doctor!'

1205 Seamus said to Paddy: 'I'm taking my pig to market next week and I want to find out how much it weighs.'

'No problem at all,' said Paddy. 'To figure out how heavy a pig is, you find a good stout plank of wood and balance it on the pole of a fence. Tie the pig onto one end of the plank, then run around to the other side and put a rock on the opposite end. Keep trying different rocks until you get one that balances with the pig. You see, it's that simple. Then all you have to do is guess the weight of the rock.'

1206 Did you hear about the Irish firing squad? – They stood in a circle.

1207 Paddy and Sean went duck hunting. Paddy shot at a flying bird, and it dropped dead at his feet. Sean turned to him and said: 'You could have saved yourself a shot there, Paddy. From that height, the fall alone would have killed it.'

1208 An Irishman came home and told his wife he had been banned from the local DIY store.

'Why?' she asked.

'Well,' he said, 'a bloke in overalls came up to me and asked if I wanted decking, so I thought I'd get the first punch in.'

1209 How did the Irish fish die? – It drowned.

1210 A drunk knocked on a door. When a woman opened it, he yelled: 'I'm Irish, I'm horny, and I want an Irish colleen!'

Before the woman could respond, he peered in and shouted: 'Begorrah! There's a beauty lying over there. I'll have her!'

'I'm going to have to ask you to leave,' said the woman frostily.

'What's the matter?' sneered the drunk. 'Are you prejudiced? I just want that girl over there. I've got plenty of money – there, see for yourself – so why can't I come in?'

'Because,' replied the woman, 'this is a funeral home.'

1211 The first Irish National Steeplechase was finally abandoned. Not one horse could get a decent footing on the cathedral roof.

1212 An Irishman was taking his driving test. The examiner asked him what a single yellow line means.

The Irishman replied: 'It means you can't park there at all.'
'And what does a double yellow line mean?'
The Irishman said: 'It means you can't park there at all, at all.'

1213 Where do an Irish family go on holiday? – A different bar.

1214 'Paddy,' asked the barmaid, 'what are those two bulges down the front of your trousers?'

'They're hand grenades,' said Paddy. 'The next time that queer Flanagan comes in here and starts feeling my balls, I'll blow his bloody fingers off!'

1215 Why did God prevent alcohol? – To prevent the Irish from ruling the world.

1216 A Donegal farmer was ploughing his field when his dim-witted son asked if he could help.

'I don't know, son,' said the farmer. 'Ploughing needs a steady hand.'
The son looked crestfallen.
'OK, then. Here, take this, and I'll watch you.'

So the son began ploughing, but his lines were all over the place. 'I don't understand,' he said. 'I was watching the plough to make sure that I didn't go crooked.'

'That's the problem,' said the farmer. 'Don't look at the plough – you have to watch where you're going. Look at the other end of the field, pick out an object and head straight for it. That way, you'll cut a straight row every time.'

With that, the farmer went back to the house, leaving the son to plough a lone furrow. When he returned, the farmer saw to his horror that the boy had cut the worst row he had seen in his life. It went all over the field in haphazard circles.

'What happened?' he asked his son. 'I've never seen such a terrible field. There's not one straight line.'

'But I did what you said: I fixed my sights on that dog playing at the other end of the field.'

1217 A cop stopped two Irish drunks in the street. He asked the first: 'Can I have your name and address?'

The first replied: 'I'm Paddy O'Grady of no fixed address.'
Then the cop turned to the second drunk and asked the same question.
The second drunk answered: 'I'm Seamus O'Toole, and I live in the flat above Paddy.'

1218 Murphy marched into the library and told the librarian: 'I've got a complaint about a book I took out last week. It has way too many characters, and there is no plot at all.'

The librarian said: 'Are you the person who took our phone directory?'

1219 Did you hear about the Irishman who got a camera for his birthday? – He just got back his first roll of film, twenty-four shots of his right eye.

1220 Following a shipwreck, two men and a woman from each of the following countries were washed up on a desert island: Italy, France, Germany, Greece, England, Bulgaria, Japan, the United States, and Ireland. One month later, and a lot has happened.

One Italian man has killed the other Italian man for the Italian woman.

The two French men and the French woman are living happily in a ménage-à-trois.

The two German men have a strict weekly schedule of alternating visits with the German woman.

The two Greek men are sleeping with each other while the Greek woman cooks and cleans for them.

The two English men are waiting for someone to introduce them to the English woman.

The two Bulgarian men took a long look at the endless ocean and a long look at the Bulgarian woman, and started swimming.

The two Japanese men have faxed Tokyo and are awaiting instructions.

The two American men are contemplating suicide because the American woman has complained constantly about her body; the true nature of feminism; how she can do everything they can do; the necessity of fulfilment; the equal division of household chores; how sand and palm trees make her look fat; but how at least her relationship with her mother is improving.

The two Irish men have divided the island into north and south and set up a distillery. They do not remember if sex is in the picture because things get foggy after the first few litres of coconut whiskey. But they're happy because at least the English aren't getting laid either.

1221 An Irishman was having sex with a Jewish girl.

He said: 'You're not very tight for a Jewish girl.'

She replied: 'You're not very thick for an Irishman.'

1222 Patrick went on the television quiz show, *Irish Mastermind*. The host asked: 'What is the capital of Ireland?'

'Pass,' said Patrick.

Next the host asked: 'What are the colours of the Irish flag?'

'Pass,' said Patrick.

Then the host asked: 'What is a leprechaun?'

'Pass,' said Patrick.

A voice from the audience shouted out: 'Good man, Paddy! Tell 'em nothing!'

1223 Mick and Sean found three hand grenades and decided they had better take them to the police station.

'What if one of them explodes before we get there?' asked Mick.

'Don't worry,' said Sean. 'We'll just lie and tell them we only found two.'

1224 Two Englishmen were talking in a bar. One said: 'Last night was a bit lively in here. I was telling a few Irish jokes when this big burly Irishman came over and started bad-mouthing me. He was ranting and raving about how I should be ashamed of myself for telling Irish jokes. He was having a real go at me. Then he started pushing me and said he was going to teach me a lesson I'd never forget. And then he went for me with a razor. It could have been pretty nasty, but luckily he couldn't find a place to plug it in.'

1225 There were just three ice skaters to go in the Olympic men's figure skating competition. First up was the Russian who gave a technically brilliant performance although his artistic interpretation left a little to be desired.

The judges' scores read: Britain 5.7, Russia 5.9, United States 5.5, Ireland 6.0.

Next on the ice was the American who was flamboyant but made a few technical errors.

The judges' scores read: Britain 5.7, Russia 5.6, United States 5.9, Ireland 6.0.

Last to skate was the Irish competitor. No sooner had he begun his routine than he tripped over and fell flat on his face. As he got to his feet, he fell over again. In the course of his two-minute performance, he fell over no fewer than nineteen times and stumbled off the ice covered in cuts and bruises.

The judges' scores read: Britain 0.0, Russia 0.0, United States 0.0, Ireland 6.0.

The other three judges turned to the Irish judge and said: 'How on earth can you give that dreadful performance top marks?'

The Irish judge replied: 'You've got to remember, it's really slippery out there.'

1226 An Irishman was travelling home late at night on the subway when he read a sign: 'Dogs must be carried on the escalator.'

Despairingly, he thought to himself: 'Now where on earth am I going to find a dog at this time of night?'

1227 Two Irishmen, Seamus and Patrick, were cast adrift in a lifeboat following a shipwreck. By a stroke of luck, they found an old lamp and when they rubbed it, a genie appeared. The genie granted them one wish.

Seamus said: 'I'd like the entire ocean to be turned into Guinness beer.' And POOF! it was done.

Patrick looked at Seamus disgustedly. 'Nice going, Seamus! Now we're going to have to pee in the boat!'

1228 A man walked up to a counter and asked for a plate of potatoes.

'You must be Irish?' said the clerk.

The man was furious. 'That is so stereotypical,' he stormed. 'If I walked in here and asked for pasta, would you naturally assume I was Italian?'

'Well, no,' admitted the clerk.

'And if I ordered a curry, would you automatically think I was Indian?'

'Of course not,' said the clerk.

'So what right do you have to assume that I'm Irish just because I walk in here and ask for a plate of potatoes?'

The clerk replied: 'Because this is a travel agent's.'

1229 Did you hear about the tragedy in Ireland? – In Dublin's biggest department store, a power outage meant that shoppers were stuck on the escalators for three hours.

1230 The boss on an Irish building site ordered one of his men to dig a hole six feet deep. After the job had been done, however, the boss explained that there had been a change of plan and that the hole wouldn't be needed after all. So he told the workman to fill it in.

The workman filled in the hole, but couldn't get all of the soil packed back into the hole without leaving a mound on top. When he told the boss of his problem, the boss snorted: 'Honestly! Where do they find you people? Obviously you didn't dig the hole deep enough!'

1231 How do we know Christ was Irish? – Well, he was 33, still lived at home with his mother, whom he thought was still a virgin, and she thought he was the son of God.

1232 Paddy and Mick were walking down the main street when they saw a little old lady shuffling along towards them.

'Hey,' said Paddy, 'isn't that Mother Theresa?'

'How can it be?' said Mick. 'She's dead.'

'That's as may be,' said Paddy. 'But, to be sure, she's the spitting image of her. I'm going to ask if it is her.' So Paddy went up to the old lady and said: 'Excuse me, but aren't you Mother Theresa?'

The old lady snarled: 'Why don't you fuck off, you big idjeet!' She then whacked him over the head with her umbrella and kicked him hard in the balls before disappearing down an alley.

As she vanished from view, Paddy groaned: 'Damn. Now we'll never know!'

ITALIANS

1233 A New York City bus stopped and two Italian men got on. They sat down and engaged in animated conversation. The woman behind ignored them at first, but then listened in horror as one of the men said:

'Emma come first. Den I come. Two asses, dey come together. I come again. Two asses, dey come together again. I come again and pee twice. Then I come once-a-more.'

The woman did not want to hear any more of this. 'You foul-mouthed swine,' she raged. 'In this country we don't talk about our sex lives in public.'

The man looked puzzled. 'Hey, cool down lady. I'm just a tellin' my friend how to spell "Mississippi." '

1234 How can you spot an Italian airplane? – They're the ones with hair under the wings.

1235 What did the barber say to the Italian kid? – Do you want your hair cut or should I just change the oil?

1236 Why do Italians wear gold chains around their necks? – So they know where to stop shaving.

1237 Two tourists in Rome were walking down the street when they noticed an Italian organ grinder with his monkey. As they passed, one of the men put a $20 bill in the monkey's cup.

'I thought you didn't like Italians,' said his friend.

'I don't really,' said the other. 'But they're so cute when they're little.'

1238 Lying on his deathbed, a Mafia godfather summoned his eldest son to his side and said: 'Luigi, I want you to have this family heirloom.' And with that, he produced a silver gun from a bedside drawer and handed it to the son.

'I'm really honoured,' said the son, 'but you know I don't like guns. If you want to leave me something, why don't you leave me your gold watch?'

'I see,' snorted the godfather. 'You don't want my gun, huh? So, let me get this straight, when you find your wife in bed with some jerk, whaddya gonna do? Shoot him, or point at your watch and say, "Hey, buddy, time's up?"'

1239 What do you call a smiling Roman with pubic hair between his teeth? — Gladiator.

1240 Three Italian mothers were attending an American football game. Each had a son playing on the same team. At the start of the game, the first boy seized his opportunity, grabbed the ball, outfoxed the opposing players, and sprinted to make a touchdown. His proud mother leaped in the air with joy. 'Thatsa ma boy! I raised him onna da pet milk. Ain't he a peach?'

Soon the second boy received the ball and, in a spectacular run down the field, made another goal for the team. Not to be outdone, his mother jumped from her seat, screaming with delight: 'Thatsa ma boy! I raised him onna da breast milk. Ain't he wonderful?'

The third boy had failed to shine, but finally someone threw him the ball. He fumbled it, then recovered, ran in the wrong direction, fell with the ball, ran some more, stumbled again, dropped it once more, retrieved it, and finally crossed the goal line at the wrong end of the field. His mother rose from her seat and shouted: 'Thatsa ma boy! I raised him onna Milk of Magnesia. Ain't he the shits?'

1241 Two Italian virgins were on the first night of their honeymoon. They had no idea what they were supposed to do, so he called his mother for help.

'Just cuddle up to each other,' advised Mama, 'and let nature take its course.'

They cuddled up on the bed, but nothing happened, so a few minutes later he phoned his mother again.

'Get into bed,' she suggested. 'Kiss each other and see where it leads.'

So they got into bed and kissed, but still nothing happened. So he phoned his mother for a third time.

Frustrated, Mama replied: 'Listen, just take the biggest thing you have and stick it in the hairiest thing she has.' And Mama slammed the phone down.

Ten minutes later her son called her back and said hesitantly: 'Right, I have my nose in her armpit. Now what do I do?'

1242 How is the Italian version of Christmas different? – One Mary, one Jesus and twenty Wise Guys.

1243 Luigi and Antonio met on the street. 'Hey, Antonio,' cried Luigi. 'Where you been for the past two weeks? No one seen you around.'

'Dona talk to me, Luigi,' said Antonio, 'I been inna jail.'

'Jail!' exclaimed Luigi. 'What for you been in jail?'

'Wella, Luigi, I was lyin' onna dis beach, and da cops come, arrest me and throw me inna jail.'

'But dey dona throw you in jail just for lyin' onna da beach!'

'Yeah, but dis beach was screamin' and akickin' and ayellin'!'

JEHOVAH'S WITNESSES

1244 A man arrived at the gates of heaven. St Peter asked: 'Religion?'

The man replied: 'Methodist.'

St Peter looked down his list and said: 'Go to room 16, but be very quiet as you pass room 9.'

Another man arrived at the gates of heaven. St Peter asked: 'Religion?'

The man said: 'Baptist.'

'OK,' said St Peter. 'Go to room 22, but be very quiet as you pass room 9.'

A third man arrived at the gates. St Peter asked: 'Religion?'

The man answered: 'Jewish.'

'Fine,' said St Peter. 'Go to room 14, but be very quiet as you pass room 9.'

The man said: 'I can understand there being different rooms for different religions, but why must I be quiet when I pass room 9?'

St Peter said: 'The Jehovah's Witnesses are in room 9, and they think they're the only ones here.'

1245 What do you get when you cross a skunk with a Jehovah's Witness? – A smell you can't get rid of.

1246 A Jehovah's Witness was doing his rounds, knocking door to door. Eventually an elderly woman invited him in for a cup of coffee.

He was so shocked, he said: 'Are you sure?'

'Yes, yes, dear, come on in,' she insisted. 'I don't see many people these days. And although my sister's coming later, she won't be here until two o'clock, so that gives us plenty of time for a nice chat. Now I want you to tell me all about the Jehovah's Witnesses.'

'I can't,' he spluttered. 'I've only been a Jehovah's Witness four years, and I've never got this far before!'

1247 Two Jehovah's Witnesses were going door to door. At one house, the woman told them bluntly that she was not remotely interested in listening to their message. She slammed the door in their faces but, to her surprise, it bounced open again. Again and again, she tried to slam the door, but still it wouldn't shut. Angrily, she yelled: 'Will you get your blasted foot out of my door!'

'My foot isn't in your door,' said one of the Jehovah's Witnesses. 'But you might want to move your cat.'

JESUS CHRIST

1248 Three wise men arrived to visit the child lying in the manger. One of the wise men was very tall and bumped his head on the low doorway as he entered the stable. 'Jesus Christ!' he exclaimed.

Joseph said: 'Write that down, Mary. It's better than Wayne.'

1249 Every night a little Catholic boy knelt beside his bed and prayed to Jesus for a new car. But after three weeks and no sign of the car, the boy became impatient. So one night he ran into his parents' bedroom, grabbed a statuette of the Virgin Mary, wrapped it in paper, tape and twine, and put it in a box at the bottom of his closet. Then he got down on his knees again, put his hands together and said: 'OK, Jesus, if you ever want to see your mother again . . .'

1250 What's the difference between Jesus and a painting? – It takes only one nail to hang a painting.

1251 What did the Virgin Mary say when she saw the wise men? – 'Typical. You wait ages then three come at once.'

1252 Jesus and Moses got together for a reunion. Moses was reminiscing. 'You know,' he said, 'it's been years since I've parted a sea.' So he raised his hands, and a sea parted. 'Hey, that was fun!' he exclaimed.

Then Jesus said: 'It's been a long time since I walked on water.' So he started to walk on water but after about ten paces, he sank and had to wade back to shore. 'That's odd,' he mused. 'I always used to be able to do it.'

So he tried again, but fared little better and had to wade back to shore once more. 'I seem to have lost the knack,' he told Moses despairingly. 'But I'm going to have one last attempt.'

For the third time Jesus tried to walk on water but once again he soon sank and had to make his way back to the shore.

'I just don't understand why I can't do it,' he wailed.

'I do,' said Moses. 'The last time you tried, you didn't have holes in your feet.'

1253 A holy priest renowned for his charitable works died and went to heaven. As a reward for a lifetime of selflessness, St Peter granted him one wish.

'I have always been a great admirer of the Virgin Mother,' said the priest, 'and I would dearly love to meet her.'

So St Peter arranged a meeting. The priest was suitably in awe. 'I have studied every portrait of you,' he said to the Virgin Mary, 'and I have always detected a slightly sad look on your face. I have often wondered what it was that made you sad. I would deem it a great honour if you could tell me your secret.'

Mary sighed: 'I was really hoping for a girl . . .'

1254 St Peter stood at the Pearly Gates and asked Jesus: 'Would you mind guarding the gate while I go on an errand?'

'Sure,' said Jesus. 'What do I have to do?'

St Peter explained: 'Just find out about the people who arrive. Ask about their background, their family and their lives. Then decide if they deserve entry into Heaven.'

'OK,' said Jesus.

The first person to appear was a wizened old man.

'What do you do for a living?' asked Jesus.

'I was a carpenter,' said the old man.

Remembering his own earthly experience, Jesus was eager to learn more. 'Did you have a family?' he asked.

'Yes, I had a son,' answered the old man. 'But I lost him.'

'You lost your son?' asked Jesus, more interested than ever. 'Can you tell me about him?'

'Well, he had holes in his hands and feet.'

Shocked, Jesus smiled and reached out his arms. 'Father?'

The old man smiled and returned the embrace. 'Pinocchio?'

JEWISH JOKES

1255 Two Jewish mothers met for coffee. 'How are the kids, Miriam?' asked one.

'To tell you the truth, my Daniel has married a slut! She doesn't get out of bed until eleven. She's out all day spending his money on heaven knows what, and when he gets home exhausted, she doesn't even have a nice hot dinner waiting for him. Instead she makes him take her out to dinner at an expensive restaurant.'

'And Rachel?'

'Ah, Rachel has married a saint. He brings her breakfast in bed, he gives her enough money to buy all she needs, and in the evening he takes her out to dinner at a nice restaurant.'

1256 Old Stanley Goldberg was on his deathbed. He called to his wife: 'Ruth, are you there?'

'Yes, I'm here,' she replied.

'What about Benjamin, my eldest son, is he here?'

'Yes, I'm here, Dad,' said Benjamin.

'And Naomi, my only daughter, is she here too?'

'Yes, Dad, I'm here too,' answered Naomi.

'And Aaron, my other son, is he here?'

'Yes, I'm here,' said Aaron. 'We're all here.'

Stanley slowly raised his head from his pillow and with his last breath said: 'Well, who's minding the shop?'

1257 Did you hear about the Jewish kamikaze pilot? – He crashed his plane into his uncle's scrap metal yard.

1258 An elderly Jewish man hated being in an old folks' home and repeatedly begged his family to take him somewhere else. His son said: 'But Dad, you've tried every other place in town except for the Catholic home on the east side. And you'd hate it there.'

'No, I wouldn't,' he said. 'Get me in.'

So the family moved him into the Catholic home. Next weekend when they all went to visit, the old man said he was having a wonderful time. 'It's great here,' he said. 'They're always laughing and joking, everybody's happy, and everybody's got a nickname.'

'A nickname?' queried the son, surprised.

'Yeah,' continued the old man. 'See that bald guy over there, they call him Curly. And that guy there who must weigh 350 pounds, they call him Tiny. And me who hasn't had sex in thirty years . . . they call me the fucking Jew!'

1259 What's the definition of a Jewish threesome? – Two headaches and an erection.

1260 Two Jews were talking. One said to the other: 'What would you do if you won the lottery?'

'I'd give you half,' said the other. 'You're my best friend.'

'What would you do if you had two houses?'

'I'd give you a house – you're my best friend.'

'And what would you do if you had two cars?'

'I'd give you a car, of course – you're my best friend.'

'What would you do if you had two chickens?'

'That's not fair – you know I've got two chickens.'

1261 After Moses and God had finished their summit on Mount Sinai, Moses had one last question. 'OK,' said Moses, 'let me get this straight: the Arabs get all the oil, we have to cut the ends off our dicks, and yet *we're* the "chosen people"?'

1262 A Jewish guy went into a baker's. 'How much are the bagels?' he asked.

'Eighty cents for two.'

'How much for one?'

'Forty-five cents.'

'Then I'll take the other one.'

1263 Old Hymie Rosenthal was suffering from a rare disease, which meant that he could drink only human milk.

'How can I get human milk?' he asked his doctor.

'Well,' said the doctor, 'Miriam Goldblum's just had a baby. Maybe she'll help.'

So every day Hymie went to Miriam's house for his daily nourishment. Miriam was a dark-eyed, big-breasted lady, who, in spite of herself, gradually became aroused as Hymie lapped at her ripe breasts. One day as he quietly lay sucking, she whispered to him: 'Tell me, Mr Rosenthal, do you like it?'

'Mmmm, wonderful,' he sighed.

'Is there . . . is there anything else you'd like?' she asked, teasingly.

'As a matter of fact there is,' murmured Hymie.

'What?' purred Miriam.

Hymie licked his lips. 'Maybe a little biscuit?'

1264 A boy came home from school with a puzzled expression. His mother was Jewish and his father was Mexican. The boy asked: 'Mom, am I more Jewish or more Mexican?'

'What does it really matter?' she said. 'But if you want to know for sure, you'll have to ask your father.'

So when his father arrived home from work, the boy asked him: 'Dad, am I more Jewish or more Mexican?'

'What kind of question is that?' said the father. 'Why do you want to know if you're more Jewish or Mexican?'

'Well, it's like this, Dad,' explained the boy. 'My friend Larry down the street wants to sell his bicycle for $50, and I don't know whether to talk him down to $25, or wait until it's dark and steal the thing.'

1265 God came down, and went to the Germans and said: 'I have Commandments for you that will make your lives better.'

And the Germans asked: 'What are Commandments?'

The Lord said: 'They are rules for living.'

'Can you give us an example?' asked the Germans.

'Thou shalt not kill,' said God.

'Not kill?' said the Germans. 'Sorry, we're not interested.'

So God went to the Italians and said: 'I have Commandments.'

The Italians asked for an example, and the Lord said: 'Thou shalt not steal.'

'Not steal?' said the Italians. 'We're not interested.'

Next God went to the French and said: 'I have Commandments.'

The French wanted an example and God said: 'Thou shalt not covet thy neighbour's wife.'

'Not covet my neighbour's wife?' said the French. 'No, we're not interested.'

So God went to the Jews and said: 'I have Commandments.'

'Commandments?' queried the Jews. 'How much are they?'

'They're free,' said God.

'We'll take ten.'

1266 If Tarzan and Jane were Jewish, what would Cheetah be? – A fur coat.

1267 A young man told his Jewish mother that he had fallen in love and was going to get married. He said: 'Just for fun, ma, I'm going to bring three women over on Thursday night, and you have to try and guess which is the one I'm going to marry.'

'Whatever,' said his mother.

So on the Thursday he brought over three young women and sat them down in the lounge. His mother immediately said: 'The one in the middle.'

'That's right,' said the son. 'How did you know?'

'Because I don't like her.'

1268 What's the hardest thing to explain to a Jew about football? – That a quarterback isn't a tax return.

1269 What do you get when you cross an Irishman with a Jew? – An alcoholic who buys his liquor wholesale.

1270 Old Hetty Goldberg was dying. She asked her husband Henry: 'How many cars have you ordered to go to the cemetery?'

'Four,' he replied.

'Does that include the hearse?'

'Yes.'

'Four is too many. Cancel one.'

'Whatever you say, darling.'

'And I want you to promise me something else.'

'Anything, darling.'

'I want you and my mother to travel together in the same car.'

'But you know we haven't spoken to each other for ten years . . .'

'I know, but it's what I want. Promise me you'll do it.'

'Well, OK, I'll do it. But let me tell you now, it will ruin the day for me.'

1271 Solly bought a cheap vase for his sister's birthday, but accidentally smashed it before he could give it to her. Then he had an idea. He gift-wrapped the vase, put it in a box, and posted it to her, with the intention of claiming money back from the postal service for the breakage.

Two days later, the sister phoned to thank him for the vase, but said that it had arrived broken.

'Oh, what a pity,' said Solly.

'Yes, isn't it?' said his sister. 'Still, it was very kind of you to wrap each piece individually . . .'

1272 Isaac was going shopping in New York for a new suit. Eventually he came across an expensive Jewish tailor's. The owner welcomed him in and immediately launched into his sales talk. 'You've come to the right place. When we make a suit here, you'll be surprised at how we go about it. No expense is spared. First, digital cameras take pictures of your every muscle and we download the pictures to a special computer to build up your image. Then we cultivate sheep in New Zealand to get the very best cloth. For the silk lining, we contact Japan for their silkworms, and we ask Hawaiian deep-sea divers to get the pearl buttons . . .'

'But,' interrupted Isaac, 'I need the suit for a Barmitzvah.'

'When?'

'Tomorrow.'

'You'll have it.'

1273 A young gay man called home and told his Jewish mother that he had decided to go back into the closet because he had met a wonderful girl whom he wanted to marry. 'I'm sure this will please you, mother, because I know you've never been happy about me being gay.'

'Oh, yes,' said his mother, 'this is indeed wonderful news. I suppose it would be too much to hope that the girl you are planning to marry would be Jewish?'

'Mother, not only is she Jewish, but she comes from a wealthy Beverly Hills family.'

'All my prayers have been answered,' announced the mother gleefully. 'You have made your mother the happiest woman on this earth. Tell me, what is the girl's name?'

'Monica Lewinsky.'

There was a pause, then his mother asked: 'Whatever happened to that nice Catholic boy you were dating last year?'

1274 Why do Jews have big noses? — Because air is free.

1275 A religious instruction teacher asked her young class to name the greatest man who ever lived. To stimulate thought, she promised a bar of chocolate to whoever gave the answer she was looking for.

Straight away a boy put up his hand and said: 'George Washington.'

'He was indeed a great man,' said the teacher, 'but not the one I'm looking for.'

Then a girl raised her hand and called out: 'John F. Kennedy.'

'He, too, was a great man,' conceded the teacher, 'but not the one I have in mind.'

Finally a Jewish boy raised his hand and said: 'Jesus Christ.'

The teacher was surprised but said, 'Yes, that's the answer I am looking for,' and handed him the chocolate.

At the end of the lesson, the teacher asked the Jewish boy how he knew the right answer.

Clutching his bar of chocolate, the Jewish boy said: 'Listen, lady, you know the answer was Moses, and I know the answer was Moses, but business is business.'

1276 A Jewish lady by the name of Mrs Goldberg was stranded late one night at a fashionable resort on Cape Cod — one that did not admit Jews. The desk clerk consulted his book and said curtly: 'Sorry, no room. The hotel is full.'

'But,' protested Mrs Goldberg, 'your sign says that you have vacancies.'

The desk clerk remained adamant. 'You know that we do not admit Jews. Now why don't you try the other side of town?'

Mrs Goldberg stiffened noticeably and said: 'I'll have you know, I converted to your religion.'

'Oh, yeah?' said the desk clerk sarcastically. 'OK, let me give you a little test. How was Jesus born?'

Mrs Goldberg replied: 'He was born to a virgin named Mary in a little town called Bethlehem.'

'Very good,' said the desk clerk. 'Tell me more.'

'He was born in a manger,' added Mrs Goldberg.

'That's right,' said the hotel clerk. 'And why was he born in a manger?'

Mrs Goldberg shouted: 'Because a jerk like you in the hotel wouldn't give a Jewish lady a room for the night!'

1277 The first Jewish woman President of the United States was elected. She called her mother: 'Mama, I've won the elections, you've got to come to the swearing-in ceremony.'

'I don't know,' said the mother. 'What would I wear?'

'Don't worry, I'll send you a dressmaker.'

'But I only eat kosher food.'

'Mama, I am going to be the President. I can get you kosher food.'

'But how will I get there?'

'I'll send a limo. Just come, Mama.'

'OK, OK, if it makes you happy.'

The great day came and Mama was seated between the Supreme Court Justices and the future cabinet members. She nudged the gentleman on her right. 'You see that girl,' she said, 'the one with her hand on the Bible? Her brother's a doctor!'

1278 Bernie and Solly were walking along the street saw a sign on a church that said: 'Attention, Jews. $5,000 if you convert.'

Bernie said: 'Y'know, $5,000 is a lot of money. I could certainly use it.'

Solly said: 'How could you even think about doing such a thing! Your grandfather was a rabbi and your entire family are devoutly religious. They'd never forgive you.'

'But they'll never know,' said Bernie, and with that he went into the church.

He emerged a few hours later. Solly said: 'Well, did you get the money?'

Bernie said: 'Huh, you Jews, always thinking about money!'

1279 What's the difference between a Jew and a canoe? – A canoe tips.

1280 What's the difference between a Jewish mother and a Rottweiller? – A Rottweiller eventually lets go.

1281 It was a terrible night: the wind was howling and the rain was lashing down. The city streets were deserted and the local baker was just about to close when a little Jewish man carrying an umbrella blown inside out entered the shop. He was wearing two sweaters beneath a thick coat and looked wet and bedraggled.

As he loosened his scarf, he said to the baker. 'May I have two bagels to go, please?'

The baker was surprised. 'Just two bagels? Nothing more?'

'That's right,' said the customer. 'One for me and one for Bernice.'

'Bernice is your wife?' asked the baker.

'What do you think?' snapped the little Jewish man. 'My mother would send me out on a night like this?'

1282 How do Jews say 'fuck you'? – 'Trust me.'

1283 An Arab spent days crossing the desert in desperate search of water. His camel had already died of thirst and it seemed that nothing could save the Arab from suffering the same fate. Then as he crawled on his hands and knees, he suddenly spotted a shiny object sticking out of the sand. Examining it, he found that it was a lamp. So he rubbed it and out popped a genie. But this was no ordinary genie – it was a rabbi genie.

'Well, kid,' said the genie. 'You know how it works – you have three wishes.'

'I don't trust you,' said the Arab. 'I'm not going to trust a Jewish genie!'

'What have you got to lose?' asked the genie. 'It looks like you're going to die otherwise.'

The Arab thought about this for a moment and realized that the genie was right. 'OK,' he said, 'I wish I was in a lush oasis with plenty of food and drink.'

And POOF! The Arab found himself in a beautiful oasis, surrounded by jugs of water and wine, and platters of exotic delicacies.

'Right, kid,' said the genie, 'what's your second wish?'

'My second wish,' said the Arab, 'is that I can be rich beyond my wildest dreams.'

And POOF! The Arab found himself surrounded by treasure chests filled with gold coins and precious gems.

'Right, kid,' said the genie. 'One wish left. Make it a good one.'

After giving the matter some thought, the Arab said: 'I wish I was white and surrounded by beautiful women.'

And POOF! The Arab was turned into a tampon.

The moral of the story is: If you do business with a Jewish genie, there's going to be a string attached.

HELEN KELLER

1284 Why did Helen Keller wear tight pants? – So you could read her lips.

1285 How did Helen Keller's parents punish her? – They stuck doorknobs to the walls.

1286 Why were Helen Keller's hands purple? – She heard it thru the grapevine.

1287 Why didn't Helen Keller scream when she fell off the cliff? – She was wearing mittens.

1288 What do you call a tennis match between Helen Keller and Stevie Wonder? – Endless love.

THE KENNEDYS

1289 Why was John F. Kennedy Jr flying on the night of his fatal crash? – Teddy Kennedy offered him a lift.

1290 How many Kennedys does it take to change a light bulb? – No one knows. Kennedys don't last as long as light bulbs.

LAS VEGAS

1291 Following an afternoon's drinking, two soldiers on Christmas leave in Las Vegas decided to go to a show. During the interval one of them needed the toilet and asked the usherette for directions. She said: 'Go up the stairs, through the double doors, turn left, carry on through the foyer, turn left at the end, down the stairs, and then left again.'

The soldier followed the directions with considerable difficulty but managed to relieve himself before finding his way back to his seat.

'Hey, you missed the best bit,' said his mate. 'While you were gone, a soldier came on-stage and pissed into the orchestra pit!'

1292 A young couple were spending their honeymoon in Las Vegas. One evening they went to a bar and asked the bartender if there was any entertainment.

'Oh, we've got entertainment, all right,' said the bartender. 'The Amazing Larry will be on any minute.'

A few minutes later, a seventy-year-old man shuffled on stage, set up a card table, and placed three walnuts on it. Then he took out his dick and hammered it down onto the walnuts – Whack! Whack! Whack! – cracking all three in half. The crowd cheered wildly, and the Amazing Larry folded up his card table and shuffled off stage again.

For their twentieth wedding anniversary the couple returned to the same bar and found the same bartender still serving. They told him how on their previous visit, all those years ago, they had seen this incredible guy called the Amazing Larry.

'You're in luck,' said the bartender. 'The Amazing Larry is on tonight.'

Sure enough, a few minutes later the same old man shuffled on stage, set up a card table but this time placed three coconuts on it. Then he took out his dick and hammered it down onto the coconuts – Whack! Whack! Whack! – smashing all three coconuts in half. To rapturous applause, he folded up his table and shuffled off the stage.

The couple said to the bartender: 'He did that twenty years ago when we were here, with walnuts. Now he does it with coconuts!'

The bartender replied apologetically: 'Well, yes, twenty years ago he did use walnuts. But you have to remember, the Amazing Larry's eyes are not what they used to be.'

LAWYERS

1293 Two doctors boarded a flight out of Chicago. One sat in the window seat, the other sat in the middle seat. Just before takeoff, a lawyer got on and took the aisle seat next to the two doctors. Ten minutes into the flight, the lawyer kicked off his shoes and was just starting to relax when the physician in the window seat said: 'I think I'll get up and get a Coke.'

'It's OK,' said the lawyer. 'To save you getting up, I'll fetch it for you.'

While he was gone, one of the doctors sneakily picked up the lawyer's shoe and put a thumbtack in it. When the lawyer returned with the drink, the other doctor said: 'That looks good. I think I'll have a Coke too.'

Once again the lawyer obligingly went to get the drink and in his absence, the other doctor gleefully picked up the lawyer's other shoe and put a tack in it. The lawyer returned and all three sat back to enjoy the rest of the flight.

As the plane was landing, the lawyer slipped his feet into his shoes and knew immediately what had happened.

'How long must this go on?' he asked despairingly. 'This fighting between our professions? This bickering? This animosity? This putting tacks in shoes and peeing in Cokes?'

1294 An eccentric woman in her late seventies informed her lawyer that she wanted to make a will. 'I have $50,000 savings in the bank,' she said. 'And I want $45,000 of that to provide for my funeral.'

'You should certainly get a fine funeral for that kind of money,' said the lawyer. 'And what do you want to do with the remaining $5,000?'

'Well,' she answered. 'As you know I'm a spinster. In fact, I have never had sex with a man in my life. So I want you to use the $5,000 to arrange for a man to sleep with me.'

The lawyer promised to do what he could.

That night he told his wife about the old woman's unusual request, pointing out that they could do with that kind of money. Taking the hint, the wife agreed to let him provide the service himself. 'I'll drive you over tomorrow morning,' she offered, 'and wait in the car till you're finished.'

The next morning the wife drove her lawyer husband to the old woman's house and waited patiently outside. After an hour and still no sign of him coming out, she honked the car horn. Moments later, her husband leaned out of the bedroom window and yelled: 'Pick me up tomorrow! She's going to let the county bury her!'

1295 In a long queue at the bank, one guy suddenly started massaging the back of the person in front of him. Shocked, the man in front turned around and snarled: 'What the hell do you think you're doing?'

'I'm sorry,' said the man behind, 'but I'm a chiropractor and I could see that you were tense, so I had to massage your back. Sometimes I simply can't help practising my art.'

'That's the stupidest thing I've ever heard,' said the other man. 'I'm a lawyer. Do you see me screwing the guy in front of me?'

1296 What do you call ten lawyers buried up to their necks in the sand? – Football practice.

1297 A lawyer's wife died. At her funeral, mourners were horrified to see that the headstone read: 'Here lies Monica, wife of Martin, L.L.D., Wills, Divorce, Malpractice, Personal Injury. Reasonable Rates.'

Suddenly Martin burst into tears. His brother-in-law said: 'So you should cry, pulling a stunt like this!'

Martin sobbed: 'You don't understand. They left off the phone number!'

1298 Lawyer's creed: a man is innocent until proven broke.

1299 What do you call a lawyer with an IQ of 50? – Your Honour.

1300 A Los Angeles lawyer died, and arrived at the Pearly Gates. St Peter said: 'What have you done to merit entrance into heaven?'

The lawyer gave the matter some thought before replying: 'A week ago, I gave a quarter to a homeless person on the street.'

St Peter asked the Angel Gabriel to check it.

'It's true,' said Gabriel. 'He did.'

'That's all very well,' said St Peter, 'but it's hardly enough to get you into heaven.'

'Wait!' said the lawyer. 'There's more. Three years ago, I gave a charity collector a quarter.'

Gabriel checked the claim and found it to be true.

St Peter whispered to Gabriel: 'What do you think we should do with him?'

Gabriel replied: 'Let's give him back his fifty cents and tell him to go to hell.'

1301 How do you stop a lawyer from drowning? – Shoot him before he hits the water.

1302 A lawyer's son graduated from university and went to join his father's firm. Eager to prove his worth to his father, he announced triumphantly at the end of his first day: 'In one day, I have cracked the Taylor case that you've been working on for the past ten years.'

'You idiot!' raged the father. 'We've lived on the funding of that case for ten years.'

1303 Inspecting the farm he had bought as a weekend retreat, a city lawyer looked down at the ground to see that his feet were in the middle of a huge cowpat.

'Help! Help!' he yelled to his wife.

'What is it?' she said, running to his rescue.

He pointed to his feet and screamed: 'I'm melting! I'm melting!'

1304 As a lawyer slowly came round from the anaesthetic following surgery, he said: 'Doctor, why are all the blinds drawn?'

The doctor explained: 'There's a big fire across the street, and we didn't want you to think the operation had failed.'

1305 Why are there only ever two pallbearers at a lawyer's funeral? – Because a garbage can only has two handles.

1306 A lawyer died and was standing in front of St Peter at the Pearly Gates. St Peter said: 'You're a lawyer, you can't come in here – you have to go to the other place.'

But, using all his courtroom expertise, the lawyer patiently pleaded his case until St Peter reconsidered. 'OK, here's what I'll do,' said St Peter. 'You will spend the same amount of time in hell as you did on Earth, and then you can spend the rest of eternity up here.'

The lawyer thought that was a reasonable deal.

'Fine,' said St Peter, 'so we'll see you in 407 years.'

'407 years? What are you talking about?' said the lawyer. 'I'm only 66.'

St Peter said: 'We go by billing hours.'

1307 What are lawyers good for? – They make used car salesmen look honourable.

1308 A man went for a job with a major company. 'I'm looking for a job as a consultant,' he said.

The employer said: 'No, sorry. We already have enough consultants.'

'OK, well, with my experience, I could be an adviser.'

'No, we've got more than we can use already.'

The applicant was becoming increasingly desperate. 'Look, I'm not proud. I can do paperwork – I'll be a clerk. If you have too many, I'll start as a janitor.'

'I'm sorry,' said the employer, 'but we just don't seem to have any openings for someone with your qualifications.'

At this, the applicant stood up, smashed his fist on the desk and stormed: 'Work for you, I'd have to be a low-life, belly-crawling, double-dealing jerk!'

'Oh,' said the employer, 'you didn't say you were a lawyer. Sit down. We may have an opening after all.'

LEPERS

1309 A leper walked into a bar and sat down, whereupon the bartender threw up all over himself and the floor.

The leper looked hurt and said: 'Hey, I know I'm not exactly handsome, but I do have feelings.'

Wiping the vomit from his mouth with his sleeve, the bartender replied: 'I'm sorry, man, but it wasn't you. That guy sitting next to you keeps dipping his crackers in your neck.'

1310 Did you hear about the male prostitute who got leprosy? – He did OK until his business fell off.

1311 How can you tell if a Valentine is from a leper? – The tongue is still in the envelope.

1312 Did you hear about the lepers playing cards? – One threw his hand in, the other laughed his head off.

1313 What's the best thing about marrying a woman with leprosy? – She can only give you lip once.

1314 Why did the leper fail his driving test? – He left his foot on the clutch.

1315 After six days of crawling through the jungle, a starving man came across a small chapel. He went in, knelt at the altar and prayed: 'Please, Lord, give me some food!' As if by magic, a lump of meat dropped at his feet. The man gleefully devoured it . . . then looked up and saw a leper painting the ceiling.

LESBIANS

1316 Have you heard about the new lesbian tennis shoe called Dike? – It has an extra long tongue and it only takes one finger to get it off.

1317 A young woman decided to come out of the closet. Nervously, she decided to approach her mother and found her in the kitchen where she was stirring stew with a wooden spoon.

Plucking up courage, she decided to blurt it out. 'Mom, I'm gay!'

The mother carried on stirring the stew without looking up. 'You mean lesbian?'

'Uh, yeah.'

Still the mother continued stirring. 'Does that mean you lick women down below?'

'Well, er, yes.'

The mother finally looked up from the pot and, waving the spoon at her daughter, said: 'Then don't you ever complain about my cooking again!'

1318 What do you call an open can of tuna fish in a lesbian's apartment? – Air freshener.

1319 What do you call two lesbians in a canoe? – Fur traders.

1320 Two lesbians were in bed. One said: 'What do you mean, my crack tastes like shit?'

'Sorry,' said the other. 'Just a slip of the tongue.'

1321 How can you tell a tough lesbian bar? – Even the pool table has no balls.

1322 What did one lesbian frog say to the other? – Well, I'll be damned. We *do* taste like chicken!

1323 Why did God invent lesbians? – So feminists wouldn't breed.

1324 A vain young guy out on the pull had just ordered a drink at a bar when two girls walked in. Fancying them both, he invited them to sit with him. He bought them drinks but when they disappeared into the toilet, the bartender warned him that they were lesbians.

The guy was so convinced that he was irresistible to all women that he continued to ply them with drinks and besiege them with corny pick-up lines. He was sure he was in with a chance.

Eventually one of the girls went off to buy a pack of cigarettes and while she was gone, the other one whispered to the guy: 'Do you fancy my friend?'

'Yeah,' he said.

'Would you like to smell her pussy?'

'You bet!'

So she breathed on him.

1325   What's the definition of frenzy? – Two blind lesbians walking through a fish market.

1326   What's the difference between a lesbian and a Ritz biscuit? – One's a snack cracker . . .

1327   What do you call a lesbian dinosaur? – Lickalotopuss.

1328   What is the leading cause of death among lesbians? – Hairballs.

1329   A famous Hollywood actress was upset to read a newspaper article that claimed she was a lesbian. When she showed the story to her teenage daughter, the girl said: 'Oh, mother, don't be ridiculous. Just ignore it. Now go shave and get ready for dinner.'

LIFE

1330   Brian ran into an old schoolmate twenty-five years on.

'Mike, how are you doing?' he asked.

'Yeah, great,' said Mike. 'I'm a fireman.'

'Really? My fifteen-year-old son wants to be a fireman,' said Brian.

'Well, if you want some advice, install a pole in your house that will go down to the basement so your kid can practise, because the hardest thing for a fireman is to jump off into space and catch that pole in the middle of the night.'

Eight years later, the two men bumped into each other again.

'Did your son become a fireman?' asked Mike.

'No,' said Brian, 'but I have two daughters who are dancers.'

1331 Two guys and a girl were sitting at a bar talking about their lives.
One guy said, 'I'm a YUPPIE – you know, Young Urban Professional.'
The second guy said, 'I'm a DINK – you know, Double Income, No Kids.'
Then they turned to the woman and asked, 'What are you?'
She replied, 'I'm a WIFE – you know, Wash, Iron, Fuck, Etc.'

1332 Bill and John met up for the first time in twenty years. 'So how's life been for
you?' asked Bill cheerily.
John replied: 'One disaster after another. My wife was killed in a freak
skiing accident, then two years later my eldest boy was fatally struck by
lightning. Then my house burned to the ground in a mystery fire and my
youngest boy died in a plane crash. My dog was run over, my sister drowned
at sea, and four months ago my doctor told me I had an incurable disease.
And to cap it all, my business has just gone bust.'
'Gee! That all sounds terrible,' said Bill. 'What business were you in?'
John said: 'I sell lucky charms.'

LIMERICKS

1333 A well-endowed guy called Apollo
Remarked as he larked in the hollow,
'Darling, my dong
Is twelve inches long.'
Said his girl, 'That's a hard one to swallow!'

1334 There once was a man from Bandoo
Who fell asleep in a canoe.
He dreamed of Venus
And played with his penis
And woke up with a hand full of goo.

1335 There once was a man from Belize
Whose pecker hung down to his knees.
The gals all adored it,
But him, he abhorred it,
Because each time it stiffened, he sneezed.

1336   There was a young actress from Crewe
Who remarked as the vicar withdrew,
'The bishop was quicker
And thicker and slicker,
And two inches longer than you.'

1337   There was a young maid from Darjeeling
Who said she had no sexual feeling
Till a sailor named Boris
Just touched her clitoris
And she had to be scraped from the ceiling.

1338   There was a young lady called Dexter
Whose husband exceedingly vexed her.
For whenever they'd start,
He'd unfailingly fart
With a blast that damn nearly unsexed her.

1339   There once was a lady from France
Who took a long train ride by chance.
The engineer fucked her
Before the conductor
While the fireman came in his pants.

1340   There was a young athlete named Grimmon
Who developed a new way of swimmin';
By a marvellous trick
He would row with his prick,
Which attracted loud cheers from the women.

1341   There was a young lady from Hitchin
Who was scratching her crotch in the kitchen.
Her mother said, 'Rose,
It's the crabs, I suppose.'
She said, 'Yes, and the buggers are itchin'.'

1342 There was a young girl from Hong Kong
Whose cervical cap was a gong;
She said with a yell,
As a shot rang her bell,
'I'll give you a ding for a dong!'

1343 A young prostitute's name is Hortense.
Her usual fee is ten cents.
But she plays anyway
When the fella won't pay
But it sure makes Hortense the whore tense.

1344 There once was a lady from Hyde
Who ate a green apple and died.
While her lover lamented,
The apple fermented,
And made cider inside her inside.

1345 Now little John Jones was a dork
Who thought he'd been brought by the stork.
His Pa was no better
He bought a French letter
And tested its strength with a fork.

1346 There was an old girl from Kilkenny
Whose usual charge was a penny.
But for half of that sum
You could roger her bum
— A source of amusement for many.

1347 A fellow from Boston named Lance
Couldn't walk well or run well or dance;
It troubled his mind
Till he happened to find
That his necktie was caught in his pants.

1348 There was a young man from Mauritius
Who said his last fuck was delicious.
'But the next time I cum,
It'll be up your bum,
Cos that scab on your cunt looks suspicious.'

1349 A shepherd from Montana's soft hills
Was always looking for thrills
Till a sheep he molested
Loudly protested
And sent him the veterinary's bills.

1350 There once was a man named Mort
Whose dick was incredibly short.
When he climbed into bed
His lady friend said
'That's not a dick, it's a wart.'

1351 Said a President thought to give pecks
To areas other than necks,
'Although it's most sultry,
It isn't adult'ry,
I'm not even sure that it's sex.'

1352 There once was a man from Rhode Isle
Who said jogging just wasn't his style.
'I'll get my workouts,' he said,
'At home, in my bed,
Cos a Miss is as good as a mile!'

1353 From the depths of the crypt at St Giles
Came a scream that resounded for miles.
Said the vicar, 'Good gracious,
Has Father Ignatius
Forgotten the Bishop has piles?'

1354 That wily old pervert St Nick
Made good use of the curve to his dick.
He glazed the whole shaft,
Painted stripes, then he laughed
As he offered young ladies a lick.

1355 There was a young fellow from Sparta,
A really magnificent farter.
On the strength of one bean
He'd fart *God Save the Queen*
And Beethoven's *Moonlight Sonata*.

1356 There once was a young man named Springer
Who got his testicles caught in the wringer.
He hollered with pain
As they rolled down the drain,
'There goes my career as a singer.'

1357 I chase all the girls when I'm spunky,
A five-days-a-week sexual junkie;
I tend not to stray
On Tues- or Wednesday,
On those nights I spank my own monkey.

1358 There once was a girl from Sri Lanka
Whose hole was as big as a tanker.
You could go for a swim
In the depths of her quim
And you needed a lamppost to wank her.

1359 A blushing young bride from Tonypandy
With her quim was incredibly handy;
On her wedding night
To her husband's delight
She filled it with three pints of brandy.

1360 A Canadian lady, Anne Tunney,
Had a habit you may think quite funny.
She would roll up a buck
In her snatch ere she'd fuck
So her husband would come into money.

MARRIAGE

1361 Three women were sitting around drinking and talking about their love lives.
Carly said: 'I call my husband the dentist. Nobody can drill like he does.'
Lauren giggled and confessed: 'I call my husband the miner because of his incredible shaft.'
All the while Maxine kept quiet until Carly asked: 'What do you call your husband?'
Maxine frowned and said: 'The postman – because he always delivers late, and half the time it's in the wrong box.'

1362 How do you know if your husband is dead? – The sex is the same, but you get the remote.

1363 Two married buddies were out drinking one night. One turned to the other and said: 'It's a real problem. Whenever I go home after we've been out drinking, I turn the headlights off before I get to the driveway, I shut off the engine and coast into the garage, I take my shoes off before I go into the house, I creep up the stairs, I get undressed in the bathroom, I ease gently into bed with disturbing the duvet and STILL my wife wakes up and yells at me for staying out so late!'
His buddy took a swig of beer and said: 'You're doing it all wrong! I screech into the driveway, slam the door, storm up the stairs, throw my shoes into the closet, jump into bed, rub my hands on my wife's ass and say, "How about a blow job?" . . . and she's always sound asleep.'

1364 What did the wife do when she saw her husband staggering around the back yard? – Reloaded.

1365 When each of her three daughters got married, their mother asked them to write to her with the truth about their new married lives. To avoid embarrassing their respective husbands with intimate details of their sex lives, mother and daughters agreed to use newspaper advertisements as a secret code.

The first wrote back after a week of marriage with the simple message: 'Maxwell House Coffee.'

The mother checked the newspaper, found the Maxwell House advertisement, and was pleased to read that it said: 'Satisfaction to the last drop.'

The second daughter sent a message after two weeks of marriage. It read: 'Rothman's Mattresses.'

So the mother looked at the Rothman's Mattresses ad, and it said: 'Full size, king size.' Mother was happy.

Then the third daughter sent her letter after a month of marriage. It read simply: 'British Airways.'

Mother looked for the British Airways ad, but this time she fainted. For the ad read: 'Three times a day, seven days a week, both ways.'

1366 Did you know that *Playboy* is introducing a new magazine for men who are married? – Every month the centrefold is the same woman.

1367 Two married men were discussing their sex lives. One asked. 'Does your wife ever let you do it doggie fashion?'

'Not exactly,' replied the second. 'She's more into doing doggie tricks.'

'Wow!' said the first. 'What does that entail? Sounds pretty kinky.'

'Sadly, it's not,' said the second. 'Whenever I make a move, she rolls over and plays dead.'

1368 Why do married men hang strobe lights from their bedroom ceilings? – To create the optical illusion that their wives are moving during sex.

1369 Five weeks after her wedding, the new bride called her sister. 'Oh, Avril,' she said, 'Neville and I had the most dreadful fight last night.'

'Don't worry,' said her sister reassuringly. 'It's not as bad as you think. All couples have to have their first fight.'

'I suppose you're right, but what am I going to do with the body?'

Dating and Marriage:

1370 • *When you are dating* . . . Farting is never an issue.
When you are married . . . You make sure there's nothing flammable near your husband – at all times.

1371 • *When you are dating* . . . He takes you out to have a good time.
When you are married . . . He brings home a six-pack and says, 'What are you going to drink?'

1372 • *When you are dating* . . . He holds your hand in public.
When you are married . . . He flicks your ear in public.

1373 • *When you are dating* . . . You enjoy foreplay.
When you are married . . . You tell him, 'If we have sex, will you leave me alone?'

1374 • *When you are dating* . . . He hugs you tenderly for no reason.
When you are married . . . He grabs your boobs any chance he gets.

1375 • *When you are dating* . . . A single bed for two feels cosy.
When you are married . . . A king-size double bed feels too cramped.

1376 • *When you are dating* . . . The sight of him naked turns you on.
When you are married . . . You think, 'Was he always that fat?'

1377 • *When you are dating* . . . You picture the two of you, growing old together.
When you are married . . . You wonder who will die first.

1378 A man came home drunk in the early hours to find his angry wife waiting for him at the door.

'Out drinking again?' she demanded. 'How much money did you spend this time?'

'$100,' he answered.

'$100!' she raged. 'That's crazy, spending that much in one night.'

'It's easy for you to say,' he countered. 'You don't smoke, you don't drink, and you have your own pussy.'

1379 What's the worst thing a woman can get on her thirtieth wedding anniversary? – Morning sickness.

1380 On the first morning after their honeymoon, the husband got up early, went down to the kitchen and brought his wife breakfast in bed. Naturally she was delighted.

'Have you noticed what I've done?' he asked.

'Of course, dear. Every single detail.'

'Good,' he said. 'That's how I want my breakfast served every morning from now on.'

1381 Three young women at a cocktail party were trying to score points off each other by boasting about their husbands.

The first said: 'My husband is taking me to the French Riviera this summer. We're going to hire a yacht and hang out with film stars.'

The second said: 'My husband has just bought me a new Mercedes. It's the most expensive car money can buy.'

Unimpressed, the third said: 'We don't have many material possessions, but one thing I can tell you about my husband: thirteen canaries can stand shoulder to shoulder on his erect penis.'

Hearing this, the first woman looked ashamed and admitted: 'I was lying. We're not really going to the French Riviera; we're going to my folks in Detroit.'

The second woman confessed: 'And my husband didn't really buy me a Mercedes — it was a Honda.'

The third wife said: 'I, too, have a confession to make. Canary number thirteen has to stand on one leg.'

Husband Ratings:

1382 • You say you are buying her a new car   +5
         It's a pickup truck   −5
         With the licence plate GR8 LAY   −10

1383 • You cook her a meal   +2
         It's out of a packet   −1
         It's still in the packet when you serve it   −5

1384 • You go out to buy her extra-light panty liners with
           wings   +3
         In the snow   +5
         But return with beer   −5

1385 • You check out a suspicious noise at night   +1
         You check out a suspicious noise and it's nothing   +1
         You check out a suspicious noise and it's something   +3
         You pummel it with a six-iron   +10
         It's her pet   −10

1386 • At a party, you stay by her side the entire time   +1
         You leave her side after a while to chat with a college
           drinking buddy   −2
         Named Selina   −4
         Selina is a dancer   −6
         Selina has implants   −8

1387 • You take your wife to a movie   +1
      You take her to a movie she likes   +3
      You take her to a movie you hate   +5
      You take her to a movie you like   −2
      It's called *DeathCop3*   .−4
      Which features cyborgs that eat humans   −8
      You lied and said it was a foreign film about orphans   −10

1388 A researcher carrying out a survey on marital sex phoned one of the participants to check on a discrepancy. He asked the husband: 'In response to the question on frequency of intercourse, you answered "once a week", but your wife has answered "several times a night".'

'That's correct,' said the husband. 'And that's the way it's going to be until the mortgage is paid off.'

1389 When his wife went missing, her husband searched everywhere for her. As well as reporting her disappearance to the police, he contacted all her friends and family in a bid to trace her. Then two days after she had vanished, he returned home to find her standing in the bathroom.

He threw his arms around her and cried: 'Where have you been? I've been worried sick.'

'These four masked men kidnapped me,' she said, 'tied me up, and had wild sex with me for a week.'

'But it's only been two days,' said the husband. 'What do you mean, a week?'

She answered: 'I'm only here to collect my toothbrush.'

1390 Three married women were talking about their sex lives.

The first said: 'My husband is like a Rolls-Royce, smooth and sophisticated.'

The second said: 'Mine is like a Porsche, fast and powerful.'

The third said: 'Mine is like an old Chevy. It needs a hand start, and I have to jump on while it's still going!'

1391 *Wife*: Oh, come on.
Husband: Leave me alone!
Wife: It won't take long.
Husband: I won't be able to sleep afterwards.
Wife: Yeah, well I can't sleep without it.

Husband: Why do you always think of things like this in the middle of the night?

Wife: Because I'm hot.

Husband: You get hot at the craziest times.

Wife: If you love me, I wouldn't have to beg you.

Husband: If you love me, you'd be more considerate.

Wife: You don't love me any more.

Husband: I do, but let's forget it for tonight, and try to get some sleep.

Wife (sobbing): You don't, you don't love me any more.

Husband: All right, I'll do it.

Wife: What's the matter? Need a flashlight?

Husband: I can't find it.

Wife: Oh, for heaven's sake, feel for it!

Husband: There! Are you satisfied?

Wife: Oh, yes, darling.

Husband: Is it down far enough?

Wife: Oh, that's just fine.

Husband: Now go to sleep. And the next time, it's your turn to get up and turn down the thermostat.

1392 Why do men chase women they have no intention of marrying? – The same reason dogs chase cars they have no intention of driving.

1393 A man arrived home from a tiring day at work, flopped down on the sofa in front of the television and called to his wife: 'Get me a beer before it starts.'

The wife sighed and got him a beer.

Fifteen minutes later, he said: 'Get me another beer before it starts.'

She fetched another beer and angrily slammed it down next to him.

He finished that beer and a few minutes later said: 'Quick, get me another beer, it's going to start any minute.'

The wife was furious. She yelled at him: 'Is that all you're going to do all evening? Drink beer and sit in front of that TV? You're nothing but a lazy, drunken, fat slob, and furthermore . . .'

The man sighed and said: 'It's started . . .'

MARTIANS

1394 One day, a spaceship landed in a farmer's field, and a Martian man and woman got out and introduced themselves to the farmer and his wife. As a friendly gesture, the farmer invited the Martian couple to his home for dinner and offered to put them up for the night. The Martians accepted, and later that evening the Martian man explained how it was customary on their planet to swap partners as a seal of friendship. The farmer, not wishing to offend his alien neighbours, readily agreed.

So the Martian man took the farmer's wife into the main bedroom while the farmer took the Martian woman into the other bedroom. In the main bedroom they had been having sex for about an hour when the Martian man asked the farmer's wife: 'Well, how do you like having sex with a Martian? How does it feel?'

The farmer's wife replied: 'To be honest, it needs to be a little bigger around.' So the Martian man twisted his right ear and, as if by magic, his penis became bigger around.

An hour later, the Martian man asked the farmer's wife again: 'How does it feel now?'

'I think it needs to be a little longer,' she answered. So the Martian man twisted his left ear and his penis immediately became longer.

The next morning, after their alien friends had left, the farmer and his wife were sitting at the breakfast table when the farmer asked her: 'How was the Martian man?'

'Fine,' she said. 'How about the Martian woman?'

'Huh,' grunted the farmer. 'Damn woman yanked on my bloody ears all night long!'

1395 After their spaceship crashed on Earth, two glowing Martians managed to survive. Trying to find a way back to Mars, they trudged through forests and fields until they eventually arrived on the edge of a big American city. Stopping at an intersection, they began to shake and moan at the mere sight of a green light.

Suddenly the light turned from green to yellow, then to red. One Martian turned to the other and said: 'Let's get out of here. If there's one thing I hate, it's a woman who's a tease.'

MASOCHISM

1396   A sadist and a masochist were put in the same prison cell.

The masochist cried: 'Oh, hurt me, pinch me, humiliate me, just cause me pain.'

The sadist said: 'No.'

1397   A young couple were making passionate love in the guy's van when suddenly the girl, being a bit kinky, yelled out: 'Oh, big boy, whip me, whip me!'

Although not surprisingly he didn't have any whips to hand, the guy was reluctant to pass up such a unique opportunity. Then, in a flash of inspiration, he opened the window, snapped the antenna off his van and proceeded to whip the girl with the antenna until they both collapsed in sadomasochistic ecstasy.

About a week later, the girl noticed that the marks left by the whipping session were starting to fester, so she went to the doctor. The medic took one look at the wounds and asked: 'Did you get these marks having sex?'

The embarrassed girl admitted that she did.

Noddin his head knowingly, the doctor added: 'I thought so because in all my years of doctoring, you've got the worst case of van aerial disease I've ever seen.'

1398   A mother found an S&M magazine under her young son's bed. She asked her husband: 'What should we do?'

'Well,' said the husband, 'I don't think you should spank him . . .'

1399   A guy was asked why he married a sadist. He said: 'Beats me!'

1400   A guy picked up a girl at an S&M bar. He said to her: 'Do you want to come back to my place and watch something raunchy on TV?'

'Do you have cable?' she asked.

'No, but I've got some old ropes that should hold you just fine.'

MASTURBATION

1401   The Queen was on a tour of one of Canada's top hospitals when she passed a room where a male patient was masturbating. 'Oh, my!' she exclaimed. 'That's disgraceful.'

'I'm sorry,' said the doctor leading the tour, 'but this man has a very serious condition where the testicles fill rapidly with semen. If he doesn't do that five times a day, they would explode and he would most likely die instantly.'

'I understand,' said the Queen sympathetically. On the next floor they passed a room where a young nurse was giving a patient a blow job. 'Oh, my!' gasped the Queen. 'What's happening in there?'

The doctor replied: 'Same problem, better health care plan.'

1402 A young guy was lying on his back on a massage table, wearing only a towel over his groin. A gorgeous Swedish girl was massaging his shoulders, then his chest, and gradually working her way down his body. As her soft, smooth hands approached the towel, he began getting sexually aroused. When the towel rose steadily, she arched her eyebrows.

'You wanna wank?' she asked.

'You bet!' he answered excitedly.

'OK,' she said. 'I come back in ten minutes.'

1403 What's the most sensitive part of your body when you're jerking off? – Your ears, listening for footsteps.

1404 A woman went to see an artistic movie with her husband, but was disturbed by a masturbation scene. She said: 'I'm sorry, but I find masturbation in a movie really offensive.'

'OK,' he said, 'I'll stop doing it.'

1405 What do you call a man who cries while he masturbates? – A tearjerker.

1406 One day, a priest spotted a young man masturbating in an alley. 'My son, you shouldn't be doing that,' said the priest. 'You should be saving that for when you get married.'

Ten years on, the priest was walking down the street when a stranger approached him. 'You probably don't remember me,' said the man, 'but ten years ago you caught me masturbating down an alley, and you gave me a piece of advice.'

'Really?' said the priest. 'What did I advise?'

'You told me to save all that for when I got married.'

'Yes, that sounds like the sort of advice I would give. And have you followed it?'

'Indeed I have, Father. But there's just one problem.'

'Oh, what is that?'

'I've got a 48-gallon drum of the stuff in the back of my pickup truck. Now that I'm getting married, what am I supposed to do with it?'

1407 What's the ultimate rejection? – When you're masturbating and your hand goes to sleep.

1408 On their first date, a guy drove his girlfriend to a quiet country lane and began reaching under her skirt.

'Get off!' she said, pushing his hand away. 'I'm a virgin, and that's how I intend to stay for the time being.'

'How about a blow job?' he inquired hopefully.

'No way. I'm not putting that thing in my mouth.'

'Well, how about a hand job?'

'I've never done that. What do I have to do?'

'It's simple,' he explained. 'Remember when you were a kid and used to shake up a Coke bottle and spray your brother with it? Well it's just like that.'

So she pulled out his dick and started shaking it. A few seconds later his head flopped back on the headrest, his eyes closed, snot started to run out of his nose, wax blew out of his ears, and he suddenly screamed in pain.

'What's wrong?' she cried.

'Take your thumb off the end!'

1409 A young married couple were sitting in the cinema. After a while, the woman said to her husband: 'The man next to me is masturbating.'

'Ignore him, honey. Come on, we'll move seats.'

'I can't,' she said. 'He's using my hand.'

1410 What do you call a successful masturbation by a ninety-year-old man? – Miracle whip.

1411 Three guys were on vacation at a ski lodge. There weren't enough rooms, so they had to share a bed. In the middle of the night, the guy on the right woke up and said, 'I had this crazy dream of getting a hand job!' Then the guy on the left woke up and, unbelievably, he'd had the same dream. A few moments later the guy in the middle woke up and said, 'That's funny, I dreamed I was skiing.'

MEN

25 Rules For Being a Man:

1412 1. Any man who brings a camera to a stag night may be legally killed and eaten by his friends.

1413 2. It is acceptable for a man to cry under the following circumstances:
- when a heroic dog dies to save its master
- the moment Angelina Jolie starts unbuttoning her blouse
- after wrecking your boss's car
- when she is using her teeth

1414 3. Unless he murdered someone in your family, you must bail a friend out of jail within twelve hours.

1415 4. If you've known a man for more than a day, his sister is off limits for ever – unless you actually marry her.

1416 5. No man shall ever be required to buy a birthday present for another man.

1417 6. On a road journey, the strongest bladder dictates pit stops, not the weakest.

1418 7. Moaning about the brand of free beer in a friend's fridge is forbidden.

1419 8. Unless you're in prison, never fight naked.

1420 9. If a man's fly is open, that's his problem; you didn't see anything.

1421 10. Women who claim they love to watch sport must be treated as spies until they demonstrate knowledge of the game and the ability to drink as much as the other sports watchers.

1422 11. Friends don't let friends wear Speedos. Ever.

1423 12. It is permissible to drink a fruity alcopop drink only when you're sunning on a tropical beach . . . and it's delivered by a topless supermodel . . . and it's free.

1424 13. Never hesitate to take the last beer or the last slice of pizza, but not both.

1425 14. Never join your girlfriend or wife in discussing a friend of yours, except if she's withholding sex pending your response.

1426 15. Never allow a telephone conversation with a woman to go on longer than you are able to have sex with her. Keep a stopwatch by the phone. Hang up if necessary.

1427   16. The morning after you and a girl who was formerly 'just a friend' have carnal drunken sex, the fact that you're feeling weird and guilty is no reason not to nail her again before the discussion about what a big mistake it was.

1428   17. Never talk to another man in a public toilet. An almost imperceptible nod is the only conversation required.

1429   18. There is no reason for guys to watch men's ice skating or men's gymnastics.

1430   19. You may exaggerate any anecdote told in a bar by 50 per cent without recrimination.

1431   20. The minimum amount of time you have to wait for another guy who's running late is five minutes. For a girl, you are required to wait ten minutes for every point of hotness she scores on the classic 1–10 babe scale.

1432   21. Agreeing to distract the ugly friend of a hot babe that your buddy is trying to hook up with is your legal and moral duty. Should you get carried away with your good deed and end up having sex with the beast, your pal is forbidden to speak of it.

1433   22. The universal compensation for friends who help you move house is beer.

1434   23. Before dating a buddy's 'ex', you are required to seek his permission, and he in return is required to grant it.

1435   24. Under no circumstances may two men share an umbrella.

1436   25. Never, ever slap another man.

1437   Away from home for two weeks on a business trip, a man booked into a modern motel. Realizing he needed a haircut before the next day's meeting, he called down to the desk clerk and asked if there was a barber on the premises.

'I'm afraid not, sir,' said the clerk, 'but down the hall is a special machine that should serve your purposes.'

Sceptical but intrigued, the businessman located the machine, inserted fifty cents, and stuck his head in the opening as per the instructions. The machine immediately started to buzz and whirl for thirty seconds. When it stopped, the man pulled out his head and looked in the mirror, which reflected the best haircut he had ever received in his life.

Further down the hall was another machine with a sign that read: 'Manicures – 25 cents.' Buoyed by his success with the haircut, he decided to give it a try. He paid the money, put his hands into the slot, and pulled them out thirty seconds later, perfectly manicured.

A little further down the hall was a third machine, bearing a sign that read: 'This machine provides what men need most when away from their wives — cost 50 cents.' The businessman had been away from home for so long that he was desperate for sex. So after checking that there was nobody around, he paid the money, then unzipped his trousers and stuck his penis into the opening. But when the machine started buzzing, he let out a shriek of agony. Thirty seconds later, it stopped and, with trembling hands, he was able to withdraw his penis . . . which now had a button sewn on the tip.

1438 Why do men name their penises? — Because they don't like the idea of a stranger making ninety per cent of their decisions.

1439 Why do men whistle on the toilet? — Because it helps them remember which end they need to wipe.

1440 Why do only ten per cent of men go to heaven? — Because if they all went, it would be hell.

1441 What's the best way to kill a man? — Put a naked blonde and a six-pack in front of him, then tell him to pick only one.

1442 What is the difference between a man and Bigfoot? — One is covered in matted hair and smells awful; the other has big feet.

1443 Why are men like guns? — Keep one around long enough, and eventually you're going to want to shoot it.

1444
Ten Things Men Know About Women:

1. They have pussies
2.
3.
4.
5.
6.
7.
8.
9.
10. They have breasts too

1445 What's a man's idea of honesty in a relationship? – Telling you his real name.

1446 What do you call a handcuffed man? – Trustworthy.

1447 What do you call a guy with a one-inch dick? – Justin.

1448 What do you call a man with ninety-nine per cent of his brain missing? – Castrated.

1449 Why did the man cross the road? – He heard the chicken was a slut.

1450 How does a man keep his youth? – By giving him money and expensive presents.

1451 Why do men marry virgins? – Because they can't stand criticism.

1452 What is the ideal breakfast for a man? – He's sitting at the table eating Eggs Benedict, his son is on the cover of the box of Wheaties, his mistress is on the cover of the new *Penthouse*, and his wife is on the back of the milk carton.

1453 A man turned to his wife and said sarcastically: 'I don't know why you wear a bra – you've got nothing to put in it.'
    She replied: 'Well, you wear underpants, don't you?'

1454 What do men and pantyhose have in common? – They either cling, run, or don't fit right in the crotch.

1455 What's the difference between a man and a condom? – Condoms have changed; they're no longer thick and insensitive.

1456 How are men like lawn mowers? – They're hard to get started, they emit noxious odours, and half the time they don't work.

1457 Men are like cycling helmets – handy in an emergency, but otherwise they just look silly.

1458 A woman bumped into an old friend and asked how her marriage was going. 'It's terrible,' she said. 'He eats like a pig, he never has a bath, and he leaves his filthy clothes lying all over the house. He makes me feel so sick I can barely eat.'

'Why don't you leave him?'

'I will. But I want to lose another fifteen pounds first.'

1459　　　　　　**Men's Mastercard Commercial:**

Cover charge $15.00

Round of drinks $23.00

Table dance $30.00

Another round of drinks $23.00

Couch dance and tips $50.00

A round of shots $34.00

Private dance in your hotel room $300.00

Being able to send her on her way and never have to hear her complain: ***PRICELESS***

1460 A man parked his car at the supermarket and was walking past an empty trolley when he heard a woman ask: 'Excuse me, did you want that trolley?'

'No,' he replied, 'I'm only after one thing.'

'Huh,' she muttered. 'Typical man!'

1461 Why can't men get mad cow disease? – Because they're all pigs.

1462 What's the one thing that keeps most men out of college? – High school.

1463 How are men like noodles? – They're always in hot water, they lack taste, and they need dough.

1464 What's the difference between men and women? – A woman wants one man to satisfy her every need; a man wants every woman to satisfy his one need.

1465 Why do men find it difficult to make eye contact? – Breasts don't have eyes.

1466 How do you know when a man's had an orgasm? – He's snoring.

1467 A guy went for a crap and kept going for three hours. Finally he got to the point where he shat his brains right out. He had no brains left at all. Finally done, he wiped his ass and for the first time in his life he put the seat down.

1468 Once upon a time a female brain cell mistakenly ended up in a man's head. She looked around nervously, but it was all empty and quiet.

'Is anyone here?' she shouted. There was no reply.

So she shouted louder: 'Is there anyone around?'

Then she heard a voice from far, far away: 'Hello, we're all down here . . .'

A Woman's Ten Favourite Men:

1469 • The doctor, because he says, 'Take off your clothes.'

1470 • The dentist, because he says, 'Open wide.'

1471 • The hairdresser, because he says, 'Do you want it teased or blown?'

1472 • The milkman, because he says, 'Do you want it in the front or around the back?'

1473 • The interior decorator, because he says, 'Once you have it all in, you'll love it.'

1474 • The banker, because he says, 'If you take it out too soon, you'll lose interest.'

1475 • The police officer, because he says, 'Spread 'em.'

1476 • The mailman, because he always delivers his package.

1477 • The pilot, because he takes off fast and then slows down.

1478 • The hunter, because he always goes deep in the bush, shoots twice, and always eats what he shoots.

1479 Strolling along the beach, a man found a magic lamp and rubbed it vigorously. As he had hoped, a genie emerged and immediately granted him one wish.

The man said: 'I want to be hard all the time and get all the ass I want.'

And POOF! he turned into a toilet seat.

1480 Why do men buy electric lawn mowers? – So they can find their way back to the house.

1481 How many men does it take to screw in a light bulb? – One. Men will screw anything.

1482 What has eight arms and an IQ of 60? – Four guys watching a football game.

1483 What's the difference between a sofa and a man watching football? – The sofa doesn't keep asking for beer.

1484   **Why a Woman's Nagging Never Works:**
The woman says: 'This place is a mess! C'mon, you and I need to clean up.
Your stuff is lying on the floor, and if we don't do the laundry right now, you'll
have no clothes to wear.'
The man hears: 'Blah, blah, blah, blah C'MON
Blah, blah YOU AND I
Blah, blah, blah, blah ON THE FLOOR
Blah, blah, blah, blah, blah RIGHT NOW
Blah, blah, blah NO CLOTHES.'

1485 How do you get a man to stop biting his nails? – Make him wear shoes.

1486 What's the difference between a penis and a prick? – A penis is fun, sexy
and satisfying. A prick is the guy who owns it.

1487 What's the difference between a man and a catfish? – One is a bottom-
feeding scum-sucker and the other is a fish.

1488 A man had six children and was so proud of his achievement that, despite his
wife's objections, he started calling her 'mother of six', both in private and in
public.
      One night the couple went to a party. When the husband was ready to go
home, he called out loudly: 'Shall we leave now, Mother of Six?'
      Irritated by his lack of discretion, his wife shouted back: 'Ready when you
are, Father of Four.'

If Men Really Ruled The World:
1489   • Any fake number a girl gave you would automatically forward
         your call to her real number.
1490   • Nodding and looking at your watch would be considered an
         acceptable response to 'I love you'.
1491   • Hallmark would make 'Sorry, what was your name again?'
         cards.
1492   • When your girlfriend really needed to talk to you during the
         game, she'd appear in a little box in the corner of the screen
         during a time-out.
1493   • Instead of beer belly, you'd get 'beer biceps'.
1494   • Valentine's Day would be moved to February 29 so it would
         only occur in leap years.

1495 • Breaking up would be a lot easier. A slap on the ass and a 'Good try, you'll get 'em next time' would pretty much do it.

1496 • The victors in any athletic competition would get to kill and eat the losers.

1497 • Condoms would be lager flavoured.

1498 • Tanks would be far easier to rent.

1499 • Telephones would automatically cut off after thirty seconds of conversation. It would be considered harmless fun to gather twenty friends, put on horned helmets, and go pillage a nearby town.

1500 What's a man's idea of foreplay? – Brushing his teeth.

1501 Why do men like having sex with the lights on? – It makes it easier to put a name to the face.

1502 Why are men like cars? – Because they always pull out before they check to see if anyone else is coming.

Manliness Test:

1503 1. In the company of females, intercourse should be referred to as:
A. Lovemaking.
B. Screwing.
C. Taking the pigskin bus to tuna town.

1504 2. You should make love to a woman for the first time only after you've both shared:
A. Your views about what you expect from a sexual relationship.
B. Your blood test results.
C. Five tequila slammers.

1505 3. You time your orgasm so that:
A. Your partner climaxes first.
B. You both climax simultaneously.
C. You don't miss the big game on TV.

1506 4. Passionate, spontaneous sex on the kitchen floor is:
A. Healthy, creative love-play.
B. Not the sort of thing your wife/girlfriend would agree to.

C. Not the sort of thing your wife/girlfriend ever needs to find out about.

1507 5. Spending the whole night cuddling a woman you just had sex with is:

A. The best part of the experience.

B. The second best part of the experience.

C. $100 extra.

1508 6. Your girlfriend says she's gained five pounds in the last month. You tell her that it is:

A. No great concern of yours.

B. Not a problem — she can join a gym.

C. A conservative estimate.

1509 7. You think today's sensitive, caring man is:

A. A myth.

B. An oxymoron.

C. A moron.

1510 8. Foreplay is to sex as:

A. Appetiser is to entrée.

B. Primer is to paint.

C. A long line is to an amusement park ride.

1511 9. You feel a gas attack coming on. Do you:

A. Hold it in with clenched buttocks.

B. Reluctantly let it go, and mutter an apology.

C. Let it rip and race around the room giving hi-fives.

1512 10. A woman who is uncomfortable watching you masturbate:

A. Probably needs a little more time before she can cope with that sort of intimacy.

B. Probably is too uptight and a waste of your time.

C. Probably shouldn't have sat next to you on the bus in the first place.

If you answered A more than seven times, check inside your pants to make sure you really are a man.

If you answered B more than seven times, check into therapy.

If you answered C more than seven times, you da man!

MEXICANS

1513 What do you throw a Mexican man when he's drowning? – His wife and kids.

1514 What do you call a Mexican with a vasectomy? – A dry Martinez.

1515 How does a Mexican get into an honest business? – Usually through the skylight.

1516 An American, a Canadian and a Mexican had been on the road for days and were starving. Arriving at a farm with dozens of different fruits on display, they ran up to the baskets and started helping themselves, only to be confronted by the irate farmer waving a shotgun. The men begged for mercy until the farmer relented.

'OK,' he said, 'I'm in a good mood so I won't kill you. Instead you must stuff one hundred of your favourite fruits up your ass. But if you laugh while you're doing it, I'll shoot you!'

Going first, the American chose cherries and reached sixty-eight before he started laughing uncontrollably. The farmer shot him.

Next, the Canadian chose grapes and reached eighty-three before he, too, burst out laughing. The farmer shot him.

When the American and the Canadian arrived in heaven, an angel asked them why they had laughed. They said: 'We saw the Mexican with watermelons.'

1517 Why do Mexicans have such small steering wheels? – So they can drive wearing handcuffs.

1518 Why did the Mexican shoot his wife? – Tequila.

1519 If you see a Mexican on a bike, why shouldn't you run him over? – It might be your bike.

1520 An American dude was driving a Cadillac in Mexico and pulled into a station for gas. A Mexican boy was quietly sitting on a fruit crate peeling an apple and showed no sign of moving.

Becoming impatient at the lack of service, the dude yelled: 'Hey, how about pumping me some motherfucking gas?'

The kid said: 'Señor, we don't like that word "motherfucker" in this country.' And he continued peeling his apple.

The dude reacted angrily. 'Boy, I want some motherfucking gas! Do you hear me?'

The kid repeated: 'Señor, we don't like the word "motherfucker" in this country.' And he carried on peeling his apple.

The dude was now seething with rage. 'You gonna pump me some motherfucking gas, or am I gonna have to pump it myself?'

The kid stood up and said calmly: 'Señor, let me show you something.' He tossed the apple into the air and with his sharp knife, cut it into sixteen slices in mid-air.

The dude said: 'You got another motherfucking apple?'

The kid tossed him another apple, whereupon the dude pulled out his .45 and made apple sauce out of it.

The kid thought for a moment and said: 'How many motherfucking gallons do you think she'll hold, senor?'

1521 Why do Mexicans refry their beans? – Have you ever known a Mexican to do something right the first time?

1522 What are the first four words in every Mexican cookbook? – 'First, steal a chicken.'

1523 How does a Mexican commit suicide? – He smells his armpits.
How does an American commit suicide? – He tells this joke to a Mexican.

1524 A Mexican was hypnotized by a fairground magician. 'You're in the desert,' said the hypnotist. 'It's unbearably hot, and you're gasping for water.'

The Mexican began panting breathlessly and licking his lips.

'Now you're at the South Pole,' said the hypnotist. 'It's bitterly cold, and you are struggling to keep warm.'

The Mexican began to shiver uncontrollably.

'Now you're in the USA,' continued the hypnotist. 'You have a good job, a nice house, you're a respected member of the community.'

The Mexican opened one eye and said: 'If you wake me up, I'll break your arms.'

1525 What do you call a black man driving a Cadillac? – Black Power.
What do you call a white man driving a Cadillac? – White Power.
What do you call a Mexican driving a Cadillac? – Grand theft auto.

1526 How can you tell a Mexican cesspool? – It's the one with the diving board.

1527 Why did the Mexican become so excited? – He discovered he could use Right Guard under his left arm.

1528 When does a Mexican become Spanish? – When he marries your daughter.

1529 A massive earthquake hit Mexico, killing two million Mexicans. Canada sent troopers to help the Mexican Army control the situation; Europe sent food and money; Saudi Arabia sent oil; the Latin American countries sent clothing supplies to help the homeless; the United States sent two million replacement Mexicans.

MIDDLE AGE

What a Difference Thirty Years Makes:

1530 *1975*: long hair
2005: Longing for hair

1531 *1975*: Moving to California because it's cool
2005: Moving to California because it's warm

1532 *1975*: Growing pot
2005: Growing pot belly

1533 *1975*: Trying to look like Liz Taylor
2005: Trying *not* to look like Liz Taylor

1534 *1975*: Seeds and stems
2005: Roughage

1535 *1975*: Getting out to a new, hip joint
2005: Getting a new hip joint

1536 *1975*: Rolling Stones
2005: Kidney stones

1537   *1975*: Screw the system
       2005: Upgrade the system

1538   *1975*: Take acid
       2005: Take antacid

1539   *1975*: Passing the driver's test
       2005: Passing the vision test

1540   *1975*: 'Whatever'
       2005: 'Depends'

MILITARY

1541   Two rednecks with the US Army – Leroy and Luke – were promoted from privates to sergeants. As they were strolling around the army base, Leroy said: 'Let's go into the Officers' Club.'

Luke said: 'But we're privates.'

Leroy pointed to his stripes and reminded him: 'We're sergeants now.'

Once inside the club, Leroy said: 'I'm gonna sit myself down with a drink.'

Luke said: 'But we're privates.'

'Are you blind?' said Leroy, pointing to his stripes. 'We're sergeants now.'

So they had a drink, and after a while a hooker sidled up to Leroy. 'You're kinda cute,' she purred, 'and I'd love to show you a good time but I've got a bad case of gonorrhoea.'

Puzzled, Leroy whispered to Luke: 'Go and look up that word in the dictionary. If it's OK, come back and give me the thumbs up.'

So Luke went back to his hut and looked up 'gonorrhoea' in the dictionary. Then he returned to the club and gave Leroy the thumbs up.

Three weeks later, Leroy was lying in the army hospital with a terrible case of gonorrhoea. When Luke came to visit, Leroy stormed: 'Luke, why did you give me the thumbs up?'

'Well,' replied Luke. 'In the dictionary it says gonorrhoea affects only the privates.' He pointed to his stripes and said: 'But we're sergeants now!'

1542 At the height of the Troubles in Northern Ireland, a 10 p.m. curfew was imposed in Belfast. Everyone had to be off the streets by that time or risk being shot. Then one night, a man was gunned down at 9.45 p.m.

The British Army conducted an immediate inquiry and the soldier involved was brought before his commanding officer.

The officer began: 'Why did you shoot that man at 9.45 when the curfew did not begin until ten?'

'I know where he lives,' replied the soldier. 'He'd never have made it.'

1543 Why is being in the military like a blow job? – The closer you get to discharge, the better you feel.

1544 Fifteen years after retiring, a US general bumped into his old orderly in a Dallas bar. For old times' sake, the general offered him a job as his valet. 'Your duties will be exactly the same as they were in the army,' he said. 'Nothing to it – you'll soon catch on.'

So on his first morning, just as he had done in Vietnam, the ex-orderly entered the ex-general's bedroom, pulled open the drapes, and gave the general a gentle shake. He then strode around to the other side of the bed, spanked his employer's wife on the bottom and said: 'OK, sweetheart, it's back to the village for you.'

1545 Why did the army private tattoo sergeant's stripes on his cock? – He loved to pull rank.

1546 A US Army platoon was conducting manoeuvres in the Florida swamps. With the men running low on water, the sergeant ordered a private to go down to the lake and fill up their canteens.

'But I saw an alligator in that lake,' protested the private. 'Real close to the edge.'

'Don't be such a lily-livered coward,' raged the sergeant. 'That alligator is ten times as frightened of you as you are of it.'

'Maybe,' said the private. 'But even if he's only twice as frightened as me, that water still won't be fit to drink!'

1547 Did you hear about the army nurse who went to bed eating popcorn? – She woke up with a kernel between her legs.

1548 Airman Harvey was assigned to the induction centre where his job was to
advise new recruits about their government benefits, especially their GI
Insurance. It soon came to the attention of his commanding officer that
Harvey was achieving almost a 100 per cent record for insurance sales,
something that had never been done before.

Curious to learn the secret of Harvey's success, the commanding officer sat
at the back of the room and listened to the airman's sales pitch. After
explaining the basics of the GI Insurance, Harvey went on: 'If you have GI
Insurance and go into battle and are killed, the government has to pay $200,000
to your beneficiaries. If you don't have GI Insurance, and you go into battle and
get killed, the government has to pay only a maximum of $6,000.

'So,' he concluded, 'which bunch do you think they are going to send into
battle first . . .?'

1549 Why did so many black GIs get killed in Vietnam? – Because every time the
sergeant shouted, 'Get down!' they stood up and started dancing.

1550 Reviewing his regiment, the colonel could not help noticing that one of the
soldiers had a huge erection. 'Give this man thirty days' compassionate home
leave,' he told the sergeant major.

A few months later, the same man was again sporting a huge erection on
the parade ground. 'Sergeant major!' said the colonel. 'Give this man another
thirty days' compassionate home leave.'

Two months later, exactly the same thing happened. This time the colonel
was angry. 'Sergeant major, haven't we given this man two periods of
compassionate home leave?'

'Yes, sir,' replied the sergeant major.

'Then what's the problem?' demanded the colonel. 'Why has he got that
huge erection again?'

The sergeant major whispered: 'I think it's you he's fond of, sir.'

MISERS

1551 Olaf and Helga lived on the edge of a lake in Canada. It was near the end of
winter, and spring was just beginning. One day Olaf asked Helga whether
she would walk across the frozen lake to the general store to pick him up
some tobacco.

'Sure, but I'll need some money,' said Helga.

Olaf thought for a moment and said: 'No, with the weather warming up, I don't know how thick the ice is. So just tell them to put it on my tab.'

1552 One summer day, a city dog was taken to a vet in Maine following an encounter with a porcupine. After almost an hour of prising, pulling, cutting and stitching, he returned the dog to its lady owner.

'How much do I owe you?' she asked.

'Forty dollars,' replied the vet.

'Forty dollars? That's outrageous!' she cried. 'That's the trouble with you Maine people – you're always trying to overcharge summer visitors. Whatever do you do in the winter when we're not being conned?'

The vet replied: 'Raise porcupines, ma'am.'

1553 A man took a huge jar of urine to a clinic and paid to have it tested. When the results came back, he was relieved to learn that it had been given the all clear. He got on the phone and said: 'It's me, Jim. Tell your Auntie Jane that there's absolutely nothing wrong with you, her, me, Uncle Michael, Grandma, or the dog.'

MISSISSIPPI

1554 A country boy from Mississippi was walking down the street with some chicken wire under his arm. His neighbour saw him and asked him what he was carrying.

'It's chicken wire, and I'm going to catch me some chickens.'

His neighbour said: 'You fool, you can't catch chickens with chicken wire!' But later that day he spotted the guy walking down the street dragging a dozen chickens.

The next morning he saw the country boy with some duct tape under his arm.

'What's that you're carrying?' asked the neighbour.

'It's duct tape. I'm going to catch me some ducks.'

'You fool,' said the neighbour, 'you can't catch ducks with duct tape.' But later that day he saw the guy walking down the street dragging a dozen ducks.

The next day the neighbour saw the country boy walking with something else under his arm.

'What are you carrying today?' asked the neighbour.

'Pussy willow,' said the country boy.

The neighbour said: 'Hold on, let me get my hat.'

1555 The old Mississippi farmer was having a miserable year. All of his crops had been lost. Fortunately, the peach orchard had done really well, but he figured the only way he was going to make ends meet was to cut out the middle man and sell the peaches directly to the customer.

So he loaded his pickup with peaches and headed into town. Eyeing a likely house, he took a basket of peaches from the truck and knocked on the front door. It was answered by a glamorous blonde wearing a slinky robe.

'Hi, honey,' she said sexily. 'What can I do for you?'

The old farmer gulped: 'I have these really nice peaches for sale.'

Noticing how rattled the farmer was, the woman decided to tease him and opened the top of her robe to reveal her breasts. 'Are those peaches full and firm like these?' she purred.

'Yes,' he stammered, sweating profusely. 'They're really good peaches.'

Then she opened the rest of her robe – wide enough to show that she wasn't wearing any panties. 'Would they be succulent and delicious like this?' she said, licking her lips seductively.

The old farmer nearly had a coronary. 'Oh, yes, they're wonderful peaches,' he sobbed.

'Honey, why are you crying?' she asked.

The farmer whimpered: 'Lady, the cut worms ruined my tomato crop, and the weevils ate all my cotton, and now I think you're going to fuck me out of my peaches.'

1556 Two fine southern ladies from Mississippi were sitting on the front porch, sipping iced tea. One of the women held out her hand ostentatiously for the other to see, and in her long southern drawl said: 'Look at this ring my husband gave me. Isn't it nice?'

The other woman replied: 'Oh, that's nice, that's real nice.'

The first woman went on: 'And just last month he took me on one of them Caribbean cruises.'

The second woman again replied: 'Oh, that's nice, that's real nice.'

'Well, sweetheart,' said the first, 'doesn't your husband ever buy you nice things or send you nice places?'

'When we first got married, he did send me to etiquette school.'

'Why did he do that?'

'Well, you see,' said the second woman, 'before, when someone told me about the jewellery their husband gave them or the trips he sent her on, I would have just said, "Who gives a shit?" But now I say, "That's nice, that's real nice."'

MONEY

1557 A little boy went up to his dad and asked: 'Dad, what's the difference between potentially and realistically?'

His father replied: 'Well, son, go ask your mother if she would sleep with Robert Redford for a million dollars. Then ask your sister if she would sleep with Brad Pitt for a million dollars. Finally ask your brother if he would sleep with Tom Cruise for a million dollars.'

So the boy went up to his mom and asked her if she would sleep with Robert Redford for a million dollars. 'My God, of course I would,' she said. 'He is good looking.'

Then the boy asked his sister if she would sleep with Brad Pitt for a million dollars. 'Are you kidding?' she said. 'Of course I would. He is so gorgeous.'

Finally the boy asked his brother if he would sleep with Tom Cruise for a million dollars. 'I sure would,' replied the brother. 'Who wouldn't for a million bucks?'

So the boy went back to his dad and said: 'I think I learned the difference between potentially and realistically.'

'So what's the difference?' asked the father.

'Well, potentially we're sitting on three million dollars; realistically we're living with two sluts and a fag!'

1558 Following a shipwreck, there were only two survivors: the boat's owner, Dr Roberts, and the steward, Oliver. The steward was terrified that they would never be found, but the owner remained perfectly calm.

'How can you be so calm?' asked Oliver. 'We're going to die on this lonely island. We'll never be discovered here.'

'Listen,' said Dr Roberts confidently. 'Five years ago I gave the United Way $600,000 and I donated another $750,000 to the United Jewish Appeal. Four years ago, I donated the same amounts, and three years ago, since I did very well in the stock market, I contributed $1,000,000 to each. Last year, business was good again, so the two charities received $1,500,000 apiece.'

'And how does that help us?' asked Oliver.

'Well,' said Dr Roberts, 'it's time for their annual fund drives. They'll find me.'

1559 What's the difference between your paycheck and your cock? – You don't have to beg your wife to blow your paycheck.

1560 A pretty young woman was examining the material in a curtain shop. 'How much does it cost?' she asked the young male clerk.

He smiled at her and said: 'One kiss per metre.'

'Fine,' she said. 'In that case, I'll take twelve metres.'

As he handed her the fabric and moved in for the kill, she pointed to a little old lady sitting in the corner and said: 'Grandma's paying the bill.'

1561 A guy went into a sex shop to return the blow-up doll he had bought the previous day. He told the storeowner: 'I blew this doll up last night, and straight away she went down on me. I want my $50 back.'

'Hell,' said the storeowner, 'if I'd known she was going to do that, I'd have charged you $75!'

1562 For his birthday a little boy asked for a ten-speed bicycle. His dad said: 'Son, we'd let you have one, but the mortgage on this house is $140,000 and your mother just lost her job. There's no way we can afford it.'

The next morning the father saw the boy heading out of the front door with a suitcase.

'Where are you going?' he asked.

The boy answered: 'I was walking past your room last night and heard you tell mom you were pulling out. Then I heard her tell you to wait because she was coming too. And I'll be damned if I'm staying here by myself with a $140,000 mortgage and no bike!'

His and her Drive-Through ATM Machines:

1563 *His*

1. Pull up to ATM.
2. Insert card.
3. Enter PIN and account.
4. Take cash, card and receipt.
5. Drive away.

1564 *Hers*

1. Pull up to ATM.
2. Back up and pull forward to get closer.
3. Shut off engine.
4. Put keys in purse.
5. Get out of car because you're too far from the machine.
6. Hunt in purse for card.
7. Insert card.
8. Hunt in purse for grocery receipt with PIN written on it.
9. Enter PIN.
10. Study instructions.
11. Hit 'cancel'
12. Reinsert card and re-enter correct PIN.
13. Check balance.
14. Look for envelope.
15. Look in purse for pen.
16. Make cash withdrawal.
17. Get in car.
18. Check makeup.
19. Look for keys.
20. Start car.
21. Check makeup.
22. Start pulling away.
23. Stop.
24. Back up to machine.
25. Get out of car.
26. Take card and receipt.
27. Get back in car.
28. Put card in wallet.
29. Put receipt in cheque book.
30. Enter withdrawal in cheque book.
31. Clear area in purse for wallet and cheque book.
32. Check makeup.
33. Put car in reverse.
34. Put car in first gear.
35. Drive away from machine.
36. Drive three miles.
37. Release handbrake.

MUSIC

1565 A classical guitarist was hired to play two solos in a movie. After the sessions he was paid handsomely and promised by the director that he would be notified when the movie was released. Three months later he was told that the movie would be making its debut at a porno house in Times Square. Although the venue was not exactly what he had been hoping for, he was determined to attend but decided to wear a raincoat and dark glasses just in case anyone recognized him. Unaccustomed as he was to porno theatres, he sat in the back row next to an elderly couple.

The movie was grossly explicit. There were scenes of oral intercourse, anal intercourse, golden showers, sado-masochism, and near the end a dog had intercourse with the film's leading lady. The guitarist, who was hugely embarrassed by the whole thing, turned to the elderly couple and explained: 'I wrote the score and I just came to hear the music.'

To which the elderly woman whispered in reply: 'We just came to see our dog.'

1566 What's brown and sits on a piano bench? – Beethoven's First Movement.

1567 What's the difference between a bull and an orchestra? – The bull has the horns in the front and the asshole in the back.

1568 Why is a conductor like a condom? – It's safer with one, but more fun without.

1569 Why is a drum machine better than a drummer? – Because it can keep a steady beat and won't sleep with your girlfriend.

1570 What did the drummer get on his IQ test? – Drool.

1571 How do you get two piccolos to play in unison? – Shoot one.

1572 What's the difference between a trombone player lying in the road and a dead squirrel lying in the road? – The squirrel might have been on his way to a gig.

1573 What do cellists and Mike Tyson have in common? – They're both hard on the ears.

1574 A guy was playing the piano at a party and one of the guests enjoyed a particular tune so much that he asked the pianist for the title.

The pianist replied: 'It's called "I Shag My Wife Up The Ass And Come All Over Her Tits."'

The guest was shocked. 'That's a bit crude,' he said, 'but nevertheless I like your playing and I'd like to you perform at my party next month. However, perhaps you could tone down some of the titles to avoid offending too many people.'

The pianist agreed, and turned up as arranged. However, his piano playing was so bad that the host felt compelled to have a word with him.

'I'm sorry,' said the pianist, 'but I really need a wank. I can't play properly until I've had one.'

'All right,' said the host. 'Go into the bathroom – there are some magazines in there that will help.'

A few minutes later the pianist emerged from the bathroom and began playing beautifully. Then a woman came up to him and said: 'Excuse me, but do you know your cock's hanging out and you've got spunk all over your pants?'

'Know it?' he said. 'I wrote it!'

1575 What's the difference between a soprano and a pit bull? – The jewellery.

1576 What do you see if you look up a soprano's skirt? – A tenor.

1577 What's the difference between a world war and a high school choral performance? – The performance causes greater suffering.

1578 Why do high school choruses travel so far? – To keep assassins guessing.

1579 A guy went to the doctor and said. 'I haven't had a bowel movement in a week.'

The doctor prescribed him a mild laxative and said: 'If it doesn't work, let me know.'

A week later, the guy was back to report: 'There still hasn't been any movement.'

So the doctor prescribed him a much stronger laxative, but this too failed to produce the desired effect. 'Oh, dear,' said the doctor, concerned. 'I think we'd better get some more information about you to try to figure out what's going on. Tell me, what do you do for a living?'

'I'm a musician,' replied the patient.

'Well, that's it!' exclaimed the doctor. 'Here's $10. Go get something to eat!'

NATIVE AMERICANS

1580 A young woman from New York was driving through a remote part of Oklahoma when her car broke down. Just then an Indian came riding by on horseback and offered her a lift to the nearest town. So she climbed up behind him on the horse and they rode off. The journey was uneventful except that every few minutes, for no apparent reason, the Indian let out a loud whoop.

When they reached town, the Indian dropped her off at the service station. As she climbed down, he whooped again and rode off.

The service station clerk said: 'What did you do to get that Indian so excited?'

'Nothing,' she replied. 'I merely sat behind him on the horse, put my arms around his waist, and held onto his saddle horn so I wouldn't fall off.'

'Lady,' said the clerk, 'Indians ride bareback!'

1581 A cowboy was riding through the desert when he came across an Indian who was lying on the ground with his dick hanging out.

'What are you doing?' inquired the cowboy.

'Me tell time,' said the Indian. 'Penis act as sundial.'

The cowboy was intrigued. 'So what time do you make it?'

'11.08.'

'Me, too. That's amazing.'

Impressed with the Indian's ingenuity, the cowboy rode off and a few miles further on he stumbled across another Indian lying on the ground with his dick out.

'I know what you're up to,' said the cowboy. 'You're telling the time. What time do you make it?'

The Indian studied the shadow from his penis. '11.21.'

'That's right,' said the cowboy. 'Unbelievable!'

The cowboy rode off until a few miles further on he spotted another Indian lying on the ground with his dick out. But this time the Indian was jerking himself off.

'What the heck are you doing?' asked the cowboy.

'Me winding clock.'

1582 Did you hear about the Indian who drank twelve gallons of Lipton's? – They found him the next day, dead in his tea-pee.

1583 One day an Indian boy asked his father why they have such long names.

The father explained: 'Whenever an Indian baby is born, the father goes outside and names the baby after the first thing he sees. Why do you ask, Two Dogs Fucking?'

1584 A Native American couple arrived in New York City. It was the first time they had ever ventured beyond their native village, and the wife, baffled by the unfamiliar streets plus the hustle and bustle of the crowds and traffic, soon became separated from her husband. The husband asked a passer-by for help in finding his missing spouse and was told to report it to the police.

At the station, the officer asked him for a description of his wife.

'What's a description?' asked the Indian.

'Well,' explained the officer patiently, 'a description is telling what something looks like. For example, my wife is twenty-four, 5ft 10in tall, weighs 140lb, and has measurements of 36–25–36. Now what can you tell me about your wife?'

'To hell with my wife!' said the Indian. 'Let's go look for yours!'

1585 What's the Indian word for 'lousy hunter'? – Vegetarian.

1586 An Indian and his squaw were driving their cart into town for some beers. On the way she gave him a blow job but then suddenly she pulled her head up and said: 'Yur pashinit.'

He grinned and pushed her head back down, but again she yanked her head back up and said: 'Yur pashinit.'

'I know, I know,' he said, smiling. 'I'm very romantic, huh?'

'No,' she said, 'yur pashinit – the beer store was back there!'

1587 An old Indian was standing on a street corner when an attractive woman passed by on her way to work. The Indian raised his hand in greeting and said, 'Chance!'

The same thing happened over the rest of the week. The woman walked past, the Indian raised his hand and said, 'Chance!'

Finally the woman could ignore it no longer. She stopped and said: 'You're an Indian, aren't you?'

He nodded.

She continued: 'I thought Indians always said "How!" as a greeting?'

The Indian said: 'Already know "how". Just want "chance".'

1588 On a red hot day, an old Indian tied his horse under the shade of a tree with the intention of completing the journey into town on foot. But a hundred yards down the road, a guy in a Chevrolet offered him a lift, and the Indian got in.

As they touched 40 mph, the Indian said: 'You go so fast, horse no get hot?'

'No,' replied the driver. 'It's air-cooled. The faster I go, the colder it gets.'

After completing his errands in town, the Indian was heading back to where he had left his horse when a Porsche driver offered him a lift. Soon they were doing 75 mph, prompting the Indian to ask: 'You go so fast, horse no get hot?'

'No,' said the driver. 'It's air-cooled. The faster I go, the colder it runs.'

The driver dropped the Indian off near the tree, and the Indian climbed on his horse and got to work with the spurs. Over miles and miles of dusty paths, he rode as fast as he could. The horse was sweating up in a terrible lather, and then just as they reached his village, the horse dropped dead.

The other Indians came out to ask what had happened.

The old Indian said: 'Near as I can tell, he froze to death.'

1589 During the space programme in the 1960s, the Apollo astronauts practised moon walking in the Arizona desert. The strange sight of the space-suited figures wandering around the landscape attracted the attention of several Indians. One of them could speak English, and the officials in charge told him what they were doing. When he informed the others, one old man wanted to write a message to send to the moon. The NASA people humoured him, and he scratched out a message. When the other Indians read it, they smiled, but didn't say anything. Since it was in native writing, the NASA people couldn't read it, but eventually they found an Indian who was willing to translate it for them. The note said: 'Watch out for these people! They're coming to take your land!'

1590 Working as a scout for the army, an Indian put his ear to the ground and said: 'Hmm, buffalo come.'

The soldier was amazed by the Indian's powers of deduction, but was unable to see any buffalo. After a minute or so, and still no sign of any buffalo, he asked the Indian: 'How do you know buffalo come?'

The Indian replied: 'Ear sticky.'

NECROPHILIA

1591 Two necrophiliacs were at work in the morgue. One turned to the other and said: 'You should have seen this woman they brought in last week. They pulled her out of the water she'd been in there for five weeks. I'm tellin' you, her clit was just like a pickle!'

'What,' asked the other, 'green?'

'No,' said the first, 'a bit sour.'

1592 What do a fur trapper and a necrophiliac have in common? – Both are looking for dead beaver.

1593 What's a necrophiliac's biggest complaint about sex? – They just kinda lay there.

1594 Two gay necrophiliacs were walking past a morgue. One said to the other: 'Hey, you wanna go in and suck a couple of cold ones?'

1595 The young male victim of a car crash was pronounced dead on arrival at hospital, and the emergency nurse was told to prepare the body for the undertaker. But as she removed the dead man's clothes, she saw that he had died with a massive erection. Hard though she tried, she couldn't take her eyes off it, and, with nobody around, she eventually yielded to temptation. She climbed on top and straddled the stiff. She found it immensely satisfying, but just as she was climbing off, a second nurse walked in and strongly reprimanded her.

'It's all right,' pleaded the first nurse. 'There's no harm done. I enjoyed it, and he's not exactly in a position to complain. I can't get pregnant. Why don't you have a go?'

'I couldn't,' said the second nurse. 'First, he's dead, and besides I'm having my period. Anyway the doctor wants you.'

At that, the first nurse left the room, and the second nurse, after gazing longingly at his upright member for a few moments, also gave in to temptation. 'So what if I'm having my period,' she thought, and she proceeded to straddle the corpse. But just as she was about to reach orgasm, she was astonished to feel him climax too. Looking down and seeing his eyelids starting to flutter, she exclaimed in shock: 'I thought you were dead!'

'Lady, I thought I was too until you gave me that blood transfusion.'

NEIGHBOURS

1596 *First neighbour.* Hi there, new neighbour, it's a nice day to be moving.
New neighbour. Sure is.
First neighbour. Tell me, what do you do for a living?
New neighbour. I am a professor at the university. I teach deductive reasoning.
First neighbour. Deductive reasoning. What's that?
New neighbour. Let me give you an example. I see you have a doghouse out back. By that I deduce that you have a dog.
First neighbour. That's right.
New neighbour. The fact that you have a dog leads me to deduce that you have a family.
First neighbour. Right again.
New neighbour. Since you have family, I deduce that you have a wife.
First neighbour. Correct.
New neighbour. And since you have a wife, I can deduce that you're heterosexual.
First neighbour. Yes.
New neighbour. And that is deductive reasoning.
First neighbour. Cool!
Later that same day . . .
First neighbour. I was talking to that new guy who moved in next door. He has an interesting job.
Third neighbour. What does he do?
First neighbour. He's a professor of deductive reasoning at the university.
Third neighbour. Deductive reasoning. What's that?
First neighbour. Let me give you an example. Do you have a doghouse?
Third neighbour. No.
First neighbour. Fag!

1597 A guy sat down at a bar, ordered a drink, and put his head in his hands.
'What's up?' asked the bartender.
'I'm in deep shit,' said the guy. 'I just got caught screwing my neighbour.'
'Who caught you?' asked the bartender. 'Your wife?'
'No,' replied the guy. '*His* wife.'

NEWFIES

1598 Two old guys were walking along on a glorious, clear Newfoundland
evening. One said to the other: 'What a beautiful night! Look at the moon.'
The other said: 'That's not the moon, it's the sun.'
'No, it's not,' insisted the first, 'it's the moon.'
'I tell you, it's the sun,' said his companion.
The pair argued bitterly until they came across a third man.
'Excuse me, sir,' they said, 'could you please help settle our argument? Tell
us what that thing is that's up in the sky shining. Is it the moon or the sun?'
The third guy looked at the sky and then looked at them and said: 'Sorry, I
don't live around here.'

1599 Did you hear about the Newfie terrorist who tried to blow up a school bus? –
He burnt his lips on the exhaust pipe.

1600 Did you hear about the Newfie Rubik's cube? – It's white on all sides and
takes five minutes to solve.

1601 Did you hear about the Newfie who read that most car accidents happen
within twenty miles of the home, so he moved?

1602 Did you hear about the Newfie who put on a clean pair of socks every day? –
By the end of the week he couldn't get his shoes on.

1603 An Ontarian, a British Columbian and a Newfie were standing at the top of a
cliff when suddenly a genie appeared before them. The genie told them that
if they jumped off the cliff, they would land in whatever they yelled as they
were jumping.
The Ontarian hared towards the edge, jumped yelling 'Money!' and
landed in a mountain of dollar notes.

The British Columbian sprinted to the cliff edge, jumped yelling 'Gold!' and landed in a pile of gold coins.

The Newfie ran as fast as he could, reached the edge of the cliff, tripped over a rock and screamed in pain as he fell downwards, 'Shiiiit!'

1604 A Newfie aunt was knitting her young nephew some socks. But then she got a letter from the boy's mother saying that he had grown another foot since she last saw him. So the aunt started knitting a third sock.

1605 A Newfie named Maurice was appearing on the television quiz show *Who Wants To Be A Millionaire?* Against all the odds, he had reached the $125,000 mark, but he had only one lifeline left, which was to phone a friend.

'You've done really well to get this far, Maurice,' said the quizmaster. 'The next question is for $250,000 if you decide to play. Are you ready?'

'Yes,' nodded Maurice.

'On screen is a photograph of a famous American sportsman as a baby. For $250,000, which sportsman is it?'

Maurice studied the picture on the screen. 'I'm pretty sure it's Jack Nicklaus,' he said. 'Yes, it's Jack Nicklaus, I'm sure it is . . . but I'd like to phone a friend to check.'

'OK,' said the quizmaster. 'Who are you going to phone?'

'My best friend Ed, who, like me, is a native of St John's, Newfoundland.'

The phone rang and Ed picked it up at the other end. The quizmaster explained the situation to Ed, and Maurice told him to look at the TV and tell him which famous American sportsman was being shown as a baby.

Without any hesitation, Ed replied: 'That's Arnold Palmer. Definitely.'

Maurice looked concerned. 'Are you sure, Ed, because I'm convinced it's Jack Nicklaus?'

'No,' said Ed. 'That's Arnold Palmer, without a shadow of a doubt.'

'Well,' said the quizmaster to Maurice. 'You've used your last lifeline, so now I need your answer.'

'OK,' said Maurice nervously. 'Despite what my buddy Ed says, I've got to go with my instincts. From the moment I saw the photo, I was certain it was Jack Nicklaus, so I'm going with Jack Nicklaus.'

'You know you don't have to play, and that if you get it wrong, you lose $93,000?'

'Yeah, I know,' said Maurice. 'But I'm going to play. Jack Nicklaus.'

'Not Arnold Palmer?' queried the quizmaster.

'No, Jack Nicklaus. Final answer.'

The quizmaster took a deep breath. 'I'm so sorry, Maurice, that is the wrong answer. You've just lost $93,000.'

Maurice held his head in his hands. As the quizmaster handed him his cheque for $32,000 and the audience started to applaud sympathetically, Maurice asked: 'So what was the correct answer? It's killing me!'

The quizmaster replied: 'Mike Tyson.'

1606 After applying for a job with a large company, a Newfie was given an intelligence test by the human resources executive.

The executive asked: 'Captain Cook went on three expeditions and died on one of them. Was it the first, the second, or the third?'

'Could I have another question instead?' asked the Newfie. 'I'm hopeless at history.'

1607 How do you know which is the Newfie on an offshore oil rig? – He's the one throwing bread to the helicopters.

1608 A Newfie was talking to his father the day after his wedding.

'So how did it go last night, son?'

'Great, Dad! Hell, the way she was acting, I think I could have fucked her!'

1609 A Newfie bought a smoke alarm for his house. After fixing it to the ceiling, he saw that the instructions said: 'Now test your alarm.' So he set fire to his sofa.

1610 An American, an Englishman and a guy from Newfoundland went on a hunting trip and were staying in a woodland cabin. They decided to go hunting one at a time while the other two stayed behind to guard the cabin.

The American went out first and came back with a fox. He said, very simply: 'I see tracks, I follow tracks, I catch fox.'

Then the Englishman went out and came back with a rabbit. He reported: 'I see tracks, I follow tracks, I catch rabbit.'

Then it was the Newfie's turn. He went out but came back covered in cuts and bruises. He said sorrowfully: 'I see tracks, I follow tracks, I get hit by train.'

1611 Two Newfies decided to go away on a weekend fishing holiday on the Canadian mainland. They spared no expense on hiring the necessary equipment, splashing out a small fortune on rods, wading suits, a rowing boat, a car, and a woodland cabin. But at the end of their three-day break, they had managed to catch just one fish.

As they were driving home, one of the Newfies turned to the other and said: 'Do you realize that this one lousy fish we caught cost us 2,000 bucks?'

'Wow!' said his friend. 'Then it's a good thing we didn't catch any more!'

1612 Talking about his ancestors, a Newfie said to his friend: 'My uncle fell off a scaffolding and was killed.'

'What was he doing up on the scaffolding?'

'Getting hanged.'

1613 A Torontonian, an American and a Newfie were all facing execution. The executioner said that since all three were to be executed that night, each could choose the method by which he would die. The choices were: lethal injection, electric chair, or hanging.

The Torontonian was afraid of needles and didn't want to be hanged, so he chose the electric chair. He sat in the chair, the switch was pulled, but nothing happened. The executioner said that if it happened a second time, the prisoner could go free. They tried a second time and again nothing happened, so they let the Torontonian go.

The American was also afraid of needles and didn't want to be hanged, so he, too, chose the electric chair. Once again the chair didn't work, and the American was set free.

Next it was the Newfie's turn to choose how he was going to be executed. The Newfie said: 'Well, I'm afraid of needles, the electric chair won't work, so you're going to have to hang me.'

1614 A two-seater private plane crashed into a large cemetery near St John's. The Newfoundland Fire Department have recovered 300 bodies and are still digging.

1615 A Newfie got a job as a keeper at the Bronx Zoo, but on his second morning the head keeper summoned him.

'You idiot!' screamed the head keeper. 'You left the door to the lions' cage open all night.'

'What's the problem?' said the Newfie, puzzled. 'Who's going to steal a lion?'

1616 Did you hear about the Newfie who went ice fishing? – He caught sixty pounds of ice, and his wife drowned trying to cook it.

1617 How many Newfies does it take to go ice fishing? – Four. One to cut a hole in the ice and three to push the boat through.

1618 How many Newfies does it take to make a chocolate chip cookie? – Two: one to hold the cookie and one to squeeze the rabbit.

1619 Walking along the harbour wall, two struggling Newfie fishermen – Karl and Henrik – saw another boat loaded with fish. So they asked its captain what his secret was.

The captain confided: 'Go out to sea until the water gets fresh. Then stop there and drop your line.'

So the pair headed out to sea. A mile out, Karl said to Henrik. 'Fill up the bucket and taste the water.'

'It still tastes salty,' said Henrik. So they carried on.

Two miles out to sea, Karl turned to Henrik again and said: 'Taste the water, my friend.'

'It's still salty,' reported Henrik. So they pressed on.

Three miles out to sea, Karl said to Henrik: 'Taste the water, old chum.'

'It's still salty,' said Henrik. So they headed further out to sea.

This continued for the next seven hours. Every mile or so, Karl would ask Henrik to taste the water, and each time Henrik would tell him that it was still salty. By now it was dark and the two Newfies were despairing of ever finding fresh water. Karl was ready to turn back but before doing so, he said to Henrik: 'Taste the water one more time.'

Henrik replied: 'I can't. There's no more water left in the bucket . . .'

1620 Two Newfie farmers were talking. The first said: 'I've got a mule that has the fits. What did you do for your mule when he had the fits?'

The second replied: 'I gave him a mixture of turpentine and kerosene.'

A week later, the two men met again. The first farmer said: 'I gave the mule that mixture and it killed him!'

The second said: 'Yeah, it killed mine, too.'

1621 A Delta Air Lines plane was flying over Arizona on a clear day. The co-pilot was giving the commentary. 'Coming up on the right, you can see the Meteor Crater, which is a major tourist attraction. It was formed thousands of years ago when a lump of nickel and iron struck Earth at about 40,000 mph. The hole measures nearly a mile across and is 570ft deep.'

A Newfie passenger turned to his wife and said: 'Wow! It just missed the highway!'

1622 A Newfie saw a sign that read: 'Press bell for night watchman.' He did so, and thirty seconds later he heard the elderly watchman clomping slowly down the stairs. The watchman took out his set of keys and laboriously opened three locks on the first gate. Next he undid two bolts, a chain and another lock on the second gate. Then he pressed ten numbers to switch off the alarm system. Finally he emerged through a set of revolving doors.

'Well?' he said. 'What do you want?'

The Newfie replied: 'I just wanted to know why you can't ring the bell yourself.'

1623 Three Newfies – Fred, Karl and Jim – were out fishing when Fred lost his balance and fell out of the boat into the sea.

'What should we do?' asked Karl in a panic.

'You'd better jump in after him,' said Jim. 'It looks like he's in trouble. That water's ice cold, and he won't survive in there for long!'

So Karl dived in and, a couple of minutes later, with the help of Jim, managed to drag Fred back into the boat.

'It doesn't look like he's breathing,' said Jim. 'Give him mouth to mouth.'

So Karl positioned his mouth over Fred's and began blowing. 'Yuk!' exclaimed Karl. 'I don't remember Fred having such bad breath!'

'Come to think of it,' added Jim, 'I don't think Fred was wearing a rotting snowmobile suit, either . . .'

1624 Erik and Lena were sitting down to their usual morning cup of coffee, listening to the weather report on the radio. The report warned: 'There will be three to five inches of snow in Newfoundland today, and a snow emergency has been declared. You must park your cars on the odd numbered side of the streets.'

Erik said: 'Jeez, OK,' and got up from his coffee.

The next day they were sitting down with their morning cups of coffee. The local weather forecast was: 'There will be up to four inches of snow today, and a snow emergency has been declared. You must park your cars on the even numbered side of the streets.'

Erik said: 'Jeez, OK,' and got up from his coffee.

Two days later, they were once again sitting down with their morning cups of coffee when the weather forecast said: 'There will be between six and eight inches of snow today, and a snow emergency has been declared. You must park your cars on the . . .' But then there was a power outage and Erik didn't get the rest of the instructions.

He turned to his wife and said: 'Jeez, what am I going to do now, Lena?' Lena replied: 'Oh, Erik, just leave the car in the garage today.'

1625 A gang of Newfie criminals targeted a bank to rob in the dead of night. Once inside the building, they quickly disabled the internal alarm system and got down to work. The robbers were expecting one or two huge safes filled with cash and valuables, but were pleasantly surprised to find instead hundreds of smaller safes scattered around the bank. The first safe's combination was cracked, but inside the robbers found only vanilla pudding. 'Never mind,' they thought, 'at least there's something for us to eat while we open all the other safes.'

The second safe also contained nothing but vanilla pudding, and it was the same with every other safe in the building. There was not a dollar, not a diamond, not an ounce of gold to be found. Every safe contained little pots of vanilla pudding. Disappointed, the gang eventually exited quietly, leaving with nothing more than queasy, full stomachs.

The following morning a St John's newspaper headline read: 'Newfoundland's Largest Sperm Bank Robbed.'

NEW YORK

1626 A high-powered New York salesman was out in the country on business when his car broke down. With darkness closing in, he went to a nearby farm and asked the farmer whether he could stay for the night. The farmer found a room for him, but in the middle of the night the New Yorker became so thirsty that he decided to go to the barn and milk a cow. Soon the farmer heard noises and went to investigate. He saw the New Yorker coming from the barn, soaking wet with white liquid dripping down his face.

'What happened?' asked the farmer.

The New Yorker replied: 'I got thirsty, so I milked your cow. It was so dark in there, I don't know how I did it. But I'm telling you, that cow has great milk! I must have drunk a gallon of it!'

The farmer said: 'But we don't have a cow. We just have a bull.'

1627 A middle-aged Boston woman was looking forward to a business trip to New York, simply so she could pick up young men. So on her first night in the Big Apple, she put on her shortest skirt and highest heels and headed for the action.

She soon spotted a couple of likely lads hanging out on a street corner, and went over and asked them for a cigarette. After flirting openly with them, she said: 'Come on then, show me what New York boys do best.'

So they beat her up and stole her purse.

1628 What's the difference between Batman and a New Yorker? – Batman can go out without Robin.

1629 An English tourist visiting New York City stopped a passer-by and asked: 'Excuse me, can you tell me where the Empire State Building is, or should I go fuck myself again?'

1630 A tourist was visiting New York City when his car broke down. He jumped out and began fiddling under the hood, but two minutes later he heard a noise and looked around to see someone taking stuff out of the car's trunk.

'Hey, buddy,' yelled the tourist. 'This is my car!'

'OK,' said the New Yorker. 'You take the front and I'll take the back.'

1631 What's the basic plot for a romance novel set in Harlem? – In the end the hero gets the heroin.

1632 A guy was tending the bar at a posh New York City party when two snooty women approached.

'So where y'all from?' he asked.

One replied haughtily: 'We are from somewhere where people do not end their sentences with prepositions.'

'Oh,' he said. 'So where y'all from, bitch?'

1633 A New York businessman was walking near a Harlem shopping mall when he spotted a little boy sitting in the gutter, crying. The boy was clutching a $100 bill in his hand. Seeing the child in such obvious distress, the guy bent down and asked him what was upsetting him.

Through the tears, the boy revealed that he came from a large family and that his father had died when he was just five. His mother was poorly educated and had to take two full-time jobs just to feed the family. Although they never got birthday presents, she had managed to skimp and save $200 to buy the kids something for Christmas. The young boy had been dropped off by his mom on the way to her second job. He was to use the money to buy Christmas presents for all his brothers and sisters and save just enough to get the bus home. But he hadn't even entered the mall when an older boy grabbed one of the $100 bills and vanished into the night.

'Why didn't you scream for help?' asked the businessman.

'I did,' replied the boy softly.

'And nobody came to help you?'

'No.'

'How loud did you scream?'

The boy shook his head, looked up and whispered meekly: 'Please help me.'

The New Yorker realised that absolutely nobody could have heard that poor boy cry for help . . . So he grabbed the other $100 and ran to his car.

NUDITY

1634 A young bride's mother had some old-fashioned views on marriage, and passed them on to her daughter.

'Never let your husband see you in the nude,' she urged. 'You should always wear something.'

'Yes, Mother,' replied the girl obediently.

Two weeks after the wedding, the girl and her husband were about to retire to bed when he asked: 'Honey, has there ever been any insanity in your family?'

'Not that I know of,' she said. 'Why do you ask?'

'Well, we've been married for two weeks now, and every night you've worn that silly hat to bed!'

1635 Even though he wasn't on a nudist beach, a man decided to go completely naked. He chose a secluded spot but, just in case anyone happened to pass by, he covered his privates with a newspaper.

After a few minutes, a little girl came along and asked: 'What's under the newspaper?'

The man replied: 'It's a birdy, and you must never ever touch it.'

Soon, lulled by the gentle sea breeze and the warm sun, he fell asleep. He woke up two hours later in hospital with a feeling of intense pain around his genital area. The doctors asked what had happened, and all he could remember was the girl at the beach.

The police duly arrived at the girl's house to ask her what she had done. She said: 'Well, I was playing with the birdy when it spat this white stuff at me. I got really mad. So I broke its neck, trod on its eggs, and burned its nest.'

1636 A male census taker rang the doorbell and was surprised when a naked woman answered the door.

'Don't be alarmed,' she said. 'I'm a nudist.'

Although embarrassed, he proceeded to ask the routine questions.

'How many children do you have?' he asked.

'Nineteen,' she replied.

'Nineteen?' he said. 'Lady, you're not a nudist – you just don't have time to get dressed!'

1637   ## Reasons For Going To Work Naked:

- Your boss is always shouting, 'I wanna see your butt in here by eight o'clock.'
- No one steals your chair.
- It diverts attention from the fact that you also came to work drunk.
- People stop stealing your pens after they've seen where you keep them.
- It gives the term 'bad hair day' a whole new meaning.
- You can say, 'I'd love to chip in, but I've left my wallet in my pants.'
- It stops those creepy guys in Marketing from looking down your blouse.
- You can take advantage of computer monitor radiation to top up your tan.
- You want to see if it's like it is in the dream.

1638 A young married couple were sunning themselves on a nudist beach when a wasp buzzed into the woman's vagina. The husband quickly covered her with his jacket, pulled on his shorts, carried her to the car and headed for the hospital. After examining her, the doctor explained that the wasp was too far in to be reached with forceps. Instead he suggested that the husband try to entice it out by putting honey on his penis, penetrating her and withdrawing as soon as he felt the wasp. The husband agreed, but was so nervous that he was unable to rise to the occasion.

Then the doctor said: 'If neither of you objects, I could give it a try.'

Under the circumstances, both agreed. The doctor quickly undressed, slapped on some honey and mounted the woman. The husband watched with increasing alarm as the doctor began thrusting forcefully and showed no signs of pulling out.

'Hey, what's going on?' demanded the husband eventually.

'Change of plan,' gasped the doctor. 'I'm going to drown the little bastard!'

1639 A man was made police chief in a nudist colony. He liked the job, but putting on the badge was murder!

1640 A New York businessman joined an exclusive nudist colony in the country. As he was exploring the site, he spotted a pretty blonde and immediately got an erection.

The blonde smiled at him: 'Did you call for me?'

'Sorry . . .?' said the man, puzzled.

'It's a rule here,' she explained. 'If you get an erection, it means you've called for me.'

And with that, she led him behind a bush and they had fantastic sex.

An hour or so later, while further investigating the facilities, he wandered into the sauna, sat down and farted. A big hairy guy appeared.

'Did you call for me?' asked the big guy.

'No,' said the businessman.

'Well, it's a rule here. If you fart, it means you've called for me.'

And before the businessman could say anything, the big guy had bent him over the sauna table and fucked the ass off him.

The businessman headed straight for reception, saying that he no longer wished to join the club and wanted his money back.

'What's the problem?' asked the receptionist. 'Aren't you impressed with our facilities?'

'Yes, they're wonderful,' he said. 'But I'm sixty-one. I only get an erection twice a month, but I fart fifteen times a day! So no, thanks.'

1641 Sign at a nudist camp: Sorry – Clothed for Winter.

1642 A man joined a nudist colony. After a few weeks, he received a letter from his mother asking him to send her a current photograph. Too embarrassed to let her know that he lived in a nudist colony, he cut a picture in half and sent her the top half.

Later he received another letter asking him to send a picture to his grandmother. The man cut another photo in half, but accidentally sent the bottom half. He was horrified when he realized he had sent the wrong part, but then remembered that his grandmother's eyesight was so bad she probably wouldn't notice.

A few weeks later he received a letter back from his grandmother. It said: 'Thank you for the picture. Change your hairstyle – it makes your nose look long.'

Cruel Things To Say To a Naked Man:

1643 • I've smoked fatter joints than that.

1644 • Aaahh, it's cute.

1645 • But it still works, right?

1646 • Does it come with an air pump?

1647 • Maybe it looks better in natural light.

1648 • Why don't we just cuddle?

1649 • You know they have surgery to fix that?

1650 • And yet your feet are so big!

1651 • I guess this makes me the early bird.

1652 • It's OK, we'll work around it.

1653 • It's a good thing you have so many other talents.

1654 • Why is God punishing me?

1655 • Can I be honest with you?

NUNS

1656 A nun was walking down a city street when a mugger dragged her into bushes and raped her. Afterwards, the attacker sneered: 'Now what are you going to tell your Mother Superior?'

The nun replied: 'I will tell her that I was walking down the street when this man dragged me into the bushes and raped me twice.'

'But I only raped you once,' protested the mugger.

The nun said: 'Surely you're not tired already?'

1657 Two nuns went on a shopping trip to France to load up with duty free. On the way back they were just about to drive through 'Nothing to declare' when a customs officer waved them to the side.

The first nun said to the Mother Superior, who was driving, 'Don't worry, just show him your cross.'

So the Mother Superior wound the window down, leaned out and shouted: 'Piss off, you bastard!'

1658 How do you get a nun pregnant? – Dress her up as an altar boy.

1659 A nun was walking through the convent grounds when one of the priests noticed that she was putting on weight. 'Gaining a little weight, are we, Sister Assumpta?' he inquired

'No, Father, just a little gas.'

A month later the same priest noticed she'd put on even more weight. 'Gaining some weight, are we, Sister Assumpta?'

'No, Father, just a little gas.'

Three months later the priest saw Sister Assumpta pushing a baby carriage around the convent. He leaned over, looked in the carriage and said: 'Cute little fart.'

1660 It was time for Father John's Saturday night bath and young Sister Mary had prepared bath towels exactly how the old nun had told her. Sister Mary was also told not to look at Father John's naked body if she could help it, to do whatever he told her, and to pray.

The next morning the old nun asked Sister Mary how the Saturday night bath had gone.

'Oh, Sister,' she said dreamily, 'I've been saved.'

'Saved?' queried the old nun. 'And how did that fine thing come about?'

'Well,' said Sister Mary, 'when Father John was soaking in the tub he asked me to wash him, and while I was washing him he guided my hand down between his legs where he said the Lord keeps the Key to Heaven.'

'Did he now?' said the old nun sharply.

Sister Mary continued: 'And Father John said that if the Key to Heaven fitted my lock, the portals of Heaven would be opened to me and I would be assured of salvation and eternal peace. Then Father John guided his Key to Heaven into my lock.'

'Is that a fact?' snapped the old nun.

'At first it hurt terribly,' added Sister Mary, 'but Father John said the pathway to salvation was often painful.'

'That wicked devil,' said the old nun. 'He told me it was Gabriel's Horn, and I've been blowing it for forty years!'

1661 Why don't gang members ever become nuns? – Because they find it difficult to say Superior after the word Mother.

1662 The girls at a convent had just come back from work experience. The Mother Superior asked the girls what they had done for the past week.

One of the girls, Mary, answered: 'I was a prostitute.'

'What?' said the Mother Superior.

'I was a prostitute,' repeated Mary.

'What?' screamed the Mother Superior.

'I was a prostitute!' yelled Mary at the top of her voice.

'Thank God for that,' said the Mother Superior. 'I thought you said you were a Protestant.'

1663 Two nuns decided they would sneak out of the convent for a night on the town. They hit all the bars and dance clubs until at about two o'clock in the morning, they decided it was time to head back to the convent.

To enter the convent grounds undetected, they had to crawl under some barbed wire. As they started crawling on their bellies beneath the barbed wire, the first nun turned to the second and said: 'I feel like a Marine.'

'Me, too,' replied the second nun. 'But where are we going to find one at this time of night?'

1664 Two old nuns were discussing their holidays. As Sister Catherine was a bit deaf, Sister Mary was communicating by means of hand gestures. 'I think I'll go to Florida this year,' said Sister Mary, 'where the oranges are that big and the bananas are that long.'

'What?' said Sister Catherine.

Sister Mary repeated loudly: 'I think I'll go to Florida where the oranges are that big and the bananas are that long.'

'What?' said Sister Catherine.

Shouting at the top of her voice and gesturing frantically, Sister Mary tried again. 'I think I'll go to Florida where the oranges are that big and the bananas are that long!'

Sister Catherine said: 'Father who?'

1665 The quiet, contemplative routine of a convent was being disrupted by a gang of workmen installing underground cables. Eventually the Mother Superior felt the need to complain to the men's supervisor. She said: 'There is too much bad language and profanity. It is inappropriate for our community. Can you please stop them?'

'I'll do my best, Sister,' promised the supervisor, 'but you have to remember that it is in their nature to call a spade a spade.'

The Mother Superior said: 'I think the term they actually use is "fucking shovel".'

1666 A preacher wanted to raise money for his church and, on being told that there was a fortune to be made in horse racing, he decided to purchase a horse and enter it in the races. However at the auction, the going price for horses was so high that he ended up buying a donkey instead. But he figured that, having bought the donkey, he might as well go ahead and enter it in the races. To his surprise, the donkey came in third. The next day the local paper carried the headline: PREACHER'S ASS SHOWS.

The preacher was so pleased with the donkey that he entered it at the next race meeting, and this time it won. The headline in the paper read: PREACHER'S ASS OUT IN FRONT. But the bishop was so upset by this publicity that he ordered the preacher not to enter the donkey in any more races. The newspaper headline read: BISHOP SCRATCHES PREACHER'S ASS.

This was too much for the bishop, so he told the preacher to get rid of the donkey. The preacher decided to give it to a nun in a nearby convent. The paper headline the next day read: NUN HAS BEST ASS IN TOWN. Reading this, the bishop fainted. When he came round, he informed the nun that she would have to get rid of the donkey, so she sold it to a farmer for $10. Next day the headline read: NUN SELLS ASS FOR $10.

In despair, the bishop instructed the nun to buy back the donkey and lead it to the plains where it could run wild and free. The headline in the paper read: NUN ANNOUNCES HER ASS IS WILD AND FREE. The bishop was buried the following day.

1667 Two nuns on a remote beach decided to go sunbathing in the nude behind a sand dune. They had been lying there for a while, soaking up the sun, when a photographer came by and immediately pointed his camera at them.

The first nun, who knew a little about photography, said: 'Aren't you going to focus?'

'Quiet, Sister,' said the second nun. 'Let him take his picture first.'

1668 Stranded for the night, a man sought refuge in a convent. Reluctantly the Mother Superior allowed him to stay over. 'But,' she pointed out, 'we have ten new nuns who may not yet be strong enough to resist temptation, so you must stay in your room and refrain from any contact whatsoever with the sisters.'

The man agreed.

The next morning, after the man had gone, the Mother Superior called all the nuns together for a meeting. 'Sisters,' she said, 'we had a man stay here last night . . .'

Nine nuns gasped, one giggled.

'. . . In his room,' added the Mother Superior, 'we found a used condom . . .'

Nine nuns gasped, one giggled.

'. . . And in this condom, we found a hole.'

Nine nuns giggled, one gasped.

1669 Recovering in hospital from an operation, a man received a visit from a nun who was there to cheer up the sick and the lame. They started talking, and she asked about his life. He told her about his wife and their fourteen children.

'My, my,' said the nun, 'fourteen children. A good and proper Catholic family. God is very proud of you.'

'I'm sorry, Sister,' he said, 'I'm not Catholic, I'm Baptist.'

'Baptist?' she replied. 'You sex maniac!'

1670 Three nuns were killed in a car crash. They went to heaven, only to find a sign at the gates, which said: 'Closed for Rebuilding.'

Uncertain as to what to do next, they knocked on the gates and St Peter emerged. 'What are you doing here?' he asked. 'There are no admissions this weekend. You'll have to come back Monday.'

'But what are we supposed to do in the meantime?' chorused the nuns. 'We're dead, so we can't go back to Earth.'

'All right, I take your point,' said St Peter. 'What I'm going to do is send you back to Earth for the weekend as whoever you want to be, and then we'll accept you into Heaven in a few days' time. How's that for a deal?'

The nuns nodded in agreement.

'OK, who do you want to be?' St Peter asked the first nun.

'Tonight, Peter, I'm going to be Mother Theresa, because she led such a selfless, devoted life.'

The second nun said: 'I'd like to go back as Joan of Arc because she was a martyr and an inspiration to so many.'

The third nun said: 'I want to be Alice Kapipelean.'

St Peter looked bewildered. 'Who?'

'Alice Kapipelean,' repeated the nun.

'I'm sorry, Sister,' said St Peter, 'but there is no record of any Alice Kapipelean having lived on Earth.'

'That's where you're wrong,' said the nun, producing a newspaper cutting. 'Here, read this. There's your proof!'

St Peter glanced at the article and said: 'No, no, Sister. You've misread it. The article says the Alaska Pipeline was laid by 500 men in six months.'

1671 Sister Mary Catherine and Sister Mary Elizabeth were walking through the park when they were jumped by two thugs. Their habits were ripped from them, and the men sexually assaulted them.

Sister Mary Catherine cast her eyes heavenward and cried: 'Forgive him, Lord, for he knows not what he is doing!'

Sister Mary Elizabeth turned and said: 'Mine does . . .'

1672 A nun was going to Chicago. While waiting in the airport for her flight, she spotted one of those weight machines that promises to tell your fortune. So, thinking that it was a good idea to know what fate had in store for her before taking to the skies, she went over to the machine and inserted a nickel. A few seconds later, a card came out that said: 'You're a nun, you weigh 128lb, and you are going to Chicago, Illinois.'

Initially impressed by its accuracy, she then started thinking that it was probably a fluke, and that all the cards were the same, but they just happened to fit her circumstances. So she decided to give the machine another go. She inserted her nickel and out came a card that read: 'You're a nun, you weigh 128lb, you're going to Chicago, Illinois, and you are going to play a fiddle.'

The nun said to herself: 'I know that's wrong, because I have never played a musical instrument in my life.' And she sat back down, convinced that the machine was a fraud.

But just then a cowboy came over and put his fiddle case on the seat next to her. After a couple of minutes, he turned to her and said: 'My fiddle needs tuning, but I've sprained my wrist. Please, Sister, could you play a few notes for me?' So the nun picked up the fiddle and instinctively began playing beautiful music.

Startled, she realised that the machine had been right. 'This is incredible,' she thought. 'I must try it again.'

So she put in another nickel, and a card came out. It said: 'You're a nun, you weigh 128lb, you're going to Chicago, Illinois, and you're going to break wind.'

'This is nonsense,' thought the nun. 'I've never, ever broken wind in public. The machine is definitely wrong this time.'

But as she stepped off the scales, she tripped and broke wind.

In stunned disbelief, she sat back down and looked at the machine. She said to herself: 'This is truly unbelievable. I've got to try it again.'

She went back to the machine, put her nickel in and collected the card. It read: 'You're a nun, you weigh 128lb, you have fiddled and farted around and missed your flight to Chicago!'

NURSERY RHYMES

1673　Jack and Jill went up the hill
And planned to do some kissing.
Jack made a pass
And grabbed Jill's ass,
Now his two front teeth are missing.

1674　Old Mother Hubbard
Went to the cupboard
To get her poor dog a bone.
But when old mother bent over,
Rover drove her
Because Rover had a bone of his own.

1675　Mary had a little lamb,
She tied it to a pylon.
10,000 volts went up its ass
And turned its wool to nylon.

1676　Georgie Porgie Pudding and Pie
Kissed the girls and made them cry.
When the boys came out to play,
He kissed them too – he's funny that way!

1677 Jack and Jill went up the hill
For just an itty bitty.
But Jill's now two months overdue
And Jack has left the city.

1678 Hey Diddle Diddle
The cat did a piddle
All over the bedside clock.
The little dog laughed to see such fun
Then died of an electric shock.

1679 Little Muss Muffet sat on a tuffet,
Her clothes all tattered and torn.
It wasn't the spider that crept up beside her
'Twas Little Boy Blue with his horn.

1680 Mary had a little lamb,
Her father shot it dead.
Now it goes to school with her
Between two chunks of bread.

1681 Jack and Jill went up the hill
So Jack could lick Jill's fanny.
Jack got a shock
And a mouthful of cock
Cos Jill's a bloody tranny!

NYMPHOMANIA

1682 A mother and daughter were raving nymphomaniacs. They screwed around with so many men that before long their holes were really loose. But then the daughter met the man of her dreams and decided to get married. Her future husband had no idea about her wild past and thought she was still a virgin. So he chose to postpone having sex with her until their wedding night. However the daughter was worried about the state of her hole and consulted her mother.

'Mom, what will Todd do if he finds about my hole?'

'Don't worry, darling,' said the mother. 'I'll show how you to keep him in the dark. All you have to do is place an apple in your hole and it will be so tight he won't even notice it.'

The daughter heeded the advice and everything went smoothly for a few months. Whenever she wanted to bathe, she would remove the apple and place it on the washbasin, reinserting it in her hole when she had finished. But one day after bathing, she forgot to put it back and left it on the washbasin. The husband came into the washroom, saw the apple and, thinking it was a treat from his wife, ate it.

'Honey, thanks for the apple,' he said later. 'It tasted great!'

The daughter was mortified and dashed to report the sorry episode to her mother. 'Todd found the apple and ate it!' she shrieked. 'What should I do? Do you think I've poisoned him?'

'Don't worry, darling,' said the mother. 'A few years ago your father ate the watermelon I left in the washroom and he lived!'

1683 Maxine was telling her friend Kay what had happened on her date the previous night when she had brought a guy home.

'The bastard called me a slut!' said Maxine.

'What did you do?' asked Kay.

'I told him to get the hell out of my bedroom and take his eight mates with him!'

1684 Two golfers were waiting on the tee when a naked woman ran across the fairway and into the woods. She was being chased by two men in white coats, another guy carrying two buckets of sand, and a little old man bringing up the rear.

One of the golfers said to the old man: 'What's going on?'

'She's a nymphomaniac from the asylum,' replied the old man. 'She keeps trying to escape, and us attendants are trying to catch her.'

'So what about the guy with the buckets of sand?'

'Oh, that's his handicap. He caught her last time.'

1685 A woman went to the doctor and said: 'Doctor, I think I'm becoming a nymphomaniac.'

The doctor said: 'Why don't you lie down and tell me about it?'

1686 A guy picked up a girl and took her back to his hotel room. She turned out to be a raving nymphomaniac and, after six times, she was still screaming for more. Eventually, after the eighth time, he said he needed to go out and buy some cigarettes.

On his way he stopped at the men's room. Standing in front of the urinal, he unzipped, but couldn't find his dick. After fishing around for it for a minute, he said: 'Look, it's OK. She's not here!'

1687 Sam was extolling the virtues of his glamorous fiancée.

One of his friends said: 'You can't be serious about marrying her. She's been with every guy in Phoenix!'

Sam thought for a second before replying: 'Phoenix isn't *such* a big town . . .'

OLD AGE

1688 One day, a farmer was in town picking up supplies for his farm. He stopped at the hardware store and picked up a bucket and an anvil, then he stopped by the livestock dealer to buy a couple of chickens and a goose. However, he now had a problem – how to carry all his purchases home.

The livestock dealer said: 'Why don't you put the anvil in the bucket, carry the bucket in one hand, put a chicken under each arm and carry the goose in your other hand?'

'Gee, thanks,' said the farmer, and off he went. While walking he met a little old lady who told him she was lost.

'Can you tell me how to get to 412 Canyon Avenue?' she asked.

The farmer replied: 'Well, as a matter of fact, I live at 401 Canyon Avenue. Let's take my shortcut and go down this alley. We'll be there in no time.'

The little old lady said: 'How do I know that when we get in the alley, you won't hold me up against the wall, pull up my skirt, and ravish me?'

The farmer said: 'Holy smokes, lady, I am carrying a bucket, an anvil, two chickens, and a goose. How in the world could I possibly hold you up against the wall and ravish you?'

The old lady answered: 'Set the goose down, cover him with the bucket, put the anvil on top of the bucket, and I'll hold the chickens . . .'

1689 A family had booked into a motel for the night but a mix-up over the rooms meant that the grandpa had to sleep in the same bed as his fifteen-year-old grandson. In the middle of the night, grandpa woke up and shouted: 'Quick! Get me a woman! Now!'

'Please, grandpa,' said the boy. 'Calm down. First, it's three o'clock in the morning, and you'll never find a woman at this hour. Second, you're eighty-three years old. And third, that's *my* dick you're holding, not yours!'

1690 What goes in and out and stinks of piss? – Your granny doing the hokey cokey.

1691 Two old ladies – Ethel and Mabel – were walking through a museum when they became separated. When they met up again, Ethel said: 'Did you see that statue of the naked man back there?'

'Yes, I did!' said Mabel. 'And frankly I was shocked. How can they display such a thing! The penis on it was so large!'

Ethel added: '. . . And cold, too!'

1692 A group of pensioners were sitting around in the nursing home comparing notes regarding their various ailments.

One said: 'My hands are so shaky I can hardly lift this cup.'

Another said: 'My cataracts are so bad I can't see to pour my coffee.'

Another said: 'I can't turn my head because of the arthritis in my neck.'

Another said: 'My blood pressure pills make me dizzy.'

Another said: 'I guess that's the price we pay for getting old.'

Another said: 'Yes, but it's not all bad. We should be thankful that we can all still drive.'

1693 An eighty-year-old rancher was about to marry a young girl of twenty-one. His trusted friend and adviser, the local banker, had serious doubts as to how long an old man would be able to satisfy such a young bride and feared for his friend's happiness. So, for the sake of matrimonial harmony, he advised the old man to bring in a hired hand to help around the ranch, knowing full well that the hired hand would probably help out in the bedroom, too, behind the old man's back. The rancher thought it was a great idea.

Four months later, the banker called on his friend. 'How's your new wife?' he asked.

'She's pregnant,' replied the old man.

The banker smiled knowingly. 'And how's the hired hand?'

'Oh, she's pregnant, too!'

1694 A boy was walking down the street when he noticed his grandfather sitting on the porch, in a rocking chair, with nothing on from the waist down.

'Grandpa, what are you doing sitting out here with nothing on below the waist?'

The old man looked at him and said: 'Well, last week I sat out here with no shirt on, and I got a stiff neck . . . This is your grandma's idea.'

1695 Two old men were talking. One said: 'I'm eighty-three and full of aches and pains. How about you?'

The other said: 'I feel like a newborn baby.'

'Really?'

'Yeah. No hair, no teeth, and I think I just wet my pants.'

1696 Three old men were discussing their lives. One said: 'I'm still a once-a-night man.' The next said: 'I'm a two-times-a-night man.' The third said: 'My wife will tell you that I'm a five-times-a-night man. You know, I really shouldn't drink so much tea before I go to bed.'

1697 An elderly couple were sitting quietly on the porch in their rocking chairs when, without warning, the old man reached over and slapped his wife.

'What was that for?' she demanded.

'That's for forty years of rotten sex!'

She said nothing, but a few minutes later she slapped him back.

'What was that for?' he asked, shocked.

'That's for knowing the difference!'

1698 How do you know when you're getting old? – When you start having dry dreams and wet farts.

1699 A general store owner hired a young female clerk who used to wear short skirts and skimpy thongs to work. One day a young man came in to the store and asked for some raisin bread. As the raisin bread was located on the top shelf, she had to climb a stepladder to reach it, affording him a great view up her skirt. He was so impressed by what he saw that when she came down, he suddenly remembered he needed more raisin bread – just so that she would have to climb back up.

By now the other male customers in the shop had cottoned on to what was happening and they, too, asked in turn for raisin bread. Each time the girl dutifully climbed the ladder for the raisin bread and each time they got an eyeful. After half a dozen climbs in quick succession, she began to get tired. From the top step, she looked down at the group of men and spotted an old man, who was yet to be served, staring up at her. Trying to save herself another trip, she asked him: 'Is yours raisin, too?'

'No,' he said, 'but it's startin' to twitch!'

1700 A young man was studying an elderly couple in McDonald's. He saw that they had ordered one meal and an extra drinks cup. Then he watched the old man carefully cut the hamburger in half before dividing the fries into two equal portions. Then the old man poured half of the soft drink into the extra cup and began to eat.

Feeling sorry for them, the young man decided to ask if he could buy them another meal so they didn't have to split everything in two.

'Oh, no,' said the old man, 'this is the way we do things. We've been married for nearly sixty years, and we always share everything.'

The young man asked the woman if she was going to eat.

'Not yet,' she answered. 'It's his turn with the teeth.'

1701 Two old men stumbled into a bar. 'Shall we have a Guinness?' suggested one. 'They say it puts lead in your pencil.'

'I suppose we could try,' said the other, 'although, to be honest, I've got nobody to write to.'

1702 An old man went into a car showroom with his young wife. When the owner of the showroom began eyeing her up, the old man proposed a wager. 'If you can do everything to my wife that I can do, I will pay you double for the car. If you can't, you will give it to me for free!'

Being something of a ladies' man, the owner readily agreed to the wager.

The old man began by giving his wife a passionate kiss, and the owner did the same. Next the old man unbuttoned her blouse and kissed her breasts, whereupon the owner did the same. Then the old man opened his fly, pulled out his pecker, and bent it in half.

'What colour car do you want?' asked the owner.

1703 An old man was proudly displaying his physique to his wife. 'What do you think of my balls?' he asked. 'Still pretty big, huh? I think of them as my Crown Jewels.'

'Yes,' said the wife. 'They're for display purposes only.'

1704 A reporter was interviewing a woman who was celebrating her 100th birthday. 'And why do you think it is that you have reached such a wonderful old age?' he asked.

'It is because I believe in moderation in all things,' she replied. 'I have always practised moderation in drink, diet and exercise, and that is why I have remained so healthy.'

'But I understand you have often been bedridden?' said the reporter.

'Of course I have,' said the old lady. 'But don't you dare put that in your newspaper!'

1705 A theatre usher saw an old man crawling on his hands and knees. He went over to him and said: 'Sir, you're disturbing several people around you. What's the problem?'

'I've lost my gum,' said the old man, continuing to rummage beneath the seats.

'Sir,' continued the usher, 'if that's your only problem, let me offer you another stick of gum so you can sit down and watch the show. A stick of gum is not worth all this commotion.'

'But you don't understand,' said the old man. 'My false teeth are in that gum!'

1706 An old man walked into an exclusive New York jeweller's with a young woman on his arm. 'I'd like the 24-carat gold necklace in the window,' he announced, 'the one priced at $20,000. Will a cheque be all right?'

'Certainly, sir,' said the sales clerk. 'But we'll have to wait a few days for it to clear. Can you come back on Monday to collect the necklace?'

'Sure,' said the old man, and he and the girl walked out arm-in-arm.

On the Monday the old man returned, to be greeted by an irate clerk. 'You've got a damn nerve coming back,' raged the clerk. 'That cheque of yours bounced all the way to Washington!'

'Yes, I'm sorry about that,' said the old man. 'I just came in to apologize – and to thank you for the best weekend of my life.'

1707 An elderly couple went for their annual medical examination. After giving the husband a thorough checkover, the doctor said: 'You appear to be in good health. Do you have any concerns at all?'

'There is one thing,' said the old man. 'After I have sex with my wife for the first time, I'm usually hot and sweaty. But after I have sex with her for the second time, I'm usually cold and shivery.'

'Hmm, that's interesting,' said the doctor. 'Let me look into it. I'll do some research and get back to you.'

Then the doctor examined the wife. After giving her the usual tests, he said: 'You seem to be in good health. Any concerns at all?'

'No, doctor,' she said.

'Oh, only your husband mentioned that after he has sex with you for the first time, he feels hot and sweaty, but after he has sex with you for the second time, he feels cold and shivery. Have you any idea why this should be?'

'The silly old fool!' said the wife. 'That's because the first time we have sex is usually in July and the second time is usually in December!'

1708   Two old men were sitting down to breakfast. One said: 'Did you know you've got a suppository in your left ear?'

'Really?' said the other. 'I'm glad you told me. Now I think I know where my hearing aid is.'

1709   What happened when the old woman streaked through the flower show? – She won the prize for Best Dried Arrangement.

1710   An old couple were watching a healing service on TV. The evangelist called for all who wanted to be healed to go to their television set, place one hand on the TV and the other on the body part they wanted to be healed. The old lady shuffled over to the TV, put her right hand on the set and her left hand on her arthritic shoulder. Then the old man got up, shuffled across to the TV, put his right hand on the set and his left hand on his crotch. The old lady scowled: 'You don't get it, do you? The purpose of doing this is to heal the sick, not raise the dead!'

1711   An old lady wanted a pet for companionship, but all the shop had left was an ugly frog. Nevertheless she decided to take it, and on the drive home the frog suddenly said: 'Kiss me.' She did, and the frog turned into a handsome prince. The prince then kissed her back, and do you know what the old lady turned into? The first motel she could find.

1712   Two old men – Sid and Bert – were sitting in the park watching a pretty girl walk by. Sid turned to Bert and said: 'You remember those bromide pills they gave us in the war to stop us chasing after women?'

'Yes,' said Bert. 'What about them?'

Sid said: 'I think mine are beginning to work.'

1713 When a sixty-eight-year-old millionaire married a twenty-year-old model, his friend was understandably envious. 'You lucky devil,' he said. 'How did you manage to get such a beautiful young wife?'

'Easy,' replied the millionaire. 'I simply told her I was ninety-six.'

1714 Two old women were out driving in a big car. Both could barely see over the dashboard. When they came to a junction, they went straight through even though the light was red. The woman in the passenger seat thought to herself: 'I must be losing it, I could have sworn we just went through a red light.'

A few hundred yards down the road, they came to another junction, and once again they sailed through on a red light. The woman in the passenger seat looked uneasily at her friend but said nothing.

Shortly afterwards they went straight through another red light. This time the woman in the passenger seat could hold back no longer. 'Ethel!' she said.

'Don't you realize we just went through three red lights? You could have killed us!'

Ethel said: 'Oh. Am I driving?'

1715 How do you get a sweet little eighty-year-old lady to say 'fuck'? – Get another sweet little eighty-year-old lady to yell 'Bingo'.

1716 An old man in a nursing home had lost the power of speech. One morning while he was sitting in his chair, a nurse walked by and noticed that he was leaning to the right. So she sat him upright and told him to sit still.

That afternoon the nurse was on her rounds when she noticed that he was leaning to the left in his chair. So she sat him upright and told him to sit still.

A couple of hours later, she saw that he was now leaning forward. Worried that he might fall out, she tied him to the chair.

When the old man's daughter came to visit that evening, she was horrified to see him strapped to the chair.

'What's the matter?' she asked.

The old man handed her a note: 'They won't let me fart.'

1717 Three old guys were sitting around complaining about their declining health.

The first guy said: 'My hands shake so bad that when I shaved this morning, I almost cut my ear off.'

The second guy said: 'My hands shake so bad that when I ate breakfast today, I spilled half my coffee on my toast.'

The third guy said: 'My hands shake so bad that the last time I went to pee, I came taking my cock out.'

1718   An old woman was feeling suicidal following the death of her beloved husband. So she decided to use his old gun to shoot herself through the heart. Not wanting to miss the vital organ and become a vegetable and a burden, she asked her doctor precisely where the heart was located on a woman.

'Just below your left breast,' he answered.

Later that night she was admitted to hospital with a gunshot wound to the knee.

1719   An old couple were banging away and he couldn't help noticing that her toes curled up as he was thrusting in and out. Afterwards he said: 'I must have been pretty good tonight. I noticed your toes curling up when I was going in and out.'

'Yes,' she said. 'That usually happens when I forget to remove my pantyhose.'

1720   An old man went to the doctor. 'Doctor, you must help me. Every time I make love to my wife, my eyes get all bleary, my legs go weak, and I can hardly catch my breath. Doctor, I'm scared.'

'Well,' said the doctor, 'I'm afraid these symptoms tend to happen during sex as you get older. Remind me, how old are you?'

'Eighty-eight.'

'And when did you first notice these symptoms?'

'Three times last night and twice again this morning.'

1721   An elderly couple went to the clinic and asked to be tested for HIV. When the counsellor asked why they felt that they should be tested at their age, the old man said: 'Well, we heard on TV that people should be tested after annual sex.'

1722   An old man went to apply for social security. The woman behind the counter asked him for his drivers' licence to prove his age, but he realized he'd left it at home.

'Never mind,' said the clerk, 'unbutton your shirt.'

So he opened his shirt to reveal tufts of silver hair.

'That silver hair on your chest is proof enough for me,' said the clerk.

Later at home the old man told the story to his wife. The wife listened patiently before replying: 'You should have dropped your pants, you might have qualified for disability too!'

Signs Your Grandparents are Still Sexually Active:

1723 • At night, they put their teeth in the same glass.

1724 • You find granny cuffed to her walker.

1725 • Not only do you hear the bed squeaking, but also joints.

1726 • Grandpa grabs his crotch and complains about 'denture-burn'.

1727 • Grandma starts baking Viagra-chip cookies.

1728 • Grandma looks at grandpa's crotch and claps twice.

1729 • Their adjustable bed is set for 'doggy-style'.

1730 An eighty-two-year-old man went to the doctor for a check-up. After examining him thoroughly, the doctor said: 'You're in great shape. You might live for ever! Tell me, how old was your father when he died?'

'Did I say he was dead?' said the old man.

The doctor was amazed. 'Well, how old was your grandfather when he died?'

'Did I say he was dead?'

The doctor was almost speechless. 'You mean to say, you're eighty-two years old, and both your father and grandfather are still alive?'

'Not only that,' said the old man, 'but my grandfather is 126 and last week he got married for the first time.'

The doctor found this unbelievable. 'After 126 years of being a bachelor, why on earth did your grandfather want to get married?'

'Did I say he wanted to?'

ORGASM

1731 A guy went into a bar and met a really nice girl. They got on so well that after a few drinks they ended up in bed back at his place. Everything was great until, still on top of him, she suddenly had an epileptic seizure and began shaking and foaming at the mouth. The ignorant guy thought this was incredible – the best sex he'd ever had. He finished but she was still thrashing about. He wasn't sure what was wrong but began to get a little nervous and decided to take her to the Emergency Room. When they arrived, she was still frothing and shaking. The nurse asked him what the problem was. He replied: 'I think her orgasm's stuck!'

1732 Unable to bring his wife to orgasm, a little Jewish man turned to his rabbi for advice. The rabbi said: 'Hire a strapping young man. While the two of you are making love, have the young man wave a towel over you. That will help your wife fantasize and should bring about an orgasm.'

So the husband agreed to try it. He hired a handsome young man to wave a towel over them while they made love, but still the wife did not reach orgasm. When the husband reported the latest failure, the rabbi suggested reversing the roles. 'Have the young man make love to your wife, and you wave the towel over them.'

So the husband stood waving the towel while his wife and the young man made love. The young man soon got into his stride and began screwing the wife with a vengeance. She responded with forceful thrusts of her own and after a few minutes let out a prolonged cry of ecstasy that travelled halfway down the street. Exhausted but grinning from ear to ear, she slumped on the bed, totally satisfied.

The husband looked at the young man and declared triumphantly: 'You see, *that's* the way to wave a towel!'

1733 Why do women have orgasms? – It gives them another reason to moan.

1734 Why do women fake orgasms? – Because they think men care.

1735 A farmer and his wife were lying in bed one evening. He was reading the latest issue of *Animal Husbandry*. Suddenly he turned to her and said: 'Did you know that humans are the only species in which the female achieves orgasm?'

'Is that right?' she said, smiling. 'Prove it!'

'OK,' he said, and to his wife's bemusement, he got out of bed and went downstairs. He returned half an hour later, sweating profusely.

'What happened to you?' she asked.

'Well,' he said, 'I'm sure the cow and the sheep didn't, but the way that pig's always squealing, how can I tell?'

1736 Norm and Kirk were drinking at a bar. As the conversation turned to women, Norm said: 'Did you know that there are four different types of female orgasm?'

'Really?' said Kirk. 'What are they?'

'There's the Positive, the Negative, the Religious, and the Fake.'

'What's the difference?'

'The Positive goes, "Oh yes! Ooh yes!" The Negative goes, "Oh no! Oh no!" The Religious goes, "Oh God! Oh God!" And the Fake goes, "Oh Kirk! Oh Kirk!"'

1737 A man and his wife were having sex. Fifteen minutes passed, then thirty, then forty-five. The sweat was pouring off them and it was becoming increasingly apparent that neither was going to reach orgasm.

Finally the wife said: 'What's the matter, darling, can't you think of anyone else either?'

PARROTS

1738 A farmer and his wife were given a male parrot by an elderly aunt. The parrot had a high sex drive and at the first opportunity flew out of the farmhouse to screw the next-door neighbour's turkey. When the neighbour complained, the farmer warned the parrot that if it happened again he would shave the parrot's head.

But the parrot couldn't help himself. Overcome with desire, he sneaked out that night and screwed the turkey again. When the farmer found out, he carried out his threat and shaved the parrot's head.

The farmer's daughter was getting married the following afternoon and, in order to please his aged aunt, the farmer sat the parrot on a piano in the church and told the bird that, as a punishment, he had to greet all the wedding guests and tell them where to sit.

The parrot proved extremely efficient, telling everyone: 'Groom's side to the left, bride's side to the right.' In fact everything was running smoothly until two bald men walked in. The parrot took one look at them and said: 'Right, you two turkey fuckers, up here on the piano with me.'

1739 A guy owned a parrot that never talked, so he went to the pet shop for advice. The pet shop proprietor said: 'Your parrot has too much hook in its beak — you have to file its beak and then it will be able to talk just fine. But you've got to be careful not to file it too far because if you take too much off, the bird will drown the first time it has a drink.'

'How much will this cost?' asked the bird's owner.

'About $100.'

'I can't afford that sort of money. Filing down a parrot's beak can't be that difficult – I'll do it myself.'

A week later the two men met in the street. 'Is your parrot talking yet?' asked the shopkeeper.

'No, he's dead,' replied the owner.

'I told you not to file the beak back too far. Did he drown when he had a drink?'

'No, he was dead before I got him out of the vice.'

1740 His marriage becoming increasingly strained, a man decided that he wanted a pet as a companion he could relate to. So he went along to the pet shop in search of a new friend and there spotted a parrot with no legs or feet sitting on a perch.

'Goodness me!' said the man to the shop owner. 'What on earth happened to that parrot?'

'I was born this way,' squawked the parrot.

The man laughed to the owner. 'It was almost if the parrot understood me!'

'I did,' said the parrot. 'I understood every word. I'll have you know I'm a highly intelligent bird. I can speak three languages and can conduct a stimulating conversation on a whole range of subjects from nuclear physics to football. I would make a great companion.'

The man was impressed by the parrot's skills but one thing puzzled him. 'How do you hang on to your perch without any feet?'

'What I do,' replied the parrot quietly, 'is wrap my little parrot penis around the perch, rather like a hook. Nobody can see it because of my feathers.'

'How ingenious!' said the man. 'You're definitely the pet for me. How much are you?'

'The price tag says $200,' replied the parrot.

'$200! I can't afford that!'

'Pssst,' hissed the parrot, beckoning the guy closer with one wing. 'Because I haven't got any feet nobody wants to buy me, so you can get me for much less. I bet the shop owner would be willing to sell for fifteen.'

So the man offered fifteen dollars and walked out with the parrot.

Over the ensuing weeks, the parrot proved the ideal companion. He was witty, interesting, understanding and dished out excellent advice. The man was delighted with him. Then one day the man arrived home from work to find the parrot waiting eagerly for him.

'Here,' said the parrot, motioning him over to the cage. 'I don't know if I should tell you this or not, but it's about your wife and the window-cleaner.'

'What?' said the man.

'Well,' said the parrot, 'when he called round today, your wife greeted him at the door in a skimpy nightdress and kissed him on the mouth.'

'What happened then?' asked the man.

'The window-cleaner came into the house and lifted up her nightdress and began petting her all over,' reported the parrot.

'Oh, no!' exclaimed the man. 'Then what?'

'Then he lifted up the nightdress, got down on his knees and began fondling her body, starting with her breasts and slowly going lower and lower . . .'

The parrot paused.

'What happened? What happened?' asked the man frantically.

'I don't know,' said the parrot. 'At that point I fell off my perch.'

1741 A man asked his pet parrot: 'What would you like for your birthday?'

The parrot said: 'I want to get laid.'

So the man took his pet to the parrot whorehouse and gave him a hundred bucks. A few minutes later, the man heard wild squawking and when he went to find out what was causing the commotion, he saw his parrot yanking out the whore parrot's colourful feathers.

'What are you doing?' demanded the man.

His parrot said: 'For a hundred bucks I want her naked!'

1742 A woman got up one morning, opened the blinds, took the cover off the parrot's cage, made a coffee and lit a cigarette. A few minutes later, the phone rang. It was her boyfriend saying that he was coming right over. She immediately put out her cigarette, pulled down the blinds, put the cover back on the parrot's cage, and got back into bed. The parrot, from under the cloth, said: 'Well, that was a short fuckin' day!'

1743 A woman went to her priest and said, 'Father, I have a problem. I have two female parrots, but they only know how to say one thing.'

'What do they say?' inquired the priest.

'They say, "Hi, we're hookers! Do you want to have some fun?"'

'That's obscene,' snorted the priest. After thinking for a moment, he said: 'I may have a solution to your problem. I have two male talking parrots, which I have taught to pray and read the Bible. Bring your parrots over to my house, and we'll put them in the cage with Francis and Peter. My parrots can teach your parrots to pray and worship, and your birds will soon stop saying that awful phrase.'

'Thank you,' said the woman. 'That sounds a splendid idea.'

So the next day she brought her female parrots to the priest's house. As he ushered her in, she saw that his two male parrots were inside the cage holding rosary beads and praying. Impressed, she walked over and put her parrots in the cage with them. A few minutes later, the female parrots squawked in unison: 'Hi, we're hookers! Do you want to have some fun?'

Shocked, one male parrot looked over at the other male parrot and said, 'Put the beads away, Frank! Our prayers have been answered!'

PERIODS AND PMS

Signs That You May Have PMS:

1744 • Everyone around you has an attitude problem.

1745 • Your husband is suddenly agreeing with everything you say.

1746 • Everyone's head looks like an invitation to batting practice.

1747 • You stop reading *Cosmopolitan* and start reading *Guns and Ammo*.

1748 • The dryer has shrunk every last pair of your jeans.

1749 • When someone asks for the salt at the table, you snap, 'All I ever do is give, give, give!'

1750 • You consider chocolate a major food group.

1751 • You buy your husband a new T-shirt . . . with a target on the front.

1752 • Everyone within your immediate reach is dead.

1753 Two couples went away for the weekend and the guys persuaded their wives to swap partners for the night. Ray knew it was the time of the month for his wife but refrained from mentioning it to Phil. The guys agreed that when they sat around the breakfast table the following morning they would tap their teaspoons on the side of their coffee mug to indicate the number of times they had sex with each other's wife.

At breakfast, Ray proudly tapped his teaspoon three times against his coffee mug and waited for Phil's response. Phil thought for a moment and then tapped his teaspoon once on the strawberry jam and three times on the peanut butter.

1754 Have you heard about the new line of Tampax with bells and tinsel? It's for the Christmas period.

1755 Two young boys went into a pharmacy, picked up a box of Tampax and walked up to the counter.
'How old are you, son?' inquired the pharmacist.
'Eight.'
'Do you know how these are used?'
'Not exactly,' said the boy, 'but they aren't for me. They're for my brother – he's four. We saw on TV that if you use these you'll be able to swim and ride a bike. And he can't do either.'

1756 What's the closest thing to a woman's period? – Your salary: it comes once a month, lasts between five and seven days, and if it doesn't come, you're fucked!

1757 A lady was placing her purchases on the conveyor belt at the supermarket checkout. However one product didn't have a price on it, so the cashier had to call for a price check. Consequently 'Price check for Tampax . . . large' was blurted out over the intercom, much to the lady's embarrassment.
Unfortunately the price checker misheard the request and thought it was for 'thumb tacks' rather than 'Tampax'. So he answered back through the intercom: 'Is it the one you stick in with your thumb or the one you have to hammer in?'

1758 How do you embarrass an archaeologist? – Give him a used tampon and ask him which period it came from.

1759 Two sanitary pads were floating down a sewer drain when they caught up with two tampons. One pad said to the other: 'Should we say hi to those two tampons?'
The other pad said: 'Nah, they're stuck up cunts.'

1760 Cinderella was desperate to go to the ball, but it was the time of the month and she didn't have any tampons. Luckily her Fairy Godmother came to the rescue and turned a pumpkin next to Cinderella's house into a tampon. The Fairy Godmother warned: 'Be sure to get home by midnight or the tampon will turn back into a pumpkin.'

So Cinderella went to the ball. The Fairy Godmother waited patiently for her return but midnight passed and there was no sign of Cinderella. Eventually Cinderella rolled in at four o'clock in the morning.

'What time do you call this?' barked the Fairy Godmother angrily.

Cinderella said: 'Sorry, but I met this amazing guy and things got really heavy between us. His name was Peter Peter . . .'

1761 Why did the US Army send so many women with PMS to Iraq? – Because they fought like animals and retained water for four days.

1762 A man walked into a pharmacy and asked where the tampons were. The sales assistant directed him to the back of the shop. A minute or so later, the man returned to the counter with a packet of tissues and some cotton buds.

The assistant was confused. 'Why did you come in here, ask for a packet of tampons, and get those items?'

The man explained: 'Last night I sent my wife down to the newsagent for a packet of cigarettes, and she came back with a packet of papers and some tobacco. So tonight she can roll her own!'

1763 Every Sunday a preacher at a small country church tried to make the Bible accessible to his congregation via his sermons. He would say: 'If you ever feel adrift in the sea of life, just turn to the Bible for guidance. All of life's experiences are immortalised in the good book.'

After one week's service, a woman went up to the preacher and said: 'I don't think every life experience is mentioned in the Bible. Nowhere in the Bible have I read about PMS.'

The preacher promised to investigate, and the following Sunday he told the woman that he had indeed found a passage in the Bible about PMS. It read: 'And Mary rode Joseph's ass all the way to Bethlehem.'

What PMS Stands For:

1764 • Precarious Mental State
1765 • Provide More Sensitivity
1766 • Punching Men Senseless
1767 • Protect My Scrotum
1768 • Pitbull in Mini-skirt and Stilettos

1769 • Pouty Mouth Syndrome
1770 • Pardon My Sobbing
1771 • Punish My Spouse
1772 • Please Meet Satan
1773 • Paint Me Sociopathic
1774 • Pass My Shotgun
1775 • Psychotic Mood Shift
1776 • Pack My Stuff

1777 A werewolf came home after a hard day at the office.

'How was work, dear?' asked his wife. 'Have you been busy?'

'I don't want to talk about work,' he snapped.

'Well, can I fix you some supper?' she said.

'For Christ's sake, no!' he yelled. 'Why can't you just leave me alone? I come in from work after a long, trying day, and all I want is to be left alone without you insinuating that I haven't done anything. And then you want to force food down my throat. Just butt out, will you!'

'Oh, dear,' she sighed. 'I guess it's that time of the month . . .'

POEMS

1778   **A Girl's Prayer:**

Lord,
Before I lay me down to sleep,
I pray for a man who's not a creep,
One who's handsome, smart and strong,
One whose willy's thick and long,
One who thinks before he speaks,
When promises to call, he won't wait weeks;
I pray that he is gainfully employed,
And when I spend his cash, won't be annoyed;
Pulls out my chair and opens my door,
Massages my back and begs to do more.
Oh! Send me a man who'll make love to my mind,
Knows just what to say when I ask, 'How big's my behind?'
One who'll make love till my body's a twitchin,
In the hall, the bathroom, the garden, the kitchen.

I pray that this man will love me no end,
And never attempt to shag my best friend.
And as I kneel and pray by my bed,
I look at the wanker you sent me instead . . .

1779 She whispered, 'Will it hurt me?'
'Of course not,' answered he,
'It's a very simple process,
You can rely on me.'
She said, 'I'm very frightened,
I've not had this before.
My friend has had it five times
And said it can be sore.'
It was growing rather painful
Tears formed in her eyes,
It was hurting quite a bit now,
It must have been a size.
'Calm yourself,' he whispered,
His face filled with a grin,
'Try and open wider
So I can get it in.'
'It's coming now,' he whispered;
'I know,' she cried in bliss;
Feeling it deep within her now
She said, 'I'm glad I'm having this.'
And with a final effort
She gave a frightened shout,
He gripped it in anguish
And quickly pulled it out.
She lay back quite contented,
Sighed and gave a smile;
She said, 'I'm glad I came now,
You made it worth my while.'
Now if you read this carefully,
The dentist you will find
Is not what you imagined;
It's just your dirty mind!

POLICE

1780 A local law enforcement officer stopped a driver for speeding, but decided to let him off with a warning. He asked the man his name and the driver replied: 'Fred.'

'Fred what?' asked the officer.

'Just Fred,' said the driver. 'I used to have a last name but I lost it.'

'What do you mean, you lost it?'

'Let me explain,' said the driver. 'I was born Fred Dingaling. I know, funny last name. The kids used to tease me all the time. But I worked hard and got good grades and trained to be a doctor. I went through college, medical school, internship, residency, and finally got my degree so I was Fred Dingaling, MD. But after a while I got bored being a doctor and went back to school to study dentistry. Again I went through school, got my degree, so now I was Fred Dingaling MD, DDS. But dentistry didn't fulfil me either and I started messing around with my assistant, who gave me VD. So I was Fred Dingaling MD, DDS with VD. Well, the ADA found about the VD, so they took away my DDS. So I was Fred Dingaling MD with VD. Then the AMA found out about the ADA taking away my DDS because of the VD, so they took away my MD, leaving me as Fred Dingaling with VD. Then the VD took away my dingaling, so now I'm just Fred.'

1781 A traffic cop stopped a woman driver for speeding and asked to see her licence.

'I'm sorry,' she said. 'I don't have a licence. I lost it for drunk driving.'

'I see,' said the officer. 'Well, can I look at your vehicle registration papers?'

'No,' said the woman, 'I'm afraid you can't. I stole this car, killed the owner, and put his remains in the trunk.'

The horrified cop immediately called for back-up and within a few minutes half a dozen police cars had arrived at the scene, sirens wailing. The police chief approached the woman cautiously, brandishing a gun. 'OK, ma'am,' he called out, 'open the trunk of the car, please.'

She opened the car trunk, but it was empty.

'Is this your car, ma'am?' asked the chief.

'Yes,' said the woman. 'Here are the registration papers.'

The chief looked puzzled. 'My officer here said you don't have a driver's licence . . .'

'Of course I have,' said the woman, reaching into her purse and producing a licence.

'I don't know what's going on here,' said the chief, scratching his head. 'My officer told me you don't have a licence, that you stole this car, murdered the owner and put the body in the trunk.'

'I don't believe it!' said the woman. 'Next you'll be telling me the lying bastard said I was speeding too!'

1782 A guy was walking down a country road late one evening when he felt the sudden need for sex. He realised that he was next to a pumpkin patch and, reasoning that a pumpkin was soft and squishy inside, he decided to cut a hole in one and satisfy his urges that way. Unfortunately he got so carried away with screwing the pumpkin that he failed to notice an approaching police car.

A policewoman got out of the car, went over to him and said: 'Excuse me, sir. But do you realise that you are screwing a pumpkin?'

The guy looked horrified and said: 'A pumpkin? Damn! Is it midnight already?'

1783 A man looked out of his window one night and saw a gang of thieves breaking into his garden shed. He called the police straight away, but the station sergeant said there was no one available to attend.

'OK,' said the houseowner, and he put the phone down. Five minutes later, he phoned the station again. 'Don't worry about sending anybody out to deal with the shed burglars at 53 Larch Avenue. I've shot them.'

Within two minutes the road was swarming with police cars. The officers caught the burglars red-handed, but the sergeant was furious. He said to the houseowner: 'I thought you said you'd shot them!'

The houseowner countered: 'I thought you said there was nobody available.'

1784 A young couple were driving down the road in a busy area when things started to get passionate. So they pulled over to the side of the road, and within a matter of seconds they were all over each other, oblivious to what was going on outside. Suddenly a policeman tapped on the window.

'Don't you know that it's against the law to have sex on a public highway?' he said.

Embarrassed at being caught, the couple apologized.

'OK,' said the cop, 'but I'm going to have to write you a ticket.' So he wrote the ticket and warned them not to do it again. After getting dressed, the girl asked her boyfriend what the policeman had written the ticket for. The boy replied: 'Doing 69 in a 30 mph speed zone.'

Signs That Your Police Partner Needs a Vacation:

1785 • Every Tuesday he insists it's his turn to be the siren.

1786 • He talks to himself. Half of him is the 'good cop' and the other half is the 'bad cop'.

1787 • He has developed a crush on one of the transvestite hookers he's arrested.

1788 • He keeps asking you if his bulletproof vest makes him look fat.

1789 • He is exchanging doughnut recipes with complete strangers.

1790 • He wants to hear less talk and more music on the police channel.

1791 A New York cop pulled a guy over for driving erratically. 'Sir, I can't help noticing your eyes are bloodshot. Have you been drinking?'

The guy answered indignantly: 'Officer, I can't help noticing your eyes are glazed. Have you been eating doughnuts?'

1792 A driver was speeding along the road when he came to a bridge. A cop with a radar gun was sitting on the other side of the bridge and pulled him over.

'Do you know what speed you were doing?' asked the officer menacingly.

'Look, I know I was probably a little over the limit, but there's a good reason for it: I'm in a real hurry.'

'What's so urgent?' asked the cop.

'I'm late for work.'

'Oh, yeah? And what line of work are you in that is so important?'

'I'm a rectum stretcher,' said the guy.

'A what?'

'A rectum stretcher. I start with a finger, then work my way up to two fingers. Eventually I get a hand in, then both hands, and I slowly stretch it till it's about six foot wide.'

'What do you do with a six-foot asshole?'

The guy said: 'You give him a radar gun and park him at the end of a bridge . . .'

1793 There was once a sheriff who, no matter what the situation, always said, 'It could have been worse' after viewing the scene of a crime. It drove his two deputies crazy.

One day, the two deputies answered an emergency call at a remote farmhouse. When they got there, they found the naked bodies of a man and a woman in the bedroom. Both had been shot dead. And in the living room was the body of a man with a gun at his side.

'No doubt about it,' said the first deputy. 'This was a double murder and suicide. The guy came home, found his wife in bed with somebody else and shot them both. Then he shot himself.'

The second deputy agreed. 'Yeah, it certainly looks like a double murder and suicide. But I'll bet you when the sheriff gets here, he'll say, "It could have been worse", just like he always does!'

'No way,' said the first deputy. 'How could it be worse? There are three people in the house, and all of them have been shot dead. Even the sheriff won't say that this could have been worse. So, yeah, you're on.'

A couple of minutes later, the sheriff arrived. He walked into the bedroom and saw the two naked bodies lying in the bed. Then he walked into the living room and saw the man on the floor with the gun by his side. 'No doubt about it,' said the sheriff, shaking his head, 'it was a double murder and suicide. This guy came home, found his wife in bed with somebody else and shot them both. But, you know, it could have been worse.'

The first deputy, angry at having lost the bet, screamed: 'Sheriff, how could it possibly have been worse? There are three people in this farmhouse, and all three of them are dead. It couldn't have been worse!'

'Yes, it could,' said the sheriff. 'You see that guy there on the floor? If he had come home yesterday, that would be me there in that bed!'

1794 A young woman phoned the police late one night and reported a sex maniac in her apartment.

'We'll be right over,' said the officer.

'Oh,' she said. 'Can you wait till morning?'

1795 A car containing three guys was driving erratically on the highway. A cop pulled it over. 'Listen,' he said, 'I don't want to give you a ticket, so I'll make a deal with you: if your three dicks add up to twenty-one inches, I'll let you off.'

The first guy whipped out his, and it measured ten inches. The second guy also had a ten-inch dick. 'OK,' said the cop. 'You just need another inch.'

The third guy produced his, and it was exactly one inch long. 'Fair enough,' said the cop. 'A deal's a deal, I'll let you go.'

Later the two ten-inch guys looked at the third guy and said, surprised:
'One inch?'

'Yeah,' he said, 'I had a boner.'

1796 Two police officers, Colin and Jessica, had been assigned to walk the beat. They had only been out on patrol a short while when Jessica said: 'Damn, I was running late this morning after my workout and after I showered I forgot to put on my panties! We have to go back to the station to get them.'

Colin replied: 'We don't have to go back. Just give the K-9 unit, Fido, one sniff and he will go fetch them for you.'

It was a hot day and Jessica didn't feel like going back to the station, so she cautiously lifted her skirt for the dog. Fido's nose quickly shot between her legs, sniffing and snorting. After ten seconds of sniffing, the dog's ears pricked up, he sniffed the wind, and raced off towards the station house.

Five minutes went by and there was no sign of Fido. Ten minutes passed, and the dog was still nowhere to be seen. After fifteen minutes, they were starting to worry. Finally after twenty minutes, they heard sirens in the distance. The sirens got louder and louder. Suddenly, pursued by a dozen police cars, Fido rounded the corner . . . with the Desk Sergeant's balls in his mouth.

POLISH JOKES

1797 An Irishman, an Italian and a Pole were sitting in a New York bar, enjoying a drink together.

The Irishman said: 'This is a great place, but where I originally come from, there's an even better bar than this — McCluskey's in Dublin. You buy a drink, you buy another drink, and McCluskey himself buys you the third drink!'

The others agreed that it sounded a great bar, but then the Italian said: 'In Rome, there's a bar called Luigi's. You buy a drink, Luigi buys you a drink, you buy another drink, and Luigi buys you another drink!'

The others agreed that it sounded a fabulous bar, but then the Pole said: 'Where I come from in Warsaw, there's this place called Warzywicki's. They buy you your first drink, your second drink and your third drink. Then they get you a date who is guaranteed to be easy!'

'Wow!' said the others. 'That's fantastic. Did that actually happen to you?'

'No,' said the Pole, 'but it happened to my sister.'

1798 Two Poles were remembering how they had first learned to swim. One said: 'My father taught me to swim the hard way – he threw me into the middle of a lake.'

'That must have been tough,' said the other.

'It was, but the really hard part was getting out of the sack!'

1799 A Polish guy living in New York took his car to a repair shop in the hope that the service manager could cure the strange noise the vehicle kept making when cornering. The job was passed on to a mechanic with a repair order that read: 'Check for clunking sound when going around corners.'

The mechanic took the car on a test drive and, sure enough, whenever he turned a corner, there was a clunking sound. Finally he found the root of the problem and returned the repair order to the service manager with a note that read: 'Removed bowling ball from trunk.'

1800 How did the Germans conquer Poland so quickly? – They marched in backwards and the Poles thought they were leaving.

1801 When a mine collapsed near Pittsburgh, one of the lucky survivors was an engineer. Recovering from his ordeal he went to a local bar. The bar was almost deserted until another man walked in a few minutes later.

'Hey, bartender,' said the engineer, 'another whiskey for me, and one for my friend here.'

'I'm sorry,' said the bartender, 'but that guy's a Polack, and we don't serve Polacks here.'

'Well, you should,' said the engineer, 'because if it weren't for him, I'd be dead. When the mine collapsed, he and I were both down there, and in the mad rush to escape, he held up the roof of the mine with his head to prevent it caving in on us. If you don't believe me, look at the top of his head. You'll see it's flat from holding the roof up. Now get the guy a whiskey – he saved my life.'

The bartender served the Pole, then called the engineer to one side and whispered: 'I saw the flat spot on his head you were talking about, but I also noticed extensive bruising under his chin. What's caused that?'

The engineer replied: 'Oh, that's where we put the jack.'

1802 At a cockfight, how can you identify the Polish guy?
He's the one with the duck.
How do you know if an Italian is there?

He bets on the duck.
How do you know if the Mafia is there?
The duck wins.

1803 The pilot of a Polish Airlines 747 was briefing his co-pilot on the landing procedures at their next destination.

'This is a short runway,' he said, 'and I'll need all your help on the flaps, thrust reversers and brakes for this one.'

'Roger that,' said the co-pilot, 'let's go.'

As they approached the airfield, the co-pilot commented: 'Wow, that's the shortest field I've ever seen.'

The pilot called for half-flaps.

'You have half-flaps,' confirmed the co-pilot.

As they got closer, the pilot said: 'Better give me three-quarter flaps.'

'Roger, you have three-quarter flaps,' said the co-pilot.

'Damn,' shouted the pilot, 'this looks even shorter than I remember. Give me full-flaps and stand by on the brakes and thrust reversers!'

'You have full-flaps and standing by,' said the co-pilot.

As the wheels touched down on the runway, the pilot immediately called for full braking and full thrust reversers. The co-pilot complied, and as the plane came to a shuddering halt inches from the end of the runway, the pilot, wiping sweat from his brow, exclaimed: 'Holy mother of God, that's the shortest runway I've ever seen in my life!'

'Yeah,' said the co-pilot, looking out both windows, 'but the son-of-a-bitch sure is wide!'

1804 Why do so many Polish names end in 'ski'? – Because they can't spell 'toboggan'.

1805 A Polish jeweller was working quietly in his shop when the peace was suddenly shattered by an elephant smashing the front window. Before the jeweller could react, the elephant had used his trunk to help himself to valuable watches, rings and necklaces.

The jeweller called the police, and the officer asked for a description of the culprit.

'It was some sort of animal,' said the jeweller. 'I'm not sure whether it was an elephant, a rhinoceros or a bear – but it was big.'

'Well,' said the policeman, 'it's not difficult to tell them apart. An elephant has big ears and a trunk, a rhinoceros has a horn, and a bear is covered in fur.'

'That's all very well,' said the jeweller, 'but, to tell the truth, I didn't get a good look at him. He had a stocking over his head.'

1806 A Polish guy was strolling along a beach in the South of France. There were many beautiful women lying in the sun, and he was desperate to meet one. But, try as he might, the women never seemed interested. As a last resort, he went over to a Frenchman who was lying on the beach, surrounded by gorgeous women.

'Excuse me,' he said, taking the Frenchman to one side, 'but I've been trying to meet one of those women for the past two hours, and I just can't seem to get anywhere with them. You're French, you know these women. What do they want?'

'Maybe I can help a leetle beet,' said the Frenchman. 'What you do ees you go to ze store. You buy a pair of tight sweeming trunks. You walk up and down ze beach. You meet girl very queekly zees way.'

'Thanks,' said the Polish guy, and he went off and bought a pair of tight red swimming trunks. He put them on, went back to the beach, paraded up and down for half an hour, but still had no luck with the ladies.

So he went back to the Frenchman. 'I'm sorry to bother you again, but I went to the store, I bought the tight swimming shorts, but I still haven't been able to meet a girl.'

'OK,' said the Frenchman, 'I tell you what you do. You go to ze store. You buy potato. You put potato in sweeming trunks and walk up and down ze beach. You will meet girl very queekly zees way.'

'Thanks,' said the Pole, and he ran off to the store. He bought the potato, put it down his tight swimming trunks, and strolled up and down the beach. But he still didn't receive even one admiring glance. After half an hour of this, he couldn't stand it any more and went back to the Frenchman.

'Look,' said the Pole, 'I got the trunks, I put the potato in them, and I walked up and down the beach – and still nothing! What more can I do?'

'Well,' said the Frenchman, 'maybe I can help you a leetle beet. Why don't you try moving ze potato to the *front* of ze sweeming trunks?'

1807 Two Polish hunters were driving through the country to go bear hunting. They came upon a fork in the road where a sign read BEAR LEFT, so they went home.

1808 A Polish guy walked into a bar to be greeted by his mates. 'Hi, Stan,' they laughed. 'You put on a great show with your missus last night. You left the light on in your bedroom and we could see everything that was going on projected on your curtains.'

'Sorry, lads,' said Stan. 'The joke's on you. I wasn't home last night.'

1809 An Italian, an American and a Polack were captured by the French for various crimes and taken to the guillotine. The executioner placed the Italian on the block and asked if he had any last words. The Italian replied: 'I pray to the Virgin Mary that I may live.' The executioner dropped the blade, and it stopped just an inch above the Italian's neck. Amazed, the French let him go.

Next the American was put in position and asked if he had any final words. He replied: 'In the name of Jesus Christ, please have mercy.' The executioner dropped the blade, and again it stopped just an inch from the American's neck. In disbelief, the French set him free.

Then the Polak was placed on the block, and the executioner asked if he had any last words. The Polak said: 'Yeah. You've got a knot in your rope.'

1810 A Polish man went to have his eyes tested. The optician showed him a wall chart and asked him whether he could read it.

'Read it?' he said. 'I know him!'

1811 Two Poles were driving east across the United States. When they got to Texas, they saw a sign that read 'Clean Restrooms Ahead'. So when they got to the filling station, they pulled in, got out of their car, and started cleaning the restrooms!

As they travelled further east, they found their progress slowed because there were so many 'Clean Restrooms Ahead' signs along the way. When they finally arrived in Alabama, they came across a sign that read 'Wanted!!! Two Mexican males for rape!'

The two Poles looked at each other and thought: 'Damn! Those Mexicans get all the good jobs!'

1812 An American, a Canadian and a Pole went out for a night on the town. The American picked up a girl and took her back to his place. The Canadian picked up a girl and they went back to her place. The Pole picked up a girl and asked if she wanted to come back to his apartment.

'I'd love to,' she said, 'but I'm on my menstrual cycle.'

'That's OK,' said the Pole. 'I came on my moped.'

1813 Did you hear about the Pole who sued the local baker for forging his signature on a hot cross bun?

1814 Out shopping, a Polish guy saw a Thermos flask in a store window. He went in and asked the clerk: 'What is the purpose of that flask?'

The clerk replied: 'It keeps hot things hot and cold things cold.'

So the Pole bought one and took it to work the next day. 'Look at this,' he said to his workmate. 'It's a Thermos flask. It keeps hot things hot and cold things cold.'

'What have you got in it?' asked his friend.

'A cup of soup and a choc ice.'

1815 A Polish man had always dreamed of owning a sports car so, when he inherited a fortune, he immediately went out and bought a Porsche . . . even though he had hardly driven a car in his life. Excitedly, he took his new toy through the gears on a quiet highway but, when he hit top speed, there was suddenly an almighty bang and a cloud of smoke.

He contacted the salesman and explained what had happened. The salesman was mystified, but, because the Pole was very rich, he agreed to swap the Porsche for a Ferrari.

The Pole set off for another deserted strip of highway where he put the Ferrari through the gears, but no sooner had he reached 140 mph than there was a huge bang and a cloud of smoke. So he returned to the salesman and told him that the same thing that had happened with the Porsche had now happened with the Ferrari. The salesman was reluctant to exchange this car, too, but eventually agreed to let the Pole have a Lotus, but only on condition that he joined him on the test run.

So the Pole found a quiet stretch of road and began putting the Lotus through its paces. When he got into sixth gear, he kept accelerating, but then the car suddenly started to shake violently. There was a loud bang and a cloud of smoke.

'What did you do?' asked the bewildered salesman.

'Well,' explained the Pole, 'I was going faster and faster, and I ran out of numbered gears. So I put it into "R" for "Race." '

1816 Did you hear about the Polack who thought his wife was trying to kill him? – On her dressing table he found a bottle of Polish Remover.

1817 A Russian, an American and a Pole were talking about the space race.
'We were the first in space,' boasted the Russian.
'So what?' snorted the American. 'We were first on the moon.'
'Ah, yes,' said the Pole, 'but we will be the first on the sun.'
'You can't land on the sun,' said the Russian. 'It's too hot.'
'We are not altogether stupid,' explained the Pole. 'We're going at night.'

1818 A double-glazing salesman phoned an elderly Polish gentleman to chase up
an unpaid bill. 'A year ago,' he said, 'our company replaced all the windows
in your house with our special weather-tight windows, and you still haven't
sent us a single payment.'
The Pole replied nervously: 'But you said they'd pay for themselves in
twelve months.'

1819 Two Indians and a Polish fellow were walking together in the Arizona desert
when one of the Indians suddenly ran up a hill to the mouth of a cave. He
stopped and hollered into the cave: 'Wooooo! Wooooo! Wooooo!' Then he
listened very carefully until he heard the answer: 'Wooooo! Wooooo!
Wooooo!' At this, he tore off his clothes and ran into the cave.
The Polish guy was puzzled and asked the other Indian what was going
on. The Indian explained: 'It is mating time for us Indians and when you see a
cave and holler, "Wooooo! Wooooo! Wooooo!", and get an answer back, it
means that she is in there waiting for you.'
Just then, the Indian spotted another cave. Running up to the entrance, he
hollered: 'Woooo! Wooooo! Wooooo!' When he heard the return 'Wooooo!
Wooooo! Wooooo!', he ripped off his clothes and went into the cave.
The Polish guy started frantically searching the desert for a cave of his
own. Eventually he found a huge one at the top of a hill – bigger than either
of the caves the Indians had gone in. Excitedly he rushed up to the entrance
and hollered: 'Wooooo! Wooooo! Wooooo!' Straight away he heard the
answering call loud and clear: 'Wooooo! Wooooo! Wooooo!' With a big
smile on his face, and full of sexual anticipation, he ripped off his clothes and
raced into the cave.
The next day's newspaper headline read: NAKED POLACK RUN OVER BY
FREIGHT TRAIN.

POLITICIANS

1820 After spending the night at a hotel with a call girl, a politician left $300 on the dressing table.

'Thanks,' she said, 'but I only charge $50.'

'You can't make a living on that,' he said.

'Oh, don't worry. I do a little blackmail on the side.'

1821 Two alligators – one big, one small – abandoned the Everglades in favour of living near the government buildings in Florida. The small one sighed: 'I can't understand why you're so much bigger than me. After all, we're the same age.'

The big one said: 'What you been eatin'?'

'Politicians, same as you.'

'Where you bin catchin' 'em?'

'Outside the State offices, same as you.'

'How you bin catchin' 'em?'

'I creep up on 'em as they get into their car, grab 'em by the leg, shake the shit out of 'em, and eat 'em.'

'That's where you're goin' wrong. You ain't getting' any real nourishment. See, by the time you get done shakin' the shit out of a politician, there ain't nothin' left but lips and a briefcase!'

1822 How do you get twenty government cabinet ministers in a mini-van? – Promote one to Prime Minister and watch the other nineteen crawl up his ass.

1823 A cannibal was visiting a neighbouring cannibal island where ordinary people cost $5 a head, but politicians cost $25.

The visiting cannibal asked: 'How come politicians cost so much?'

The chief said: 'Do you know how hard it is to clean one of those?'

THE POPE

1824 The Pope had been diagnosed as having a potentially fatal testicular disease and after treatment he was told that he had to have sex with a woman in order to confirm that the treatment had been successful. He called all his cardinals together and explained the situation. They agreed that it was absolutely necessary but the Pope remained uneasy, eventually consenting to go ahead only after insisting on four conditions.

'Firstly,' said the Pope, 'the girl has to be blind so she cannot see it's the Holy Father and tell the whole world. Secondly, she must be deaf so that she doesn't recognize the Holy Father's voice and tell the whole world. Thirdly, as a precaution, she has to be dumb so she cannot tell the whole world.'

At this point one of the cardinals stood up and said: 'Leave it to me, your Holiness, I know just the woman for you.'

As the cardinal was about to leave, the Pope said: 'Wait a minute. I told you there are four conditions.' The Pope beckoned the cardinal over and whispered in his ear: 'Big tits!'

1825 What happened to the Pope when he went to Mount Olive? – Popeye nearly killed him.

1826 The Pope called his mother after being elected. 'Hi, Mom, I have good news and bad news.'

'What's the good news?' she asked.

'I've just been elected Pope.'

'What's the bad news?'

'I have to move into an Italian neighbourhood.'

1827 On a tour of the United States, the Pope agreed to grant absolution to three sinners.

First up was George W. Bush.

'What is your sin?' asked the Pope.

'I have sent hundreds of young Americans to a needless death in Iraq.'

'Kneel down,' said the Pope. 'I'll bless you and grant you absolution.'

Next up was Bill Clinton.

'What is your sin?' asked the Pope.

'I cheated on my wife.'

'Kneel down, I'll bless you and grant you absolution.'

When the third person appeared, the Pope asked: 'What is your name?'

'Monica Lewinsky.'

The Pope stroked his chin. 'Hmm. Perhaps you should remain standing . . .'

1828 What's black and white and tells the Pope to sod off? – A nun who's just won the lottery.

1829 Colin bragged to his boss that he knew everyone in the world worth knowing, but his boss didn't believe him.

'OK,' said Colin, 'I'll prove it. Jump into my car. We're going to Michael Jordan's house.'

Twenty minutes later, they pulled up outside a huge house and Colin knocked on the door. Michael Jordan answered. 'Hi, Colin, how are ya?' he beamed. And he invited Colin and his boss in for a drink.

When they left, Colin turned to his boss and said: 'Now are you convinced that I know everyone?'

'No,' said the boss churlishly. 'You probably paid Michael to pretend he knows you.'

So Colin got back in the car and headed for Jack Nicholson's house. Jack answered the door and said: 'Hi, Colin. Good to see ya again. How're ya doin'?' Colin introduced Jack to his boss and they chatted for over an hour.

When they left, Colin said to his boss: 'Now do you believe me when I tell you I know everyone?'

The boss remained unconvinced. 'You just got lucky. Jack's a friendly guy.'

So a week later, they flew to Rome. 'If I can prove that I know the Pope, then will you believe me?' asked Colin.

'I guess so,' conceded his boss.

Telling his boss to wait in St Peter's Square, Colin said he was going up to talk to the Pope.

'You'll never get through security,' laughed the boss.

'You watch me,' said Colin confidently.

And a few minutes later, the crowd cheered as the Pope appeared on the Vatican balcony . . . with Colin at his side. Suddenly the watching boss had a heart attack and a crowd gathered around him. Seeing the commotion, Colin ran back down to the square to find his boss propped up by paramedics.

'What happened?' asked Colin.

The boss gasped: 'I was doing fine till you and the Pope came out on the balcony, and the guy next to me said: "Who the hell's that on the balcony with Colin?"'

PORNOGRAPHY

1830 Delivering a crusading speech against porn videos, a US mayoral candidate stormed: 'I rented one of these cassettes and was shocked to find five acts of oral sex, three of sodomy, a transsexual making love to a dog, and a woman accommodating five men at once. If elected, I will ban such filth. Any questions?'

Half a dozen people shouted: 'Where did you rent the tape?'

1831 How do you know when a male porn star is working at the gas station? – Right before the gas stops pumping, he pulls out the nozzle and sprays it all over the car.

1832 Did you hear about the chain of sex shops that have introduced a line of inflatable dolls modelled on Palestinian women? – When you get them home, they blow themselves up.

1833 A blonde decided to add a little spice to her life by renting out an X-rated adult video. So she went to the video store and, after searching around for a while, selected a title that sounded suitably raunchy. Then she drove home, lit some candles, slipped into something comfortable, and put the tape in the VCR. However, to her dismay, there was nothing but static on the screen, so she called the video store to complain.

'I just rented an adult movie from you and there's nothing on the tape but static.'

'Sorry about that,' said the store clerk. 'We've had problems with some tapes. Which title did you rent?'

The blonde said: 'It's called *Head Cleaner*.'

PREGNANCY

1834 A holiday rep went to the doctor and discovered she was pregnant.

'When did you last have a check-up?' asked the doctor.

'I don't remember,' said the rep, 'but I know the last one was a Spaniard.'

1835 Two women were sitting in the doctor's waiting room. 'I want a baby more than anything,' said the first, 'but it doesn't seem like it's ever going to happen.'

'I used to feel the same way,' said the second. 'But then everything changed. That's why I'm here. I'm going to have a baby in three months.'

'You must tell me what you did,' said the first.

'I went to the faith healer in the mall,' replied the second.

'But I've tried that. My husband and I went to him for nearly a year and it didn't help at all.'

The second woman smiled and whispered: 'Try going alone next time.'

1836 After spending months searching for a suitable maid, a wealthy Washington couple finally found a girl who met their requirements. So they were bitterly disappointed when, just six weeks after taking the job, she announced that she would have to quit because she was pregnant.

The childless couple were desperate to keep her and made her an offer. 'If we adopt your baby, will you stay?'

'Well, yes,' she replied.

So they adopted the girl's baby, but a year later she again handed in her notice because she was pregnant. They still didn't want to lose her, so again they offered to adopt her baby. And again she agreed to stay.

Twelve months later, she announced once more that she would have to leave her post because she was pregnant. Unable to contemplate life without their trusted maid, the couple offered to adopt this baby, too, if she would stay. The girl agreed.

Nine months later, the girl handed in her notice for a fourth time. 'You're not pregnant again?' asked the couple.

'No,' replied the maid.

'So why do you want to go?'

'There are too many babies to look after.'

1837 A teenage girl confessed: 'Mom, I'm pregnant.'

'How?' gasped her mother. 'What did I tell you about sex?'

'That I should take measures. Well, that's what I did! I took measures and went with the biggest.'

1838 A man told the doctor: 'My wife's pregnant, but we haven't had sex in over a year. I don't understand it.'

The doctor said: 'It's what we in the medical profession call a grudge pregnancy.'

'What's a grudge pregnancy?' asked the man.

The doctor replied: 'Well, somebody's obviously had it in for you.'

1839 The pre-natal class was full of pregnant women and their partners. The instructor was teaching the women how to breathe properly and was issuing sound advice for a healthy pregnancy.

'Ladies,' she announced, 'exercise is good for you. Walking is especially beneficial. And gentlemen, it wouldn't hurt you to take the time to go walking with your partner.'

The room fell silent until a man raised his hand: 'Is it all right if she carries a golf bag while we walk?'

1840 What two things in the air will get a woman pregnant? – Her legs.

1841 A doctor was doing the rounds of a maternity ward. 'And when is Mrs Black's baby due?' he asked.

'March 12,' replied the nurse.

'Right,' said the doctor. 'And how about Mrs White? When is her baby due?'

'She's due on March 12 too,' said the nurse.

'Oh, and Mrs Brown?' asked the doctor.

'She's also due on March 12,' said the nurse.

'And Mrs Green?' said the doctor, raising his eyebrows. 'Don't tell me she's due on March 12 as well?'

'I don't think so,' said the nurse. 'She didn't go on the church picnic.'

1842 A recently married church minister informed his congregation that his wife was pregnant and asked for a pay rise that would give him a reasonable salary. After deliberation, the congregation agreed that the increase in family size warranted a pay rise.

However, after the minister's wife gave birth to six children over the next six years – each one accompanied by a pay rise – the congregation called a meeting to complain that the cost had become prohibitive. The minister tried to defend his sizeable salary by declaring: 'Having children is an act of God!'

'Snow and rain are acts of God, too,' said a man at the back of the room, 'but most of us wear rubbers.'

1843 A young woman was so excited to learn she was pregnant that she had to tell her friends right away. It was nearly midnight when she got round to phoning the last one.

'I can't believe I have a person inside me!' she shrieked.

'So do I,' said the friend. 'Can I call you back in an hour?'

PREMATURE EJACULATION

1844 A guy was having problems with premature ejaculation, so he decided to go to the doctor for advice. The doctor listened to his story and suggested: 'When you feel like you are getting ready to ejaculate, try startling yourself.'

That afternoon the guy went out and bought a starting pistol. Rushing home early from work, he found his wife lying on the bed, naked and waiting. Before she could say a word, he jumped on her eagerly and soon they found themselves in the 69 position. Moments later, he felt the sudden urge to ejaculate and fired the starting pistol.

The following day he went back to the doctor.

'How did it go?' asked the doctor.

'Not that well,' answered the guy. 'When I fired the pistol, my wife peed in my face, bit three inches off my penis, and my neighbour came out of the wardrobe with his hands in the air!'

1845 A man went to a psychiatrist and said: 'Doctor, I suffer from premature ejaculation. Can you help me?'

The psychiatrist said: 'No, but I can introduce you to a woman with a short attention span.'

1846 A guy bumped into his ex-girlfriend, from whom he had parted on bad terms.

He said: 'You know, I was with another woman last night, but I was still thinking of you.'

'Why?' she asked, surprised. 'Because you miss me?'

'No, because it stops me coming too soon!'

PRIESTS

1847 Three Boy Scouts, a lawyer, a priest and a pilot were on a plane that was about to crash. The pilot said, 'Look, we only have three parachutes, let's give them to the three Boy Scouts. They're young and have their whole lives ahead of them.'

The lawyer snarled: 'Fuck the Boy Scouts!'

The priest said: 'Do we have time?'

1848 An Irish priest in a small village near Limerick kept chickens. He had a cock rooster and a dozen hens but one day the rooster went missing and he appealed for its return at Mass.

'Has anybody got a cock?' he asked the congregation. All the men stood up. 'Dear God, no,' exclaimed the priest, flustered. 'That wasn't what I meant. Has anybody seen a cock?' All the women stood up. 'No, no. That wasn't what I meant either. Has anybody seen a cock that doesn't belong to them?' Half of the women stood up. 'No, no. That wasn't what I meant at all. Let me rephrase the question. Has anybody seen my cock?' All of the nuns stood up.

1849 A young priest got up one morning and went to breakfast. On his way, he passed two nuns and said cheerily: 'Good morning, Sisters.'

The nuns replied: 'You got out on the wrong side of bed this morning!'

Taken aback by their reply, he walked on and met a monk. 'Good morning, Brother,' said the priest.

'You got out on the wrong side of bed this morning!' replied the monk.

Confused, the priest then bumped into a fellow priest. 'Good morning, Father,' he said.

The other priest said: 'You got out on the wrong side of bed this morning!'

By now the young priest was furious. He continued his walk to the dining hall without greeting anyone. But then the bishop saw him and said: 'Father . . .'

The priest glared at the bishop and snapped: 'No, I did not get out on the wrong side of bed this morning!'

The bishop was puzzled. 'I don't know what you mean.'

The priest realized his mistake. 'I am sorry, your holiness. What is it you want?'

The bishop looked at him and said: 'All I was going to ask was why you were wearing Sister Mary's shoes?'

1850 Some years ago, the Catholic Church required women to wear a head covering in order to enter the sanctuary. One Sunday, a lady arrived without her head covering, and the priest refused her admission. Undeterred, she returned a few minutes later, wearing her blouse tied around her head.

The shocked priest said: 'Madam, I cannot allow you to enter this holy place without you wearing a blouse.'

'But, Father,' she protested, 'I have a divine right.'

'I see that,' said the priest. 'And your left one's not bad either, but you still have to wear a blouse to enter this church!'

1851 A priest was pulled over by a cop for speeding. Seeing an empty wine bottle in the car and smelling alcohol on the priest's breath, the police officer asked: 'Father, have you been drinking?'

'Only water, my son,' replied the priest.

'Then why can I smell wine?' said the officer.

The priest looked at the wine bottle and exclaimed: 'Oh, my Lord, He's gone and done it again!'

1852 A young woman went to confession. 'Bless me Father, for I have sinned,' she said. 'Last night my boyfriend made love to me seven times.'

The priest said: 'You must go home and suck the juice of seven lemons.'

'And will that absolve me?' asked the young woman.

'No,' replied the priest, 'but it will take that smug look off your face.'

1853 Two priests died at the same time and met St Peter at the Pearly Gates. St Peter said: 'I'd like to let you guys in now, but unfortunately our computers are down. You'll have to go back to Earth for a week or so, but I'm afraid you can't go back as humans. What do you want to be?'

The first priest said: 'I've always wanted to be an eagle, soaring above the Rocky Mountains.'

'So be it,' said St Peter, and the priest flew off.

The second priest thought about the proposition for a minute, then said: 'Will you be keeping track of us, St Peter?'

'No,' said St Peter. 'Like I told you, the computer is down. There's no way we can keep track of what you are doing. This week's a freebie.'

'In that case,' said the second priest, 'I've always wanted to be a stud.'

'So be it,' said St Peter, and the second priest disappeared.

A week went by, the computer was repaired, and God told St Peter to recall the two priests. 'Will you have trouble locating them?' he asked.

'The first one should be easy,' answered St Peter. 'He's somewhere over the Rocky Mountains, flying with the eagles. But the second one could prove more difficult.'

'Why?' asked God.

'Because he's on a snow tyre somewhere in Alaska.'

1854 Staying the night in a hotel, a priest made a pass at the maid. At first she objected, but he sweet-talked her into bed by insisting: 'It's all right; it's written in the Bible.'

Waking the next morning, the maid began to wonder where exactly in the

Bible it says that it's all right for a priest to sleep with hotel staff. So the priest picked up the copy of the Bible from the bedside table and showed her the inside cover. Written in pencil were the words, 'The maid is easy.'

1855 A new priest was so nervous before giving his first mass that he could hardly speak. Afterwards he confessed his feelings to the watching monsignor who suggested: 'Whenever I feel anxious about getting up on the pulpit, I put a glass of vodka next to my glass of water. And if I start to feel nervous, I take a sip of the vodka. It calms me down, and none of the congregation is any the wiser.'

So next Sunday at mass the priest took the monsignor's advice. At the beginning of the sermon, he got nervous and took a drink of vodka. It loosened his tongue so effectively that his nerves vanished at once. Returning to his office at the end of mass, he found the following note from the monsignor pinned to his door:
1. Sip the vodka, don't gulp.
2. There are ten commandments, not twelve.
3. There are twelve disciples, not ten.
4. Jesus was consecrated, not constipated.
5. Jacob wagered his donkey, he did not bet his ass.
6. We do not refer to Jesus Christ as 'the late J.C.'.
7. The Father, the Son, and the Holy Ghost are not referred to as 'Daddy, Junior, and the Spook'.
8. David slew Goliath, he did not kick the shit out of him.
9. When David was hit by a rock and was knocked off his donkey, don't say he was stoned off his ass.
10. We do not refer to the cross as the 'Big T'.
11. The Virgin Mary is not called 'Mary with the Cherry'.

1856 A young man went to confession and said: 'Father, it has been one month since my last confession. I have had sex with Pussy Green every week for the last month.'

The priest said: 'You are forgiven. Go out and say three Hail Marys.'

Ten minutes later, another man entered the confessional. 'Father,' he said, 'it has been two months since my last confession. I have had sex with Pussy Green twice a week for the last two months.'

The priest was intrigued. 'Who exactly is this Pussy Green?'

'A new woman in the neighbourhood,' replied the sinner.

'Very well,' said the priest. 'Say twelve Hail Marys.'

At Mass the next day, as the priest was preparing to deliver his sermon, a tall, beautiful woman swanned down the aisle. She was wearing a green mini-dress with matching shiny emerald green shoes.

The priest and the altar boy gasped in admiration as the woman sat before them with her legs spread slightly apart. The priest turned to the altar boy and whispered breathlessly: 'Is that Pussy Green?'

The equally smitten altar boy said: 'No, I think it's just the reflection off her shoes.'

1857 A priest was making the rounds of his parish on a bicycle when he came upon a small boy trying to sell a lawnmower.

'How much do you want for the mower?' asked the priest.

'I'm just trying to make enough money to buy a bicycle,' said the boy.

After a moment of consideration, the priest suggested: 'How about taking my bicycle in trade for it?'

The boy said: 'You've got a deal.'

The priest took the mower and tried to start it. He pulled on the string a few times, but the mower refused to respond. In frustration, he called the boy over and said: 'I can't get this mower to start.'

The boy said: 'That's because you have to swear at it to get it started.'

The priest was shocked. 'I'm a man of the church. I can't curse and swear. In fact, it's been so long since my salvation that I don't know if I could even remember how to swear.'

The boy smiled at him and said: 'Just keeping pulling on that string. It'll come back to ya!'

1858 At confession, a young guy told the priest: 'Father, I have a steady girlfriend but I'm ashamed to say I've cheated on her. Last month I went to her uncle's house to visit her, but she wasn't around. The only person there was her aunt, so I slept with her.'

'That's a bad thing to do,' said the priest.

'But that's not all,' continued the young man. 'Last week I went to my girlfriend's office, but she wasn't there. The only person around was one of her colleagues, and I ended up having sex with her.'

'That's bad,' said the priest.

'But there's more,' said the young man. 'Yesterday I went to my girlfriend's house, but she wasn't there. In fact nobody was home except her sister. We were alone and I slept with her.'

'That's very bad,' said the priest, dropping his pants.

'Father, what are you doing?' demanded the young man.

The priest answered: 'Well, your girlfriend's not here either!'

1859 O'Reilly lived alone in the countryside with only his pet dog for company. When the dog died, O'Reilly went to the parish priest and said: 'Father, my poor dog has died. Could you be saying a Mass for the poor creature?'

The priest replied: 'I'm afraid not. We cannot have church services for an animal. It would set an unhealthy precedent. But there's a new denomination in the next village, and there's no tellin' what they believe. Maybe they'll do something for the poor creature.'

'Very well, Father,' said O'Reilly. 'I'll go right away. Do you think $5,000 is enough to donate for the service?'

The priest exclaimed: 'Sweet Mary, Mother of Jesus! Why didn't you tell me the dog was Catholic?'

PRISON

1860 A group of prisoners were in a rehabilitation meeting at which they had to admit to fellow inmates what crime they had committed.

The first prisoner said: 'I'm Gavin, and I'm in for murder.' The others nodded approvingly and patted him on the back for having the courage to speak up.

The second said: 'I'm Pete, and I'm in for armed robbery.' Again the others congratulated him for being brave enough to admit to his crimes.

The third said: 'I'm Dennis, but I'm not telling you what I'm in for.'

The group leader intervened. 'You must,' he said. 'It's the only way you'll progress.'

'All right, then,' said Dennis. 'I'm in for screwing dogs.'

'That's disgusting!' shouted the others. 'How low can you go?'

'Chihuahuas,' replied Dennis.

1861 A nerdy accountant was sent to jail for embezzlement and, to his horror, was put in a cell with a big greasy biker.

That night the biker announced menacingly: 'I want to have some sex. You wanna be the husband or the wife?'

The accountant was terrified by both prospects, but decided to go for what he thought was the lesser of the two evils.

'I'll be the husband,' he stammered.

'Well,' snarled the biker, 'get over here and suck your wife's dick.'

1862 Two white guys and a black guy were sharing a cell in a US jail. The first white guy said he was doing ten years for armed robbery, but said he was lucky the gun hadn't gone off or he'd be doing life. The second white guy said he was doing twelve years for attempted murder, but reckoned he was lucky the victim had lived or he'd be doing life. The black guy said he was doing twenty years for riding his bike without a light, but figured he was lucky it wasn't night time.

1863 A man had just come out of prison after serving a forty-year sentence. In the first bar he went to, a filthy, greasy, long-haired, bearded guy came over and sat down. The ex-con couldn't help staring at him.

After a while the hairy guy asked: 'Why are you staring at me?'

The ex-con replied: 'What the hell are you?'

'I'm a hippie,' he said.

'What's a hippie?'

'Well, we believe in free love, no rules of life, and generally just hanging out doing our own thing. It's a form of philosophy.'

'Thank God!' exclaimed the ex-con. 'Forty years ago I got sent to prison for having sex with a buffalo, and I was afraid you might be my son!'

1864 Two hardened prisoners in a maximum-security prison were talking.

The first said: 'I've got two tickets for the warden's ball. Do you want to buy one?'

'No, thanks, mate. I can't dance.'

'It's not a dance, it's a raffle!'

PSYCHICS AND MEDIUMS

1865 A frog phoned the Psychic Hotline and was told, 'You are going to meet a beautiful young woman who will want to know everything about you.'

The frog said, 'That's great! Will I meet her at a party, or what?'

'No,' replied the psychic. 'Next term – in her biology class.'

1866 A ventriloquist decided to set up in business using his dummy as a medium. One day a woman approached him and said she wanted to contact her dead husband.

'How much would it cost me to get in touch with my husband via your dummy?' she asked.

The ventriloquist said: 'If you only want to hear him speak, it's $30. If you want to have a conversation with him, it's $50. And I charge $75 if you want a conversation with him while I'm drinking a glass of water.'

1867 Strolling through a fairground, a guy arrived at a palm reader's table. 'For fifteen dollars I can read your love line and tell your romantic future,' said the mysterious old woman.

The guy agreed, and the reader took one look at his open palm and said: 'I can see that you have no girlfriend.'

'That's true,' said the guy.

'Oh, my goodness, you are extremely lonely, aren't you?' added the woman.

'Yes,' he admitted. 'That's amazing. Can you tell all of this from my love line?'

'Love line? No, from the calluses and blisters.'

PUBIC HAIR

1868 As her fellow passengers got off to do some sightseeing on a senior citizens' coach tour, one old lady surprised the driver by going up to him and whispering in his ear: 'Driver, I believe I have just been sexually harassed.'

The driver thought she was probably imagining it but, to keep her quiet, he promised to investigate it as soon as he could.

Later that day, when the passengers were unloading at another stop, a second old lady whispered in the driver's ear: 'Sir, I think I have just been sexually harassed.'

This time, the driver knew he had to do something. A few passengers had remained on the coach, so he decided to ask them whether they had seen or heard anything untoward. He found one little old man crawling along the floor of the coach underneath the seats.

Bending down to question him, the driver said: 'Excuse me, sir. Can I help you?'

The old man looked up and said: 'Well, sonny, sure you can. I've lost my toupee and I'm trying to find it. I thought I'd located it twice, but they were parted in the middle, and mine's parted on the side.'

1869 What's the similarity between a woman's pubic hair and parsley? – You have to push it to one side before you start to eat.

1870 What do you call a female police officer that shaves her pubic hair? – Cunt stubble.

1871 A little girl was licking a lollipop at the hairdresser's and accidentally dropped it into a heap of cut hair lying on the floor.
The hairdresser said: 'Oh, have you got hair on your lollipop?'
The girl said: 'No, I'm only three.'

1872 When Terry walked into a bar for the first time in two months, his friends couldn't help noticing that he had a radiant glow. His skin seemed particularly smooth; in fact he looked years younger.
'Have you joined a fitness club?' they asked.
'No, I've got a new girlfriend.'
'How does a new girlfriend give you such healthy-looking, smooth skin on your face?'
Terry explained: 'She's got the hairiest pussy I've ever seen. She's like a wire brush down there. So going down on her is the quickest way I know to exfoliate and moisturize my face at the same time!'

1873 A woman was towelling off in front of the mirror when she noticed a few grey pubic hairs. She bent down and said to her privates: 'I know you haven't been getting much lately, but I didn't know you were so worried about it.'

1874 What's got 400 legs and no pubic hair? – The front row of a Hanson concert.

1875 A guy met a hooker on the street. He said: 'Let's go down this alley. I've got fifteen bucks.'
'Fifteen bucks!' she scoffed. 'For fifteen bucks, all you can do is look at it.'
Reluctantly he agreed.
So they went down the alley, and she dropped her panties. He sank to his knees but it was so dark that he lit his lighter to get a better view of her

pussy. 'Gee,' he said. 'Your pubic hair . . . it's so thick, so matted, so lustrous. It's beautiful.'

'Thank you,' she said.

'Can I ask you a personal question?' he said.

'Sure.'

'Can you pee through all that hair?'

'Sure.'

'Well, then, you'd better start, because you're on fire!'

PUERTO RICANS

1876 A muscular Puerto Rican was sitting in his favourite bar minding his own business when a little gay guy came in and sat next to him. The Puerto Rican glanced at the gay guy but carried on drinking his beer. Neither said anything to the other, but the gay guy kept throwing admiring looks in the direction of the Puerto Rican. Seven beers later, the gay guy finally summoned up the courage to say something to the Puerto Rican. Whispering in his ear, he asked the Puerto Rican if he would like a blow job.

The Puerto Rican immediately jumped down from his stool and began pummelling the gay guy black and blue before dragging him outside and dumping him in the parking lot, barely clinging to life. The Puerto Rican then quietly returned to his bar stool as if nothing had happened. When he had finished his beer, he asked the bartender for another.

The bartender said: 'If you don't mind me asking, what was all that about? I've never seen you so angry. What did that little guy say to you?'

The Puerto Rican replied disgustedly: 'He said something about a job.'

1877 Why is there so little Puerto Rican literature? – Because spray paint wasn't invented until 1949.

1878 How many Puerto Ricans does it take to grease a car? – Just one if you hit him right.

1879 How many people does it take to bury a Puerto Rican? – Five. One to lower the body, and four to lower the radio.

1880 How do you shoot a Puerto Rican in the head? – Aim for his radio.

1881 How do you starve a Puerto Rican to death? – Hide his food stamps under his work shoes.

1882 What's the difference between a Puerto Rican and a park bench? – A park bench can support a family of four.

1883 How do you get twelve Puerto Ricans into a Volkswagen Beetle? – Throw in a welfare cheque.

1884 How do you get twelve Puerto Ricans out of a Volkswagen Beetle? – Throw in a job application.

1885 Two Puerto Ricans in a car without any music. Who's driving? – The police.

1886 Why aren't there any Puerto Ricans on *Star Trek*? – Because they're not going to work in the future either.

1887 A prostitute had a price list – $10 to do it on grass, $20 to do it on the couch, $30 to do it in bed.
     One morning an American came in and gave her $10. She escorted him to the backyard and they did it on the grass.
     Later in the day a Canadian came in and gave her $20. She took him through to the living-room and they did it on the couch.
     In the evening a Puerto Rican came in and handed her $30.
     The prostitute said: 'Man, you got class.'
     He said: 'Class my ass, I want it three times on the grass.'

1888 How do you save a drowning Puerto Rican? – Throw him an anchor.

1889 What do you call a hitchhiking Puerto Rican? – Stranded.

1890 How do you get a Puerto Rican out of the bath? – Turn on the water.

1891 What's the Puerto Rican national anthem? – 'Row, Row, Row Your Boat'.

1892 Why are Puerto Ricans like sperm? – Thousands of them get in, but only one of them works.

1893 An American, a Mexican and a Puerto Rican were walking down the street when a genie suddenly appeared and granted each of them a wish.

The Mexican wished that he and all other Mexicans could return to live happily in their homeland.

The Puerto Rican wished that he and all other Puerto Ricans could return to live happily in their homeland.

Finally it was the American's turn. Before making his wish, he said to the genie: 'Let me get this straight. I can wish for anything I want, and all the Mexicans and Puerto Ricans are already gone?'

'That's right,' said the genie.

'OK,' said the American, 'then I'll have a Coke.'

1894 What do you get at a Puerto Rican garage sale? – Your stuff back.

1895 What runs faster than a Puerto Rican with a TV? – His brother with your VCR.

1896 What do you call an American surrounded by two hundred Puerto Ricans? – Warden.

RABBIS

1897 A rabbi and a priest were walking down the street together when they fancied a drink. The only problem was, neither of them had any money. Standing outside a bar, the priest said: 'Leave it to me. I know how we can get free drinks.'

While the rabbi stood watching at the door, the priest walked into the bar and ordered a drink. After finishing it, he was about to leave when the bartender gave him his tab.

The priest said: 'But, my son, I've already paid for the drink.'

The bartender said: 'I'm terribly sorry, Father, but it's been really busy in here. I must have forgotten.'

Then it was the rabbi's turn. He walked in, ordered his drink and after finishing it, he was about to leave when the bartender handed him his tab.

The rabbi said: 'Excuse me, but I paid you when I ordered the drink.'

'I'm terribly sorry, rabbi,' said the bartender. 'I don't know what's wrong with me, but that's the second time it's happened to me today.'

'That's OK,' said the rabbi. 'No offence taken. Now, if you just give me change for the twenty I gave you, I'll be on my way.'

1898 A rabbi kept a jar full of foreskins on his desk as mementos of the many circumcisions that he had performed over the years. One day he took the foreskins to a leatherworker and asked him what he could do with them. The leatherworker said: 'Come back in two days.'

The rabbi returned two days later, and the leatherworker presented him with a wallet. 'One lousy wallet!' snorted the rabbi. 'Was that all you could make out of that entire jar of foreskins?'

'Listen,' said the leatherworker. 'You rub it a little bit, and it turns into a briefcase.'

1899 Although good friends for a number of years, a priest and a rabbi were always arguing the finer points of their respective theologies, each trying to prove the other wrong. One day the car in which they were travelling was involved in a bad smash, somersaulting four times before ending up on its roof. The priest and the rabbi crawled from the wreckage, just relieved to be alive.

As the priest crossed himself, he noticed the rabbi doing the same. 'Praise be!' shouted the priest. 'You've seen the light!'

'What do you mean?' asked the rabbi.

'You,' said the priest. 'You've crossed yourself. You have seen the true way. This is wonderful!'

'Cross myself?' said the rabbi. 'No way. I was just checking everything was OK: spectacles, testicles, wallet, and watch.'

1900 A Catholic priest, a Methodist preacher and a rabbi were discussing how they divided up their collection money.

The priest said: 'I draw a line down the centre of the room, then I throw the collection money up in the air. Whatever lands on the left side of the line belongs to God; whatever lands on the right is mine.'

The preacher revealed: 'I draw a circle in the middle of the room. Whatever lands in the circle is God's, and the rest is mine.'

The rabbi said: 'I take the collection money, throw it high in the air, and tell God to take what he wants. Whatever comes back down is mine.'

1901 A man got off a plane in Boston, Massachusetts, and went to the men's room. It was crowded but he managed to find a vacant urinal.

Suddenly the man next to him said: 'You're Jewish, aren't you?'

'Yes.'

'And you come from Springfield?'

'Yes, that's right.'

'And your parents went to Temple Emmanuel?'

'Yes. How do you know so much about me?'

'Because Rabbi Minski of Temple Emmanuel is the only rabbi I know who performs circumcisions by cutting at an angle . . . and you're pissing in my shoe!'

REDNECKS

1902 Jesse, an old army buddy, came to stay at Bubba's house. After sharing a few beers, supplies began to run low, so Bubba went to the store to get some more drink. As he was leaving the house, he told his wife, Lindy-Lou, to show Jesse her best southern hospitality while he was out. Lindy-Lou said she would.

Forty minutes later, Bubba came back with the beer and found Jesse screwing Lindy-Lou on the kitchen floor.

Bubba yelled: 'What are you doing, Lindy-Lou?'

She replied: 'You told me to show Jesse my best southern hospitality.'

'For God's sake, woman,' raged Bubba, 'arch your back — poor Jesse's balls are on the cold floor.'

1903 What is a redneck's favourite food? — Pump kin.

1904 One day Bubba decided to go hang-gliding. Shortly after he'd taken to the air, Zeke and Mary-Lou were sitting on their porch when she spotted the biggest bird she'd ever seen. Zeke immediately grabbed his shotgun and fired off three shots, but the monster bird continued to sail silently over the treetops.

'I reckon ya missed him, Zeke,' said Mary-Lou.

'Yeah, maybe,' said Zeke. 'But at least he let go of ole Bubba, didn't he?'

1905 A young guy graduated from the University of Alabama with a degree in journalism. His first assignment for the newspaper that hired him was to write a human interest story. Being from Alabama, he went back there to do his research. His first call was at an old farmer's house, way back in the hills. After explaining the purpose of his visit, he asked the farmer: 'Has anything ever happened around here that made you happy?'

The farmer thought for a minute and said: 'Yep! One time one of my neighbour's sheep got lost. We formed a posse and found it. We all screwed it and took it back home.'

'I can't print that!' the young guy exclaimed. 'Can you think of anything else that has happened which made you or a lot of other people happy?'

After another moment's thought, the farmer said: 'Yep! One time my neighbour's daughter, a good-looking girl, got lost. We formed a big posse and found her. After we all screwed her, we took her back home.'

The young man said: 'I can't print that either. Has anything ever happened around here that made you sad?'

The farmer lowered his head and a tear came into his eye. A few seconds later, he looked up at the young reporter and said timidly: 'I got lost once . . .'

Signs That a Redneck has Been Using Your Computer:

1906   ● The monitor is up on blocks.

1907   ● Outgoing faxes have tobacco stains on them.

1908   ● The keyboard is camouflaged.

1909   ● The password is 'Bubba'.

1910   ● The six front keys have rotted out.

1911   ● The extra RAM ports have truck parts stored in them.

1912   ● The numeric keypad only goes up to three.

1913   ● There's a gun rack mounted on the CPU.

1914   ● There's a Coors can in the CD-ROM drive.

1915   ● The mouse is referred to as a 'critter'.

1916   Big Bubba decided it was time his fourteen-year-old son Billy Bob learned the facts of life. So he took him to the town brothel, an outwardly respectable establishment fronted by a beauty parlour.

The middle-aged Madame said: 'Bubba, you've been such a good customer down the years, I'll see to the boy personally.'

She was as good as her word and led Billy Bob up to a quiet room where she proceeded to have sex with him. Afterwards she said: 'As this was your first time, I'm going to see that you get the full treatment before you leave. I'm going to give you a manicure.'

Two weeks later, Bubba and Billy Bob bumped into her in the main street. Billy Bob was uncharacteristically shy.

The Madame said: 'Billy Bob, don't you remember me?'

'Yes, ma'am,' replied Billy Bob quietly. 'You're the lady that gave me the crabs, then cut off my fingernails so I couldn't scratch 'em.'

1917 What do a tornado and a redneck divorce have in common? – Somebody's gonna lose a trailer.

1918 A redneck patient was told by his doctor: 'Until the penicillin cleans out your infection, you ain't to have no relations whatsoever.'
'OK,' said the redneck, 'but what about friends and neighbours?'

1919 A young hillbilly and his new bride visited the doctor because they didn't know how to go about having kids. The doctor showed them a sex manual, but they just looked bewildered. Realizing he would have to communicate in simpler terms, the doctor slowly explained the birds and bees to them, but still they looked blank. Exasperated, the doctor grabbed the bride, laid her on the examining table and screwed her.
'Now do you understand?' asked the doctor.
'Yes, sir,' replied the hillbilly. 'Just one question though: how often do I have to bring her in?'

1920 What do you call a redneck with an IQ of 120? – A suburb.

1921 Ellie-Mae passed away and Bubba called 911. The 911 operator told him she'd send someone out right away.
'Where do you live?' asked the operator.
'At the end of Eucalyptus Drive,' answered Bubba.
'Can you spell that for me?'
There was a long pause, then Bubba said: 'How 'bout if I drag her over to Oak Street, and you pick her up there?'

1922 Two rednecks were courting in cattle country. One evening as they were sitting on the porch watching the sun go down, the young guy spotted his prize bull doing the business on one of his cows. Sighing contentedly, he plucked up the courage to say: 'Ellie-Mae, I'd sure like to be doing what that bull is doing.'
'Go ahead,' said Ellie-Mae. 'It *is* your cow.'

1923 Did you hear about the divorced redneck? – He wondered if his ex-wife was still his sister.

1924 An Alabama State Trooper pulled over a pickup truck and said to the driver: 'Got any ID?'
The driver said: ' 'Bout what?'

1925   Why do drivers' education classes in redneck schools use the car only on Mondays, Wednesdays, and Fridays? – Because on Tuesday and Thursday, the sex education class uses it.

1926   Bubba decided he wanted to get married to his sweetheart.

'Bubba, you can't get married yet,' said his mother. 'You're the baby of the family.'

'But, Ma,' protested Bubba, 'I just had my 37th birthday last week.'

'We know that, Bubba,' said his father, 'but your ma and me think you should put off getting married until after you graduate from high school.'

1927   Why is it so difficult to solve a redneck murder? – No dental records.

1928   A woman from Arkansas was in the welfare office filling out forms. The welfare officer asked her how many children she had.

'Ten boys,' she said.

'And what are their names?' he asked.

'Leroy, Leroy, Leroy, Leroy, Leroy, Leroy, Leroy, Leroy, Leroy and Leroy.'

'All named Leroy? Why would you give all your kids the same name?'

'That way, when I wants them all to come in from the yard or for dinner, I just yells "Leroy". And they all come.'

'What if you just want a particular one of them to do something?'

'Then I calls him by his last name.'

1929   What do you call the sweat produced when two rednecks are having sex? – Relative humidity.

1930   Billy-Bob was riding in Jed's truck. Suddenly Jed pulled over, got out, pointed to a field and said misty eyed: 'That's where I first had sex.'

'How was it?' asked Billy-Bob.

'Great,' replied Jed. 'Until I looked up and saw her mom was watching.'

'Holy shit! What did she say?'

'Baaaa.'

1931   Two Alabama State Troopers were chasing a suspect car towards Georgia. When the suspect crossed the Georgia line, the first Trooper immediately pulled over.

His colleague said: 'Why did you stop?'

The first Trooper replied: 'He's in Georgia now. They're an hour ahead of us, so we'll never catch him.'

1932 A small wild animal park in Arkansas acquired a rare species of gorilla. Unfortunately they only had the one – a female – as a result of which there seemed little prospect of establishing a breeding programme. Within weeks, the gorilla was in heat, but with no male available, the park chiefs could only watch in frustration. Then one of them came up with an idea: redneck men are not renowned for being choosy and, if the money was right, maybe one of them could be persuaded to impregnate the gorilla. So they decided to approach Ed, a part-time redneck intern at the park.

The park manager called Ed into his office. 'Ed, I know this is a strange request, but would you be willing to have sex with the gorilla for $500?'

Ed said he'd like to go away and think about. The next day he returned with his answer.

'Yes, sir, I'll do it . . . but on three conditions. First, I don't want to have to kiss the gorilla. Second, you must never tell anyone about this . . .'

'And thirdly?'

'You gotta give me another week to come up with the $500.'

1933 Arkansas police were conducting a campaign to round up all stray dogs and those without a licence. Billy-Bob was driving along in his good ole pickup truck when a police officer pulled him over.

'What's the problem, officer?' asked Billy-Bob.

The officer pointed to Ole Blue, Billy-Bob's hunting dog, which was sitting in the passenger seat, and said: 'Does that dog have a licence?'

Billy-Bob replied: 'No, sir, he don't need one. You see, I do all the driving myself.'

RESTAURANTS

1934 A customer at a restaurant noticed that all the staff had spoons in their shirt pockets. So he asked the waiter at his table: 'Why the spoons?'

The waiter explained: 'The restaurant's owners hired a consulting firm to revamp all of our processes. After several months of analysis, they concluded that the spoon was the most dropped utensil – approximately three spoons per table per hour. So if our personnel were better prepared, we could reduce the number of trips back to the kitchen and save fifteen man-hours per shift.'

The customer was impressed, all the more so when he accidentally dropped his spoon and the waiter was able to replace it with his spare.

Then the customer spotted that all the waiters had a piece of string hanging from their flies. Curious, he asked his waiter: 'Can you tell me why you have that string right there?'

'Certainly,' said the waiter, lowering his voice. 'That consulting firm I mentioned also found that we can save time in the restroom. By tying this string to the tip of you know what, we can pull it out without touching it and eliminate the need to wash our hands, thus shortening the time in the restroom by 76.26%.'

'But after you get it out,' asked the customer, 'how do you put it back?'

'I don't know about the others,' whispered the waiter, 'but I use the spoon.'

1935 A drunk staggered into a diner and ordered a couple of eggs. The waiter, fearing that they had run out, went into the kitchen to check with the chef.

'Have we got any more eggs left?' he asked.

The chef replied: 'I'm right out of fresh eggs. There's just two rotten eggs left.'

The waiter said: 'That's OK. Give him the rotten eggs. He's so drunk he won't know the difference.'

So the chef scrambled the rotten eggs, and heaped on hash browns, sausage and toast. The drunk was so hungry he wolfed down the breakfast without saying a word.

When the drunk went to pay, he said to the cashier: 'Where did you get those eggs?'

She said: 'We have our own chicken farm.'

'Do you have a rooster?' asked the drunk.

'No,' she said.

'Well,' advised the drunk, 'you'd better get one, because some skunk is screwing your chickens.'

1936 A hobo in a greasy spoon diner asked the waitress for a meatloaf dinner and some kind words. She brought the meatloaf, but didn't say a thing.

'Hey, what about the kind words?' he asked.

She said: 'Don't eat the meatloaf.'

1937 A man walked into a hamburger bar and ordered a regular meal. But halfway through his meal he found a small hair in the hamburger and called the waitress to complain. The waitress took him to see the cook who was flattening meat patty under his armpit.

'That's disgusting!' said the man.

The waitress said: 'You think that's disgusting, you should see him make donuts!'

You Might be Under-Qualified for a Fast-Food Job If:

1938   • When a customer asks for his change, you instinctively say, 'Would you like fries with that?'

1939   • Your uniform doubles as your 'going out' clothes.

1940   • There is more grease on your body than in the fryer.

1941   • You can't count to twenty with your shoes on.

1942   • You squeeze your zits into the coleslaw bowl.

1943   • Your name tag serves as an invaluable reminder.

1944   • You think to yourself, 'Here's a job with a future.'

1945   A waiter in a restaurant carried a bowl of soup to the table with his fingers dangling in the soup.

'What are you doing with your fingers in my soup?' demanded the customer.

'It keeps them warm,' said the waiter.

'Well, why don't you poke them up your ass?'

'I do . . . in the kitchen.'

1946   A guy walked into a downmarket New York diner and saw a sign hanging over the counter which read: 'cheese sandwich $1.50; chicken sandwich $2.00; hand job $5.00.'

Checking his wallet for the necessary money, he walked up to the counter and beckoned to one of the attractive women serving a line of eager-looking middle-aged men.

'Yes?' she inquired with a knowing smile. 'Can I help you?'

'I was wondering,' whispered the man, 'are you the one who gives the hand jobs?'

'Yes,' she purred. 'I am.'

The man said: 'Well, wash your fucking hands – I want a cheese sandwich!'

1947   A woman was dining in a restaurant in a small country town in the Mid-West. She had ordered chicken, but part-way through her meal she began to choke uncontrollably on a chicken bone. Two country boys spotted her plight and went over to help. The first quickly dropped his overalls and bent over the woman's table, enabling the second country boy to begin licking his butt. The woman was so grossed out by the sight of one guy licking the other's butt that she puked all over the floor, dislodging the chicken bone from her throat.

The first country boy immediately pulled his overalls back up and said to the other: 'You're right, Eddie, that hind-lick manoeuvre works like a charm.'

RIDDLES

1948 How can you tell if a crab is an insomniac? – It only sleeps in snatches.

1949 What was John Lennon's last hit? – The pavement.

1950 Why did Mark Chapman shoot John Lennon? – Yoko ducked.

1951 What fruit has seven dents? – Snow White's cherry.

1952 What's the difference between love, true love and showing off? – Spit, swallow and gargle.

1953 What's the definition of eternity? – The time between when you cum and she leaves.

1954 What do you do when the dishwasher quits working? – Slap her.

1955 What do you call five dogs with no balls? – The Spice Girls.

1956 Why do Montana stadiums have Astroturf? – To stop the cheerleaders grazing.

1957 What did Cinderella do when she got to the ball? – Gagged.

1958 What do Lifesavers do that a man can't? – Come in eight flavours.

1959 Why can't Miss Piggy count to 70? – Because she gets a frog in her throat at 69.

1960 Why did the bee cross his legs? – Because he couldn't find the BP station.

1961 What goes 10, 9, 8, 7, 6, 5, 4, 3 . . .? – Bo Derek getting older.

1962 What's the best thing about line dancing? – One grenade gets them all.

1963 What slides down toilet walls? – George Michael's latest release.

1964 How do you know a man is a really bad dancer? – When he can still step on Dolly Parton's toes.

1965 If they bring shrimps home on shrimp boats, fish home on fish boats, and clams home on clam boats, what do they bring crabs home on? – The captain's dinghy.

1966 How did the Dairy Queen get pregnant? – The Burger King didn't cover his whopper.

1967 What is thirty feet long, has ten teeth, and smells of piss? – The front row at an Andy Williams concert.

1968 What has balls and screws old ladies? – A bingo machine.

1969 What has hindsight? – A stag during the rutting season.

1970 How do you piss off Winnie the Pooh? – By sticking your finger in his honey.

1971 Who invented break dancing? – A guy trying to steal hubcaps off a moving car.

1972 What looks like Blu-tak, feels like Blu-tak, tastes like Blu-tak, but isn't Blu-tak? – Smurf poo.

1973 What goes 'Mark!' – A dog with a harelip.

1974 How did the teenager know he had bad acne? – His dog called him Spot.

1975 What is an innuendo? – An Italian suppository.

1976 What's ten inches long, two inches thick, and starts with a P? – A really good crap.

1977 If Eve wore a fig leaf, what did Adam wear? – A hole in it.

1978 Why was the washing machine laughing? – Because it was taking the piss out of the underwear.

1979 What do you get if you cross Tina Turner with an orangutan? – An ugly orangutan.

1980 Why does it suck to be an egg? – You only get laid once, you only get eaten once, it takes fifteen minutes to get hard, three minutes to get soft, and the only chick who will sit on your face is your mother.

1981 Why does Tigger have no friends? – Because he plays with Pooh.

1982 What's white, sticky, and falls from the sky? – The coming of the Lord.

1983 What's the noisiest thing in the world? – Two skeletons screwing on a tin roof.

1984 What is the lightest thing in the world? – A penis: even a thought can raise it.

1985 What's green and smells like pork? – Kermit's finger.

1986 Why did the lump of snot cross the road? – Because he was being picked on.

1987 What's the difference between sin and shame? – It's a sin to put it in, but it's a shame to pull it out.

1988 What's round, hard, and sticks so far out of his pyjamas that a man can stick his hat on it? – His head.

1989 What's red and white and sits in trees? – A sanitary owl.

1990 What's the difference between a pickpocket and a peeping Tom? – A pickpocket snatches watches.

1991 What's a hospice? – About three gallons.

1992 Why did Raggedy Anne get thrown out of the toy box? – Because she kept sitting on Pinocchio's face, moaning, 'Lie to me!'

1993 Why did Humpty Dumpty push Mrs Dumpty off the wall? – To see her crack.

1994 Who has blonde hair, surgically enhanced 32E breasts, and is the richest woman in Switzerland? – Osama bin Laden.

ROYALTY

1995 The Kings of Spain, France and England were taking part in a public competition to discover which of them had the biggest penis. As the King of Spain whipped his out, the Spanish crowd cheered 'Viva España!' Next the French King dropped his pants, and his dick was even bigger. 'Vive la France!' roared the French supporters. Finally the King of England produced his massive member. After a stunned silence, everyone exclaimed: 'God Save the Queen!'

1996 When Prince Charles turned up for an official visit to Mansfield, the mayor was surprised to see him wearing a large hat made from red fur. Eventually the mayor asked: 'Excuse me, sir, but if you don't mind me asking, why are you wearing such unusual headgear today?'

'Well,' explained Charles, 'when I told Daddy that I was going to Mansfield, he said: "Wear the fox hat."'

1997 Camilla Parker Bowles bought Prince Charles a bookmark for his birthday. It was to stop him bending the pages over.

1998 Keen to arrange a royal marriage for his daughter, a king advertised her availability on the Internet. Before allowing her to meet the applicants in person and in order to determine the character of the potential suitors, the king took the precaution of spraying her private parts with green glitter.

The first guy turned up, but when the king inspected his dick the following morning, it was covered in green glitter. The suitor was immediately struck off the list. It was the same with the next ten men: the next morning their members were all covered with green glitter. Finally, a guy came along who passed the green glitter test. There was not a trace of glitter on his dick. The king was thrilled, and offered the man his daughter's hand in marriage. The guy let out a whoop of delight . . . and revealed a mouth full of green glitter.

RUSSIANS

1999 A Russian walked into a bar and ordered a beer.

'That will be one rouble,' said the bartender.

'One rouble!' protested the customer. 'Last week it was only fifty kopecks!'

'Well,' replied the bartender, 'it's fifty kopecks for the beer and fifty kopecks for the perestroika.'

Reluctantly, the customer handed the bartender a rouble. To his surprise, the bartender gave him back fifty kopecks and said: 'We're out of beer.'

2000 An Englishman, a Swede and a Russian were studying a painting of Adam and Eve in the Garden of Eden.

'Look at that beautiful garden,' said the Englishman. 'Only an Englishman could grow a garden as beautiful as that.'

'Nonsense,' said the Swede. 'They're naked and proud of it – they must be Scandinavian.'

'Rubbish,' said the Russian. 'No clothes, no house, one apple between them, and they're told it's paradise – definitely Russian.'

2001 A Russian man decided he wanted to buy a car, so he phoned the factory and asked: 'How long do I have to wait for a car if I place my order immediately?'

The salesman said: 'Your car will be delivered in five years. Let me see now . . . that will be Friday 8 October, 2010.'

'Will that be morning or afternoon?' asked the customer.

The salesman was stunned. 'When you've waited five years, what does it matter whether the car arrives in the morning or the afternoon?'

The customer said: 'Because the plumber is coming in the morning.'

2002 What's 100 feet long and lives on potatoes? – A Russian meat queue.

2003 A man waiting in a Moscow theatre queue tapped the guy in front of him on the shoulder. 'Are you a member of the Secret Police?' he asked.

'No.'

'Are any of your family in the Secret Police?'

'No.'

'Do you have any friends in the Secret Police?'

'No, I don't.'

'Good. In that case, would you mind getting off my bloody foot?'

2004 There were two friends in Moscow, both of whom were habitual drunks. One of them – Alexei – was happy, the other – Vladimir – was sad.

Alexei said: 'What is troubling you, my friend?'

Vladimir answered: 'When I get home drunk, my wife locks the door. I have to walk the streets for many hours, and get into trouble with the police. They want to get rid of me at work. So you see, nothing to cheer about.'

'I had that problem in the past,' revealed Alexei, 'but found a solution. I am undressing naked at the stairways, press the bell button. When my wife opens the door, I throw my clothes inside. She is afraid of the scandal, so she lets me in.'

'That sounds good plan,' said Vladimir. 'I will try it.'

A few weeks later, they met again, but Vladimir was more miserable than usual. 'What happened?' asked Alexei. 'Did you try my method?'

'Let me tell you,' replied Vladimir sombrely. 'I undressed, I pressed the button. The door opened. I threw in all of my clothes. The door closed. And then I heard: "Next station – Red Square." '

2005 A customer asked a sales assistant in a Russian department store: 'Don't you have any shoes here?'

The assistant said: 'No, we don't have any electrical goods here. No shoes is the next floor up.'

SCHOOL

2006 The science teacher stood in front of the class and said: 'Children, if you could have one raw material in the world, what would it be?'

Little Jimmy raised his hand and said: 'I would want gold, because gold is worth a lot of money and I could buy a Corvette.'

The teacher nodded, and then she called on little Jenny.

Little Jenny said: 'I would want platinum, because platinum is worth more than gold and I could buy a Ferrari.'

The teacher smiled, then called on little Johnny.

Little Johnny stood up and said: 'I would want silicone.'

The teacher asked: 'Silicone? Why silicone?'

Little Johnny said: 'Because my mom has two bags of the stuff and you should see all the sports cars outside our house!'

2007 At school one day, the teacher said: 'Today, we are going to learn multi-syllable words. Now, does anybody have an example of a multi-syllable word?'

Little Johnny put up his hand: 'Me, Miss Johnson, me, me!'

'All right, Johnny,' said the teacher. 'What is your multi-syllable word?'

'Mas-tur-bate,' he replied.

'My!' said Miss Johnson, blushing. 'That's a mouthful!'

Little Johnny said: 'No, Miss Johnson, you're thinking of a blow job.'

2008 What was Dolly Parton voted in school? – Most likely to breast-feed Ethiopia.

2009 One morning, the teacher noticed a small boy squirming at the back of the class, scratching his crotch and not paying attention. When she asked him what the problem was, he said that he'd recently been circumcized and was quite itchy. The teacher told him to go to the principal's office and to phone his mother and ask her what he should do about it.

The boy went to the principal's office and then returned to his class. A few minutes later, there was a sudden commotion at the back. Investigating, the teacher found him sitting at his desk with his penis hanging out.

'I thought I told you to call your mother?' said the teacher.

'I did,' said the boy. 'She told me if I could stick it out till noon, she'd come and pick me up from school.'

2010 *Teacher.* Why weren't you at school yesterday?

Little Johnny. My grandpa got burnt.

Teacher. I'm sorry to hear that. He wasn't burnt too badly, was he?

Little Johnny. Oh, yes. They really know what they're doing at those crematoriums.

2011 One day, during a lesson on English grammar, the teacher asked for a show of hands from those who could use the word 'beautiful' twice in the same sentence.

First, she called on Monica who responded with: 'My father bought my mother a beautiful dress, and she looked beautiful in it.'

'Very good, Monica,' said the teacher. Then she asked David for his answer, and he said: 'The beautiful flowers make the whole garden look beautiful.'

'Excellent, David,' said the teacher. Then she asked Little Johnny for his sentence.

Little Johnny answered: 'Last night at the dinner table, my sister told my father that she was pregnant, and he said: "Beautiful, just fucking beautiful!"'

2012 After class, a busty thirteen-year-old girl went up to the male teacher and said: 'Can you give me a cigarette?'

'No, of course not,' said the teacher. 'Do you want to get me into trouble?'

'OK,' she said. 'But I'd still rather have a cigarette.'

2013 Little Jenny had little interest in Sunday School and usually slept through class. One day the teacher called on her while she was napping. 'Tell me, Jenny,' she said. 'Who created the universe?'

When Jenny didn't stir, Johnny, who was sitting in the chair behind her, jabbed her in the backside with a pin.

'God Almighty!' shouted Jenny.

'Very good,' said the teacher, and Jenny fell back asleep.

Twenty minutes later, the teacher asked Jenny: 'Who is our Lord and Saviour?'

Jenny remained sound asleep until Johnny came to her rescue again by prodding her sharply with the pin.

'Jesus Christ!' shouted Jenny.

'That's right,' said the teacher, and Jenny went back to sleep.

Ten minutes later, the teacher asked Jenny a third question: 'What did Eve say to Adam after she had her twenty-third child?'

Once again, Johnny jabbed her with the pin. This time Jenny jumped up and shouted: 'If you stick that fucking thing in me one more time, I'll break it in half and stick it up your arse!'

The teacher fainted.

2014 The dean at an exclusive girls' school was lecturing students on sexual morality. 'In moments of temptation,' she said, 'ask yourself this: is an hour of pleasure worth a lifetime of shame?'

A girl at the back asked: 'How do you make it last an hour?'

2015 The young female teacher walked into the classroom and noticed that someone had written the word 'Penis' in tiny letters on the chalkboard. She hastily rubbed the word off and began class. The next day the word 'Penis' was written again, this time in slightly larger letters. Not wishing to draw attention to the incident, she quickly rubbed out the offending word and started class. This went on for the rest of the week. Each morning, the word 'Penis' would be written on the board in ever-increasing size and each time she would rub it off vigorously. When the teacher arrived at school the following Monday, she expected to be greeted by the same word on the board, but instead found the message: 'The more you rub it, the bigger it gets.'

2016 It was the first day of a new school year. Three boys arrived late for class, and the teacher asked the first boy: 'Why are you late?'

The boy replied: 'I've been on Honeysuckle Hill.'

'Take your seat,' said the teacher.

Then she asked the second boy why he was late.

'I've also been on Honeysuckle Hill,' he answered.

And when the teacher asked the third boy why he was late, he gave the same answer. As the boys were sitting down, a girl walked in to class.

'Let me guess,' said the teacher. 'You too were on Honeysuckle Hill?'

'No,' the girl replied. 'I am Honeysuckle Hill.'

2017 Little Johnny was sitting in his Catholic school classroom. The nun said: 'Do you know where little boys and girls go when they do bad things?'

'Sure,' said Johnny. 'They go out back of the school yard.'

2018 A kindergarten teacher was taking her class through the alphabet by asking them to name words that began with each letter. However she was anxious to avoid the answers of one child, Darryl, who had a tendency to use rude words.

She began with 'A', and everyone put up their hands. Ignoring Darryl, who was almost certain to say 'ass', the teacher instead asked Lisa, who came up with 'apple'. She then moved on to 'B'. Again the whole class raised their hands but, rather than hear Darryl shout something like 'bitch', the teacher opted for Alvin, who offered 'bridge'. But as the teacher pressed on through the alphabet, the children's enthusiasm began to wane until, by the time she reached 'R', only Darryl had his hand raised. She realised she had no choice but to hear Darryl's suggestion.

'OK, Darryl,' she said, taking a deep breath, 'what word starts with "R"?'

'Rat,' replied Darryl.

'Rat?' repeated the teacher incredulously, but hugely relieved. 'That's it? Rat?'

'Yeah,' said Darryl. 'Big-ass mother-fuckin' rat with a twelve-inch dick!'

2019 The male biology teacher at a girls' private school asked during class: 'Miss Hodgson, would you name the organ in the human body which, under the appropriate conditions, expands to six times its normal size, and define the conditions?'

A shocked Miss Hodgson replied loftily: 'I don't think that is a proper question to ask me. I assure you that my parents will hear of this.' And with that, she sat down, red-faced.

Unperturbed, the teacher called on Miss Upton and asked the same question. Miss Upton, with calm composure, replied: 'The pupil of the eye, in dim light.'

'Correct,' said the teacher. 'Now, Miss Hodgson, I have three things to say to you: one, you have not done your homework; two, you have a dirty mind; and three, you will someday be faced with a dreadful disappointment!'

2020 A young female teacher was giving a lengthy assignment to sixth grade, a task which required her to write high on the chalkboard. As she did so, she could hear one of the boys giggling.

'What's so funny, Eric?' she asked.

'I just saw one of your garters, Miss.'

The teacher was furious. 'Get out of my classroom, and don't come back for three days!'

As the class settled down again, she realized she had omitted a word from the top line and reached up high on the chalkboard. Once again, she heard a boy giggling.

'What's so funny, Billy?'

'I just saw both of your garters, Miss.'

The teacher was even angrier than before. 'Get out of my classroom, and don't come back for three weeks!'

She was now so flustered that she dropped the eraser. As she bent over to pick it up, she heard more giggling. She stood up to see little Johnny leaving the classroom.

'Where do you think you're going?' she barked.

Little Johnny replied: 'From what I just saw, my school days are over!'

2021 A reunion brought four old schoolfriends together for the first time in thirty-five years. While one guy went to the toilet, the other three started boasting about how successful their sons were in their chosen careers.

'My boy is doing so well,' said one. 'He owns his own factory making furniture. Why, just the other day he gave his best friend a whole load of brand new furniture. I'm so proud of him.'

The second said: 'My son is doing every bit as well. He has worked his way up to being manager at a leading car sales firm. Why, just the other day he gave his best friend a Ferrari. I'm so proud of him.'

The third said: 'My son's a great success. He's a bank manager. Why, just the other day he gave his best friend the money to buy a house. I'm so proud of him.'

Just then the fourth guy returned from the toilet. The others said they had just been talking about how successful their sons were. The fourth guy shook his head despairingly. 'I'm afraid my son hasn't amounted to much. You see, he's gay. But I guess he must be doing something right because just the other day he was given a house, furniture and a Ferrari by his friends.'

SCOTS

2022 Two girls came across a drunken Scotsman lying asleep by the side of the road. One girl said: 'I've always wondered what a Scotsman wears under his kilt.' She looked, and was so impressed that she decided to reward him, tying a red ribbon from her hair around his penis. With that, the girls went on their way.

When the Scotsman eventually woke up, he needed to pee and went behind a tree. Noticing the ribbon on his dick, he shook his head and mumbled: 'I don't know where you've been, laddie, but it's nice to know you won first prize!'

2023 How do you disperse an angry Scottish mob? – Nae bother: just go round with a collection box.

2024 How do you take a census in Scotland? – Throw 10p in the street.

2025 How do you spot a Scottish trawler? – It's the one not being followed by seagulls.

2026 Why are so many Scottish churches circular? – So that nobody can hide in the corners during the collection.

2027 A Scotsman returned home from a medical check-up to tell his wife: 'There's good news and bad news.'
'Tell me the bad news first,' she said eagerly.
'I've got sugar in my urine, so there's a strong chance I'm diabetic.'
'And what's the good news?'
'Think of the money I'll save by pissing on my cornflakes!'

2028 What have the Scottish football team and a three-pin plug got in common? – They're both useless in Europe.

2029 What do you call a Scotsman at the World Cup finals? – Ref.

2030 Did you hear about the Scotsman who got a cab to take him and his girlfriend home? – The girl was so beautiful he could barely keep his eyes on the meter.

2031 An Englishman went to a small hotel in the Scottish Highlands and ordered a whiskey.
'That will be ten pence,' said the landlord.
'Ten pence!' exclaimed the Englishman. 'That's amazingly cheap. A whiskey would cost me thirty times that in London!'
'Aye,' said the landlord, 'but the folks around here willnae pay prices like that.'
The Englishman took his drink and sat down at a table. Two old men were playing dominoes on the next table, and he couldn't help noticing that neither of them had a drink.
'Why aren't you fellows drinking?' he asked. 'The prices here are an absolute bargain.'

'Is that so?' said one of the old men. 'Well, a Londoner might call them a bargain, but Hamish and I are waiting for Happy Hour.'

2032 Did you hear about the Scotsman who got caught making nuisance phone calls? – He kept reversing the charges.

2033 A Scotsman was sitting in a bar in Cuba, minding his own business, when a man with a bushy black beard walked in. The man went up to the bar and ordered a shot of whiskey. After knocking it back, he headed for the door.

'Hey,' said the bartender, 'aren't you going to pay for that?'

The man turned around and replied: 'Excuse me, Castro's Army.'

'Sorry,' said the bartender. 'That's fine.'

And the man left without having to pay.

A few minutes later, another man with a bushy black beard wandered in and ordered a shot of whiskey. After drinking it, he was about to leave when the bartender called out: 'Hey, aren't you going to pay for that?'

The man turned around and said: 'Excuse me, Castro's Army.'

'That's OK, then,' said the bartender.

And the man left without having to pay.

Having observed all this, the Scotsman had an idea. He walked up to the bar, ordered a shot of whiskey and, after drinking it, he headed for the door.

'Hey,' yelled the bartender, 'aren't you going to pay for that?'

The Scotsman turned around and said: 'Excuse me, Castro's Army.'

The bartender asked: 'Where is your bushy black beard?'

Thinking quickly, the Scotsman lifted his kilt and said: 'Secret Service.'

2034 A woman was sitting alone in a train carriage until a little old Scotsman wearing a kilt came in and sat down opposite her. She was so fascinated by his kilt that eventually she plucked up the courage to ask: 'I've always wanted to know what a man wears under one of those . . .?'

'I'm a man o' few words,' replied the Scotsman. 'Give me yer hand.'

SEATTLE

2035 A British tourist arrived in Seattle on a wet day. He asked a small boy: 'Does it always rain like this?'

The kid said: 'How should I know? I'm only six!'

2036 Pat left Cork for Seattle where he found a job on a building site. When his first payday came, he went out on the town, got blind drunk and ended up in a brothel. The next day he bared his soul at confession. The priest told him to say twenty Our Fathers, twenty Hail Marys, and to put $20 in the poor box.

A few weeks later, Pat moved to San Francisco where he heard there was better-paid work. On his first payday, he went out on the town, got blind drunk and ended up in a brothel. The next day he went to confession. After listening to Pat's sins, the priest told him to say a couple of Our Fathers and to drop a dollar in the poor box.

'But Father,' said Pat, 'I did the same thing in Seattle and had to say twenty Our Fathers, twenty Hail Marys, and put $20 in the poor box.'

'Ah, sure,' scoffed the priest, 'what do they know about drinkin' and fuckin' in Seattle?'

SEX

2037 An elderly couple were enjoying an anniversary dinner together at their favourite country restaurant. As they finished, the husband leaned over and asked his wife: 'Do you remember the first time we had sex together, over fifty years ago? We went behind this restaurant where you leaned against the fence and I made love to you.'

'Yes,' she said contentedly. 'I remember it well.'

'Well,' he suggested, 'how about taking a walk round there right now and doing it again for old time's sake?'

'Ooh, Henry, you devil!' she smiled. 'That sounds like a wonderful idea.'

So they tottered round to the back of the restaurant and made their way to the fence. The old lady lifted her skirt, took her knickers down, and the old man dropped his trousers. Then she leaned back on the fence and the old man moved in. Suddenly they erupted into the most frenzied sex; they were bucking and jumping like eighteen-year-olds, and he was hanging onto her hips for dear life. When it was all over, they slumped to the ground in an exhausted heap.

'Oh, Miriam!' he gasped. 'That was amazing. That's the best sex we've ever had — no, the best sex anyone's ever had! How come you weren't that athletic fifty years ago?'

The wife replied, panting: 'Because back then the fence wasn't electrified!'

2038 A guy told his doctor: 'I've got this sex problem.'

'OK,' said the doctor. 'Tell me about your average day.'

'Well, it starts in the middle of the night. My wife always wakes me at three o'clock in the morning for sex, and then again at five o'clock so we can spend a couple more hours making love before I go to work . . .'

'Oh, I see . . .'

'No, Doc, that's not it. Because then I get on the train to work and there's always this beautiful girl I meet every morning. And we sneak into an empty compartment and have sex.'

'Now I see . . .'

'No, you don't, Doc. When I get to work, my secretary really fancies me and I have to screw her in the storeroom during morning break.'

'Oh, now I see . . .'

'No, Doc, there's more. For lunch I go to the local sandwich bar where this really sexy woman works. And we always pop into the back room for a quickie.'

'Now, I think I see . . .'

'No, no, Doc. Then in the afternoon I have to shag my attractive lady boss because if I don't, she says she'll fire me. Then when I get home, my wife gives me a blow job before dinner and then we have sex afterwards.'

The doctor scratched his head: 'So what's your problem?'

'It hurts when I wank.'

2039 A man returned home from the night shift and, feeling horny, went straight up to the bedroom. He found his wife with the sheet pulled over her head, fast asleep, but not to be denied, he crawled under the sheet and screwed her feverishly. Afterwards, he hurried downstairs for something to eat and was startled to find breakfast on the table and his wife pouring coffee.

'How'd you get down here so fast?' he gasped. 'We were just making love!'

A look of horror crossed the wife's face. 'Oh, my God!' she exclaimed. 'That's my mother up there! She came over and complained of a headache, so I told her to lie down for a while.'

The wife rushed upstairs. 'Mother, I can't believe what happened! Why didn't you say something?'

The old woman replied: 'I haven't spoken to that jerk for fifteen years and I wasn't about to start now!'

2040 When they have sex, what do most men like their wives to do? – The shopping.

2041 A couple were having sex for the first time and after a while the guy asked the woman to open her legs a little wider. She did so, and they carried on, but a few minutes later he said again: 'Can you open your legs a little wider?' Again she obliged, but shortly afterwards he said: 'A little wider, please.'

Although she was becoming increasingly irritated by his request, she did as he wanted and they continued until, thirty seconds later, he pleaded: 'Can you open them just a little wider?'

She'd had enough. 'What are you trying to do? Get your balls in, too?'

He said: 'No, I'm trying to get them out!'

2042 A guy complained to a friend that sex with his wife had become boring.

'Why don't you try something a little different?' suggested the friend.

'Like what?'

'Well, why don't you try playing doctor for an hour? That's what I do with my wife.'

'A whole hour! How the hell do you manage to make it last that long?'

'It's easy. I just keep her in the waiting room for fifty-eight minutes.'

2043 Two young women were talking over lunch about their dates when one turned to the other and asked: 'What's the best sex you've ever had?'

'Oh, definitely with a guy I went out with last year. He was so imaginative.'

'Like how?' inquired her friend eagerly.

'Well, I remember once he sat me on top of the washing machine when it was on fast spin and made me take all my clothes off.'

'That must have been an amazing sensation,' enthused her friend.

'Yeah, it sent incredible vibrations through my whole body. I just had one roaring orgasm after another and that was before he even entered me. Mind you, I'll never be able to use that launderette again.'

2044 Sex is the only activity where you start at the top and work your way to the bottom, while getting a raise.

2045 A man told his colleagues at work that his wife had given him an ultimatum: no sex until he quit smoking.

'How long do you think you'll be able to hold out?' they asked.

He answered: 'Until my girlfriend dies or I get arthritis of the wrist.'

2046 Sleeping with a man is just like a soap opera. Just when it's getting interesting, they're finished till next time.

2047 A girl picked up a guy at a nightclub and, with her parents out of town, seized the opportunity to invite him back home. When they got to her bedroom, the guy noticed that the room was full of fluffy toys. There were hundreds of them: fluffy toys on top of the wardrobe, fluffy toys on the windowsill, fluffy toys on the floor, fluffy toys all over the bed, and fluffy toys on three rows of shelves. Later, after they'd had sex, he turned to her and asked: 'So how was I?'

She said: 'You can take anything from the bottom shelf.'

2048 Two friends, John and Rob, were talking over a beer.

After a while Rob said: 'John, would you like to participate in group sex?'

'Who's involved?' asked John hesitantly.

'Me, you, and your wife.'

'No, thanks,' said John.

'Fine,' said Rob. 'Then I'll take your name off the list.'

2049 How do you make your girlfriend scream while having sex? – Call her and tell her.

2050 A small boy caught his parents having sex. 'Dad, what are you doing?' he asked.

Embarrassed, the father spluttered: 'Er, I'm filling your mother's tank.'

'Well,' said the boy, 'you better get a model that gets better mileage, because the postman filled her this morning.'

2051 Sex is nobody's business except for the three people involved.

2052 One night a guy and his girlfriend went back to his house to have sex, but on the doorstep he warned her: 'I still live with my parents, and me and my eleven-year-old brother share bunk beds. So we'll have to be quiet. I've thought up some code words we can use: if you want me to change positions, say "lettuce", and if you want to go faster, say "tomato".'

Stealthily they climbed into the top bunk and began making love. As the passion heightened, the girl began moaning: 'Lettuce, lettuce, tomato, lettuce, tomato, tomato, tomato . . .'

Suddenly the kid brother on the bottom bunk called out: 'Can you stop making sandwiches? You're getting mayonnaise all over me.'

2053 A guy had been dating a girl for over a year when he decided it was time to take their relationship a stage further.

'How do you feel about sex?' he asked cautiously.

'It's fine,' she said, 'as long as it is infrequent.'

He looked at her, puzzled. 'Is that one word or two?'

2054 A newly married man came home from work to find his new bride stretched out on the sofa, wearing a negligee.

'Guess what I've got planned for dinner?' she purred. 'And don't you dare tell me you had it for lunch today.'

2055 A virile construction worker saw himself as a stud, and he had no trouble persuading a pretty girl to come back to his apartment. Inevitably they ended up in bed. After sex, he rolled over and lit a cigarette but his smug smile vanished when she jumped out of bed and snapped: 'You may look like Mel Gibson, but you're lousy in the sack!'

Indignant at this affront to his pride, he countered: 'I don't see what makes you such an expert after only thirty-five seconds!'

2056 A man and a woman were having sex in a dark forest. After fifteen minutes of fumbling, he said: 'Damn, I wish I had a flashlight.'

She said: 'So do I. You've been eating grass for the past ten minutes!'

2057 A newly married couple arrived home from their honeymoon and moved into the upstairs apartment that they had rented from the groom's parents. That night, the father of the groom was woken up by his wife.

'Listen, Tony!' she whispered.

He listened, and heard the sound of the bed upstairs creaking in rhythm. The wife said: 'Come on, Tony. Let's make love.' So Tony climbed on top of his wife and they had sex.

Fifteen minutes later, just as he was trying to fall back to sleep, the bed upstairs began creaking in rhythm again. 'Come on, Tony,' said his wife. 'Let's make love again.' Once more, Tony climbed on top of his wife and shafted her with all the energy he could muster.

Twenty minutes later, as he was drifting off to sleep, the bed upstairs began creaking in rhythm again. 'Come on, Tony,' purred his insatiable wife. 'Let's do it again!'

Tony grabbed a broom, pounded on the ceiling and yelled: 'Cut it out, kids! You're killing your old man down here!'

How Sex Can Burn Off The Calories:

2058 *Taking off the clothes*
With her agreement	12 cal
Without her agreement	166 cal

2059 *Taking off the bra*
With both hands	8 cal
With one hand	11 cal
With one hand being slapped	53 cal
With the mouth	91 cal

2060 *Putting on the condom*
With erection	6 cal
Without erection	335 cal

2061 *Preliminaries*
Trying to find the clitoris	14 cal
Trying to find the G spot	107 cal
Without giving a damn	0 cal

2062 *Positions*
Missionary	13 cal
Doggie-style	19 cal
69 lying down	20 cal
69 standing up	137 cal
Hostess trolley	223 cal
Italian chandelier	934 cal

2063 *Having an orgasm*
Real	115 cal
Fake	404 cal

2064 *Post orgasm*
Staying in bed	5 cal
Jumping off the bed	30 cal
Explaining why she jumped off the bed	828 cal

2065 *Getting the second erection*
Between 16 and 19 years of age	14 cal
From 20 to 29	36 cal
From 30 to 39	97 cal

From 40 to 49	376 cal
From 50 to 59	919 cal
Over 60	3623 cal

2066 *Putting on the clothes*

Quietly	4 cal
Hurriedly	99 cal
With her husband opening the door	5190 cal

2067 Thor, the Norse God of Thunder, decided to slip down to Earth for a spot of sex. He picked up a girl in a bar and went back to her place. Blessed with unrivalled stamina, he then subjected her to a three-day non-stop sex session, at the end of which she was utterly exhausted. After saying his farewells, he felt guilty that he might have injured her in some way, so he went back to apologize and explain why he had been able to keep going for so long.

He said: 'I'm sorry, I'm Thor . . .'

The girl yelled: 'Oh, you're thor, are you? Well, tho am I. In fact, I can't even pith!'

2068 Jack and Sam were chatting in a bar. Jack said: 'What would you do if you heard the world was to end in fifteen minutes?'

'I'd shag everything that moved,' said Sam. 'What would you do?'

Jack said: 'I'd stand perfectly still.'

2069 Define 'egghead' – What Mrs Dumpty gives to Humpty.

2070 Two guys were getting drunk and horny at a bar. One said: 'When I get home I wanna give my woman a different kind of sex – something that'll blow her mind.'

The other suggested: 'Why don't you try rodeo sex?'

'Rodeo sex? What's that?'

'It's when you mount your woman from behind, start going nice and slowly, take her hair, pull her head back slightly and whisper in her ear, "Your sister was better than you," . . . and try to hold on for eight seconds!'

2071 A man was walking through the park when he came across an old lamp. He rubbed it, and the genie that appeared granted him three wishes.

'To be honest,' said the man, 'I can't think of anything I really need. I have all I want in life.'

The genie tried to prompt him. 'How about a million dollars? Everyone could do with more money.'

'Not me,' said the man. 'I lead a relatively simple life.'

'What about a fast car?' said the genie. 'I could get you a top of the range Ferrari with a click of the fingers.'

'I don't drive,' said the man.

'How about sex?' suggested the genie. 'How many times do you make love in a week?'

'Once or twice,' replied the man.

'There you go!' said the genie. 'I can make your sex life much more active.'

'Well, OK,' said the man indifferently. 'But I thought once or twice a week was pretty good for a priest in a town this small.'

2072 Tarzan had been living alone in the jungle for thirty years, the only outlet for his sexual frustrations being a hole in a tree. Then one day Jane arrived on a news assignment from NBC and watched him thrusting vigorously into a jungle oak. Touched by his obvious needs, she threw herself to the ground and yelled: 'Take me, Tarzan!'

Tarzan gazed at her lying there, came over to her and kicked her hard in the crotch.

'Ow! What the hell did you do that for?' she screamed.

'Always check for squirrels.'

Why Chocolate Is Better Than Sex:

2073 ● Chocolate satisfies even when it's gone soft.

2074 ● You can safely have chocolate while you're driving.

2075 ● You can make chocolate last as long as you want it to.

2076 ● You can have chocolate even in front of your mother.

2077 ● If you bite the nuts too hard, the chocolate won't mind.

2078 ● You can have chocolate on top of your desk during working hours without upsetting your co-workers.

2079 ● Chocolate is so good to swallow.

2080 ● You can ask a stranger for chocolate without getting your face slapped.

2081 ● You don't get hairs in your mouth with chocolate.

2082 ● With chocolate there's no need to fake it.

2083 ● Chocolate doesn't make you pregnant.

2084 ● When you have chocolate it doesn't keep the neighbours awake.

2085 Carl walked into a bar and saw Ray sitting there with a huge smile on his face. 'What are you so pleased about?' he asked.

'Well, Carl, I gotta tell you . . . Yesterday I was out waxin' my boat, just waxin' my boat, and this gorgeous redhead came up to me. Tits out to here, Carl. Tits out to here! She said, "Can I have a ride in your boat?" I said, "Sure, you can have a ride in my boat." So I took her way out, Carl. I turned off the key and I said, "It's either screw or swim!" She couldn't swim, Carl. She couldn't swim!'

Two days later, Carl walked into the bar and saw Ray sitting there with an even bigger smile on his face. 'What are you so happy about today?' he asked.

'Well, Carl, I gotta tell you . . . Yesterday I was out waxin' my boat, just waxin' my boat, and this heavenly blonde came up to me. Tits out to here, Carl. Tits out to here! She said, "Can I have a ride in your boat?" I said, "Sure, you can have a ride in my boat." So I took her way out, Carl. Way out much further than the last one. I turned off the key and said, "It's either screw or swim!" She couldn't swim, Carl. She couldn't swim!'

Three days later, Carl walked into the bar and saw Ray crying over his beer. 'What are you so sad for?' he asked.

'Well, Carl, I gotta tell you . . . Yesterday I was out waxin' my boat, just waxin' my boat, and this stunning brunette came up to me. Tits way out to here, Carl. Tits way out to here. She said, "Can I have a ride in your boat?" I said, 'Sure, you can have a ride in my boat." So I took her way out, Carl, way way out, much further than the last two. I turned off the key, looked at her tits and said, "It's either screw or swim!" She pulled down her pants and . . . she had a dick, Carl! She had this great big dick, Carl. And I can't swim!'

2086 Why does Mike Tyson cry after sex? – The mace.

2087 What is the square root of 69? – Eight something.

2088 What is 69 and 69? – Dinner for four.

2089 What is 6.9? – 69 ruined by a period.

2090 A guy went up to a girl in a bar and said: 'You want to play Magic?' 'What's that?' she asked.
'We go to my house, fuck, and then you disappear.'

2091 What's the speed limit of sex? – 68, because at 69 you have to turn around.

2092 A couple had been dating for some time, but while he was desperate to sleep with her, she wanted to save herself for marriage. One evening as they started kissing on the sofa, he could feel the sap rising once more.

'Come on, just a feel,' he said, caressing her thighs.

'No,' she replied. 'I've told you before, I'm saving myself for marriage.' They carried on kissing passionately.

'Oh, go on, one quick feel,' he pleaded, flicking his tongue into her mouth. 'No.'

'Just one feel, that's all I want. I promise, nothing more.'

'Oh, all right. But that's all, just one. I'm saving myself for marriage.' So he slid his hand down her panties and rummaged around. Things were really heating up now, and he could contain himself no longer.

'Can't we . . . please?'

'No,' she moaned. 'I'm saving myself for marriage.'

'Please . . .?'

'No, definitely not. Not until we're married.'

'How about if I agree to put just the tip in?'

'No way. I'm saving myself.'

'I promise, just the tip, no more, and we'll stop after that.'

Finally she weakened. 'OK, but just the tip, no more, and that's all. Promise?'

'Promise.'

So he pulled down her panties and poked the tip in, but the sensation made him lose control and he shoved it all the way in. As he began pumping her furiously, she started moaning and groaning. Suddenly she shouted: 'OK, go ahead, put it all the way in!'

Mortified, he replied: 'No, absolutely not, a deal's a deal!'

2093 Two guys were driving along when they saw two dogs mating in someone's front garden. The driver remarked: 'That's great. My wife and I do that every night.'

The passenger said: 'My wife is more conservative – she likes the old-fashioned way. But if you tell me how you get your wife to do that, I'd like to try it.'

'It's easy,' said the driver. 'I just give her a couple of martinis and she's game for anything.'

'Right,' said the passenger, 'I'll try that tonight.'

When the two men met the next morning, the driver asked: 'So how was it?'

'It was great,' said the passenger, 'but it took my wife ten martinis.'

'Ten martinis?'

'Yeah, after two she was more than willing to make love that way, but it took eight more to get her out on the front lawn.'

SEXUAL ORGANS

2094 *Name*: *Expecteria Trouserius* (Trouser Snake)

Location: Throughout the world

Description: Varying from pink to black. Fangless, but with a highly venomous spit. Size varies from three to twelve inches, depending on its mood and subspecies.

Symptoms: The snake attacks mainly women in the front lower abdomen, resulting in an inconspicuous bump, then a severe swelling, followed by excruciating pain after nine months. However it has been known to attack men in the rear lower abdomen, which can be fatal.

Habitat: Usually found in bedrooms, but also open spaces, the back seats of cars, and in fact can pop up in the most unexpected places.

Antidote: Various types of vaccine available for women. But once the venom is injected into the body, only drastic measures will ensure complete recovery.

What to do when attacked:

Sucking the wound: This method is the most popular with the victim, but is not known to have achieved any success.

Milking the snake:

1. Place four fingers of the right hand around the neck of the reptile, with the thumb in the front.
2. Grip firmly and move the hand in an upward and downward motion.
3. This will see the snake become highly aggressive and start spitting.
4. The time taken for this milking process depends entirely on the milker and the last time the snake attacked.
5. Once milked, the snake should remain harmless for about twenty minutes.

2095 A young woman bought a mirror at an antique shop and hung it on her bathroom door. One evening, while getting undressed, she playfully said: 'Mirror, mirror on my door, make my bust-size 44.'

Instantly there was a brilliant flash of light and her breasts grew to an enormous size. Excited, she ran to tell her husband and a few minutes later they both returned to the bathroom. This time, the husband said: 'Mirror, mirror on the door, make my penis touch the floor.'

Again, there was a blinding flash of light . . . then both his legs fell off.

2096 As regular drinking buddies, Des and Jim often found themselves standing next to one another in the urinal. One day, Des, emboldened by several beers, admitted: 'I'm not gay or anything, Jim, but I can't help admiring your dick. It really is a huge specimen.'

'It wasn't always like this,' said Jim. 'I went to Harley Street in England to get a new penis a few years back. It cost me $3,000.'

Des was so impressed that he booked himself on the next flight to London. The surgeon fitted him with a new penis, and Des was mightily pleased with the result. When he next met up with Jim, he was keen to show off his new equipment.

'You were robbed,' he told Jim at the urinal. 'I went to that place you recommended in Harley Street, and he only charged me $1,500.'

'Do you mind if I take a look?' asked Jim.

'Be my guest.'

Jim looked over and laughed: 'No wonder he charged you less. That's my old one!'

2097 A guy entered a clock and watch shop and saw the most gorgeous girl clerk serving behind the counter. He calmly walked up to her, unzipped his pants and flopped his dick out on to the counter.

'What are you doing, sir?' she asked. 'This is a clock shop!'

'I know,' he said, 'and I'd like two hands and a face put on this!'

2098 What do a Rubik's cube and a penis have in common? – The longer you play with them, the harder they get.

2099 Frustrated by a world of moral decay, a man decided that he wanted a pure, innocent woman for his wife. So he went to church in the hope of finding someone who had not been corrupted by modern society. After two weeks, he met a charming girl and took her back to his place for the ultimate test. Whipping out his manhood, he asked her: 'What's this?'

'A cock,' she replied.

Disappointed by her vulgar response, he decided she was not the girl for him.

Two weeks later he met another fine upstanding church girl and resolved to put her to the same test. So when he took her home, he whipped out his manhood and asked her: 'What's this?'

'A cock,' she answered.

Deeply dejected, he concluded that she, too, failed to meet his requirements.

Two weeks later, he met another sweet girl and invited her home. He whipped out his manhood and asked her: 'What's this?'

She giggled and said: 'A pee-pee.'

That was exactly the sort of innocent answer he was looking for, and the pair began dating. Soon they married and settled down to enjoy their life together. But whenever she saw him naked, she giggled and said: 'That's your pee-pee.' Whilst he found it endearing at first, it eventually began to grate a little, so he thought he ought to correct her.

'Look,' he explained, 'this is not a pee-pee, it's a cock.'

She laughed and said: 'No, it's not. A cock is ten inches long and black.'

2100 A husband's penis was so small that, for the first seven years of their married life, he made love to his wife with a gherkin. Since they always had sex in their dark, she was none the wiser until one night she suddenly put the lights on and saw him with the pickle in his hand.

'Oh, my God!' she exclaimed. 'Is that what you've been shafting me with all these years? How could you? It's disgusting!'

'Shut up!' he yelled. 'How dare you accuse me of anything when I've never even asked where our three kids came from!'

2101 Three US educational institutions were commissioned by the government to discover why the human penis is shaped the way it is. The University of California allocated a budget of $750,000 for research and after three years of study concluded that the reason the head of the penis is wider than the shaft is because it fits better in the vagina. This prevents leakage of semen and increases the probability of successful fertilisation. The University of Texas spent $500,000 on a two-year research programme. Their results showed that the penis widened near the tip to maximize the number of nerve endings stimulated during sex. This would lead to increased sensitivity and a better chance of impregnation. The Texas A & M University spent $3.95 on a copy of *Playboy* and ten minutes in the staff toilet, and discovered that the penis widens at the tip in order to prevent your hand from slipping off the end.

2102 A man went to a party, got drunk and passed out. He woke the next day to find two lines around his penis – a red one and a brown one. So he went to the doctor who took samples of both lines.

After conducting the necessary tests, the doctor announced: 'There is good news and bad news. The good news is the red line was lipstick. But the brown line is bad news.'

'Why?'

'It was chewing tobacco.'

2103 A man said to his wife: 'You know, I was thinking of going down to the bar tonight and entering that Big Dick Contest.'

'Oh, honey, please don't,' she begged. 'I don't want you taking that thing out in public.'

'But the first prize is $150,' he said.

'I don't care. I just don't want you showing that monster to everybody. Understand?'

The subject was dropped, but the next night she caught him counting out $150. 'Did you go down and enter that Big Dick Contest after I expressly told you not to?'

'Please forgive me, darling . . .'

'You mean, you took that thing out for everybody to see?'

He smiled at her tenderly and said: 'Only enough to win.'

2104 A man walked into the doctor's office and said: 'Doctor, I have five penises.'

'I see,' said the doctor. 'How do your trousers fit?'

'Like a glove.'

2105 A guy went to the doctor and said: 'Doc, you've got to help me. My penis is orange.'

The doctor asked the guy to drop his pants and was alarmed to see that the patient's penis was indeed orange. 'This is very strange,' admitted the doctor. 'Sometimes things like this are caused by a lot of stress in a person's life.'

Probing as to the possible causes of stress, the doctor asked: 'How are things at work?'

'I was fired six weeks ago,' said the guy.

'Aha,' said the doctor. 'That is most probably the cause of the stress.'

'I don't think so,' said the guy. 'The boss was a real asshole. I had to work unpaid overtime every week, and I had no say in what was happening. I found a new job earlier this week where I can set my own hours, I'm getting paid double what I got at the old place, and the boss is a really great guy. I start there Monday.'

'Hmmm,' mused the doctor. Pursuing another avenue, he asked. 'How's your home life?'

The guy replied: 'I got divorced eight months ago.'

'Aha,' said the doctor. 'That's why you're stressed.'.

'No way,' said the guy. 'For years, all I listened to was nag, nag, nag. I'm just so relieved to be rid of the bitch!'

By now the doctor was really struggling to find a cause for the orange penis. In desperation, he asked: 'Do you have any hobbies or a social life?'

The guy replied: 'No, not really. Most nights I sit at home, watch some porno flicks and munch on Cheetos . . .'

2106 What is the part of Popeye that never rusts? – The one he puts in Olive Oyl.

2107 A muscular guy called Michael met a woman named Sharon at a bar and after several drinks they went back to his place. As they were making out in the bedroom, Michael stood up and started to undress. After taking his shirt off, he flexed his biceps and said: 'See that, baby? That's one thousand pounds of dynamite!'

With Sharon drooling in expectation, Michael then dropped his jeans and pointed to his bulging thighs. 'See that baby? That's one thousand pounds of dynamite!'

Sharon could hardly wait for the action to begin. Finally, Michael dropped his underpants but, after a quick glance, Sharon grabbed her jacket and ran screaming towards the door. Michael grabbed her just as she was about to leave and demanded: 'Why are you in such a hurry to go?'

Sharon replied: 'With two thousand pounds of dynamite and such a short fuse, I was afraid you were about to blow!'

2108 What did the left testicle say to the right testicle? – 'The guy in the middle thinks he's so hard!'

2109 Two drunks were sitting next to each other in a bar. When one staggered back from the washroom, he forgot to button up his fly so that as he sat on his bar stool, his penis flopped out onto the bartop.

Seeing this, the other drunk screamed, 'Snake!' and whacked the penis with a bottle.

The first drunk yelled: 'Hit it again! It just bit me!'

2110 Why does a penis have a hole in the end? – So that men can be open minded.

2111 An old man went to the doctor and said: 'I want you to take a look at my penis, doc.'

The doctor examined it but said: 'I can't see anything wrong with it.'

'I know that,' said the old man, 'but ain't it a beauty!'

2112 A guy on a business trip bought a cool pair of snakeskin boots. When he got home, he went upstairs, stripped naked except for his boots, and called his wife. She entered the bedroom to find him standing there.

'Do you notice anything special?' he asked.

'Yeah,' she said, bored. 'It's limp.'

'It's not limp,' he protested. 'It's admiring my new boots.'

'Well,' she said, 'next time buy a hat.'

2113 What did the elephant say to the naked man? – 'Cute, but can you breathe through it?'

2114 A stranger went into an empty bar in Georgia and ordered a beer. As he was looking around, he saw a table about 6ft by 4ft with some lines marked between six and ten inches from one edge. Next to each line was a set of initials.

The stranger asked the bartender: 'What are all those marks on that table?'

'It's a game the locals play,' said the bartender. 'They pull out their dicks, stretch them as far as they can, and mark a line.'

Being hung like a horse, the stranger reckoned he could beat all the lines on display and asked if he could have a go.

'Sure,' said the bartender.

So the stranger pulled out his dick and was a clear winner by at least two inches. He was just marking his line in triumph when the bartender pointed out: 'No, mate, the locals start from the other side!'

2115 A guy was nervous about making a move on his new girlfriend because he thought his penis was rather on the small side. So he asked his friend for advice. The friend said: 'Don't worry. Just get her in the mood and everything will be fine. I'm sure she won't think your dick is small.'

So on their next date the guy drove his girlfriend to a secluded spot. After kissing her tenderly, he plucked up the courage to open the zip on his jeans and guide her hand down onto his organ.

'No thanks,' said the girl. 'I don't smoke.'

2116 At the greeting card shop, a woman was spending a long time poring over the cards, trying to find something appropriate.

Seeing that she was having trouble finding what she wanted, a clerk came over and asked: 'May I help you?'

'I don't know,' said the woman. 'Do you have any "Sorry I laughed at your dick" cards?'

2117 A white man couldn't help noticing a black man's impressive cock as he stood at the adjacent urinal.

'I wish I had one like yours,' sighed the white man.

The black man said: 'You can – just tie a string around it and hang a weight on the end of the string. Put the weight down your pant leg and you can have one like mine.'

'Thanks. You've been really helpful.'

A few weeks later, the two men bumped into each other again.

'How's it going?' asked the black man.

'Great,' said the white man. 'I'm halfway there.'

'Really?'

'Yes, it's definitely turning black.'

2118 The rule of the tool: if the mass of the ass is proportional to the angle of the dangle, then the torque on the pork determines the heat of the meat.

2119 When a ninety-year-old man announced that he was going to marry a woman of thirty-three, his daughter urged him to have a medical examination first to see if he was still capable sexually.

The doctor said: 'Let me see your sexual organs.'

The old man stuck out his tongue and his little finger.

2120 A guy had a work physical. The doctor said: 'You've got a tiny dick. Has it caused any difficulties?'

'No, I've got a wife and three kids. But I do sometimes have a problem finding it in the daytime.'

'Hmmm,' said the doctor. 'What about at night?'

'Nights are no problem, because there's two of us looking for it then.'

2121 'Hi, darling,' breathed an obscene phone caller. 'If you can guess what's in my hand, I'll give you a piece of the action.'

'Listen, chum,' said the woman on the other end. 'If you can hold it in one hand, I ain't interested.'

Letter of Complaint to the Management

I, the Penis, hereby request a raise in salary for the following reasons:

2122 I do physical labour.

2123 I work at great depths.

2124 I plunge head first into everything I do.

2125 I do not get weekends or public holidays off.

2126 I work in a damp environment.

2127 I work in a dark workplace that has poor ventilation.

2128 I work in high temperatures.

2129 My work exposes me to contagious diseases.

The Reply

Dear Penis, after assessing your request and considering the arguments you have raised, the administration rejects your request for the following reasons:

2130 You do not work eight hours straight.

2131 You fall asleep after brief work periods.

2132 You do not always follow the orders of the management team.

2133 You do not stay in your designated area and are often seen visiting other locations.

2134 You must be stimulated in order to start working.

2135 You leave the workplace rather messy at the end of your shift.

2136 You don't always observe necessary safety regulations, such as wearing the correct protective clothing.

2137 You will retire well before you are sixty-five.

2138 You are unable to work double shifts.

2139 You sometimes leave your designated work area before you have completed the assigned task.

2140 And if that were not all, you have repeatedly been seen entering and exiting the workplace carrying two suspicious-looking bags.
Sincerely,
The Management

2141 Suddenly in middle age, Ralph's penis began to grow at an alarming rate. Soon it was twenty inches long and making his life uncomfortable. Eventually he sought medical advice and a urologist told him that the condition could be cured through corrective surgery.
'How long will Ralph be on crutches?' asked his wife.
'Crutches? Why would he need crutches?' said the urologist.
The wife said: 'Well, you are planning to shorten his legs, aren't you?'

2142 Little Johnny told his schoolfriend: 'Annie Roberts cheats!'
'Why do you say that?' asked his friend.
'Well,' said Johnny, 'she said she'd show me hers if I showed her mine – but it turns out she hasn't got one!'

2143 Which is the least sensitive part of the penis? – The man attached to it.

2144 A guy with a twenty-five-inch dick wanted it made smaller because it was too big for women to cope with. So he went to see a witch who told him to go to the woods where he would find a frog. 'You must ask the frog to marry you,' said the witch. 'And when the frog says "no", your dick will shrink by five inches.'
So the guy headed off into the woods. He found the frog sitting at the base of a tree. 'Frog,' he said, 'will you marry me?'
The frog said: 'No.' And, sure enough, the guy's dick shrank five inches. But twenty inches was still too long, so again he asked the frog to marry him.
'No,' answered the frog. And the guy's dick shrank five inches.
The guy was going to leave it at that, but then he thought that fifteen inches was still too long. Ten would be ideal. So he went up to the frog for a third time.
'Frog, will you marry me?'
The frog glared at him. 'How many times do I have to tell you? No! No! No!'

2145 A boy asked his father: 'What does a vagina look like?'
'Well, son, before sex it looks like a perfect pink rosebud with a sweet perfume.'

'So what does it look like after sex?'

'Well, son, have you ever seen a bulldog eating mayonnaise?'

2146 How can you tell when your girlfriend wants you? – When you put your hand down her pants and it's like you're feeding a horse.

2147 A man was sitting on a train opposite a girl in a short skirt. Although he tried not to stare, he couldn't take his eyes off her, particularly when it became obvious that she wasn't wearing any knickers. Realizing what was going on, she asked him: 'Are you looking at my pussy?'

'Er, yes. I'm sorry.'

'It's OK,' said the girl. 'My pussy's very talented. Watch this. I'll make it blow a kiss to you.'

Sure enough, it blew a kiss at him.

'That's not all,' she boasted. 'I can also make it wink.'

Sure enough, she made it wink at him.

'Come and sit next to me,' she said, patting the seat. 'Would you like to stick a couple of fingers in?'

'My God!' said the man. 'Can it whistle, too?'

2148 When his mother walked out of the shower, Little Johnny saw his mother's vagina. He asked her what it was and she replied embarrassed: 'Oh, that's mommy's black sponge.'

A few days later, Johnny spilt a glass of milk on the kitchen floor and said: 'Mommy, I need your black sponge to mop up the milk.'

She replied awkwardly: 'Uh, I lost it.'

A couple of days later, he came running up to her and said: 'Mommy, I found your black sponge!'

Mystified, she asked: 'Where?'

Little Johnny said: 'It's over at Mrs Taylor's house, and Daddy's washing his face in it!'

2149 Who designed the female genitals? – The local council: who else would put a playground right next door to a sewer?

2150 What's the difference between eating pussy and driving in a snowstorm? – When you eat pussy, you can always see the asshole in front of you.

2151 After a wild night's partying, three women decided to see who had the biggest snatch. So they took off all their clothes and began fingering themselves and each other.

A few minutes later, the first one squatted on a glass top table and then they measured the slimy outline she left behind.

The second one then squatted on the table and they measured the slimy outline she left, which was even bigger.

Finally the third one squatted on the table but when she stood back up, the others said: 'You didn't leave an outline.'

'Ah,' she said, 'smell the rim.'

2152 What's white, smells, and can be found in panties? – Clitty litter.

2153 Spotting a sexy woman in a bar, a guy went over to her and said: 'Hey, baby, let me suck on your nipples.'

She snapped: 'Watch it, buddy, I'll have my boyfriend kick your ass.'

The guy simply laughed and said: 'OK, why don't I just give you a French kiss?'

'Listen,' she barked, 'if you say one more thing to me, I'll have my man kill you.'

The guy was undeterred. 'OK. This is my final offer. I'll hold you upside down, pour beer into your pussy and drink from it.'

In a rage, the girl marched straight over to her boyfriend.

'See that guy over there,' she said. 'He told me he was going to lick my tits.'

'I'll kill him!' yelled the boyfriend.

'Wait! Then he said he was going to French kiss me.'

The boyfriend moved menacingly towards the guy, ready to rip him apart.

'And,' she added, 'he also said he'd hang me by my ankles, pour beer down my twat and drink from me.'

The boyfriend stopped in his tracks. 'Sorry, babe,' he said, 'I can't mess with anyone who can drink that much beer.'

2154 Three fleas were sleeping on a woman. One was on her head, the second was in her armpit and the third was in her pussy. The next morning the three fleas met up on a passing dog and compared notes as to how they had slept.

The first said: 'I slept on this really hard place. It had some hair, but it was very uncomfortable.'

The second said: 'I slept in a place that was kinda wet, but it was warm and comfortable.'

The third flea said: 'I slept in this dark cave and it was really nice. But as I was sleeping this big bald monster came in, woke me up, slammed me up against the wall a few times, and then spat in my damn face!'

2155 A woman with three vaginas went to the doctor about her embarrassing problem. The doctor responded by sewing up two of the holes, leaving just the middle one open.

'Am I cured?' she asked.

'Not as such,' he replied. 'But it will stop you getting fucked left, right and centre.'

2156 A guy was eating a girl out when he stopped for a second and moaned: 'God, this pussy's big! God, this pussy's big!'

'I know,' she said, 'but why did you say it twice?'

He said: 'I didn't.'

2157 An explorer in the Amazon jungle was searching for a lost tribe whose women were reputed to have vaginas that were three inches wide and twelve inches long. When he finally caught up with the chief of the tribe, the explorer asked whether this story was true.

'Yes, it is,' said the chief.

The explorer was amazed. 'However do you manage to have sex with women with vaginas that are three inches wide and twelve inches long?'

The chief replied calmly: 'They stretch.'

2158 An old maid wanted to travel by bus to the pet cemetery with the remains of her cat. As she boarded the bus, she whispered to the driver: 'I have a dead pussy.'

The driver pointed to the woman in the seat behind him and said: 'Sit with my wife. You two have a lot in common.'

2159 A man went into a chemist's and started chatting to the pharmacist. In the course of the conversation, the pharmacist asked him if he had seen the shop's newest product, the Artificial Vagina.

'An artificial vagina?' said the customer. 'I don't believe you!'

'Well, I'll show you one,' said the pharmacist, fetching a box from beneath the counter.

'Blimey!' said the customer, examining the product. 'It looks just like one!'

'Give it a real test,' said the pharmacist. 'Smell it.'

'Bloody hell! It smells just like one, too!'

'A final test: just feel it.'

So the customer fingered it. 'It's amazing – it feels just like a real one. I'll buy it.'

'Should I wrap it up?'

'No, I'll eat it here.'

2160 A young white trash couple were having sex in a muddy cornfield one evening.

The guy said: 'Can you check to see if it's in you or if it's in the mud?'

She reached down and checked. 'It's in the mud.'

'Well, could you put it back in you?' he asked.

She put it back in, and they continued having sex for a while until he asked again: 'Can you check to see if it's in you or if it's in the mud?'

She checked again, and said: 'It's still in me, big fella!'

He said: 'Um, could you put it back in the mud?'

SHEEP

2161 A Californian tourist was visiting Wyoming when he saw a flock of sheep being cared for by a handsome, strapping young man.

The tourist went over to the young man said: 'With looks like yours, you could be in movies. What are you doing working as a mere shepherd?'

The guy replied: 'I do it for the sex.'

'For the sex?' said the California, dumbfounded. 'What do you mean?'

'Well,' said the shepherd, 'I pick me out a sheep, I take its two back legs and stick them in my boots, then I take the two front legs and put them over the fence. I tell you, it's the best sex I've ever had!'

The next stop on the tourist's itinerary was Montana, and there again he spotted a strong, handsome young man tending a flock of sheep. The curious Californian asked the guy why he devoted his life to looking after sheep when there were surely opportunities for him in Hollywood.

'I do it for the sex,' replied the shepherd.

'How do you mean?' asked the Californian.

The guy from Montana explained: 'I find me a pretty sheep, and I take its two hind legs and I stick them in my boots. I take the two front legs and throw them over my shoulders. The sex is fantastic.'

The Californian said: 'But in Wyoming, they throw the front legs over a fence.'

'What?' said the guy from Montana in disbelief. 'You mean they don't kiss?'

2162 Did you know they just discovered a new use for sheep in Montana? – Wool!

2163 Why do guys in Montana have sex with sheep on the edge of cliffs? – So they push back harder.

2164 What do you call a hillbilly who owns sheep and goats? – Bisexual.

2165 Three guys were riding in a pickup when they saw a sheep caught in the fence with its hind end up in the air.

The guy from Ohio said: 'I wish that was Angelina Jolie.'

The guy from Pennsylvania said: 'I wish that was Sarah Michelle Gellar.'

The guy from Montana said: 'I wish it was dark . . .'

SMALL ADS

What 'women seeking men' Classifieds Really Mean:

2166 • 40-ish means: 49

2167 • Adventurer: Has had dozens of partners

2168 • Affectionate: Possessive

2169 • Artist: Unreliable

2170 • Beautiful: Pathological liar

2171 • Commitment-minded: Pick out curtains . . . now!

2172 • Communication important: Just try to get a word in

2173 • Contagious smile: Bring your own penicillin

2174 • Educated: College dropout

2175 • Emotionally secure: Medicated

2176 • Employed: Has part-time job stuffing envelopes at home

2177 • Enjoys art and opera: Snob

2178 • Free spirit: Substance abuser

2179 • Friendship first: Trying to live down reputation as slut

2180 • Fun: Irritating

2181   • Gentle: Comatose

2182   • Good listener: Monosyllabic

2183   • Humorous: Caustic

2184   • Intuitive: Your opinion doesn't count

2185   • Light drinker: Lush

2186   • Looks younger: If viewed from far away in bad light

2187   • Loves animals: Cat lady

2188   • Non-traditional: Ex-husband lives in the basement

2189   • Open-minded: Desperate

2190   • Outgoing: Loud

2191   • Passionate: Loud

2192   • Poet: Manic depressive

2193   • Reliable: Frumpy

2194   • Self-employed: Jobless

2195   • Smart: Insipid

2196   • Spiritual: Involved with a cult

2197   • Stable: Boring

2198   • Tall, thin: Anorexic

2199   • Tanned: Wrinkled

2200   • Wants soulmate: One step away from stalker

2201   • Writer: Pompous

2202 A woman walking past a shop spotted an advert in the window: GOOD HOME WANTED FOR CLITORIS LICKING FROG.

So she went in and said to the guy behind the counter: 'I've come about the clitoris licking frog.'

He said: 'Oui, madame . . .'

SMELLS

2203 Wandering through a department store, two women stopped at the perfume counter where they picked up a sample bottle. One sprayed the perfume on her wrist and smelled it.

'That's nice, isn't it?' she said, waving her arm under her friend's nose.

'Yeah,' said her friend. 'What's it called?'

'*Viens à moi*.'

'*Viens à moi*? What's that mean?'

A clerk offered some help, explaining: '*Viens à moi*, ladies, is French for "come to me".'

The first woman took another sniff. 'That doesn't smell like come to me!'

2204 A girl was sitting in a train carriage when an old guy entered and sat opposite her, eating a tray of king prawns. His manners were appalling. He was belching and swearing and he took great delight in flicking the shells on the floor and at the girl. Finally he screwed up the polystyrene tray and threw it at her. While he roared with laughter, she calmly picked the prawn shells off the floor, threw them and the tray out of the window, and pressed the emergency stop.

'You dumb bitch!' he yelled. 'That's gonna cost you $100!'

'Yeah,' she replied, 'but when the police smell your fingers, it's gonna cost *you* ten years!'

2205 Every day at work, a man sidled up to a woman, took a deep breath, and told her that her hair smelt nice. After a week of this, the woman reported him to her boss for sexual harassment.

The boss was mystified. 'What's wrong with someone telling you that your hair smells nice?'

The woman replied: 'He's a midget!'

2206 When a guy couldn't get a dance, his mate decided to tell him the truth. 'It's the smell from your socks,' he said. 'Go home and change them, and you'll have no trouble.'

So the guy went home but when he returned to the dance he still had no luck with the girls.

'Did you change your socks?' asked his friend.

'Of course I did,' he said, pulling them from his jacket pocket.

2207 A woman asked her husband to go to the video store and get *Scent of a Woman*. He came back with *A Fish Called Wanda*.

2208 A young guy spotted a gorgeous girl in a nightclub, so when the DJ played a slow number, he moved in and asked her for a dance. As they danced cheek to cheek, he said: 'You smell really terrific. What's that you have on?'

'Chanel No. 5,' she replied.

Keen to return the compliment, she said: 'You smell good too. What is it that you have on?'

'Well,' he said, 'I've got a hard on, but I didn't think you could smell it.'

2209 An old man was giving an old woman cunnilingus. But after ten seconds, he raised and his head and said: 'I can't carry on. The smell is too bad.'

'I'm sorry,' she said. 'The smell must be down to my arthritis.'

'How can arthritis cause such a bad smell?' he queried.

'It's in my shoulders,' she said. 'It means I can't wipe my ass properly.'

2210 A guy was alone in an elevator with a woman when he turned to her and said: 'Can I smell your pussy?'

'No, you can not,' she snapped.

'Oh, it must be your feet, then.'

2211 An Oklahoma City bar was sponsoring the ultimate politically incorrect contest by offering a cash prize to the guy who could bring on stage the wife or girlfriend with the smelliest pussy. No sooner had the announcement been made than a local factory worker went up to the MC and said: 'Buddy, that money's as good as mine. In a few minutes I'll bring my wife on stage – and, believe me, she has the smelliest pussy in the whole damn world!'

Five minutes later, true to his word, the guy dragged in a huge, bloated woman. 'Look at her!' roared the MC. 'She's so fat and bloated she can't even walk! And, my God, her pussy stinks! I can smell her from here!'

When the woman reached the stage, the MC was prepared to concede the contest even before the guy pulled up her skirt and dropped her panties. And when he did remove her underwear, the stench was so vile that the audience began gagging and retching. The MC hurriedly handed over the prize money and said: 'You win. No contest. But how the hell do you live with the smell of her pussy?'

'It's not really that difficult,' replied the guy. 'You kinda get used to it. The first three weeks after she died were the worst.'

SOCIAL WORKERS

2212 Two social workers were walking through a rough part of town one evening. Passing an alley, they heard moans and groans, and, on investigating, they found a man lying semi-conscious in a pool of blood.

'Help me,' he begged, his eyes almost shut, his face battered and bruised. 'I've been mugged and viciously attacked.'

The social workers turned on their heels and walked away. One remarked to her colleague: 'You know, the person that did this really needs help.'

2213 A social worker asked a colleague: 'What time is it?'
'Sorry,' said the colleague, 'I don't know. I don't have a watch.'
'That's OK. The main thing is, we talked about it.'

2214 In a perfect world, what question would a social worker ask of clients? – 'Do you want fries with that?'

2215 A man was rushed to hospital after suffering a heart attack. The doctor told him bluntly that his only hope of survival was to have a heart transplant. Just then, a nurse ran in and said: 'You're in luck. Two hearts have just become available. One belongs to a lawyer and the other to a social worker. Which one do you want?'
The patient said: 'The lawyer's.'
The doctor was surprised: 'Are you sure? Wouldn't you like to know a little more about the two people concerned before making your decision?'
'I already know enough,' said the man. 'We all know that social workers are bleeding hearts, and the lawyer's probably never used his. So I'll take the lawyer's.'

2216 How many social workers does it take to change a light bulb? – None, but it takes twelve to write a paper entitled 'Coping With Darkness'.

2217 A social worker was confronted by a mugger with a gun.
'Your money or your life!' snarled the mugger.
'I'm sorry, I'm a social worker, so I have no money and no life.'

SODOMY

2218 When three explorers were captured by a tribe in the Amazon jungle, the chief announced that he was going to punish them. He called the first explorer to the front of the tribe and asked ominously: 'Death or Booka?' The explorer didn't want to die, so he opted for 'booka'. Hearing this, the tribe began screaming 'Booka! Booka!' and dancing around excitedly. The chief then ripped the explorer's pants off and shafted him in the ass.

Then the chief called forward the second explorer and asked: 'Death or Booka?' Not wanting to die, he, too, opted for 'booka'. The tribe again screamed 'Booka! Booka!' and danced around. The chief ripped the second explorer's pants off and shafted him in the ass.

Then the chief called forward the third explorer and asked: 'Death or Booka?' The third guy had a little more self-respect and reckoned that even death would be preferable to being violated before hundreds of tribesmen, so he opted for death. At this, the chief turned to the tribe and screamed: 'Death by Booka!'

2219 A guy was sitting in a bar when a stranger walked up to him and said. 'If you woke up in the woods, scratched your butt and found Vaseline all over it, would you tell anyone?'

The guy looked at him in amazement and said: 'Hell, no!'

'If you felt further into your crack,' continued the stranger, 'and pulled out a used condom, would you tell anyone then?'

'Of course not!'

'Wanna go camping?'

2220 A man walked into a public toilet and began using one of the urinals. Looking to his left, he saw a very short man peeing too. Suddenly the short man looked up and the taller man was totally embarrassed about staring at the little fellow's dick.

'Sorry,' said the taller man, 'I'm not gay or anything, but you have the longest penis I've ever seen, especially for someone so small.'

'Well,' said the little man, 'that's because I'm a leprechaun. All leprechauns have huge penises.'

'That's incredible!' said the taller guy. 'I'd give anything to have one that long!'

'Well, with me being a leprechaun and all, I can grant you your wish! If you let me take you into that cubicle over there and screw you, your wish will come true.'

'Oh, I don't know about that,' said the man hesitantly. 'But I guess no one will ever find out . . . so go on, then, what the hell!'

Soon the leprechaun was behind the taller man, humping away energetically. 'Say,' said the leprechaun, 'how old are you?'

Finding it difficult to turn while being shafted so ferociously, the taller man said over his shoulder: 'Er, thirty-six.'

'Fancy that,' said the little man. 'Thirty-six and still believes in leprechauns!'

2221   The firemen finally brought a huge fire under control, and Chief Smith had all of his men accounted for except Olsen and Ravazzio. After a few minutes' search, the chief looked down an alley, and there was Ravazzio, leaning over a trash can. His pants were down to his ankles, and Olsen was banging away from behind.

The chief yelled: 'What the hell is going on?'

Olsen said: 'Ravazzio passed out from smoke inhalation.'

The chief said: 'Smoke inhalation? You're supposed to give him mouth-to-mouth resuscitation!'

Olsen said: 'I did, chief, but then one thing led to another . . .'

SOUTH AFRICANS

2222   A white South African went on holiday to Australia. Lying on the beach, he pointed out to sea and asked one of the locals: 'What are those black dots?'

'They're buoys,' replied the Australian.

'And what are they doing?'

'They're holding up the shark nets.'

'Gee, what a country!' said the South African. 'We'd never get away with that back home.'

SPEECH IMPEDIMENTS

2223   *Stammerer.* I hea . . . hea . . . heard tha . . . that you can hel . . . hel . . . help me.

Speech therapist. Certainly. Sit back in the chair, relax, look straight into my eyes and count slowly to ten.

Stammerer. O . . . one, t . . . two, th . . . th . . . three, f . . . f . . . four, f . . . f . . . five, s . . . s . . . six, s . . . seven, eight, nine ten. That's wonderful. I'm cured. My nervous stammer has gone.

Speech therapist. That's excellent. My fee is $500.

Stammerer. H . . . h . . . how m . . . m . . . much?'

2224   A guy who owned a horse stud farm got a call from a friend. 'I know this midget with a speech impediment who wants to buy a horse. I'm sending him over.'

The midget arrived, and the owner asked if he wanted a male or female horse.

'A female horth,' replied the midget. So the owner showed him one.

'Nith looking horth, can I see her mouth?' So the owner picked up the midget and showed him the horse's mouth.

'Nith mouth. Can I see her eyesth?' So the owner picked up the midget and showed him the horse's eyes.

'OK, what about the earsth?' The owner was getting a bit fed up with this, but he picked up the midget one more time and showed him the horse's ears.

'OK, finally, I'd like to see her twat.' With that, the owner picked up the midget and shoved his head up the horse's twat. Then he pulled him out.

Shaking his head, the midget said: 'Perhapth I should rephrase. I'd like to see her run!'

2225 Sitting in a bar, a man noticed a group of deaf and dumb people using sign language. He also spotted that the bartender was using sign language to speak to them. The man was impressed to learn that the bartender had actually been taught to sign by the customers, who were regulars at the bar.

After admiring this scene for a few minutes, the man became aware that the people in the group were waving their hands about wildly. The bartender then looked over, signed, 'Now, cut that out! I warned you!' and threw the group out of the bar.

'Why did you do that?' inquired the man.

The bartender replied: 'If I've told them once, I've told them a hundred times: no singing in the bar!'

2226 Three men were being treated for their stuttering by a gorgeous speech therapist who, struggling to make progress, decided on a reward system as an incentive. She said that she would have sex with whoever could tell her where he was born without stuttering.

The first guy said: 'B-B-B-Belfast,' and sat down, disappointed.

The second guy said: 'D-D-D-Dublin,' and he, too, sat down, dejected.

The third guy stood up and said: 'London.'

So she immediately grabbed him and took him into the next room. Half an hour later, he returned grinning from ear to ear. Before restarting the session, the therapist asked if there was anything any of them wanted to say.

The third man raised his hand and said: '. . . d-d-d-derry.'

2227 A lady golfer was about to tee off when a man tapped her on the shoulder and held up a card, which said: 'I am a deaf mute. Please may I play through?'

The woman yelled back: 'Certainly not. You'll wait your turn like everyone else. What makes you think you should receive preferential treatment?' And with that, she sent her drive down the fairway.

A few minutes later she was lining up her putt on the green when a golf ball hit her on the head, knocking her out cold. She came round to see the deaf mute standing over her and holding up four fingers.

2228 A man saw an old schoolfriend driving up to a smart house. 'Hey, you must have done well for yourself. What line of work are you in?'

The friend, who had a fearful stutter, replied: 'Oh, j-j-j-just by selling c-c-c-copies of the B-b-b-bible d-d-d-door to d-d-d-door.'

'Wow! You must really sell a lot of Bibles. What's your secret?'

'I j-j-just knock on p-p-people's d-d-d-doors, show them a c-c-copy of the B-b-b-bible and ask them if they w-w-would rather b-b-buy it or have me r-r-r-read it to them.'

2229 A doctor was examining a young female patient.

'Big breaths,' he said.

'Yeth,' she replied. 'And I'm still only thixtheen.'

2230 A huge muscular guy with a bad stutter went to a counter in a department store and asked: 'W . . . w . . . w . . . where's the m . . . m . . . m . . . men's dep . . . p . . . p . . . partment?'

The clerk behind the counter just looked at him and said nothing.

The guy repeated himself: 'W . . . w . . . w . . . where's the m . . . m . . . m . . . men's dep . . . p . . . p . . . partment?'

Again, the clerk didn't answer him.

The guy asked several more times: 'W . . . w . . . w . . . where's the m . . . m . . . m . . . men's dep . . . p . . . p . . . partment?'

Still the clerk ignored him. Eventually the guy stormed off.

The customer who was waiting in line behind the big guy asked the clerk: 'Why wouldn't you answer his question?'

The clerk answered: 'D . . . d . . . d . . . do you th . . . th . . . th . . . think I w . . . w . . . w . . . want to get b . . . b . . . b . . . beaten up?'

SPERM

2231 A man and a woman were waiting at the hospital donation centre.

The man decided to strike up a conversation and asked her: 'What are you here for?'

'I'm here to donate some blood,' she replied. 'They're giving me five dollars for it.'

'Right,' said the man. 'I'm actually here to donate sperm. But they pay me $25.'

The woman looked thoughtful for a moment and they chatted some more before going their separate ways. A couple of months later, the same man and woman met again at the donation centre.

'Hi,' he called out. 'Here to donate blood again?'

The woman shook her head with her mouth closed: 'Unh, unh.'

2232 How does a guy know if he has a high sperm count? – If the girl has to chew before she swallows.

2233 The first day at the London sperm bank was pretty unsuccessful. Only two men made appointments – one came on the bus and the other missed the tube.

2234 A guy wearing a black ski mask walked into a sperm bank, pointed a gun at the woman behind the counter and yelled: 'Open the safe!'

The woman protested: 'But this isn't a real bank, it's a sperm bank.'

The robber insisted: 'Open the safe or I'll shoot!'

Terrified out of her mind, she opened the safe.

'Now,' barked the robber, 'take one of the bottles and drink it.'

'But these are sperm samples,' she pleaded.

'Just drink it!' screamed the robber, his eyes flashing menacingly through his woollen mask. 'Or I'll shoot you dead.'

Trembling with fear, the woman gulped down the contents.

'Now take another bottle and drink it,' he ordered.

'But I just drank one,' she stammered.

'Drink it or I'll shoot you!'

Somehow she managed to drink the bottle.

As she swallowed the last drop, the guy took off his mask. It was her husband.

'You see, honey,' he said. 'It isn't so difficult, is it?'

2235 Why does it take one million sperm to fertilize one egg? – Because they won't stop to ask for directions.

2236 The newly born sperm was receiving instructions in conception. The instructor said: 'As soon as you hear the siren, run for the tunnel and swim in a straight line until you reach the entrance of a damp cavern. At the end of the cavern you will find a red, sticky ball, which is the egg. Address it and say, "I'm a sperm." She will answer, "I'm the egg." From that moment on, you will work together to create the embryo. Do you understand?'

The sperm nodded in the affirmative, and the instructor said: 'Then good luck, chaps!'

Three days later, the sperm was taking a nap when he heard the siren. He woke up immediately and ran to the tunnel. A multitude of sperm swam behind him. He knew he had to arrive first. When he was near the entrance to the cavern, he looked back and saw that he was way ahead. Then he was able to swim at a slower pace until he reached the red, sticky ball. When, at last, he got to the red, sticky ball, he brightened up, smiled and said: 'Hi, I'm a sperm.'

The red, sticky ball smiled and said: 'Hi, I'm a tonsil.'

SPORTS

2237 It was the final of the Olympic heavyweight-wrestling tournament between a Russian and an American. The Russian started as favourite by virtue of his infamous 'pretzel' hold, from which no wrestler had ever escaped. The fight was evenly balanced until suddenly, without warning, the Russian managed to trap the American in a deadly pretzel. The American coach held his head in despair. The end, it seemed, was imminent. In fact the coach was turning to collect his gear when a roar erupted from the crowd. He turned to see the Russian flying through the air. As the Russian landed, the American immediately pinned him to win the gold medal. The crowd went wild.

Afterwards the coach asked the American: 'How did you get out of that pretzel hold? No one has ever done it before.'

The American wrestler admitted: 'I was ready to give up when he got me in that hold, but then I opened my eyes and saw this pair of balls right in front of my face. I thought I had nothing to lose, so with my last ounce of strength, I bit them as hard as I could. You'd be amazed how strong you get when you bite your own balls!'

2238 A swarm of flies were playing soccer in a saucer in a restaurant kitchen. After they had finished, one fly turned to another and said: 'You'll have to improve your game for tomorrow.'

'Why's that?'

'We're playing in the cup.'

2239 What's the difference between a hockey game and a High School reunion? – At a hockey game you see fast pucks.

2240 A guy was drinking in a bar when he met up with a slim, attractive girl who turned out to be a female jockey. They ended up in bed together, and she promised to give him tips for the race meeting at which she was riding the following day. She said that she would tip him the winner of each race she was riding in by giving him a sign as she rode out of the paddock.

Her first mount was in race two, and as she rode out of the paddock, she began rubbing both tits. The guy studied the racecard, saw Two Abreast, put $50 on, and it romped in at 5–1.

An hour later, she came out for race four, rubbing her finger around her eye. The guy noticed that Eyeliner was running in that race, put $50 on, and it came in at 3–1.

For the last race, she came out standing in her stirrups and rubbing her fanny. The guy was puzzled by this and backed nothing. Afterwards they met up and he thanked her for the winners in races two and four.

'What about Itchy Mick in the last at 20–1?' she asked.

'Damn!' said the guy. 'I thought you were telling me the cunt was scratched!'

2241 Why is David Beckham like Ferrero Rocher? – They both come in a posh box.

2242 What's the difference between David Beckham and Posh? – Posh Spice doesn't kick back when she's taken from behind.

2243 In a bid to speed up their pit stops, the Ferrari Formula One team sacked their entire pit crew and replaced them with local gang members who, it was said, could get the wheels off a car in less than four seconds without any proper equipment.

Come the day of the next Grand Prix and the gang members, working in the pits, did indeed change the tyres on Michael Schumacher's Ferrari in under four seconds. But there was a problem: within ten seconds they had resprayed and re-numbered the car and sold it to the McLaren team.

SURGERY

2244 A woman went to her doctor to tell him that she wanted an operation because the lips of her vagina were much too large. She asked the doctor to keep the operation a secret as she was embarrassed and didn't want anyone to find out. The doctor agreed to her request.

Coming round from the anaesthetic after the operation, she was alarmed to find three bunches of flowers in vases next to her bed. Outraged, she immediately summoned the doctor.

'I thought I asked you not to tell anyone about my operation!'

'Don't worry,' he said. 'I didn't tell a soul. The first bunch of flowers is from me – I felt bad because you had to go through this all by yourself. The second bunch is from the nurse who assisted me with the operation, and she'd previously had a similar operation herself.'

'What about the third bunch?' demanded the woman.

'That's from the guy upstairs in the burn unit. He wanted to thank you for his new ears!'

2245 What's the worst thing about getting a lung transplant? – The first couple of times you cough, it's not your phlegm.

2246 A young man went into hospital for some minor surgery, and the day after a friend dropped by to see how he was doing. The friend was amazed at the number of nurses who entered the room at short intervals with refreshments, offers to fluff his pillows, give back rubs, etc. 'Why all the attention?' asked the friend. 'You look fine to me.'

'I know!' grinned the patient. 'It's been like this ever since the nurses heard that my circumcision required twenty-seven stitches.'

2247 A married couple were involved in a terrible accident that left the woman with a badly burned face. The doctor told the husband that it was impossible to graft any skin from her body because she was so slim. So the husband offered to donate some of his own skin. However the only skin on his body that the doctor felt was suitable was on his buttocks. The husband and wife agreed that they would tell nobody where the skin came from, and also asked the doctor to honour their secret.

When the surgery was completed, everyone was astounded at the woman's new beauty. Indeed she looked more beautiful than ever. All her friends and family kept going on about her youthful looks. One day, alone with her husband, she was overcome with emotion at his generosity.

'Darling,' she said, 'I just want to thank you for everything you did for me. You have saved my life. There is no way I could ever repay you.'

'Honey,' he replied, 'think nothing of it. I get all the thanks I need every time I see your mother kiss you on the cheek.'

2248 Two surgeons were chatting in the bar after a round of golf. When the conversation turned to work, one said: 'I operated on Mr Reid the other day.'

'What for?' asked the other.

'About $19,000.'

'What did he have?'

'Oh, about $19,000!'

2249 The surgeon said to the patient: 'I have good news and bad news regarding your operation. The bad news is that it's an extremely risky procedure, and your chances of survival are a hundred to one.'

'Oh, my God!' cried the patient. 'So what's the good news?'

The surgeon replied: 'The good news is that my last ninety-nine patients died.'

2250 Following a dreadful accident with a chainsaw, a man's penis was mangled and ripped from his body. The doctor assured the patient that whilst modern medicine could repair the damage, the surgery would not be covered by his insurance since it was classified as cosmetic. When the patient asked what the cost of a new penis was likely to be, the doctor quoted him $3,500 for a small, $7,000 for a medium and $15,000 for a large. Naturally the man said he wanted a large, but the doctor advised him to talk it over with his wife before coming to a final decision.

So the man phoned his wife and explained the different options. The doctor came back into the room a few minutes later and found the man looking thoroughly dejected.

'Well, what have the two of you decided?' asked the doctor.

The man answered: 'She'd rather have a new kitchen.'

2251 Sam and John were out chopping wood when John accidentally cut his arm off. Sam wrapped the arm in a plastic bag and took the severed limb and John to a local surgeon. The surgeon examined the wound and said: 'You're in luck. I'm an expert at reattaching limbs. Come back in four hours.'

Sam returned four hours later and the surgeon said: 'I got done faster than I thought. John is down at the pub playing darts.' So Sam went to the pub and, sure enough, John was there playing darts.

A few weeks later John cut his leg off in another accident. Sam put the leg in a plastic bag and took it and John to the same surgeon. The surgeon studied the injury and said: 'Legs are a little tougher. Come back in six hours.'

Sam returned six hours later and the surgeon said: 'I finished early. John's out playing soccer.' Sam went to the local pitch and there was John playing soccer.

A few weeks later accident-prone John cut his head off. Sam put the head in a plastic bag and took it and the rest of John back to the surgeon. The surgeon considered the situation and said: 'Heads are really tough. Best come back in twelve hours.'

Sam returned twelve hours later, but the surgeon said: 'I'm sorry, John died.'

Sam said: 'I understand – heads are tough.'

The surgeon said: 'Oh, no, the surgery went fine. He suffocated in that plastic bag.'

Things You Don't Want To Hear During Surgery:

2252 ● Better save that – we'll need it for the autopsy.
2253 ● Accept this sacrifice, O Great Lord of Darkness!
2254 ● Hand me that . . . uh . . . that uh . . . thingie.
2255 ● Come back with that! Bad dog!
2256 ● Ooops! Hey, has anyone ever survived 500 ml of this stuff before?
2257 ● You know, there's big money in kidneys, and this guy's got two of them.
2258 ● What do you mean, he wasn't in for a sex change?
2259 ● I wish I hadn't forgotten my glasses.
2260 ● Well, folks, this will be an experiment for all of us.
2261 ● OK, sho I've had a few drinksh (hic).
2262 ● Wait a minute, if this is his spleen, what's that?
2263 ● Damn! Page 39 of the manual is missing.
2264 ● Sterile, schmerile. The floor's clean, right?
2265 ● What do you mean, he's not insured?
2266 ● Don't worry, it's probably sharp enough.
2267 ● The foot bone's connected to the leg bone . . .
2268 ● Fire! Fire! Everyone get out!

2269 • Has anyone seen my watch?
2270 • Damn! There go the lights again.
2271 • Everybody stand back! I lost my contact lens!
2272 • So which leg should it have been?
2273 • Let's hurry. I don't want to miss *Baywatch*.
2274 • Hey, Bill, unzip the bag on that one — he's still moving.
2275 • What do you mean, 'You want a divorce'?

TATTOOS

2276 A girl told her boyfriend to prove his love for her by getting her name, Wendy, tattooed on his penis. He agreed, and when erect, it spelt out her name in full, but when limp it just said Wy.

After their wedding, they went to a nudists' beach in Jamaica for their honeymoon. There, the husband spotted a black guy with Wy on his penis.

'You must have a wife named Wendy too?' said the husband.

'No, mine says, "Welcome to Jamaica man have a nice day."'

2277 A man went to a tattoo parlour and had the words 'yes' and 'no' tattooed on his dick. When he got home, he stripped off and showed his wife the aroused organ and its new tattoo.

'What do you think?' he asked.

'What do I think?' she yelled. 'You tell me how to cook, how tell me how to dress, you tell me how to wear my hair, you tell me how to clean the house . . . and now you're gonna put words in my mouth!'

2278 Two guys were sitting in a bar discussing their ideal date.

One said: 'I always look for a woman with long blonde hair, long slim legs and a short skirt. Because when I see a woman like that, I reckon here's a girl who knows what she wants and knows how to get it.'

The other said: 'I always look for a woman who has a tattoo.'

'Why a tattoo?'

'Because when I see a woman with a tattoo, I think here's a girl who's capable of making a decision she'll regret in the future.'

2279 A man went to a tattoo artist and asked him to put a tattoo of a $100 bill on his penis.

'Why on earth do you want a tattoo of a $100 bill on your penis?' asked the artist.

The man explained: 'First, I like to play with money. Second, I like to watch the money grow. And third, and most importantly, the next time my wife wants to blow $100, she can stay home to do it.'

2280 A guy and his new date were undressing in the bedroom. First, she spotted a NIKE tattoo on his shoulder. Then, as he took off more clothes, she saw a REEBOK tattoo on his ankle. 'This guy's got a training shoe fetish,' she thought.

Then when he removed his last item of clothing, she recoiled in horror. For there on his penis was the tattoo AIDS. 'No way am I going near that!' she shrieked.

'Relax,' he said. 'In a minute it'll say ADIDAS.'

TEXAS

2281 A New Yorker was travelling in Texas around Christmas time. In the small town square he admired the nativity scene but was puzzled by one thing: the three wise men were wearing firemen's helmets.

Unable to work out why, he decided to ask the old woman who served at the town store.

'Excuse me, ma'am,' he said, 'I'm not from these parts and I don't understand why the three wise men are wearing firemen's helmets.'

She snarled: 'You darn Yankees, you never read your Bibles!'

'I do,' he protested, 'but I don't recall anything in the Bible about firemen.'

She grabbed a Bible from beneath the counter and frantically leafed through the pages. Then waving the book under his nose, she barked: 'See, it says right here, "The three wise men came from afar . . ."'

2282 A professor at the University of Texas asked his students: 'Who believes in ghosts?' About half of them raised their hands. Then he asked how many thought they had seen a ghost. Around fifteen put their hands up. Next he asked how many present had touched a ghost. Five students raised their hands. 'Finally, there's one more question I want to ask: how many of you have made love to a ghost?' Everyone looked around the hall to see if there would be any response until right at the back Bubba raised his hand.

The professor was overjoyed. 'All the years I've been giving this lecture no one has ever claimed to have had sex with a ghost. Come on up here, young feller, and tell us about your experience.'

A grinning Bubba made his way to the front of the hall.

'So, Bubba,' said the professor, 'tell us what it's like to have sex with a ghost.'

Bubba suddenly looked bewildered. 'Heck! From way back there I thought you said "Goats"!'

2283 Three married guys died and met St Peter at the Pearly Gates. St Peter asked the first guy: 'Did you ever cheat on your wife?'

The guy answered truthfully: 'Every chance I got.'

St Peter pointed to two doors, telling the guy to enter the second one. He then turned to the second guy and asked him: 'Did you ever cheat on your wife?'

'A couple of times,' the guy muttered.

St Peter ordered him through door two. Then he asked the third guy: 'Did you ever cheat on your wife?'

The guy gave it some thought and said: 'Well, there was one time. You see, I was in this saloon in Texas, and I noticed they had only one cowgirl working there to look after all the guys. I asked the bartender how come, and he said: "She's all we need. That filly can suck a baseball bat through a garden hose!" So that's when I cheated on my wife.'

St Peter told the guy to enter door number one.

The guy asked: 'What's the deal? You sent the others to door number two.'

'I know,' said St Peter, 'and they're both going to hell. But you and I are going to Texas!'

2284 A businessman from California was chatting to a girl in a Texas bar. After a few drinks, he invited her to his hotel room, and she readily agreed. As she eagerly stripped off, he asked her how old she was.

'Thirteen,' she replied.

'Thirteen!' he exclaimed in horror. 'My God! Get those clothes back on at once and get the hell out of here. Are you crazy?'

As she grabbed her things and headed for the door, she turned to him and said: 'Superstitious, huh?'

Things You Won't Hear In Texas:

2285 • Duct tape won't fix that.

2286 • Actually, I'll have a Heineken.

2287 • We don't keep firearms in this house.

2288 • You can't feed that to the dog.

2289 • I thought Graceland was a bit tacky.

2290 • No kids in the back of the pickup, it's just not safe.

2291 • Honey, did you mail that donation to Greenpeace?

2292 • Oh, I just couldn't. She's only sixteen.

2293 • We're vegetarians.

2294 • Do you think my gut is too big?

2295 • Honey, we don't need another dog.

2296 • Spitting is such a vile habit.

2297 • Trim the fat off that steak.

2298 • No more for me, I'm driving tonight.

2299 A Texan went to Toronto on vacation. On the cab ride from the airport to his downtown hotel, he passed Queens Park.

'What's that?' asked the Texan.

'Oh, that's Queens Park,' said the cab driver. 'It's our provincial government — it's like your state government. Those buildings are nearly two hundred years old and are pretty big.'

'That's nothing,' said the Texan. 'We have buildings much older than that back home and at least twice as large!'

Shortly afterwards they passed First Canadian Place.

'What's that?' asked the Texan.

'It's the biggest office complex in the country,' replied the cab driver. 'It took nearly four years to build.'

'That's nothing,' sneered the Texan. 'In Houston we have buildings twice that big and built in less than half the time!'

By now the cabby was becoming irritated by the Texan's boasting. Soon they drove past the CN Tower. The Texan leaned out of the window and stared up at the 1,850ft tower.

'What's that?' he asked.

The cab driver said: 'Damned if I know. It wasn't there yesterday!'

2300 Why doesn't Texas slide off into the Gulf? — Because Oklahoma sucks.

2301 Gabriel came to the Lord and said: 'I have to talk to you. We have some Texans up here in heaven who are causing problems. They're swinging on the Pearly Gates, my horn is missing, their dogs are riding in the chariots, and they insists on wearing baseball caps and cowboy hats instead of their halos. Also they refuse to keep the stairway to heaven clean – there are watermelon seeds all over the place.'

The Lord said: 'I made them special, Gabriel. Heaven is home to all my children. If you want to know about real problems, let's call the Devil.'

So they phoned down to hell, and asked the Devil what sort of problems he was experiencing. 'Hang on a second, will you,' said the Devil. 'I have to sort something out.' They heard shouting in the background. When the Devil returned to the phone, he groaned: 'You'll never believe the day I'm having! Those damn Texans have put out the fire and are trying to install air conditioning!'

2302 A Texan farm-girl answered the door and found her father's neighbour standing there. 'My paw ain't home,' she said, 'but I know what you want. You want our bull to service your cow. Well, my paw charges $150 for his best bull.'

'That's not what I want,' said the neighbour tetchily.

'Well, we also have a young bull – my paw charges $100 for him.'

'That's not what I want,' growled the neighbour.

'In which case, we do have an old bull in the pasture. My paw charges $50 for him.'

'That's not what I want, either!' snarled the neighbour. 'I came to see your pa about your brother, Elmer. He's gone and got my daughter pregnant!'

The girl said: 'Oh, I guess you'll have to see my paw about that then, 'cos I don't know what he charges for Elmer.'

2303 A rich old Texan woman was feeling generous at Thanksgiving. So she called up the local military base and asked to speak with the lieutenant.

She said: 'Please send up four nice young men to eat dinner at my mansion on Thanksgiving. But don't send any Jews. Please, no Jews.'

The lieutenant thanked her for her generosity.

On Thanksgiving the woman opened the door to find four young black soldiers standing there. 'There must be some mistake,' she spluttered.

'No, ma'am,' said one. 'Lieutenant Goldstein doesn't make mistakes.'

You Know You're a True Texan When:

2304 • Your idea of a traffic jam is ten cars waiting to pass a tractor on the highway.

2305 • 'Vacation' means going to the family reunion.

2306 • You've seen all the biggest bands . . . ten years after they were popular.

2307 • You measure distance in minutes.

2308 • You know several people who have hit a deer.

2309 • Your school classes were cancelled because of cold.

2310 • Your school classes were cancelled because of heat.

2311 • You think of the four major food groups as beef, pork, beer, and Jell-O salad with marshmallows.

2312 • You think sexy lingerie is a T-shirt and boxer shorts.

2313 • You know which leaves make good toilet paper.

2314 Three Texas surgeons were arguing about which was the most skilful.

The first said: 'Three years ago, I reattached seven fingers on a pianist. He went on to give a recital before the Queen of England!'

The second boasted: 'That's nothing. I attended a man in a car smash. All his arms and legs were severed from his body. Two years later, thanks to my surgical expertise, he won a track and field gold medal at the Olympic Games!'

The third said: 'A few years back, I operated on a cowboy. He was high on drink when he rode his horse head-on into a Santa Fe freight train travelling at 100 mph. All I had to work with was the horse's ass and a ten-gallon hat. Last year, he was re-elected President of the United States!'

THERAPY

2315 *Girl*: I have committed a great sin. I called a boy a bastard.

Psychiatrist: That's not a nice thing to call someone. What did he do to deserve it?

Girl: Well, he kissed me.

Psychiatrist: You mean, like this?

Girl: Yes!

Psychiatrist: Well, that's no reason to call him a bastard.

Girl: But he put his hand inside my bra.

Psychiatrist: You mean, like this?

Girl: Yes!

Psychiatrist: Well, that's no reason to call him a bastard.

Girl: But he took my clothes off.

Psychiatrist: You mean, like this?

Girl: Yes!

Psychiatrist: Well, that's no reason to call him a bastard.

Girl: But he had sex with me.

Psychiatrist: You mean, like this?

Girl: Yes!

Psychiatrist: Well, that's still no reason to call him a bastard.

Girl: But he told me has AIDS.

Psychiatrist: The bastard!

2316 Two married women, Lynn and Christine, were discussing their sex lives over lunch.

'To tell you the truth,' confessed Lynn, 'Jay and I have been having some problems.'

'Really?' said Christine. 'So have Frank and I. In fact, we're thinking of going to see a sex therapist.'

'Oh, we could never do that,' said Lynn. 'We'd be too embarrassed. But if you go, I'd be interested to hear how got on.'

A couple of months later the two friends met for lunch again.

'So how did the sex therapy work out?' asked Lynn.

'Things couldn't be better!' said Christine. 'We began with a physical examination, and afterwards the doctor said he was sure he could help us. He told us to stop at the grocery store on the way home and buy a bunch of grapes and a dozen donuts. He told us to sit on the floor naked and to toss the grapes and donuts at each other. Whenever a grape went into my vagina, John had to get it out with his tongue. Every donut that I ringed his penis with, I had to eat. It's put a real spark back into our sex life.'

Encouraged by this report, Lynn managed to persuade her husband to book an appointment with the same therapist. After the physical examinations were completed, the doctor called Lynn and Jay into his office.

'I'm afraid there is nothing I can do for you,' he said.

'Wait a minute,' interrupted Lynn. 'You did such a wonderful job for our friends, Christine and Frank, surely there must be something you can suggest to boost our sex life? Please can you help us? Anything at all.'

'Well, OK,' said the doctor. 'On your way home, I want you to stop at the grocery store and buy a bag of apples and a box of Cheerios . . .'

2317 How many Freudian analysts does it take to change a light bulb? – Two. One to change the bulb and one to hold the penis, I mean ladder.

2318 After hearing a couple complain that their sex life wasn't as exciting as it used to be, a sex therapist suggested they try some new positions. 'For example,' he said, 'you might try the wheelbarrow.'

'The wheelbarrow? What's that?' asked the husband.

The therapist explained: 'You just lift her legs, penetrate, and off you go.'

The husband liked the sound of that and was keen to try out the new position as soon as they got home. 'Well, OK,' agreed the wife hesitantly, 'but on two conditions. First, if it hurts, you'll stop right away. And second, you must promise you won't go past my mother's.'

2319 A guy went to a psychiatrist. After listening to his problems, the psychiatrist declared: 'I think your problem is low self-esteem. It's very common among total losers.'

2320 The mother of a problem child was advised by a psychiatrist: 'You worry about your son too much, and it is causing you needless anxiety. I'm going to put you on a course of tranquillizers.'

On her next visit, the psychiatrist asked: 'Have the tranquillizers calmed you down?'

'Oh, yes,' replied the woman. 'They have worked wonders.'

'And how is your son now?'

'Who cares?'

2321 A man walked into a therapist's office, looking thoroughly depressed. 'Doc, you've got to help me. I can't go on like this.'

'What's the problem?' asked the therapist.

'I'm 39 years old and I still have no luck with the ladies. No matter how hard I try, I just seem to scare them away.'

'This is not a serious problem,' said the therapist. 'You just need to work on your self-esteem. Each morning, I want you to get up and go straight to the bathroom mirror. Tell yourself that you are a good person, a fun person, an attractive person. But say it with real conviction. Within a week you'll have women swarming all over you.'

The man seemed happy with this advice but when he returned to the therapist three weeks later, he was looking just as miserable as before.

'Did my advice not work?' asked the therapist.

'It worked all right,' said the man. 'For the past three weeks I've enjoyed some of the best moments in my life with the most fabulous-looking women.'

'So, what's your problem?'

'I don't have a problem,' said the man. 'My wife does!'

2322 A psychiatrist was travelling home from work by train when he noticed the old man opposite talking to himself then laughing aloud. Every so often the man would raise his hand, stop talking, and then start all over again.

Intrigued by what was clearly a fascinating case, the psychiatrist eventually asked: 'Can I help in any way? I'm a trained psychiatrist.'

'Thanks, but no,' said the old man. 'It's nothing out of the ordinary. You see, to keep myself awake on the journey, I tell myself jokes.'

'But why do you keep raising you hand?' asked the psychiatrist.

'Oh, that's to stop me telling a joke I've heard before.'

2323 When over a hundred people turned up for a group therapy session, the speaker decided to break the ice by asking how often those present had sex. First he asked for a show of hands from anyone who had sex almost every night. A few people raised their hands. Then he asked how many had sex once a week. A larger number of hands were raised. Next he asked how many had sex once every two weeks or once a month. More hands were raised. After polling his group several more times, the speaker spotted one guy sitting at the side of the auditorium with a huge grin on his face. The speaker had noticed that the guy never raised his hand, so he asked him how often he had sex.

The grinning guy replied: 'Once a year.'

The puzzled speaker inquired: 'Why are you so happy getting sex only once a year?'

Still beaming, the guy said: 'Tonight's the night!'

2324 A guy went to a therapist who asked: 'How is your sex life?'

The man admitted: 'I have a lot of issues with sex.'

'Hmm. What kind of issues?'

'Oh, mostly *Hustler* and *Penthouse*.'

2325 Unable to find a man who could satisfy her physically, a woman sought the advice of a sex therapist.

In desperation, she asked him: 'Isn't there some way to judge the size of a man's equipment from the outside?'

'The only foolproof way is by the size of his feet,' counselled the therapist.

So the woman headed downtown and cruised the streets until she spotted a young guy with the biggest feet she had ever seen. She took him out to dinner, wined and dined him, and then took him back to her apartment for a night of passion.

When the guy woke up the next morning, she had already left for work. But on the bedside table was a $50 bill and a note that read: 'With my compliments, take this money and go out and buy a pair of shoes that fit you.'

2326 A guy went to a psychiatrist. 'Doc, you've got to help me. My wife is unfaithful to me. Every Friday night, she goes to Larry's bar and picks up men. She sleeps with anybody who asks her! I'm going crazy. What should I do?'

'Relax,' said the psychiatrist. 'Take a deep breath and calm down. Now, tell me, where exactly is Larry's bar?'

2327 A man told a psychiatrist: 'I have this recurring dream in which five women rush into the room and start tearing off my clothes.'

'What do you do?' asked the psychiatrist.

'I push them away.'

'I see, and how can I help you?'

'Please, break my arms.'

2328 A seventy-eight-year-old couple went to a sex therapist's office. The old man asked: 'Will you watch us having sexual intercourse?'

The therapist was puzzled by the request, but agreed. When they had finished, he said: 'There's nothing wrong with the way you have intercourse. That will be $50.'

This happened several weeks in a row. Each time the couple would make an appointment, have intercourse with no problems, pay the therapist and leave. Eventually the therapist asked: 'What exactly are you trying to find out?'

The old man said: 'We're not trying to find out anything. She's married and we can't go to her house. I'm married and we can't go to my house. The Hilton charges $110, the Holiday Inn charges $90. We do it here for $50, and I get $43 back from Medicare!'

TOILETS

2329 A male passenger travelling by plane was desperate to use the toilet, but because there was a long queue and he couldn't hold it in any longer, the flight attendant suggested he use the ladies' washroom instead.

'But, whatever you do,' she warned, 'don't press any of the buttons.'

Of course, once he was inside and sitting down, his relief was such that his curiosity got the better of him and he pressed the WW button on the wall, whereupon warm water sprayed on to his bare bottom. It was a pleasurable experience, so he pressed the WA button, causing warm air to dry his wet bottom. Next he pressed the PP button and a soft disposable powder puff dusted his bottom lightly with talc.

'Man, this is great,' he thought as he reached out for the ATR button.

He woke in hospital just as the anaesthetic was wearing off. Confused, he buzzed the nurse.

'Where am I?' he asked. 'What happened? The last thing I remember was being on a plane and feeling intense pain as I sat in the ladies' room.'

The nurse said: 'Yes, you must have been having a great time until you pressed the Automatic Tampon Removal button. By the way, your penis is under your pillow.'

2330 While taking a class, a schoolteacher noticed a puddle under a little girl's chair.

'Oh, Samantha!' said the teacher. 'You should have put your hand up.'

'I did,' said Samantha, 'but it still trickled through my fingers.'

2331 What's the difference between toilet paper and toast? – Toast is brown on both sides.

2332 A man went to the doctor because he was getting a burning sensation every time he pooped. The doctor told him that in order to get rid of it, he would need to clean out his colon once a week for the next month. He gave the man a cleaning rod and shoved it up his butt for the first cleaning.

The man took the rod home and a week later attempted the cleaning himself. Unable to get it at the right angle, he called his wife to help. So she shoved it up and cleaned out his colon for him. As she finished, he suddenly gasped.

'What is it, darling?' she asked, concerned.

'I just realized,' he said. 'When the doctor did it, he had both hands on my shoulders!'

2333 A guy was in the urinal of a bar when he heard two voices coming from one of the cubicles.

'Get lost, will you?' said one voice.

'No, it's my turn,' said the other.

'But you had it earlier.'

'Let me have it, you bastard.'

'No way, I'm not finished!'

Back in the bar, the guy relayed this conversation to the bartender. The bartender said: 'Oh, don't worry. It's just those Siamese twins having a wank.'

2334 Three men were standing side-by-side using the urinal. The first man finished, zipped up, and began washing and scrubbing his hands furiously. He did right up to his elbows and got through about twenty paper towels. When he had finished, he turned to the other two and said: 'I graduated from the University of Michigan and they taught us to be clean.'

The second guy finished, zipped up, quickly wet the tips of his fingers, grabbed one paper towel and commented: 'I graduated from the University of California and they taught us to be environmentally conscious.'

The third man zipped up and as he was walking out the door, said: 'I graduated from Penn State and they taught us not to pee on our hands.'

2335 A guy was sitting in the men's room cubicle at a highway stopover when he heard a voice coming from the next cubicle.

'Hi, how are you doing?' asked the voice.

Embarrassed at the sudden intrusion of privacy, the guy replied hesitantly: 'Er . . . yeah . . . I'm OK!'

'And what are you up to?' asked the voice from next door.

The guy didn't really know what to say. 'Pretty much the same as you, I guess!'

Then the voice said: 'Look, I'll call you back. There's some idiot in the next cubicle answering all the questions I'm asking you!'

2336 A drunk staggered into the bar toilet. A few minutes later, a blood-curdling scream was heard from inside the toilet. Then another. The bartender decided to investigate.

'What's the problem?' the bartender called out.

A drunken voice from within replied: 'I'm just sitting here on the toilet and every time I try to flush, something comes up and squeezes the hell out of my balls!'

The bartender opened the door, looked in and said: 'You're sitting on the mop bucket!'

2337 Sitting in a public toilet, a man discovered when it was too late that there was no toilet paper. So he called to the guy in the next cubicle: 'Do you have any toilet paper in there?'

'Sorry, no.'

'What about paper tissues?'

'No, none of those either. Sorry.'

'How about newspaper? Is there a sheet of newspaper you could give me?'

'Sorry, pal, I don't have any newspaper.'

'OK. Can you give me two fives for a ten?'

2338 A small boy, just potty trained, hit everything but the toilet whenever he went to the bathroom. So his mother always had to go in and clean up after him. After six weeks of this, she decided to take him to the doctor.

After examining him, the doctor concluded that the boy's penis was too small, and suggested an old wives' cure of two slices of toast each morning. This, the doctor hoped, would make the boy's penis grow sufficiently for him to be able to hold it properly and aim straight.

Next morning the boy ran down to breakfast and saw twelve slices of toast on the table.

'But, mom,' he yelled, 'the doctor said I only had to eat two slices.'

'I know,' said his mother, 'the other ten are for your father.'

2339 A group of third, fourth and fifth graders accompanied by two female teachers went on a field trip to the local racetrack to learn about thoroughbred horses and the supporting industry. During the tour some of the children needed to go to the toilet, so it was decided that the girls would go with one teacher and the boys with the other.

As the teacher assigned to the boys waited outside the men's toilet, one of the boys came out and told her that he and some of his friends couldn't reach the urinals. Left with no choice, the teacher went inside and began hoisting the little boys up by their armpits, one by one.

As she lifted one up by the armpits, she couldn't help noticing that he was unusually well-endowed for an elementary school child. 'I guess you must be in the fifth,' she said.

'No, ma'am,' he replied. 'I'm in the seventh, riding King's Treasure. Thanks for the lift anyway.'

2340   While out at lunch with his manager, Sean Connery excused himself to go to the washroom. A few minutes later he returned and the front of his trousers were soaking wet.

His manager said: 'Sean, what's up? Do you need an operation or something?'

The actor said, 'No, it's just that whenever I go into a public restroom and I'm taking a piss, the guy next to me always turns and says, "Hey, are you Sean Connery . . . ?"'

TOYBOYS

2341   A middle-aged woman spotted a cute young man working in her local supermarket. When she reached the checkout, she asked whether someone could carry her shopping to the car and was delighted to see the manager nominate the young man for the task.

Once outside in the car park, she whispered suggestively: 'Young man, I have an itchy fanny.'

He said: 'You'll have to point it out to me, madam. All those Japanese cars look the same to me!'

2342   A farmer's neglected wife sneaked behind the barn to watch the young hired hand taking a pee. Staring in disbelief at his huge dick, she said: 'Boy, I'd sure like to have some of that!'

'Well,' he said innocently, 'you'd best run and get a cup 'cos I'm about through.'

TRAVEL

2343   Two women met in the gymnasium of a cruise ship. One said: 'This is my first cruise. My husband saved up for months to send me on this trip. Have you been on a cruise before?'

'Yes,' said the other, 'I've been on over thirty cruises. That's not surprising, though – my husband works for Cunard.'

'Mine works hard too,' said the first, 'so there's no need to swear!'

2344 Two old ladies were sitting waiting for a bus. One said: 'I hate it when the buses run late. I've been sitting here so long that my butt has fallen asleep.'

'I know,' said the other. 'I heard it snoring.'

2345 A father was worried sick because his twenty-year-old daughter had hitch-hiked alone all the way from Los Angeles to Washington. 'You could have been attacked or raped,' he warned.

'I was never in any danger,' she insisted. 'As soon as someone offered me a ride, I said I was going to Washington because that's where they have the best treatment for sexually transmitted diseases.'

2346 A guy got on a bus, sat in the front seat, spat on the floor and said: 'What a driver!' After he had spat and cursed half a dozen times, the driver ordered him off at the next stop.

The guy promptly spat on the sidewalk and said: 'What a driver!'

A man who had got off at the same stop said: 'I didn't think the bus driver was that bad.'

'I'm not talking about him,' said the first guy. 'When I was walking to the bus stop, I saw this ugly fat broad trying to park a pink Cadillac convertible in a space that was about a foot longer than the car. I shouted: "Lady, if you can get that car into that space, I'll eat your snatch!" Ptui! What a driver . . .!'

2347 After seeing a young couple having sex in a carriage, a train ticket inspector summoned the police. The young man was arrested for having a first-class ride with a second-class ticket.

2348 An old man got on a crowded bus and no one gave him a seat. As the bus shook, the old man's cane slipped on the floor and he fell. As he got to his feet, a nine-year-old boy sitting nearby said: 'Hey, mister, if you put a little rubber thingy on the end of your stick, it wouldn't slip.'

The old man replied: 'Well, sonny, if your daddy had done the same thing nine years ago, I'd have a bloody seat today!'

UGLINESS

2349 A guy went into a pharmacy and asked for a vial of cyanide
'Why do you want a vial of cyanide?' asked the pharmacist.
The man replied: 'I want to kill my wife.'
'I'm sorry,' said the pharmacist, 'but there's no way I can sell you cyanide so that you can kill your wife.'
With that, the guy reached into his wallet and pulled out a photo of his wife. The pharmacist looked at the photo of the ugliest woman he had ever seen, blushed and answered: 'My mistake, sir, let me get it for you. I didn't realize you had a prescription.'

2350 A guy phoned his lawyer and said: 'Is it true that people are suing cigarette companies for causing them to get cancer?'
'Yes, it's true,' said the lawyer. 'I have three such cases ongoing.'
'And am I right in thinking that someone is now suing fast food restaurants for making him fat?'
'That's right,' said the lawyer.
'In that case,' said the guy, 'can I sue Budweiser for all them ugly women I've slept with?'

2351 A guy starting a new job was told by his boss: 'Marry my daughter and I'll make you a partner in the firm, give you an expense account, a Mercedes, and a million-dollar salary.'
Naturally suspicious, the guy asked: 'What's wrong with her?'
The boss showed him a picture of the daughter and she was truly hideous. 'It's only fair to tell you,' added the boss, 'she's not only ugly, she's stupid too.'
'No way,' said the guy. 'I don't care what you offer me – it won't be enough to make me marry her.'
'Listen,' persisted the boss, 'I'll give you an annual salary of $5 million and build you a mansion on Long Island.'
This was tempting. So the guy accepted, figuring that he could always put a bag over her head during sex. And they duly got married.
Twelve months later, the guy was in the process of hanging a Picasso original on the wall of their new mansion. Climbing the ladder, he called to his wife: 'Bring me a hammer.'
She mumbled to herself, 'Get the hammer, get the hammer,' and handed him the hammer.

'Fetch me some nails,' he added.

She mumbled to herself, 'Get the nails, get the nails,' and fetched the nails.

As he hammered the nail into the wall, he accidentally hit his thumb. 'Fuck!' he yelled.

She mumbled to herself: 'Get the bag, get the bag.'

2352 A good looking man strolled into a singles bar, bought a drink and settled down ready to use his best chat up lines. But for the next two hours every woman he approached gave him the brush-off. Then suddenly a really ugly guy walked in and within seconds he was surrounded by beautiful, available women. A few minutes later he sauntered out with a stunning brunette on each arm.

The handsome guy was thoroughly despondent. Turning to the barman, he said: 'Tell me, why haven't I been able to pull all night when that really ugly man comes in and walks out with the most beautiful women in the bar?'

'I don't know what his secret is,' said the barman. 'But he does the same thing every night. He walks in, orders a drink, and just sits there licking his eyebrows . . .'

2353 How do you know if you're really ugly? – Dogs hump your leg with their eyes closed.

2354 A guy was out driving when he was pulled over by the police.

'Have you been drinking, sir?' asked the officer.

'Well, yes, a bit. But how did you know? Was I weaving all over the road?'

'No,' said the officer, 'you were driving splendidly. It was the fat, ugly chick in the passenger seat that gave you away.'

UNDERWEAR

2355 Three women walking down the street were stopped by a man conducting a survey. He asked: 'Ladies, would you mind telling me how you know if you've had a good night out?'

The first replied: 'I come home, get into bed, and if I lay there and tingle all over, I know that I had a good night.'

The second answered: 'I come home, have a shower and a glass of wine, get into bed, and if I tingle all over, I know I've had a good night.'

The third one said: 'If I get home, rip off my knickers, throw them against the wall, and they stick, then I know it was a good night.'

2356 Two women got blind drunk on a hen night. Staggering home, they became desperate for a pee and decided to relieve themselves in a cemetery. When they had finished, one used her panties to wipe herself and then threw them away. The other woman was wearing expensive knickers, so rather than ruin them, she wiped herself clean with a card from a nearby wreath.

The next morning the two husbands were discussing their wives' behaviour over the phone. One said: 'I think we need to start keeping a closer eye on the girls. My wife came home last night without any knickers on.'

'Tell me about it,' said the other husband. 'My wife came home with a card stuck to her fanny that read: "We will never forget you."'

2357 Why do women wear black underwear? – They're in mourning for the stiff they buried the night before.

2358 Three small boys were sitting in the park. One said: 'My Daddy smokes, and he can blow smoke rings.'

The second said: 'Well, my Dad smokes, and he can blow smoke out of his ears.'

Determined not to be outdone, the third said: 'My Dad can blow smoke out of his ass!'

'Have you actually seen him do that?' asked his friends.

'Not exactly, but I've seen the tobacco stains on his underpants.'

2359 One day a girl decided to buy some crotchless panties to surprise her boyfriend. When the boyfriend got home, she was waiting for him, lying spreadeagled on the bed wearing only her bra and her new panties.

'Come here, baby,' she purred seductively.

The guy backed off. 'No way. If your pussy can do that to your panties, I ain't going anywhere near it!'

2360 When a wife returned home from a shopping expedition with some expensive new underwear, her husband was horrified by the price tag.

'Don't be so mean,' she said. 'After all, you wouldn't expect to find fine perfume in a cheap bottle, would you?'

'No,' he replied. 'And nor would I expect to find gift-wrapping on a dead beaver!'

2361 A woman sent her clothing to a Chinese laundry, but when it came back, there were still stains on her panties. So the following a week she enclosed a note: 'Use more soap on panties.' The laundryman responded with a note of his own: 'Use more paper on ass.'

2362 A nun went to her first confession and told the priest: 'Father, I never wear any panties under my habit.'

'That's not so serious,' said the priest. 'Say five Hail Marys, five Our Fathers, and do five cartwheels on your way to the altar.'

VAMPIRES

2363 Why do vampires drink blood? – Because coffee keeps them awake all day.

2364 How can you tell if a vampire is lazy? – He uses leeches.

2365 Why did the vampire give his girlfriend a blood test? – To see if she was his type.

VASECTOMY

2366 After having their eleventh child, an Alabama couple decided that enough was enough. So the husband went to the doctor and told him that he and he and his wife didn't want any more children. The doctor told him there was a procedure called a vasectomy that could provide the solution. The doctor instructed him to go home, get a huge firework called a cherry bomb, light it, put it in a beer can, then hold the can up to his ear and count to ten.

The guy said to the doctor: 'I may not be the smartest man on this earth, but I don't see how putting a cherry bomb in a beer can next to my ear is going to help me.'

So the couple drove across the state border into Georgia to get a second opinion. The Georgia physician was just about to tell them about the procedure for a vasectomy when he noticed that they were from Alabama. Instead the doctor told the man to go home, get a cherry bomb, light it, place it in a can, hold it to his ear and count to ten.

Figuring that both physicians couldn't be wrong, the guy went home, lit a cherry bomb, and put it in a beer can. He held the can up to his ear and began counting '1,2,3,4,5 . . .' at which point he paused, placed the beer can between his legs and resumed counting on the other hand.

2367 A man went to his doctor and said: 'I'm thinking about having a vasectomy.'

'That's a pretty big decision,' said the doctor. 'Have you talked it over with your family?'

'Yeah, and they're in favour, fifteen to two.'

VERMONT

2368 Three guys were trying to sneak into the Olympic Village in Athens for souvenirs and autographs by posing as competitors.

The first guy grabbed a small sapling, stripped off the branches and roots, walked up to the registration table and said: 'Chuck Wagon, Canada, javelin.' They gave him his hotel keys, meal tickets and passes, and wished him good luck.

The second guy grabbed a manhole cover, walked up to the registration table and said: 'Dusty Rhodes, Australia, discus.' He, too, was admitted to the village and wished good luck.

The third guy – a simple country boy – walked up to the registration table with a roll of barbed wire under his arm. He said: 'Foster Bean, Vermont USA, fencing.'

2369 Three Americans were sitting in a bar. The guy from Maine said: 'My wife is so dumb, she carries an automatic garage door opener in her car and she doesn't have an automatic garage door!'

The guy from Maryland said: 'My wife is so dumb, she has a cellular phone antenna on her car and she doesn't even have a cellular phone!'

The guy from Vermont said: 'My wife is so dumb, she carries a purse full of condoms and she doesn't even have a dick!'

2370 Two Vermont farmers bought a truckload of watermelons, paying one dollar apiece for them. They drove to market and sold all the melons for the same price they'd paid for them. After counting the money at the end of the day, they realized that they'd finished up with no more money than they'd started with. 'See!' said one. 'I told you we should have got a bigger truck!'

2371 A Vermont couple's sex life was so bad that they went out and bought a sex manual. 'Honey,' said the husband, 'I want to perform oral sex with you like it says in the book, but it smells so bad. Why don't you go out and buy some of that feminine deodorant spray?'

The wife agreed, and returned an hour later, very excited. 'You should see the flavours they have!' she said. 'Strawberry, cherry, banana . . .'

'What flavour did you get?'

'Tuna.'

VIAGRA

2372 A middle-aged guy went to his doctor and asked for a prescription of the strongest Viagra available because he had got two young nymphomaniacs staying at his house for a few days.

Later that week he went back to the doctor and asked for painkillers.

'What's the problem?' asked the doctor. 'Is your penis in that much pain?'

'No,' said the guy. 'It's for my wrists – the girls never showed up.'

2373 An old man went to the drug store and asked the pharmacist for Viagra.

'How many?' asked the pharmacist.

'Just a few,' said the old man, 'but can you cut each one into quarters?'

'That's too small a dose – tiny quarters of Viagra won't get you through sex.'

'That's OK,' said the old man. 'I don't think about sex any more. I'm too old. I just want it to stick out far enough so that I don't pee on my shoes.'

2374 Did you hear about the new Viagra eye drops? – They make you look hard.

2375 Did you hear about the first death from an overdose of Viagra? – A man took twelve pills and his wife died.

2376 Did you know that Viagra now comes in a nasal spray? – It's for dickheads.

2377 An old man stood up slowly and put on his coat.
'Where are you going?' asked his equally aged wife.
'I'm going to the doctor's.'
'Are you sick?'
'No, I'm going to get some of those Viagra pills.'
At this, the wife climbed from her rocker and put on her coat.
'Where are you going?' he asked.
'I'm going to the doctor's too. If you're going to start using that rusty old thing, I'm going to get a tetanus shot!'

2378 A man suffered serious sunburn after falling asleep on a Spanish beach. His wife rushed him to hospital where the doctor rubbed lotion over him and prescribed Viagra.
'Viagra?' exclaimed the wife. 'What good is Viagra in his condition?'
The doctor replied: 'It will keep the sheets off him.'

2379 Did you hear about the guy who took a course of iron tablets along with Viagra? – Now his dick always points due north.

2380 A woman went to the doctor to discuss her husband's sexual problems. The doctor said: 'Just give him these Viagra pills in his next meal and stand back.'
The woman went home, handed the pills to her Italian cook, who was preparing for a large dinner party, and said: 'Just put two of these in my husband's dinner tonight.'
Rushed off her feet, the cook was irritated by the request, and instead threw the whole packet into the soup. As the guests were sitting down to dinner, she rushed out of the kitchen and told the lady of the house that there was a problem. So the woman followed the cook into the kitchen and demanded to know what was going on.
Breaking down in tears, the cook admitted: 'I was in such a rush, I threw all of those pills into the soup. Now I don't know what to do. The meat balls have doubled in size and the vermicelli is standing straight up!'

2381 What happens when a lawyer takes Viagra? – He grows taller.

2382 What do you get when you smoke pot and take Viagra? – Stiff joints.

2383 What do the vacuum cleaner 'Dirt Devil' and Viagra have in common? – They both put the power of an upright in the palm of your hand.

2384 Did you hear about the guy who left his Viagra tablet in his shirt pocket when he sent it to the laundry? – Now the shirt is too stiff to wear.

2385 A woman asked her husband whether he'd like some breakfast. 'Bacon and eggs, perhaps a slice of toast? Maybe a nice half of grapefruit and a cup of fresh coffee?'

He declined. 'It's this Viagra – it's really taken the edge off my appetite.'

At lunchtime, she asked him again whether he would like anything. 'How about a bowl of homemade soup and a chicken sandwich? Or how about a plate of snacks and a glass of milk?'

'No, sorry,' he said. 'It's this Viagra – it's really taken the edge off my appetite.'

At dinnertime, she asked again if he wanted anything to eat. 'I could rustle up a tasty stir fry, I could put a pizza in the oven, or even go down the road and fetch a burger. What do you say? It would only take a few minutes.'

'Thanks, but no,' he replied. 'It's this Viagra – it's really taken the edge off my appetite.'

'Well, then,' she snapped, 'would you mind getting off me? I'm fucking starving!'

2386 Did you hear about the new type of Viagra, Viagra Lite? – It's for people who only want to masturbate.

2387 A guy picked up his Viagra prescription at the pharmacy. He arrived home full of anticipation but decided to wait until his wife got back before taking one. In the meantime he left the pack open and unattended on the table, and his inquisitive pet parrot ate all the pills. When he realized what had happened, the man was seized with panic at what effect a heavy dose of Viagra might have on the parrot. So he shut the bird in the freezer to cool off.

When his wife eventually arrived home, he forgot all about the parrot, and it was another four hours before he opened the freezer door. To his immense relief, the parrot was still alive, breathing heavily and dripping with sweat.

'My God!' exclaimed the man. 'You've been in there for hours yet not only are you still alive, you're sweating like crazy!'

'Of course I'm sweating!' said the parrot. 'Have you ever tried to prise apart the legs of a frozen chicken?'

VIBRATORS

2388 An old lady was walking down the street, shaking like hell. When she came across a sex shop, she looked in the window. Still shaking, she went in and stammered to the guy behind the counter: 'Do you sell those big black dildos?'

'Yes,' replied the guy.

'Well,' said the little old lady, 'can you tell me how to turn the damn things off?'

2389 What do tofu and a dildo have in common? – They're both meat substitutes.

2390 How do you know if a woman used a vibrator while she was pregnant? – The kid stutters.

2391 On his first day working at a sex shop, a young guy was left alone for the afternoon while his boss visited a supplier. The guy was nervous about dealing with the customer's questions, but the boss assured him he would be fine.

The first customer was an elderly white lady. 'How much for the white dildo?' she asked.

'$35,' he said.

'And how much for the black one?'

'Same price, $35.'

'Right,' she said. 'I think I'll take the black one. I've never had a black one before.' So she paid him and off she went.

Shortly afterwards, an elderly black woman came in and asked: 'How much for the black dildo?'

'$35,' he said.

'How much for the white one?'

'Same price, $35.'

'Hmmm, I think I'll take the white one. I've never had a white one before.' So she paid him and left.

An hour later, a young blonde woman came in and asked: 'How much are your dildos?'

'$35 for the white and $35 for the black.'

'Hmmm,' she said. 'And how much is that tartan one on the shelf?'

The young guy replied: 'Well, that's a very special dildo. It'll cost you $250.'

The blonde thought for a moment and said: 'I'll take the tartan one, I've never had a tartan one before.' So she paid him and left.

Finally the boss returned and asked: 'How did you get on while I was gone?'

The young guy replied: 'I did really good. I sold one black dildo, one white dildo, and I sold your thermos for $250!'

Why a vibrator is better than a man:

2392   ● It's happy to keep going until you are satisfied.
2393   ● You can get another one that has better options whenever you want without being called a slut.
2394   ● It doesn't care that you gained 10lbs.
2395   ● It doesn't fall asleep and snore in your ear afterwards.
2396   ● You don't have to cook it breakfast and pretend to be interested in it the next morning.
2397   ● You don't have to tell the vibrator it's the best you ever had.
2398   ● You know exactly where it's been.
2399   ● It never drinks too much and embarrasses you.

VIRGINITY

2400   Maria had just got married and, being a traditional Italian, she was still a virgin. So on her wedding night, staying at her mother's house, she was nervous and apprehensive. Her mother reassured her: 'Don't worry, Maria. Tony's a good man. Go upstairs and he'll take care of you.'

So Maria went upstairs to the bedroom where Tony took off his shirt and exposed his hairy chest. Maria immediately ran downstairs to her mother and said: 'Mama, Mama, Tony's got a big hairy chest!'

'Don't worry, Maria, all good men have hairy chests. Go upstairs. He'll take good care of you.'

So Maria returned to the bedroom just as Tony was removing his jeans to reveal a pair of hairy legs. Maria ran straight downstairs to her mother, shouting: 'Mama, Mama, Tony's got hairy legs!'

'Don't worry, Maria, hairy legs are good in men. Go upstairs. Tony will take good care of you.'

So Maria returned to the bedroom where Tony was now taking off his socks and on one foot he was missing three toes. Maria ran back downstairs. 'Mama, Mama, Tony's got a foot and a half!'

Her mother said: 'Stay there and stir the pasta. This is a job for Mama.'

2401 What do you say to a virgin when she sneezes? – Goes-in-tight.

2402 A virgin wanted to marry a farmer boy. One day she went to his parents' house for dinner and afterwards they were walking through the fields when she saw two horses mating.

'What are they doing?' she asked.

'They're making love,' said the boy.

'What's that long thing he's sticking in there?'

'Oh, uh, that's his rope.'

'Well, what are those two round things on the other end?'

'Er, those are his knots.'

'OK, OK,' said the girl, happy with the explanation. 'I get it.'

As they continued to stroll, they came to a barn and went in. The girl announced: 'I want you to make love to me the way those animals were.'

Excited and surprised, he readily agreed, but suddenly she grabbed his balls and squeezed them hard.

'Whoa! What are you doing?' he shrieked in pain.

'I'm untying the knots so I'll get more rope.'

2403 A young guy was cuddling up on the sofa with his girlfriend, but just as he slid his hand up her skirt, his mother walked in. With a face like thunder, she ordered him into the kitchen.

'Henry,' she said, 'I never want to see you doing that again.'

'Why not?'

'Because up between them legs is a black hole and it's got teeth in it! If you put your hand near it again, it'll bite your fingers off!'

'OK, Mom,' he agreed reluctantly, 'I promise.'

The young sweethearts continued dating and eventually they got married. On their wedding night, they climbed into bed together but then he rolled over and started to go to sleep.

The frustrated bride pleaded: 'Henry, I've been waiting years for this day. Make love to me.'

'No way,' he said. 'My mother told me that up between your legs you've got a black hole with teeth in it and if I go near it, it will bite me!'

Laughing, she rolled over, picked up a bedside torch and shone it between her legs.

'Can you see any teeth up there?' she demanded.

'No,' he answered meekly.

She moved even closer and shone the torch once more. 'Well, can you?'

'No,' he admitted, looking again. 'There's no teeth. But I'm not surprised, judging by the state of your gums!'

2404 A shy male virgin was introduced to a girl who would teach him a few things. They ended up in a hotel room for the night, and the girl took off her clothes and asked him: 'Do you know what I want?'

'No,' he said.

So she lay down on the bed, and asked him again: 'Now do you know what I want?'

'No,' he answered.

Not sure quite what she had to do to get the message across, she then spread her legs as far as she could. 'Now do you know what I want?' she purred.

'Yeah, I know what you want,' he said. 'You want the whole damn bed to yourself!'

2405 The groom-to-be said: 'I'm not sure if my future bride is a virgin or not.'

His friend said: 'There's an easy test for that. All you need is some red paint, some blue paint and a shovel. You paint one of your testicles red and the other one blue. On your honeymoon, if she laughs and says, "Those are the funniest balls I've ever seen," you hit her with the shovel!'

2406 A young male virgin – a shy college freshman – was fortunate enough to have an experienced roommate who offered to fix him up with the campus floozy. The roommate said all you've got to do is show her a good time, and she'll be over you like a rash.

So the shy virgin wined her and dined her, and on the way home parked his car in a dark lane. Plucking up courage, he blurted out: 'I sure would like to have a little pussy.'

The girl replied: 'Me, too. Mine's the size of a bucket.'

2407 A young girl was having a heart-to-heart talk with her mother on her first visit home since starting university.

'Mom, I have to tell you,' the girl confessed. 'I lost my virginity last weekend.'

'I'm not surprised,' said her mother. 'It was bound to happen sooner or later. I just hope it was a romantic and pleasurable experience.'

'Well, yes and no,' replied the student. 'The first eight guys felt great, but after them my pussy got really sore.'

VOMIT

2408   A cop stopped his police car when he spotted a young couple sitting by the side of the road. The guy was lying on his side with his pants pulled down while the girl was fingering him vigorously in his asshole.

'What the heck is going on here?' asked the cop.

'This is my date,' explained the girl. 'When I told him I wouldn't spend the night with him, he started knocking back the booze. Now he's too drunk to drive me home, so I'm trying to sober him up by making him puke.'

The cop said: 'That's not gonna make him puke.'

'Yeah?' she replied. 'Wait till I switch this finger to his mouth!'

2409   A timid little man found was allocated a window seat of an airplane next to a burly biker. The little man was a nervous flyer and began to feel sick moments after take-off, by which time the biker was already sound asleep. Just as he was summoning the courage to wake the biker so that he could get to the washroom, the little man threw up violently in the biker's lap. The awful stench woke the biker and he opened his eyes to find himself covered in vomit. The little man quickly patted him on the shoulder and said: 'There. Are you feeling better now?'

2410   Ken was planning a night out with his pals, but his wife was threatening to block the idea because the last time he'd gone out on the town he'd got so drunk that he had puked up all over his shirt.

'But, honey,' he pleaded, 'I promise not to touch a drop of alcohol all night.'

Eventually she relented, but only on condition that he stayed off the booze. However once he was with his mates, Ken's promises flew out of the window and he proceeded to get blind drunk. After about three hours of solid drinking, he threw up all over his shirt.

'Shit!' said Ken. 'My wife's gonna kill me for getting drunk and puking over my new shirt!'

Fortunately his buddy Ray had an idea. 'When you get home, have a $20 bill in your hand and tell her that some other guy puked on you, and that he gave you the twenty bucks to get your shirt cleaned.'

Ken thought it was a great idea. When he walked into the house money in hand, his wife was waiting for him.

She let him have it with both barrels: 'I knew you'd get so drunk that you'd throw up all over your new shirt!'

'Honey, let me explain,' said Ken. 'This drunken idiot at the bar puked up on me and gave me twenty bucks to have the shirt cleaned.'

His wife snatched the money out of his hand and noticed that he was holding two $20 bills. 'Is that so? Then where did the other $20 bill come from?'

'Oh,' said Ken. 'That's from the guy who shit in my pants.'

WEDDINGS

2411 A drunken wedding ended in a brawl and a court appearance. The judge was having difficulty getting to the truth of what had actually happened until the best man offered to outline the facts.

'Your honour,' he began, 'I was the best man at the wedding. It is the tradition in these parts that the best man gets the first dance with the bride. After I'd finished the first dance, the music kept going, so we kept dancing to the second song and then the third, when suddenly the groom jumped over a table and kicked the bride right between her legs.'

'That must have hurt!' exclaimed the judge.

'Hurt?' said the best man. 'He broke three of my fingers!'

2412 A couple applied for a wedding licence. 'Can I have your name, please?' asked the clerk.

'Emma Jones,' replied the woman grumpily.

'Jeremy Jones,' answered the man.

'Oh. Any connection?' asked the clerk.

'Only the once,' snapped the woman, patting her stomach. 'When he put me in this state.'

2413 When a girl was planning to get married, she asked to wear her mother's wedding dress. Touched by the request, the mother gave her the dress and, when the daughter walked downstairs for the first time, the dress a perfect fit on her petite frame, it made the mother burst into tears.

'Don't think of it as losing a daughter,' said the girl reassuringly. 'You're gaining a son.'

'That's got nothing to do with it,' sobbed the mother. 'I used to fit into that dress!'

2414 Leaving their wedding reception, a young honeymoon couple hailed a cab to take them to their country hotel. The driver wasn't sure how to get there and said he'd ask for directions when they got nearer their destination. Meanwhile the lovers started getting really passionate in the back seat.

Seeing a fork in the road, the driver said: 'I take the next turn, right?'

'No way,' panted the groom. 'Get your own. This one's all mine.'

WEIGHT

2415 A country boy had trouble getting dates but eventually his mates found a twenty-stone girl who was willing to go out with him. But they advised: 'Compliment her on something. Chicks always like to hear good things about themselves.'

A few days later, they bumped into the country boy on his father's farm. 'How did the date go?' they asked.

'It was a total disaster,' he said. 'She just stormed off even though I took your advice about paying her a compliment.'

'What did you say to her?'

'I told her that for a fat, ugly broad, she didn't sweat much.'

2416 What do fat women and mopeds have in common? – Both are fun to ride but you don't want your friends to see you on them.

2417 A woman said to her husband: 'Be honest, does this skirt make my bum look big?'

'Of course not, darling,' he replied. 'Don't be silly.'

Flattered, she was about to kiss him when he added: 'It's all that bloody chocolate you eat that makes your bum look big.'

Signs That It's Time To Diet:

2418 • You are diagnosed with the flesh-eating virus, and the doctor gives you twenty-five more years to live.

2419 • You put mayonnaise on an aspirin.

2420 • You dive into a swimming pool and your friends say, 'One at a time, please.'

2421 • You go to the zoo and the elephants throw you peanuts.

2422 • You dance, and it makes the band skip a beat.

2423 • You go into a restaurant, and the waiter asks you whether you want a bill or an estimate.

2424 • Your driving licence says 'Picture continued on other side'.

2425 • You learn you were born with a silver shovel in your mouth.

2426 • You could sell shade.

2427 • Your blood type is Ragu.

2428 A young woman having a physical examination was very embarrassed because she had put on a lot of weight. As she removed her last item of clothing, she blushed. 'I'm so ashamed, Doctor. I guess I've let myself go.'

The doctor checked her eyes and ears. 'Don't feel ashamed, Miss. You don't look that bad.'

'Do you really think so, Doctor?' she asked.

The doctor held a tongue depressor in front of her face and said: 'Of course. Now just open your mouth and say moo.'

2429 What do you call an anorexic with a yeast infection? – A quarter-pounder with cheese.

2430 A fat man went to a health farm where he was offered three weight-loss plans – one for $100, another for $200, and the third for $500. Choosing the cheapest plan, he had a shower and was shown into a sauna. There, sitting naked on a chair, was a pretty young woman with a sign over her head, which said: 'If you can catch me, you can have sex with me.'

The man immediately began chasing the woman around the room. His time ran out before he could catch her, but he was delighted to learn that the exertion had caused him to lose eight pounds of fat.

The next day he tried out the $200 plan. After showering, he was again taken to the sauna where another pretty woman, totally naked but for high heels, was sitting under the sign that said: 'If you catch me, you can have sex with me.'

Thinking that the high heels would slow her down, he set about the chase with confidence, but again he failed to catch her before running out of time. Nevertheless he lost another five pounds of fat.

For his final day at the health farm, he decided to splash out on the most expensive plan. After showering, he was shown into the sauna, but was disappointed to find the room empty. Then a chronically obese, ugly woman waddled into the room, stark naked. Hanging round the rolls of fat on her neck was a sign saying: 'If I catch you, I get to have sex with you.'

2431 A mother took her five-year-old son with her to the bank on a busy lunchtime. They got into line behind an obese woman wearing a business suit complete with pager. As the mother waited patiently, the boy looked at the woman in front and said loudly: 'Gee, she's fat!'

The woman instinctively turned around and looked at the boy. His mother mildly reprimanded him.

A minute or so later, the boy spread his hand as far as they would go and announced: 'I bet her butt is *that* wide!'

The woman turned around and glared at the boy. His mother gave him a good telling off.

A couple of minutes later, the boy stated loudly: 'Look how the fat hangs over her belt.'

The woman angrily turned around and told the mother to control her rude child. The mother issued threats to the boy. He promised to behave.

After a brief lull, the large woman reached the front of the queue. Just then her pager began to emit its distinctive tone, at which the little boy yelled in panic: 'Run for your life, mom, she's backing up!'

2432 How do you make five pounds of fat look great? – Put a nipple on it.

2433 How do you fuck a fat chick? – Roll her in flour and find the wet spot.

2434 There was this Texan who loved big women – the fatter the better. One day he took a really huge woman to bed, climbed on top of her and began having sex with her. They had been going at it for a while when he suddenly said: 'Would you mind if we turned the light off?'

The woman was indignant. 'Why am I that ugly?'

'No,' he answered, 'it's just that while we're fucking, my ass keeps hitting the light bulb!'

2435 A woman sat opposite a fat man on a train and told him bluntly: 'If that stomach was on a woman, I'd think she was pregnant.'

The fat man replied: 'It was. She is.'

2436 What's the best way to get a youthful figure? – Ask a woman her age.

2437 What do you call a pig that weighs more than 150lb? – A divorcee.

2438 Lonely, middle-aged and divorced, a guy decided out of the blue to phone a gorgeous ex-girlfriend whom he hadn't seen for twenty years. For over an hour they talked about the wild nights they used to have together and then, to his amazement, she suggested they meet up and maybe rekindle some of the old magic.

'Gee,' he said, 'I don't know if I could keep up with you now. I'm a lot older and a bit balder than when you last saw me!'

She giggled suggestively and said: 'I'm sure you'll rise to the occasion.'

'Yeah,' he said defensively. 'Just so long as you don't mind a man with a waistband that's a few inches wider these days.'

She laughed and told him to stop being so silly. 'I think tubby, bald men are cute,' she teased. 'Anyway, I've put on a couple of pounds myself.'

He hung up.

WIDOWS

2439 A New York woman was still grieving after losing her husband four years earlier. Her social life was virtually non-existent until a friend persuaded her to go to a dinner party where she met a man to whom she was instantly attracted. After dating for a few months, she agreed to go away with him for a long weekend in the Catskills. On their first night, he stripped off completely but she kept on a pair of black lace panties.

'What's with the panties?' he asked.

She said firmly: 'You can fondle my breasts, you can caress my body, but down there I am still in mourning.'

It was the same the following night: he stood there naked while she kept her black panties on, insisting that she was still in mourning down there.

On their third and final night away, his frustration proved too much. She undressed right down to her black panties, but this time he stood before her naked except for a black condom on his erection.

'Why are you wearing a black condom?' she asked.

He said: 'I'm going to offer my condolences.'

2440 A woman had her husband cremated and brought the ashes home. Picking up the urn, she poured him out on the counter. While tracing her fingers through the ashes, she started talking to him:

'Marlon, you know that fur coat you promised me? I bought it with the insurance money.

'Marlon, remember that diamond necklace you promised me? I bought it with the insurance money.

'Marlon, remember that new car you promised me? I bought it with the insurance money.

'And Marlon, remember that blow job I promised you? Here it comes.'

2441 An undertaker explained to a widow that it was impossible to fit her late husband's body into the coffin because rigor mortis had set in and left the corpse with an erection. As a result, they couldn't close the lid.

'We could order a bigger coffin,' suggested the undertaker, 'but it will cost you an extra $1,000.'

'No, that's too expensive,' sighed the widow. 'I simply can't afford it.'

'Well, I suppose there is one other possible solution,' said the undertaker hesitantly. 'We could cut off his penis.'

'No, no,' said the widow. 'I want all of him there when we bury him.'

'I understand that,' said the undertaker, 'but we could remove his penis and insert it in his rectum. That way he would be complete.'

After thinking over the proposition for a few minutes, the widow agreed. 'OK,' she said, 'but I want to see the body immediately before the funeral.'

The undertaker and the surgeon went about their business and laid the body out as arranged for the day of the funeral. The corpse was made-up immaculately and the penis was neatly inserted in his rectum. As the mourners began to gather, the widow went to pay her last respects to the body in the coffin. Saying her private goodbyes, she noticed that a tear had trickled out of his eye and smudged his make-up. Leaning over, she whispered: 'Hurts, doesn't it, you bastard!'

2442 Phil, Dave and Rob were working on very high scaffolding when Phil suddenly fell off and plunged to his death. As the ambulance departed with his body, Dave and Rob realized that they would have to inform his wife. Dave said he was good at the sensitive stuff, so he volunteered to tell her.

Two hours later, he returned with a six-pack of beer. 'So did you tell her?' asked Rob.

'Yep,' said Dave.

'Where did you get the six-pack?'

'She gave it to me.'

'What?' exclaimed Rob. 'You just told her that her husband was dead and she gave you a six-pack?'

'Yep,' said Dave.

'Why?'

'Well,' said Dave, 'when she answered the door, I asked, "Are you Phil's widow?" "Widow?" she said. "No, no, you're mistaken. I'm not a widow." So I said, "I'll bet you a six-pack you are!"'

2443 Two widows were talking in a nursing home. One said: 'Rose has just cremated her fifth husband.'

'That's the way it goes,' said the other. 'Some of us can't find a husband, and others have husbands to burn.'

WOMEN

2444 A man was walking along a beach in California when he stumbled across an old lamp. As he rubbed it, a genie popped out and granted him a wish.

'Let me see,' said the guy. 'I've always wanted to go to Hawaii, but I'm scared of flying and get seasick. So could you build me a bridge to Hawaii so that I can go there on vacation?'

The genie scratched his head. 'A bridge from California to Hawaii? That's an impossible engineering feat. For a start, how would the bridge supports ever reach the bottom of the Pacific? Then there's all the concrete and steel that would be needed. No, it can't be done. Sorry, you'll have to think of another wish.'

The guy thought for a few moments. 'Well, I've been divorced three times, and I guess I just don't understand women. They say I'm not sensitive enough or appreciative of their needs. But I can never read their minds and work out what makes them happy. Could you make me understand women?'

The genie said: 'You want that bridge two lanes or four?'

Things You Should Never Say
To a Woman During An Argument:

2445 • You're so cute when you're angry.

2446 • Don't you have some laundry to do or something?

2447 • You're just upset because you're putting on weight.

2448 • Wait a minute, I get it. What time of the month is it?

2449 • You sure you don't want to consult the great Oprah on this one?

2450 • Sorry, I was just picturing you naked.

2451 • Looks like someone had an extra bowl of bitch flakes this morning.

2452 • Is there any way we can do this via e-mail?

2453 • Whoa, time out! Football is on.

2454 • Who are you kidding? We both know that thing ain't loaded.

2455 If a motorcyclist runs into a woman, who's to blame? – The motorcyclist: he shouldn't have been riding in the kitchen.

2456 Why don't women wear watches? – There's a clock on the stove!

2457 What would have happened if it had been three Wise Women instead of Wise Men? They would have asked for directions, arrived on time, helped deliver the baby, cleaned the stable, made a casserole, and brought practical gifts. But what would they have said as they left?
'Did you see the sandals Mary was wearing with that gown?'
'That baby doesn't look anything like Joseph!'
'Virgin, my arse! I knew her in school!'
'Can you believe they let all those disgusting animals in there?'
'I heard that Joseph isn't even working right now.'
'And that donkey they are riding has seen better days too!'
'Want to bet on how long it will take until you get your casserole dish back?'

2458 What paralyses women from the waist down? – Marriage.

2459 Why do women have a hole between their legs? – So oxygen can get to their brain.

2460 What's hard and long and screws women? – An I.Q. Test.

2461 A guy walked over to a beautiful woman in a bar and said: 'Do you mind if I ask you a personal question?'

'It depends,' she replied.

'OK. How many men have you slept with?'

'I'm not going to tell you that,' she said. 'That's my business!'

'Sorry,' he said. 'I didn't realize you made a living out of it.'

2462 What is a woman's idea of a perfect lover? – A man with a nine-inch tongue who can breathe through his ears.

2463 Why do female skydivers wear jockstraps? – So they don't whistle on the way down.

2464 Why can't women read maps? – Because only the male mind can comprehend the concept of one inch equalling a mile.

2465 If you go to bed eight hours before you have to wake up, and your wife wants to have an hour of sex, how much sleep will you get? – Seven hours, fifty-nine minutes: who cares what she wants!

The Seven Most Important Men in a Woman's Life:

2466 1. The Doctor – who tells her to 'take off all her clothes'.

2467 2. The Dentist – who tells her to 'open wide'.

2468 3. The Milkman – who asks her 'do you want it in the front or the back?'

2469 4. The Hairdresser – who asks her 'do you want it teased or blown?'

2470 5. The Interior Designer – who assures her 'once it's inside, you'll LOVE it!'

2471 6. The Banker – who insists to her 'if you take it out too soon, you'll lose interest'.

2472 7. The Primal Hunter – who always goes deep into the bush, always shoots twice, always eats what he shoots, but keeps telling her 'keep quiet and lie still!'

2473 Recent scientific tests have proved that the most intelligent gene can be found in women. Unfortunately ninety-eight per cent of them spit it back out.

2474 Why don't women have brains? – They don't have a cock to keep them in.

2475 What do you do if your boiler explodes? – Buy her some flowers.

2476 Why do men fart more than women? – Women don't shut up long enough to build up pressure.

2477 How many men does it take to change a light bulb? – None. Let the bitch cook and clean in the dark.

2478 Seeing Adam looking dejected, God went over to him and asked: 'What's the matter?'

'There's no one for me to talk to,' moaned Adam.

God revealed: 'Actually, Adam, I've got some good news for you. I'm going to give you a companion, and it will be a woman. This person will gather food for you, cook for you, and when you discover clothing, she will wash it for you. She will always agree with whatever you say. She will bear your children and never ask you to get up in the middle of the night to take care of them. She will not nag you and will always be the first to admit she was wrong when you've had a disagreement. She will never have a headache and will freely give you love and passion whenever you need it.'

Adam was impressed, but inquired cautiously: 'What would a woman like this cost?'

God said: 'An arm and a leg.'

'What can I get for a rib?' asked Adam.

The rest is history . . .

Reasons Why Beer Is Better Than Women:

2479 • You can enjoy a beer all month.

2480 • A beer won't get upset if you come home with beer on your breath.

2481 • You can share a beer with your friends.

2482 • You always know that you are the first one to pop a beer.

2483 • A beer is always wet.

2484 • After you have a beer, you're committed to nothing more than dumping the empty bottle.

2485 • Beer looks the same in the morning.

2486 • Beer doesn't have a mother.

2487 • If you change beers, you don't have to pay alimony.

2488 • Beer labels come off without a fight.

2489 ● When you go to a bar, you know you can always pick up a beer.

2490 ● If you pour a beer right, you will always get good head.

2491 ● Beer stains wash out.

2492 ● When beer goes flat, you throw it out.

2493 ● Beer doesn't mind being on the wet spot that IT left.

2494 ● A beer doesn't get jealous when you grab another beer.

2495 ● You can't catch anything but a buzz from beer.

2496 A Space Shuttle mission to the moon had a crew of two monkeys and a woman. Three hours into the mission, NASA announced: 'Monkey number one, Monkey number one, to the television screen.' The monkey sat down and was told to release the pressure in compartment two, increase the temperature in engine four, and release oxygen to the reactors. So the monkey released the pressure, increased the temperature, and released oxygen.

Thirty minutes later, NASA called again. 'Monkey number two, Monkey number two, to the television screen.' The monkey sat down and was told to add carbon dioxide to room four, stop the fuel injection to engine three, add nitrogen to the fuel compartment, and analyse the solar radiation. So the monkey added the carbon dioxide, stopped the fuel injection, added nitrogen, and performed a detailed analysis.

Twenty minutes later, the woman was called to the screen. Before NASA could issue any orders, she said: 'I know! I know! Feed the monkeys, don't touch anything . . .'

2497 A recent survey asked a hundred sexually active women if their twat twitched after sex. Ninety-six per cent replied: 'No, he just rolls over and goes to sleep.'

2498 What should you give a woman who has everything? – Penicillin.

2499 What does it mean when a woman is in your bed gasping for breath and calling your name? – You didn't hold the pillow down long enough.

2500 A psychiatrist was sitting in a bar chatting to a friend. 'See that guy over there?' said the psychiatrist. 'He claims to understand women.'

'Is he a colleague of yours?' asked the friend.

'No,' said the psychiatrist. 'He's one of my patients.'

Clues That a Woman Should Call It a Night:

2501 • You believe that dancing with your arms overhead and wiggling your ass while yelling 'Woo-hoo' is truly the sexiest dance move around.

2502 • On your last trip to the toilet, you had begun to look like a drag queen.

2503 • You start crying and telling everyone you see that you love them sooooo much.

2504 • You've suddenly decided you want to kick someone's ass, and you honestly believe you can do it.

2505 • You've found a deeper, more spiritual side to the geek sitting next to you.

2506 • You loudly accuse the bartender of giving you just lemonade, but that's only because you can no longer taste the vodka.

2507 • The man you're flirting with used to be your geography teacher.

2508 • The urge to take off articles of clothing, stand on a table and sing or dance becomes strangely overwhelming.

2509 • You start every conversation with a booming, 'DON'T take this the wrong way, but . . .'

2510 • You fail to notice the toilet lid is down when you sit on it.

2511 • Your hugs begin to resemble wrestling take-down moves.

2512 • You have absolutely no idea where your bag is.

2513 • Your eyes just don't seem to want to stay open on their own, so you keep them half closed and think it looks exotically sexy.

2514 • You take off your shoes because you believe it's their fault that you're having problems walking straight.

2515 • You've suddenly taken up smoking and become really good at it.

2516 • You're due to start work in three hours.

2517 • You think you're in bed, but your pillow feels strangely like the kitchen floor.

2518 A boy at school overheard the older kids talking about pussy and their bitch. That evening the boy asked his father: 'Dad, what's a pussy?'

His father was watching baseball on TV and didn't want to be distracted, so he quickly grabbed a copy of Penthouse, turned to the centrefold, drew a circle around the vagina and said: 'Son, that's a pussy.'

The boy took this in and a few moments later asked: 'Then, dad, what's a bitch?'

The father replied: 'That's everything outside the circle.'

Things You'll Never Hear a Woman Say:

2519   • I'm bored. Let's shave my fanny.

2520   • Shouldn't you be down at the pub with your mates?

2521   • That was a great fart! Do another one!

2522   • You're so sexy with a hangover.

2523   • Let's start subscribing to *Penthouse*.

2524   • Just for a change, can we try anal sex tonight?

2525   • I think buying a big motorbike is a great idea.

2526   • I know you're already late for work, but can I gag on it just
        one more time?

2527   • Anywhere you like, it's really good for my skin.

2528   • This diamond is way too big.

2529   • I'm wrong, you must be right again.

2530   'Good afternoon, ladies,' said Sherlock Holmes to three women sitting on a
London park bench.

'Do you know those women?' asked his faithful companion, Dr. Watson.

'No,' said Holmes as the pair continued walking, 'I don't know the
spinster, the prostitute and the new bride.'

'Good heavens, Holmes! If you don't know them, how can you be so sure
that they are what you say?'

'Elementary, my dear Watson,' explained Holmes, glancing back. 'Do you
see how they are eating bananas?'

'So?'

'Well, Watson, the spinster holds the banana in her left hand and uses her
right hand to break the banana into small pieces which she puts into her mouth.'

'I see what you mean, Holmes. That's amazing! What about the
prostitute?'

'She holds the banana in both hands and crams it into her mouth.'

'Holmes, you've surpassed yourself! But how do you know the other
woman is a new bride?'

'Simple,' said Holmes. 'She holds the banana in her left hand and uses her
right hand to push her head towards the banana.'

2531   How are women like tornadoes? – They both moan like hell when they come
and take the house when they leave.

2532   Why do women have arms? – Have you any idea how long it would take to
lick a bathroom clean?

2533 How is a carton of milk like a woman? – You need to push the flaps back before you can get to the good bits.

38 Things Women Can't Do:

2534 1. Know anything about a car except its colour.

2535 2. Go 24 hours without sending a text message.

2536 3. Understand a movie plot.

2537 4. Lift.

2538 5. Throw.

2539 6. Catch.

2540 7. Park.

2541 8. Fart.

2542 9. Read a map.

2543 10. Resist Ikea.

2544 11. Sit still.

2545 12. Play pool.

2546 13. Eat a kebab whilst walking.

2547 14. Pee out of a train window.

2548 15. Argue without shouting.

2549 16. Get told off without crying.

2550 17. Understand fruit machines.

2551 18. Clear their throat noisily.

2552 19. Walk past a shoe shop.

2553 20. Not comment on a stranger's clothes.

2554 21. Use small amounts of toilet paper.

2555 22. Let you sleep with a hangover.

2556 23. Drink a pint gracefully.

2557 24. Throw a punch.

2558 25. Do magic.

2559 26. Enjoy porn.

2560 27. Eat a really hot curry.

2561 28. Get to the point.

2562 29. Take less than twenty minutes in the bathroom.

2563 30. Avoid credit card debt.

2564 31. Dive into a pool.

2565 32. Assemble furniture.

2566 33. Roll a bogey between finger and thumb.

2567 34. Set a video recorder.

2568 35. Not try and change you.

2569   36. Buy a purse that fits in their pocket.
2570   37. Choose a video quickly.
2571   38. Get this far without having argued about at least one of the
       above.

2572 Which is the odd one out – a TV, a fridge, a washing machine, or a woman?
      – A TV, because the other three leak when they're fucked.

2573 What's the difference between pink and purple? – The grip!

If Women Ruled the World:

2574 ● Men would get 'reputations' for sleeping around.
2575 ● Singles bars would have metal detectors to weed out men
        hiding wedding rings in their pockets.
2576 ● A man would no longer be considered a 'good catch' simply
        because he is breathing.
2577 ● Women with cold hands would give men prostate
        examinations.
2578 ● PMS would be a legitimate defence in court.
2579 ● Men would not be allowed to eat gas-producing foods within
        two hours of bedtime.
2580 ● Men would HAVE to get *Playboy* for the articles because
        there'd be no pictures.
2581 ● Men would learn phrases like 'I'm sorry', 'I love you' and 'Of
        course you don't look fat in that outfit'.
2582 ● All toilet seats would be nailed down.
2583 ● Overweight men would be encouraged to wear girdles.
2584 ● Men who designed women's shoes would be forced to wear
        them.
2585 ● Fewer women would be dieting because their ideal weight
        standard would increase by 40lbs.
2586 ● During a mid-life crisis, men would get hot flushes and women
        would date nineteen-year-olds.
2587 ● Shopping would be considered an aerobic activity.

Men's Advice to Women:

2588 ● Learn to work the toilet seat: if it's up, put it down.
2589 ● Don't cut your own hair. Ever.
2590 ● Don't make us guess.

2591 • If you ask a question you don't want an answer to, expect an answer you don't want to hear.

2592 • Don't feel compelled to tell us how all the people in your stories are related to one another: we're just nodding, waiting for the punchline.

2593 • Sometimes he's not thinking about you. Live with it.

2594 • Get rid of your cat. And no, it's not different – it's just like every other cat.

2595 • Anything you wear is fine. Really.

2596 • Never buy a 'new' brand of beer because it was on sale.

2597 • Crying is like blackmail. Use it if you must, but don't expect us to like it.

2598 • The quarterback who just got pummelled isn't trying to be brave. He's just not crying. Big difference!

2599 • Ask for what you want. Subtle hints don't work.

2600 • 'Yes' and 'No' are perfectly acceptable answers.

2601 • Nothing says 'I love you' like sex in the morning.

2602 • If we're in the backyard and the TV in the den is on, that doesn't mean we're not watching it.

2603 • Foreign films are best left to foreigners.

2604 • Check your oil.

2605 • Please don't drive when you're not driving.

2606 • Anything we said six or eight months ago is inadmissible in an argument.

2607 • When the waiter asks if everything's OK, a simple 'yes' is fine.

2608 • If you think fat, you probably are. Don't ask us.

2609 • Yes, pissing standing up is more difficult than peeing from point blank range: we're bound to miss sometimes.

2610 • Whenever possible, please try to say whatever you have to say during commercials.

2611 • Don't fake it. We'd rather be ineffective than deceived.

2612 • Let us ogle. If we don't look at other women, how can we know how pretty you are?

2613 • Women wearing Wonderbras or low-cut blouses lose their right to complain about having their boobs stared at.

2614 Why hasn't a woman walked on the moon? – Because it doesn't need cleaning.

2615   ## I'm Glad I'm a Woman:

I'm glad I'm a woman, yes I am, yes I am,
I don't live off Budweiser, Beer Nuts and Spam.
I don't brag to my buddies about my erections,
I won't drive to hell before I ask for directions.
I don't get wasted at parties, and act like a clown,
And I know how to put that damned toilet seat down.
I won't grab your hooters, I won't pinch your butt,
My belt buckle's not hidden beneath my beer gut.
And I don't go around 'readjusting' my crotch,
Or yell like Tarzan when my headboard gets a notch.
I don't belch in public, I don't scratch my behind,
I'm a woman, you see – I'm just not that kind!
I'm glad I'm a woman, I'm so glad I can sing,
And that I don't have body hair like shag carpeting.
It doesn't grow from my ears or cover my back,
When I lean over you can't see three inches of crack.
And what's on my head doesn't leave with my comb,
I'll never buy a toupee to cover my dome.
Or have a few strands pulled from over the side,
I'm a woman, you know – I've got far too much pride!
And I honestly think it's a privilege for me,
To have these two boobs and squat when I pee.
I don't live to play golf and shoot basketball,
I don't swagger and spit like some Neanderthal.
I don't long for male bonding, I don't cruise for chicks,
Join the Hair Club for Men, or think with my dick.
I won't tell you my wife just does not understand,
Or stick my hand in my pocket to hide that gold band.
Or tell you a story to make you feel sad and weep,
Then screw you, roll over and fall sound asleep.
Yes, I'm so very glad I'm a woman, you see,
Forget all about that old penis envy.
I'm a woman by chance and I'm thankful, it's true,
I'm so glad I'm a woman and not a man like you!

WORK

2616 A woman called her boss one morning and told him she was staying home because she didn't feel well.

'What's the matter?' he asked.

'I have a case of anal glaucoma,' she replied wearily.

'What the hell is anal glaucoma?'

'I just can't see my ass coming in to work today.'

2617 Two guys were discussing the new office secretary. Don said to Mike: 'I dated her last Wednesday and we had great sex. She's a lot better in bed than my wife.'

Three days later, Mike told Don: 'I dated the new secretary, too, and we had great sex as well, but I still think your wife is better in bed.'

2618 As an executive entered the office elevator, a woman inside muttered, 'T-G-I-F.' He smiled and replied, 'S-H-I-T.' The woman looked bemused and repeated, 'T-G-I-F,' but once again the man answered, 'S-H-I-T.'

The woman said: 'Do you know what I'm saying? T-G-I-F means, "Thank God it's Friday." '

'I know,' replied the man. 'But S-H-I-T means, "Sorry, Honey, it's Thursday." '

2619 A secretary came in late for work for the fourth morning in a row. The boss called her into his office. 'Look, Tracy,' he said, 'I know we had a fling a while back, but that's all over now. I can't be seen to be doing you any favours, so I expect you to behave like any other employee. Who told you that you could come and go as you please around here?'

She replied: 'My lawyer.'

2620 A railway worker was writhing in agony on the station floor.

'Are you OK?' asked a concerned passenger.

'I'll be all right in a few minutes,' he groaned.

'Why? What's wrong?'

'I'm busting for a shit, but I don't start work for another ten minutes!'

2621 Two women were discussing the trials of work. One said: 'We have introduced Friday as a casual day, so that we can wear what we like to the office. It actually makes us more focused, which is essential in the insurance business.'

The other said: 'At work we now have one day a week where we just leave the phones ringing and don't answer them, which is good because it really can get quite stressful at the Samaritans.'

2622 After being made redundant at a Belfast factory, two men signed on for unemployment benefit. The first man told the clerk that he was a panty stitcher and was awarded £200 a week in benefits. The second man told the clerk he was a diesel fitter and was given £250 a week in benefits.

When the first man learned that his friend was receiving more money, he complained bitterly to the clerk. 'Why should a diesel fitter get more than a panty stitcher?' he demanded.

The clerk explained: 'The additional money is a new grant given to skilled workers. Engineers such as diesel fitters are eligible.'

'He was never an engineer,' stormed the man. 'He was in quality control. After I'd stitched a pair of panties, I'd give them to him. If he could pull them over his arse, he'd say, "Yeah, diesel fitter."'

2623 A guy had a tomcat that howled all night, so he took it to the vet to have it castrated. But even after the operation it still howled all night.

The guy asked the cat: 'Why do you keep making that noise?'

The cat said: 'Well, now I'm a consultant.'

2624 Three senior managers were arguing about sex. One insisted that sex was fifty per cent work and fifty per cent fun; another claimed that it was seventy-five per cent work and twenty-five per cent fun; and the third thought it was ninety per cent work and only ten per cent fun. Just then the young office junior walked by, so they asked him what he thought the answer was.

After a moment's thought, he declared: 'Sex is 100 per cent fun.'

'How do you work that out?' asked one of the managers.

'Easy,' replied the junior. 'If there was any work involved, you'd be making me do it for you!'

Excuses For Missing Work:

2625 • If it's all the same to you, I won't be coming in to work. The voices told me to clean all the guns today.

2626 • When I got up this morning, I took two Ex-Lax in addition to my Prozac. I can't get off the john, but I feel good about it.

2627   • I can't come in today because I'll be stalking my previous boss who fired me for not showing up for work. OK?

2628   • Constipation has made me a walking time bomb.

2629   • I just found out I was switched at birth. Legally, I shouldn't come to work knowing that my employee records may now contain false information.

2630   • The dog ate my car keys. We're going to hitchhike to the vet.

2631   • I am extremely sensitive to a rise in interest rates.

2632   • The psychiatrist said it was an excellent session. He even gave me this jaw restraint so I won't bite things when I am startled.

2633   • My mother-in-law has come back as one of the Undead, and we must track her to her coffin to drive a stake through her heart and give her eternal peace. One day should do it.

2634   • I am converting my calendar from Julian to Gregorian.

2635   • I have a rare case of forty-eight-hour projectile leprosy, but I know we have that deadline to meet . . .

2636   • I prefer to remain an enigma.

2637   Two young guys from Cleveland drove down to New Orleans. A few miles outside New Orleans, they picked up a girl and offered her a lift into the city.

'What do you two boys do, then?' she asked in a sexy voice.

Trying to impress her, the driver said: 'I'm with GM.'

'Yeah?' she said.

'Yeah, I'm general manager with General Motors.'

Inventing something equally impressive, the guy in the passenger seat said: 'And I'm with GE.'

'Yeah?'

'Yeah, I'm general manager of General Electric. What about you?'

'I'm with VD,' said the girl.

'Are you the general manager?' asked the driver.

'No, I'm just the li'l ole southern distributor.'

2638   To give his wife a break during the long school holidays, a man agreed to take his young daughter into work for the day. When they got home in the evening, the little girl said: 'I saw you in your office with your secretary. Why do you call her a doll?'

Aware that his wife was listening, the husband said: 'Well, it's because my secretary works really hard. I'd be lost without her. I guess that's why I call her a doll.'

'Oh,' said the little girl. 'I thought it was because she closed her eyes when you laid her on the couch.'

ZOOS

2639 A guy went to the zoo one day, but while he was standing in front of the gorilla enclosure, the wind gusted and got some grit in his eye. As he pulled down his eyelid to dislodge the particle, the gorilla went crazy, bent open the bars, and beat the guy senseless.

When the guy recovered consciousness, the worried zookeeper explained what had happened, revealing that in gorilla language, pulling down your eyelid means, 'Fuck you!' However the explanation failed to appease the guy and he vowed revenge.

The next day he purchased two large knives, two party hats, two party horns, and a large sausage. Putting the sausage in his trousers, he hurried to the zoo and went over to the gorilla's cage. He then tossed a knife, a party hat and a party horn into the gorilla enclosure. Knowing that the great apes are natural mimics, the guy put on the party hat. The gorilla looked at him, looked at the hat lying on the ground, and put it on. Next the guy picked up the horn and blew on it. The gorilla picked up his horn and did the same. Then the man picked up his knife, whipped the sausage out of his pants, and sliced it neatly in two.

The gorilla looked at the knife in his cage, looked at his own crotch, and pulled down his eyelid.

2640 Two old ladies were standing by the giraffe enclosure at the zoo. As a male giraffe stood by the fence, one of the old ladies announced mischievously: 'I bet I could squeeze his balls from here.' With that, she reached over and squeezed the giraffe's balls hard. The giraffe's eyes opened wide, and it bolted over the fence, out of the enclosure and ran off into the distance.

The zookeeper came rushing over. 'What happened?' he yelled.

'I squeezed the giraffe's balls,' replied the little old lady.

The keeper said: 'Well, you'd better squeeze mine too. I'm going to have to catch the bastard!'

2641 Did you hear about the guy who had a job at the zoo circumcising elephants?
– The wages were poor but the tips were huge.

2642 Joe the gorilla had lived at the zoo for eight years but during that time he had shown no interest whatsoever in the female gorilla, Jemima. In a desperate attempt to persuade Joe to mate, zoo officials called in the services of a gorilla behavioural expert. After studying Joe for a number of days, the expert recommended stimulating the gorilla's genitals with a long wooden pole. He was convinced this would put the animal in the mood for sex. The keeper promised to give it a try.

Three weeks later, the expert asked the keeper if there had been any change in Joe's behaviour since using the long pole.

'There certainly has,' said the keeper. 'Now we can't get him away from the TV when the snooker is on.'

INDEX